MEETING GORBACHEV'S CHALLENGE

December 1989
For Dale and
Polly Wise
with the very best
of holiday wishes.
Jonathan Dean

D1519222

Also by Jonathan Dean

WATERSHED IN EUROPE: Dismantling the East–West
Military Confrontation

Meeting Gorbachev's Challenge

How to Build Down the NATO–Warsaw Pact Confrontation

Jonathan Dean
Arms Control Advisor
Union of Concerned Scientists

St. Martin's Press   New York

First published in the United States of America in 1989

Printed in the U.S.A.

ISBN 0–312–03266–8 cloth
ISBN 0–312–03267–6 paper

Library of Congress Cataloging-in-Publication Data
Dean, Jonathan.
Meeting Gorbachev's challenge.
Includes index.
1. Nuclear arms control—United States.   2. Nuclear
arms control—Soviet Union.   3. Europe—Military policy.
4. North Atlantic Treaty Organization.   I. Title.
JX1974.D415   1989   355'.03304   89–10560
ISBN 0–312–03266–8
ISBN 0–312–03267–6 (pbk.)

This book, too, is dedicated to the two to whom I owe most, my father, Kenneth Dean, and my wife, Theodora—and also to the men and women on both sides who in coming years will be called on to find answers to the problems described here

Contents

List of Appendices

List of Maps

Map 1 The Atlantic-to-Urals area

Source: John M. Collins, *U.S.-Soviet Military Balance 1980–1985* (New York: Pergamon Press, 1985) p. 123.

Foreword

This book assesses the prospects for the new Atlantic-to-the-Urals, NATO/Warsaw Pact force-reduction talks, which began in March, 1989, in Vienna. More generally, it assesses the prospects for building down the NATO/Warsaw Pact military confrontation in Europe by negotiated and unilateral measures.

Will the new Vienna talks—their official name is Negotiation on Conventional Armed Forces in Europe, or C.F.E. for short—bring deep cuts in the size and costs of the NATO–Warsaw Pact military confrontation in Europe? Their precursor, the NATO/Pact talks on Mutual and Balanced Force Reductions, or M.B.F.R., also based in Vienna, lasted fifteen years and failed to make a dent.

The NATO/Pact confrontation remains very large indeed. With a combined total of 7 million soldiers and airmen, 80,000 tanks, 60,000 artillery pieces and 10,000 nuclear warheads, this peacetime concentration of armed forces is the largest and the deadliest in human history. It is also the costliest. The United States spends at least half of its annual $300 billion military budget on defending Europe; the European NATO states together spend about $160 billion a year.

The convergence of two fundamental developments—the slow fading of the political origins of the military confrontation in Europe and the rapid rise of a new leadership in the U.S.S.R. committed to radical reform of the Soviet system—seems to have created an unprecedented opportunity for negotiated build-down of the confrontation.

The closeness in the positions of the two alliances as the C.F.E. talks started was encouraging. It suggested that a first agreement might be reached within three to four years. NATO's opening position was to call for equality between the alliances in major ground force weapons— tanks, artillery, and armored troop carriers—at a level only slightly below its current holdings of those armaments. Gorbachev appeared ready to make the very large cuts in the armaments of the Soviet Union and its allies needed to come to the new level NATO was proposing. But he challenged NATO to make much larger reductions than it planned—35 to 40 percent instead of 5 to 10 percent—and said the Pact would come down to that point.

This book argues for cutbacks that are deeper still, amounting to a reduction of 50 percent in the armaments and manpower of NATO forces in Europe with the Pact's forces coming down to the new NATO levels. The cutbacks would be phased in over the decade of the 1990s.

One major aim of these cuts is to define an equal plateau of reduced military effort on which both alliances might rest for several decades, during which NATO countries could observe how well or how poorly the Soviet Union implements its reforms.

Both supporters of a negotiated build-down of the NATO/Pact confrontation and sceptics are calling for clarity as to the final outcome of the negotiation process on which East and West have embarked. But there are too many uncertainties as regards the long-term shape of Soviet society now that pent-up forces for change have been released to make well-founded estimates of the internal state and foreign policy of the Soviet Union decades hence. Thus it is too early to define some desirable ultimate outcome of the force reduction process.

To meet the reasonable demands of western publics and political leaders for a sense of direction, NATO governments should instead seek to define an intermediate goal more favorable than the current confrontation but short of the ideal. The NATO countries should be looking for a less stressful and less risky position in which they can securely observe long-term developments in the U.S.S.R. Further reductions might follow in the course of time, but only if there were enduring, positive change in the Soviet system and in Soviet actions abroad.

This book therefore deals with the possibility of cutting back the military confrontation in Europe, not with eliminating it. It deals with a world in which the East/West confrontation continues, together with the military alliances that are its manifestation.

The new NATO force posture after reductions must provide safeguards against negative changes in Soviet policy and actions. It can accomplish this by reorganizing its standing forces to emphasize increased cooperation among European NATO members. There would be a continuing but smaller American troop presence and a more effective European reserve structure, backed by a continuing but smaller NATO nuclear deterrent on which the United States, the United Kingdom, and France would cooperate.

The primary answer to uncertainties about the future actions of the Soviet Union is agreements that leave the NATO countries far more secure than they now are. Moreover, properly designed agreements would interpose a lengthy delay before even a new, expansionist Soviet leadership could feel confident that its forces could prevail in Europe.

But because so much is uncertain about the future of the U.S.S.R., in recommending action now to build down the NATO/Pact confrontation, we must make some assumptions. This book rests on the assumption that the reform line in the Soviet Union associated with the leadership of Mikhail Gorbachev will continue for the next five to six years at least. It also assumes that, even if Gorbachev is replaced for political reasons or reasons of health, the present reform line may lose some steam but it will continue, driven by the economic pressures which were its origin. In that event, positive trends in arms-control policy will also continue, although at a more conservative pace. A decidedly negative turn in Soviet policy cannot be ruled out, of course. But even if that occurred, the present openness of Soviet society assures that the West would have considerable political warning and thus time to react.

Beyond reducing the risks of the confrontation, the second major aim of the proposed deep cuts is to achieve real annual savings—up to 30 percent or more over the ten-year period—in the $300-billion defense budgets of NATO member-states, including major savings in American expenditures for Europe's defense.

Important as these objectives are, success in these C.F.E. talks and in the parallel talks on strategic nuclear reductions will be only one part of a larger task for the Bush administration and its successors.

The main task of American administrations in securing the peace over the next decade is to consolidate the trend toward build-down of the U.S./Soviet military confrontation on a worldwide basis.

The Gorbachev reform movement in the U.S.S.R. has mainly domestic causes. But it also marks the success of the policy of containment of Soviet expansion followed by the West for the past forty years. The cost of this success has been high for the western alliance, and especially the United States. It includes tragic losses in two wars, Korea and Vietnam; a foreign policy, national economy, and national research effort in which the military component has played a dominant and by normal standards excessive role; and an enormous and rapidly increasing national debt. It is time for us to realize that containment has succeeded and that we can afford to cut back on the high rate of investment for national security.

The Soviet reform movement presents a remarkable and possibly unique opportunity to do so. The United States must use that opportunity not only to achieve deep mutual cuts in nuclear and conventional forces but to establish an enduring pattern of negotiated controls over all areas of East/West military competition. That effort should include an understanding, formal or informal, between the United States and the Soviet Union on mutual restraint in military intervention in the Third World encompassing agreed restrictions on providing arms and military advisers. It should also include some mutual restraint on naval forces that takes into account the widely differing geostrategic position of the United States and the Soviet Union.

Effective defenses will continue to be necessary for the United States. But the Bush administration should take the lead in moving away from the post-World War II international system dominated by military considerations (and especially by nuclear weapons). It should move instead toward a different global system in which mutual restraint in military forces is combined with a degree of cooperation in damping down regional conflicts and in managing an increasingly stressed natural environment.

If the U.S./Soviet military rivalry in Europe, in strategic nuclear arms worldwide, and in the Third World fades and is replaced to a degree by mutual restraint and cooperation on a widening range of specific issues, then the two former rivals will have to find some surrogate to intervene in regional quarrels where they once might have played a more direct role. Such a surrogate is needed to assure that these quarrels do not spread and intensify uncontrollably. The situation points inescapably to the revival and rebuilding of the United Nations Security Council, which has itself been paralyzed by the postwar U.S./Soviet rivalry. In disappointment and frustration, Americans have turned hard against the U.N. and have been slow to recognize this logic. The Soviet leadership, in contrast, has already made clear that it grasps the point.

We suggest here how the twenty-three member-states of the NATO alliance and the Warsaw Treaty Organization can proceed to make deep cuts in the East/West military confrontation in Europe. It is not enough merely to desire a more peaceful world of reduced military tension and military costs. To dismantle this enormously destructive time bomb is a sensitive and complicated task; we have to know what specific steps to take—and which to reject. In one sense, then, this is a "How-To-Do-It" book. Our intent is to give some useful suggestions to governments and negotiators. We also aim to help the interested public understand the issues that negotiators in the force-reduction talks will be trying to solve over the coming years, to follow the course of the new Vienna talks more closely, and to develop views of its own on these subjects, a process which has already taken place with regard to the strategic nuclear confrontation. The book should remain topical for many years to come. If the C.F.E. conference succeeds, it will be followed by others dealing with much the same issues.

The task of build-down in Europe is enormously difficult. The East/West military confrontation has lasted for more than forty years and has deep roots. Many serious-minded people in the West think that its continuation, even at high cost in money and risk, is the only effective guarantor of peace and stability in Europe. They fear that tampering with this intricate system of military stalemate may bring instability and even trigger conflict. If the system works, they argue, don't change it.

These worries could prove well-founded. Some forms of troop reduction could increase instability and the incentives for preemptive attack in a crisis. In a worst-case situation, negotiated force reductions could elicit uncontrollable political pressures in the West leading to the wholesale withdrawal of American troops from Europe; to the stripping away of Europe's remaining American, British, and French nuclear deterrent; to German neutrality; to the dissolution or paralysis of the western military coalition; and to lasting intimidation of western Europe by the Soviet Union, which will remain a military superpower even if an agreement to reduce strategic nuclear forces is negotiated.

As we have pointed out, no one, including the Soviet leadership under General Secretary Mikhail Gorbachev, knows where the forces that have been unleashed by the Soviet programs of openness and restructuring will lead the Soviet Union. The Soviet Union may revert to an expansionist policy. Given this gnawing and persisting uncertainty, some argue that it would be better for the West to wait, to keep up its defenses, and to observe whether in fact the Soviet Union ultimately moves to an enduring pattern of pluralism, and only then to lower its guard.

Others say that if negotiations for force reductions succeed and improve the East/West military balance, the large Soviet withdrawals that would result could plunge eastern Europe into turmoil. Will there be serious, widespread unrest? Will the governments gradually lose control, perhaps even in East Germany, the most sensitive of all the Warsaw Pact states because of its common border—and common nationality—with the Federal Republic of Germany? Will arguments among eastern European states, civil wars, or a push for German unity destabilize Europe? In short, will the governments of the two alliances solve their immediate problem—reducing the risks and costs of the East/West confrontation in Europe—only to create even more danger-

ous instabilities, instabilities that could culminate in the very war that
the confrontation was able to avert, thus fulfilling the nightmares of
those who believe that the present structure with all its risks and costs
should continue?

   This is a powerful negative vision. It must be looked at seriously. But
as we shall see in the concluding chapter, shrinking the forces of the two
alliances does not mean abolishing the alliances or their power to
contribute to order in Europe. Moreover, other institutions are emerging to take on part of this role. The time is foreseeable though distant
when the European Community, already an economic superpower, will
emerge as a political superpower as well, and take on the capacity to
defend itself. The ongoing negotiating process of the Conference on
Cooperation and Security in Europe—the parent organization of the
new C.F.E. talks—may in time also develop some all-European institutions bridging the two alliances.

   Moreover, the risks in continuing the status quo in Europe are high.
The threat of nuclear retaliation around which the defenses of both
alliances are in essence organized is a very dangerous way to deter war.
If it fails, as all forms of deterrence eventually have, the result will be
general catastrophe. The European military confrontation is not static
but dynamic. The next wave of competitive improvements in forces will
see the deployment by both alliances of many hundreds of conventionally armed surface-to-surface missiles with ranges of up to 500 kilometers. Because the best targets for these weapons are the missile sites,
airfields, ports, rail junctions, and field headquarters of the opposing
alliance, there will be a high incentive to use them preemptively at the
outset of conflict—without the inhibitions of using nuclear weapons.
The NATO/Pact confrontation will become more unstable.

   In the early 1960s the countries of the western coalition reached the
decision that it was unnecessary and undesirable to await the transfor-
mation of the totalitarian Soviet system before entering into arms-
control agreements with the U.S.S.R. Correctly, they concluded that
agreements with the U.S.S.R. and its allies could benefit western
security and also promote the internal evolution in the U.S.S.R. and
eastern Europe that they desired. These are major reasons why
negotiation for a strategic nuclear reduction agreement will continue in
the Bush administration.

   The failure of the West to energetically investigate Soviet proposals
for force cuts in Europe in favor of proceeding with competition
between the alliances in force improvements could also have negative
effects on internal developments in the U.S.S.R., by discrediting the

Soviet leaders who are actively pushing arms control with the West as part of their overall program. We may be sceptical that actions by the West have much influence on the reform process inside the Soviet system, or, indeed, that they should be designed to have an influence. But in agreeing on well-conceived measures of arms control with the Soviet Union and its allies, we are encouraging the reform process while gaining a clear security benefit for ourselves.

In the West, if governments do not vigorously seek the possible benefits of a build-down in the military confrontation, there is considerable risk that pressures for unilateral western budget and troop cuts by individual NATO member states will intensify. This could eventually bring a reduction in NATO forces at the high additional cost of disunity over the purpose, and perhaps even the existence, of the western alliance. This outcome can be avoided and alliance unity maintained by taking the route of negotiation, or, on occasion, of unilateral action coordinated within the alliance. In that event, the forces of the NATO alliance would also shrink. But the new NATO would not be a hollow shell. It would be healthy and capable of maintaining and justifying strong transatlantic cooperation in defense, economics, and coordination of foreign policy.

The expense of the East/West military confrontation has been huge—perhaps four trillion dollars for each alliance over the past forty years—and it has hobbled economic growth on both sides. It would be irrational for the West to continue to pay such high premiums to insure its security if safe lower levels can be negotiated. The East/West military confrontation is not an impersonal natural force with an autonomous existence of its own, but a man-made artifact that men can build down.

This book describes how C.F.E. negotiators might go about the task of making reductions in conventional and nuclear forces in Europe. It describes how they might decide which weapons to cut back and how many, how to dispose of the armaments they withdraw, and how to establish a system of early-warning measures and verification controls that will ensure against surprise attack and preparation for mobilization.

The book also deals with the organization of defense in Europe after an agreement or series of agreements have reduced the level of armed forces on both sides. For we are talking here about a process that will extend into the future. The NATO and Warsaw Treaty alliances may eventually be connected by some common institutions—in the framework of the on-going Conference for Security and Cooperation in

Europe—for information exchange, the management of verification and compliance, and the reduction of risk. But the two alliances are likely to continue to provide much of the framework for defense, stability, and political change in Europe.

Because this book deals with the many practical problems of building down the military confrontation in Europe, it may create the cumulative impression that the central task is so complex as to be impossible. This impression would be wrong. Present trends in East/West relations are favorable; the political confrontation in Europe has peaked and is on a downward slope. That downward movement can be reversed, but not easily. Sooner or later, by one means or another, the downward movement will encompass the NATO/Pact military confrontation also. It would appear therefore that our choice is not over the general trend, but over its articulation in specific actions and approaches.

In writing this book, I owe a great deal to the advice of Stanley Resor, former Undersecretary of Defense and M.B.F.R. negotiator; no one in the United States has maintained over long years a clearer vision of reducing force levels in Europe. I owe thanks to Dr. Edward Warner of the Rand Corporation, one of the country's best-informed defense analysts, for information on the air balance in Europe; to James Blackwell of the Meridian Corporation for always practical advice on verification; and to Gordon Adams and his colleagues at the Center on Budget and Policy Priorities, a public-interest organization located in Washington, D.C., for estimating the savings in the U.S. defense budget that might be achieved with deep cuts in the forces assigned to the defense of Europe. Of course, none of these experts is responsible for what I have written here.

My deepest thanks go to Deborah McGill for her discerning editorial skill in making the complicated less so, and to Ellen Dicks, a world leader in patience and precision, for preparing the text. Emma Arguelles and Christopher Bolkcom did the difficult work of preparing the numerical charts.

JONATHAN DEAN

1 Beginning the Build-Down in Europe: Negotiating the I.N.F. Treaty

On June 1, 1988, the most turbulent chapter in the history of East/West arms control culminated in Moscow with the televised exchange by President Ronald Reagan and General Secretary Mikhail Gorbachev of documents ratifying the treaty on intermediate-range nuclear forces (I.N.F.). The "Treaty Between the United States of America and the Union of Soviet Socialist Republics on the Elimination of Their Intermediate-Range and Shorter-Range Missiles" marks the first successful effort to build down the East/West military confrontation in Europe. Thus any attempt to judge the prospects for continuing the build-down process and for significantly cutting back the vast force concentration on that continent must begin with I.N.F.[1]

In this chapter, we review the course of the I.N.F. talks to explain values and apprehensions which are still strong today and play important roles in the relations within and between the rival NATO and Warsaw Pact alliances. The following chapter will analyze the specific military and political legacies of the agreement for further attempts to cut back the confrontation.

The I.N.F. treaty now being implemented calls for the destruction of all U.S. and Soviet ground-based missiles (sometimes called surface-to-surface missiles) with ranges between 500 and 5,500 kilometers and prohibits the production of new missiles within those ranges.

I.N.F.'s genesis goes back three decades, to the late 1950s, when the United States deployed intermediate-range, nuclear-armed ballistic missiles in western Europe and the Soviet Union responded in kind on its own soil. The United States had then offered to deploy its own newly developed Thor and Jupiter intermediate-range missiles in western Europe in order to deal with an early outbreak of uneasiness by European NATO governments over the reliability of American nuclear support.

European concerns had at that point been triggered by the Soviet Union's successful launch of the Sputnik satellite in October, 1957.

Many European and American officials assumed that this technological feat meant that the U.S.S.R. would soon be able to deploy nuclear-armed ballistic missiles of intercontinental range which could strike the home territory of the United States.

Recurrent doubts by European officials and government leaders in the readiness of the United States to use nuclear weapons in the defense of Europe at the cost of exposing the United States to Soviet nuclear attack—and American efforts to assuage these doubts lest they lead to successful Soviet intimidation of western European governments—have been an important element of the U.S./European relationship throughout the cold war period. In a sense, these doubts were the unavoidable price the Europeans paid for their decision not to mortgage their war-ravaged economies to the attempt to match Soviet strength in conventional forces. The decision created a relationship of uncomfortable dependence on a remote superpower whose political processes were beyond the control of Europeans.

The post-Sputnik predictions proved to be right. Strategic-range intercontinental ballistic missiles were developed and deployed, first by the Soviet Union and then by the United States, the latter in far greater numbers. Yet even before missiles of strategic range were in place, an imbalance was exposed in intermediate-range weapons. The United States could use its nuclear-capable land- and carrier-based aircraft deployed in and around Europe—what the Soviet Union came to call "forward-based systems"—together with its intermediate-range missiles to attack the Soviet Union on its home territory. But if the Soviet Union wished to retaliate without launching its strategic missiles and escalating the conflict to all-out nuclear war, it could do so only by attacking America's allies—not the United States itself. This difference in the degree of nuclear threat to the three principal actors involved— the U.S., the U.S.S.R., and Europe—sparked a deep controversy among them that continues today.

The deployment in Europe of American intermediate-range missiles in the late 1950s led ultimately to the Cuban missile crisis in October, 1962. By placing intermediate-range nuclear missiles in Cuba, the Soviet Union was in part attempting to redress the imbalance of threat we have just described. In the aftermath of this confrontation, Premier Nikita Khrushchev withdrew Soviet intermediate-range missiles from Cuba and President John F. Kennedy withdrew American Thor and Jupiter missiles from western Europe. This outcome resolved the immediate conflict between the U.S. and the U.S.S.R. over Soviet missiles in Cuba. But it left about 600 Soviet intermediate-range missiles targeted on western Europe, a fact of grave concern to western European political leaders.

The shock of the Cuban missile crisis led the United States and the Soviet Union to bring the talks on limiting nuclear tests to a rapid conclusion and provided much of the motivation for the SALT I negotiations. The partial test-ban treaty signed in 1963 by the United States, the Soviet Union, and the United Kingdom prohibited nuclear tests by the signatories at sea and in the air; it was the first nuclear arms-control agreement since the beginning of the cold war. SALT I, signed in 1972, froze the number of intercontinental delivery systems of the U.S. and the U.S.S.R.

Western European leaders repeatedly pressed for the inclusion of Soviet intermediate-range missiles in SALT I and then in SALT II. But at the same time they did not want the United States to reduce its forward-based systems and tactical-range nuclear weapons, both of which were considered to hold in check the Warsaw Pact's superiority over NATO in conventional weapons. Yet there was no practical possibility in SALT I of restricting Soviet intermediate-range missiles without also restricting U.S. forward-based systems. Consequently, SALT I did not cover deployments of either Soviet intermediate-range missiles or American forward-based systems. The imbalance in Europe remained: with forward-based systems the United States posed a threat to the Soviet Union which the Soviet Union lacked the means to counter without escalating conflict or attacking western Europe with its conventional forces or nuclear weapons. (With the dependable, accurate, and easily concealed long-range sea-launched cruise missiles the Soviet Union is now developing, it may finally be obtaining an "equalizer" for this important United States advantage.)

Ironically, the SALT I treaty not only failed to deal with intermediate-range missiles but actually encouraged their development. Let us consider first the effect the treaty had on the Soviet Union.

At the time of the treaty, the Soviet arsenal of intermediate-range weapons—SS-4s and SS-5s—was aging. The missiles were slow to ready for launch and had only one rather inaccurate warhead. But the missile which the Soviets had developed as a follow-on—the variable-range SS-11 missile—had in the meanwhile been designated a strategic missile in SALT I because of its potential to reach intercontinental range; consequently, its numbers were restricted. In the early 1970s, possibly even before SALT I was signed, Moscow decided to proceed with the development of a different alternative to the SS-4 and SS-5: the SS-20.

Even if the Soviet leadership had had in mind only a replacement for the SS-4 and SS-5, it produced a weapon of far greater potential. The SS-20, though not strategic, could travel farther than other intermediate-range missiles in the U.S.S.R.'s arsenal or in NATO's. Its three warheads could be programmed to strike different targets with unusually high accuracy. The SS-20 could be moved from one launch site to another fairly easily, and its solid fuel gave it quick launch capacity. (The SS-4 and SS-5, in contrast, took from eight to twenty-four hours to charge and their highly volatile liquid fuel had to be topped up every five hours to keep them in ready status. The United States' Thors and Jupiters, too, had been liquid fuelled.) When the first SS-20 rolled out in 1977, NATO governments declared that the deployment would change the nuclear balance in Europe. They saw in the SS-20 a counter-force weapon that could be used for preemptive strikes on NATO command posts, ports, and nuclear-weapons sites.

Soviet leaders were probably unprepared for the loud public outcry that greeted their new weapon in the West. Particularly in the aftermath of the December, 1979, Soviet invasion of Afghanistan, NATO countries came to see the SS-20 as a quantum jump in Soviet nuclear armaments that signified the U.S.S.R.'s intention to achieve regional nuclear superiority. Whether this was indeed the case is open to question; despite the important improvements incorporated in the SS-20, many western experts doubted that the deployment had decisive military significance. If the U.S.S.R. truly wished to dominate Europe, they reasoned, it already had a highly usable strategic nuclear arsenal to brandish.

Some Soviet officials and academicians seem now to consider the deployment of the SS-20 a mistake, because whatever military advantages it offered were outweighed by the strong impression it created of Soviet aggressiveness and because fielding it elicited for the first time in a generation the deployment of a new American intermediate-range missile in Europe. In an interview with the weekly Soviet magazine *New Times* (November 20, 1987), Deputy Foreign Minister Aleksander Bessmertnykh said the decision to deploy SS-20s in 1977 was not "optimal. ... We had quite enough SS-4 and SS-5 missiles in Europe. Then we began to deploy SS-20s. Technically, they are more perfect. But the question is how they fitted into our military-strategic concept of the European theater."

How did the SALT I treaty motivate the United States to develop and deploy a new generation of intermediate-range nuclear missiles? The U.S. had more than one reason to favor such missiles. One was the growing effectiveness of Warsaw Pact air defenses, which undermined longstanding qualitative advantages of NATO attack aircraft and their capacity to penetrate eastern European airspace. Most western military experts believed that missiles were the best answer to the penetration problem. Another reason was simply the availability of the new technology. This goes far to explain Soviet as well as American missile procurements during the 1970s. Planning in the United States for modification of the Pershing I (which had been deployed in Federal Germany since the 1960s) to increase the missile's range and accuracy began in the early 1970s. Full field development was approved by President Jimmy Carter in 1977, the year the SS-20 was deployed.

More compelling than any of these incentives, however, was the SALT I treaty's recognition that the Soviet Union, after twenty-five years of assiduous effort, had achieved parity—that is, a rough equality—with the United States in strategic nuclear weapons. SALT I's codification of U.S./Soviet strategic parity—the most momentous military development of the U.S./Soviet cold-war military competition—created fresh doubts in the minds of European NATO experts as to the reliability of American nuclear protection for Europe.

NATO's strategy of flexible response, formally approved in the late 1960s, holds that the alliance will use any necessary means, including first use of nuclear weapons, to repel a Soviet attack on Europe. The underlying theory was that, rather than to move directly to all-out nuclear war by ordering use of strategic weapons, an American president might be more likely to decide to use nuclear weapons in the defense of Europe if American nuclear weapons of various types and ranges were already available in Europe. This circumstance would make NATO deterrent strategy more credible to the Soviet leadership and thus more effective. Moreover, deployment in Europe of American nuclear weapons of various kinds might deter the Soviets from using counterpart weapons in an attack.

As we have seen, the original reason for deploying American intermediate-range Thor and Jupiter missiles in Europe at the end of the 1950s had been to reassure Europeans of the reliability of the American response to counter evidence that the Soviet Union was developing missiles of intercontinental range. These intermediate-range missiles also had the advantage that, with them, the United States could inflict serious damage on targets in the Soviet homeland itself— in the hope of eliciting a negotiated end to hostilities rather than escalation to strategic nuclear war.

But, once having withdrawn its intermediate-range missiles from Europe after the Cuban missile crisis, would the United States have the nerve instead to launch strategic weapons against military targets in the U.S.S.R. in defense of Europe, thus making itself a target of Soviet retaliation? Charles de Gaulle and many other NATO leaders had feared the answer was no as soon as the Soviets developed the capacity to reach U.S. territory with even a few intercontinental ballistic missiles. When the Soviets pulled even with the United States in strategic nuclear capability, these worries were intensified. Tactical-range United States nuclear weapons were not an answer. They could not strike Soviet territory and German public opinion was becoming increasingly restive about the consequences of their possible use on German territory.

European NATO leaders and American officials were concerned that these doubts could weaken U.S.–European links and they began to consider the advantages of replacing the intermediate-range systems that President Kennedy had withdrawn. In 1977 Federal German Chancellor Helmut Schmidt, who had failed to obtain firm United States assurances that Soviet intermediate-range missiles would be covered in the emerging SALT II agreement, suggested in a speech he gave in London that if the United States could not negotiate a cutback of Soviet intermediate-range missiles, then the NATO alliance might instead have to deploy intermediate-range missiles of its own. The Schmidt speech is often cited as the turning point in the West's decision to deploy new I.N.F. missiles in response to the SS-20s. It was the first public mention by a NATO leader of what came to be known as NATO's "two track" strategy: prepare to deploy as you negotiate.

The SALT II treaty, signed in 1979, once again did not cover either American forward-based systems or Soviet intermediate-range missiles. As European NATO governments saw it, both the U.S.S.R. and the U.S. were benefiting from nuclear arms control, but not western Europe. Expecting ratification of the SALT II treaty, European NATO governments insisted that the next U.S./Soviet nuclear arms-control negotiation bring them benefits, too, by finally restricting Soviet intermediate-range missiles.

NATO'S TWO-TRACK DECISION

At a special meeting of foreign and defense ministers in Brussels on December 12, 1979, NATO made a formal commitment to the two-track strategy Chancellor Schmidt had alluded to two years earlier: (1) The alliance would negotiate in the then-projected SALT III talks for limits on future deployments of American intermediate-range nuclear missiles still in development in return for reductions in the number of Soviet I.N.F. already deployed; and (2) it would proceed with development of American I.N.F. (the Pershing II ballistic missile and the ground-launched cruise missile) and would deploy 572 of the new American I.N.F. missiles (108 Pershing II and 464 ground-launched cruise missiles) if those negotiations did not succeed by late 1983.

In the communiqué of the meeting at which this decision was formally made, NATO foreign and defense ministers justified the decision by pointing to several developments. One was the expansion of Soviet intermediate-range nuclear capability brought about by deployment of the SS-20 missiles (and also of a new aircraft—the Backfire bomber, whose prospective deployment had played a major role in the SALT II talks). Another concern was the aging of NATO tactical-range nuclear armaments and the absence from the NATO arsenal of land-based intermediate-range nuclear delivery systems. Last, the ministers pointed to the Soviets' achievement of parity with the United States, which, they said, had undermined the credibility of NATO's strategy of flexible response.

Did the NATO decision violate an explicit or implicit commitment by President Kennedy not again to deploy American medium-range missiles in Europe? The Soviets never raised this claim with any real insistence, and if such a commitment existed, it could be said to have been nullified by the Soviet deployment of the new and far more capable SS-20 missiles.

To make their decision to field new missiles more palatable to the European public, the NATO ministers announced unilateral withdrawal from Europe of 1,000 American nuclear warheads. The NATO ministers also decided that, for each new single-warhead American missile deployed, the United States would withdraw one more nuclear warhead from its European stockpile. They proposed equal ceilings for the U.S. and the Soviet Union, stating that their objective was "a more stable overall nuclear balance at lower levels of nuclear weapons on both sides."

This language reflected the fact that NATO ministers were not at that point by any means thinking of eliminating Soviet and American I.N.F. but rather of deploying some American missiles and bringing the arsenal of Soviet missiles down to that number. But the ministers set no specific level of deployment as a goal of negotiation. In fact, there had been no time to fully mesh the work of the two separate committees of western officials who had developed deployment plans and arms-control positions. Filling the perceived gap in NATO's deterrent capability had priority.

A SLOW BEGINNING FOR THE I.N.F. TALKS

When in mid-December of 1979 the NATO ministers endorsed bilateral U.S./Soviet negotiations on I.N.F., they assumed that this negotiation would take place in the framework of SALT III talks. But that same month the Soviet Union invaded Afghanistan. In consequence President Carter asked the Senate to suspend consideration of the SALT II agreement. With SALT II unratified and hopes for SALT III extinguished, the I.N.F. negotiations were left in limbo. Yet Chancellor Schmidt, on a visit to the Soviet Union in June of 1980, succeeded in persuading General Secretary Leonid Brezhnev to undertake separate U.S./Soviet talks on I.N.F.

Preliminary exchanges began in October, 1980, in the last months of the Carter administration, and ended after a few weeks. (The talks were then called negotiations on "theater nuclear forces". This designation was changed by the Reagan administration because of European uneasiness over the word "theater," which implied that western Europe might be an area of foreign military operations from a distant and secure United States.) The criteria for an I.N.F. agreement that the United States presented were drawn from principles approved by NATO in connection with its 1979 decision on the two-track strategy.

Even this brief U.S./Soviet encounter raised the main issues of the subsequent negotiations. These were:

(1) Which Soviet and U.S. nuclear delivery systems should be included? From the outset, the U.S. position, approved by the NATO allies in all aspects, was to limit the scope of the negotiations to land-based I.N.F. of both countries. The United States wanted to postpone (actually, to avoid) consideration of sea-based missiles and of aircraft, because this would complicate discussion, given the many different types deployed by the two countries, and also because in these categories the United States had a technological advantage. The Soviets wanted to include both sea-based missiles and aircraft. In particular, they insisted on coverage of all U.S. fighter-bombers, including not only intermediate-range F-111s but also the short-range F-4s and carrier-based A-6s and A-7s in the classic forward-based systems that they had tried to cut in both sets of SALT talks.

(2) Geographic coverage. To prevent circumvention and to meet the interests of Asian countries, the United States wanted to cover in an agreement the highly mobile I.N.F. in the whole of the Soviet Union—both Europe and Asia, thus including Soviet nuclear weapons directed at Japan and China. The Soviet Union wished to include only armaments deployed in Europe west of the Urals.

(3) Third-country forces. The Soviet Union insisted that, because the British and French had nuclear forces that would not be covered by the negotiations, the United States would have to make deeper reductions to take British and French forces into account. Reviving a classic Soviet position which the United States had rejected in the SALT I and SALT II talks, Soviet negotiators insisted on "equal security" for the Soviets—in this particular case, equality between total Soviet I.N.F. and the total number of I.N.F. of all countries that could be launched from Europe against the Soviet Union. The consequence would be to permit the United States fewer weapons than the Soviet Union. American negotiators refused, insisting on full parity of the U.S. with the U.S.S.R. and insisting that Britain and France were sovereign countries with which the Soviet Union could negotiate further reductions if it wished.

(4) Verification. From the outset, the United States stressed the need for full verification given the mobility and reload capability of SS-20s, although U.S. negotiators advanced a specific verification approach only in the spring of 1986 and a detailed text only in the spring of 1987. The Soviets were reticent on the subject; they customarily argued either that National Technical Means (satellite photography and sensors) would be sufficient for verification or (as in other arms control negotiations) that it was premature to deal with verification measures until the outlines of a specific agreement had emerged and participants knew precisely what they had to verify.

After President Ronald Reagan assumed office in January, 1981, the European NATO governments, worried by his militantly anti-Soviet election campaign and by the emerging public sentiment against deployment in western Europe of the new American I.N.F., brought great pressure on the new administration to resume I.N.F. negotiations. The talks picked up at the end of November, 1981; by then, two of the four years NATO had said it would wait before deploying new I.N.F. in Europe had already elapsed.

Just before the I.N.F. negotiations resumed, President Reagan intensified the public-diplomacy character of the talks by inaugurating the practice, subsequently actively followed by both governments, of announcing a new negotiating position before presenting it at the table. What President Reagan proposed in 1981 was "the zero option": the United States would not deploy I.N.F. in Europe if the Soviet Union would eliminate all of its I.N.F. (SS-4s, SS-5s, and SS-20s) throughout its territories. In a draft treaty presented in Geneva in February, 1982, the United States proposed in addition a freeze on the shorter-range Soviet SS-21, SS-22, and SS-23 missiles. Aircraft were to be left to later negotiation, and British and French forces were not to be taken into account.

Administration officials, among them Secretary of State Alexander Haig after he left office, have said that the proposal for reduction to zero of both United States and Soviet I.N.F. was made for publicity— to take the high ground in propaganda—with no real expectation that the Soviet Union would ever agree.

After eighteen months of negotiation without outcome, European NATO governments, whose publics, under the impact of Soviet criticism, had come to consider the zero option inequitable and non-negotiable, now pressed the Reagan administration to propose a less extreme position. In March, 1983, President Reagan publicly offered the Soviets an alternative to the zero option (which nevertheless remained on the table). Under the new proposal, the United States would limit its I.N.F. deployments in Europe to a specific number of warheads—somewhere between 50 and 450—provided that the Soviet Union reduced the total of all its intermediate-range nuclear warheads on a global basis to the same level. As before, British and French nuclear forces would be excluded.

As NATO's 1983 deadline for deploying American I.N.F. neared, the Soviet Union appeared ready to offer still more to keep the missiles out. The Soviet negotiator in Geneva offered to go down to about 120 SS-20s in Europe in return for zero U.S. deployment, cuts roughly equivalent to deleting an equal number of warheads from the existing Soviet arsenal and from the planned U.S. arsenal. The number of British and French nuclear armaments would not be limited. Instead, they would be credited to the U.S. total of strategic weapons in other U.S./Soviet talks on reducing strategic systems. Also in the fall of 1983, Soviet General Secretary Yuri Andropov offered for the first time to freeze Soviet SS-20 deployments in Asia.

Given their position at the outset, the Soviets had shown considerable flexibility: an agreement on this basis would have meant more than a 50-percent cut in Soviet I.N.F.—a result far beyond western expectations when the talks began in 1980, and one that would probably have met the original western European desire to obtain some reduction of Soviet I.N.F. in U.S./Soviet nuclear arms control talks.

On November 23, 1983, the day after the Federal German Bundestag confirmed the Pershing II deployment and the same day the first nine Pershing IIs reached an American unit in southern Germany, Soviet negotiators walked out of the I.N.F. negotiation in Geneva. Shortly thereafter they walked out of all other arms control negotiations, including the Vienna M.B.F.R. talks on the reduction of NATO and Warsaw Pact forces.

The reason for the breakdown was quite clear. Most American and NATO officials were unwilling to accept any outcome that did not entail some deployment of United States I.N.F. For its part, the Soviet Union took the categorical position of rejecting even a minimal U.S. deployment with only limited military significance.

By the time the I.N.F. talks broke down, the issue had ceased to be one of East/West force balance. It had become a question of whether the European NATO governments, primarily the governments of the United Kingdom and Federal Germany, where the first deployments were to take place, were strong and determined enough to carry out the deployments in the face of powerful opposition from their own citizens and from the Soviet Union. Most western officials felt that, whether the original NATO decision to deploy had been right or wrong and whether the projected deployment of American I.N.F. would in fact bring additional security, giving in to Soviet pressure against deployment would be a serious political defeat for NATO—one that would leave it in dangerous disarray. In response to the arrival in Europe of the Pershings the Soviet Union announced "countermeasures," including deployment of SS-12 and SS-23 missiles forward from the U.S.S.R. into East Germany and Czechoslovakia. For the peoples of Europe, the only result of the I.N.F. negotiations thus far had been to increase nuclear deployments on both sides.

RAPID MOVEMENT AT THE NEW NEGOTIATIONS

Soon after the breakdown at Geneva, the Soviet Union indicated interest in returning to the negotiating table. But it was not until after the reelection of President Reagan in November, 1984, that agreement was reached to resume talks on I.N.F., combining them with talks on strategic weapons in a format expanded to include the issue of weapons in space. Soviet leaders insisted that all three subjects be addressed as a single package; no final agreement on any one subject could be concluded until all were resolved. Mikhail Gorbachev became the General Secretary of the Soviet Communist Party in March, 1985, just as the talks resumed in Geneva. Shortly thereafter, and in direct connection with the emergence of Gorbachev as Soviet leader, there began a series of important Soviet moves toward the American position on I.N.F.:

(1) Soviet leaders, reversing course, agreed to keep separate the I.N.F. talks from resolution of other subjects under negotiation in Geneva, including that of weapons in space. There were many ups and downs in the Soviet position on this issue of a separate agreement. Briefly, General Secretary Gorbachev agreed to it at his summit conference with President Reagan in Geneva in November, 1985, only to revoke it in October, 1986, after the breakdown of the Reykjavik summit, and then to revalidate it in February, 1987.

(2) The Soviets agreed to confine the talks to United States and Soviet armaments only. In General Secretary Gorbachev's proposal for elimination of all nuclear weapons, announced in January, 1986, he dropped the Soviet insistence that U.K. and French nuclear weapons be accounted for in an I.N.F. agreement. He confirmed this position at the 1986 Reykjavik summit.

(3) At the 1985 Geneva summit General Secretary Gorbachev agreed to focus on reduction of land-based missiles; Soviet negotiators subsequently dropped demands for inclusion of American nuclear-capable aircraft in the I.N.F. treaty, the most recent relinquishment of the U.S.S.R.'s longstanding objective to restrict American forward-based systems. (Yet the Soviets were to bring up the subject again in connection with the new NATO/Warsaw Pact force-reduction talks.)

(4) The Soviets moved from proposing that the United States have zero I.N.F. in Europe and the Soviets about 120 warheads—their last offer before breaking off the negotiations in 1983—to a zero–zero outcome for Europe.

(5) Although the Soviets insisted at the outset that the scope of the I.N.F. talks be confined to Soviet SS-20 missiles deployed in Europe west of the Urals, they had subsequently agreed to freeze their SS-20s in Asia. Then, at the October, 1986 Reykjavik summit, they agreed to reduce the number of Soviet I.N.F. in the Asian

U.S.S.R. to 100 warheads. In July, 1987, they agreed to reduce the number of warheads in Asia to zero if the United States did the same with its own small holdings in American territory, making the elimination of I.N.F. complete.

(6) Recognizing a particular interest of European NATO countries, the United States had proposed in 1981 that, in order to prevent circumvention of an agreement to eliminate missiles in the 1,000 to 5,500-kilometer range—SS-4s, SS-5s and SS-20s—and American Pershing II and ground-based cruise missiles, an I.N.F. agreement must also include a freeze on missiles with ranges of 500 to 1,000 kilometers (that is, Soviet SS-23 and SS-12 missiles and the American Pershing I).

At the Reykjavik summit, the Soviets conceded on this point, then withdrew their assent. In late February, 1987, they offered to take up the whole issue in separate negotiations. But in April, 1987, when Secretary of State George Schultz travelled to Moscow, they offered to get rid of these missiles in Europe. In July, 1987, General Secretary Gorbachev broadened this proposal to include elimination of the shorter-range missiles in Asia. Soviet negotiators then made Gorbachev's offer dependent on the elimination of seventy-two Pershing IA missiles owned and operated by Federal German forces with their warheads in American custody. In August Chancellor Helmut Kohl, under considerable pressure from all sides, including the large majority of his own people, agreed to destroy the German Pershing IAs once destruction of Soviet and American I.N.F. was completed.

(7) After maintaining for years that primary reliance in verifying an I.N.F. agreement should be on "National Technical Means", that is, on satellite imaging and electronic sensors, and that it would be premature to deal with verification until reductions had been spelled out, the Soviets agreed in principle at the Reykjavik summit to American suggestions for verifying an I.N.F. accord, including exchange of data and on-site monitoring. Detailed U.S. proposals on these subjects were presented at Geneva in March, 1987, and the Soviets agreed to most; the two sides began work on the procedures to implement these concepts the following September. (The United States dropped a proposal for "suspect-site" challenge inspections anywhere in the United States or the Soviet Union after objections from some American security agencies and after the need for such inspection had been diminished by the Soviet's agreement to eliminate I.N.F.)

SIGNIFICANCE OF THE AGREEMENT

How did this outcome, remarkable by any previous standard of U.S./
Soviet arms control negotiation, come about? And what changed the
position of the U.S.S.R. between 1983, when it walked out of the talks
in Geneva, and 1985, when it began a steady move toward the NATO
position as represented by the United States? Several factors played a
role in the outcome; the absence of any one of them might have brought
a different result.

The success of NATO governments in convincing their citizens that
deployment of the Soviet SS-20s represented a dangerous new threat
had unintended consequences for NATO. It revived and intensified
public worries about the possibility and consequences of limited
nuclear war in Europe. At the same time, it obscured the fact that
NATO wanted a modernized American I.N.F. not just to check the SS-
20s, but also to give the U.S. an additional option for retaliation short
of strategic nuclear war if the U.S.S.R. invaded Europe. Failure to get
this rationale across to the European public left the European NATO
governments without convincing grounds to support their strong
preference to retain some American I.N.F. when the Soviet Union
moved to accept elimination of all I.N.F. missiles.

The NATO governments made a second serious miscalculation of
the state of public opinion when they decided to make the American
nuclear missiles land-based rather than sea-based. NATO officials
urged land-basing, in part, because they believed doing so would
provide greater reassurance to European publics of American support
in a crisis. But NATO officials had wrongly projected their own doubts
over flexible response onto European publics. At that time, the
European publics needed no additional assurance that the U.S. would
use nuclear weapons in their defense. Rather, they needed assurance
that the new missile deployments would not bring war closer and that,
in the event of war, the superpowers would not use their intermediate-
range nuclear missiles to do battle against each other on European soil
while keeping their own home territories out of the nuclear war. These
fears, heightened but not originated by astute Soviet propaganda,
resulted in huge public demonstrations against both the new American
"Euromissiles" and the Soviet SS-20s.

Pressures from European publics and their leaders had led President
Carter, in 1980, to agree to enter into bilateral negotiations on I.N.F.
notwithstanding his refusal to ratify SALT II. And they led President
Reagan to continue the talks after he took office, in 1981. The

vehement opposition of many Europeans to the stationing of intermediate-range nuclear missiles anywhere in Europe and the calls for the
elimination of I.N.F. by opposition parties in Belgium, the Netherlands, and Luxembourg, Federal Germany, the U.K., Norway, and
Denmark may well have played a major role in the decision of the
NATO governments to press for the zero option as the NATO goal
even though the governments actually preferred a less radical outcome.

At the same time, public opposition to I.N.F. deployments in
western Europe persuaded the Soviet leadership that the deployments
could be blocked and encouraged the Soviets to withdraw from the
Geneva negotiations in 1983. Their withdrawal was admittedly a
mistake, but the clear evidence of a desire for positive change in East/
West relations on the part of so many West Europeans, especially
Federal Germans, seems to have eased deep-seated Soviet worries
about irredentist German militarism and probably contributed to the
general shift of the Soviet position on arms control beginning in 1985.

One key factor in the zero-I.N.F. outcome was the willingness of
European NATO governments to deploy American I.N.F. despite
strong domestic resistance and intense Soviet pressures, including the
forward deployment of Soviet missiles in East Germany and Czechoslovakia and threats of an "ice age" in relations between the two
Germanies. The actual deployment of the American missiles may have
influenced the Soviets to offer more for the missiles' elimination than
they might have otherwise—to the extent of dismantling all of their
own SS-20s.

Still, the scope of Soviet moves in negotiations on strategic nuclear
armaments, on chemical weapons, and on I.N.F. has been impressive.
The U.S.S.R.'s pledges to destroy not only the SS-20s, SS-4s, and SS-5s
in Europe but also those in Asia, to destroy its SS-23s and SS-12s in
addition, to submit to stringent verification, to withdraw its forces from
Afghanistan, and to make the significant unilateral reductions in
conventional forces that Gorbachev announced in December, 1988 (see
Chapter 3 for details) argue for broader motives than purely military
ones. Some western officials believe that the Reagan defense build-up
was the decisive factor; yet the Soviet Union had no apparent difficulty
in adding warheads and strategic delivery systems to keep up with
increases in U.S. strategic forces.

Instead, a sea change in Soviet policy toward the West seems to have
swept the I.N.F. negotiations up in its forward rush. Most observers see
the motive for this change as domestic. The U.S.S.R. needed to
improve relations with western governments in order to make cutbacks

in its military outlays and bring about reform of the Soviet economic system. From this viewpoint, concluding an I.N.F. treaty (technically the most separable part of the current or prospective East/West arms control agenda and less complex than either U.S./Soviet strategic reductions or reductions in conventional forces in Europe) was a logical first step, though a costly one. Some western observers also believe that the present Soviet political and military leadership has a serious desire to keep conflict in Europe non-nuclear if war should break out and that the elimination of I.N.F. serves that goal.

A minority of western observers saw the Soviet position on I.N.F. as part of a deliberate effort to render unworkable the NATO strategy of flexible response, in order to improve prospects for a conventional attack by the Warsaw Treaty countries on western Europe or for purposes of political intimidation, given the U.S.S.R.'s numerically superior conventional forces.

Continued caution in interpreting Soviet actions is highly advisable. Still, this negative assessment of Soviet objectives seems a narrow, Eurocentric view, given the many other Soviet arms control moves outside Europe already mentioned here, which argue convincingly for a general Soviet effort, of whatever duration, to improve relations with the West. However, the specific concerns of this group of critical western officials remain strong and we will return to them in the next chapter.

The I.N.F. agreement has considerable significance for East/West arms control in general. For many NATO observers, the treaty has vindicated the alliance's much-criticized two-track strategy. For a worried minority of NATO defense experts and political conservatives the treaty has seriously weakened American nuclear protection of Europe and left our allies militarily and politically vulnerable to the U.S.S.R. For the Soviet Union, the I.N.F. treaty marks the success— this time, probably enduring—of a long effort, begun in the late 1950s, to prevent deployment in Europe of missiles that the United States could use for rapid, destructive strikes at vital targets within the Soviet Union—including Moscow—without having to call upon American strategic nuclear forces.

The favorable terms of the I.N.F. treaty have increased western hopes for Soviet flexibility in making cutbacks of strategic weapons and conventional forces. Already, because of the treaty, considerable progress toward a U.S./Soviet agreement on strategic reductions has been made. The verification procedures established for I.N.F. have been adopted by mutual assent for use in a strategic arms reduction agreement.

The success of the I.N.F. talks probably resulted more from the emergence of a conciliation-minded Soviet leadership than from a particular western negotiating approach. Whether the treaty also marks a true turning point in East/West relations is largely dependent on whether this conciliatory Soviet attitude persists.

One result of the treaty is clear now. The entire I.N.F. episode has done more than nearly any other single development of the past forty years to change the nature of the defense relationship between the United States and the European members of NATO. In the following chapter we shall consider how that relationship has changed, in order to understand the bearing it will have on future arms control efforts, including negotiations to build down forces in Europe.

2 Military and Political Consequences of the I.N.F. Treaty

As the first direct move to build down the military confrontation in Europe, the I.N.F. treaty has set the stage for the new round of NATO/Pact force-reduction talks. In this chapter, we shall analyze first the military and then the political consequences of the treaty.

WHAT THE I.N.F. TREATY DOES NOT DO

The I.N.F. treaty leaves untouched ground-launched missiles with ranges greater than 5,500 kilometers or less than 500 kilometers. It does not affect air- and sea-launched missiles, nuclear-capable artillery, or rockets with ranges under 500 kilometers. It does not affect the nuclear delivery systems of third countries, like those of the United Kingdom and France. Nor does it affect American or Soviet surface-to-air weapons or missiles designed for launch in the atmosphere or space; these include weapons designed to destroy satellites and missiles. Finally, although the treaty calls for the destruction of all intermediate-range missiles, it does not require destruction of the nuclear warheads and guidance systems with which they are equipped.

In the ratification hearings held by the United States Senate beginning in February, 1988, critics of the I.N.F. treaty pointed out what they considered to be two disturbing gaps in the treaty's provisions. First, they worried about what the U.S.S.R. might do with the warheads and guidance systems removed from its I.N.F. missiles. In particular they were concerned about a new mobile intercontinental ballistic missile in the Soviet arsenal, the SS-25, which, though not interchangeable with the SS-20, has a first stage outwardly similar to it. They wondered, what was to stop the Soviets from secretly arming SS-25s with guidance systems and warheads salvaged from the destroyed SS-20s and thus creating a new intermediate-range missile?

Such a conversion is theoretically possible. It would be out of keeping with Soviet strategy to date, however, because, undertaken in secrecy, it would not serve to induce restraint and caution in the NATO

18

alliance. And such an effect on NATO was clearly the aim of the Soviet Union when it deployed intermediate-range missiles in the first place, starting in the late 1950s. Moreover, if the Soviet Union intended to convert SS-25s to SS-20s, why at the same time would it energetically pursue a strategic reduction treaty that could restrict or diminish its SS-25 stockpile?

Senate critics of the treaty have also claimed that the U.S.S.R. stands to benefit from the absence of provision for inspection on short notice of suspect sites. They reason that, unrestrained by such a provision, the U.S.S.R. could hide existing SS-20 missiles or produce them covertly.

This scenario, like the preceding one, ignores the fact that deterrence cannot be achieved in secrecy. It also entails some practical difficulties. For example, while it is possible that some SS-20s could be concealed and even that clandestine manufacture could take place at undeclared sites, actual use of the missiles would require personnel recently trained in their deployment and at least a minimum array of ground-based guidance and control systems. These systems could not be set up without considerable risk of observation. Without thorough testing, the missiles could not be used with much confidence, because the solid propellant which fuels them deteriorates over time. The intrusive inspection requirements that will accompany the next strategic nuclear reduction agreement would make clandestine storage or production of I.N.F. missiles still more difficult. Moreover, as a result of the I.N.F. agreement, the U.S. and the U.S.S.R. are likely to increase their coverage of each other's territory by national technical means, especially satellite photography, further eroding the possibility of militarily significant evasion.

WHAT THE I.N.F. TREATY DOES DO

The I.N.F. treaty eliminates all land-based U.S. and Soviet missiles of intermediate range (500 to 5,500 kilometers, or 300 to 3,400 miles). The ban is "global," covering not only missiles based in the European theater but all missiles of this type in the possession of the two countries, including Soviet missiles in Asia. It covers undeployed as well as installed weapons. Missiles and their launchers must be unambiguously destroyed in accordance with detailed procedures. Missile warheads must be disassembled; their guidance systems and nuclear material may be kept for use in other weapons.

In numerical terms, the I.N.F. treaty is very favorable to the United

States and its allies. It provides for withdrawal of four deployed Soviet warheads for every American one. In all, the U.S. will eliminate 859 missiles and the U.S.S.R. 1,836, more than twice as many. The weapons covered by the treaty are shown in the table below:

	Missiles deployed	Missiles undeployed	Warheads deployed
United States			
Intermediate-Range			
Pershing II	120	127	120
Ground-Launched			
Cruise Missile	309	133	309
Subtotal	429	260	429
Shorter-Range			
Pershing IA*	0	170	0
Subtotal	0	170	0
Total	429	430	429
Soviet Union			
Intermediate-Range			
SS-20	405	245	1,215
SS-4	65	105	65
SS-5	0	6	0
Ground-Launched			
Cruise Missile**	0	84	0
Subtotal	470	440	1,280
Shorter-Range			
SS-23	167	33	167
SS-12	220	506	220
Subtotal	387	539	387
Total	857	979	1,667

* Does not include 72 Pershing IA missiles and 28 reloads under control of the Federal Republic of Germany (warheads under U.S. control), which will also be dismantled.
** Tested but never deployed.

It is true that I.N.F. reductions represent no more than 4 percent of the total nuclear warhead holdings of the United States and the Soviet Union. However, that statistic is not in any sense an indicator of the treaty's military significance.

The treaty's advantage to western Europe is great. As we saw in the first chapter, from the late 1950s on, the U.S.S.R. had more than 600 intermediate-range missiles aimed at western Europe, a continuing source of worry to European NATO governments. They feared that the Soviet Union might use these missiles to launch a "theater" nuclear war against western Europe. Doing so would avoid a direct Soviet assault on American territory while keeping intact the Soviet strategic arsenal, thus decreasing the chances that the United States would retaliate for the attack on Europe by escalating to strategic nuclear war. With the deployment of the triple-warhead SS-20, Europe's concerns grew. The SS-20 launching system is mobile, thus less vulnerable to NATO's counterfire, and thus more likely to survive to fire again. It is more accurate than the SS-4s and -5s and can be readied for firing more quickly. Now this entire class of Soviet missiles is being eliminated.

The treaty contains a further bonus for NATO in the elimination of Soviet missiles with ranges of 500 to 1,000 kilometers, a category in which the U.S.S.R. had great numerical superiority over NATO. In recent years, as these Soviet missiles improved in accuracy, NATO commanders have feared that they might be used at the outset of a Pact attack with conventional or chemical warheads for strikes against NATO nuclear storage sites, airfields, anti-aircraft missile installations, and command centers. This strategy would allow the Soviets to preempt much of NATO's nuclear capability without resorting to nuclear weapons themselves, and at the same time deal a decisive blow to NATO's air assets, whose full use would be essential to the defeat of a Pact attack. NATO has been so worried about this possibility that it has been planning an expensive new generation of missile defenses in anticipation. The I.N.F. treaty largely eliminates the need to invest in such defenses.

For the Soviets, the main military benefit of the treaty is the removal of Pershing II missiles, the most accurate ballistic missile in the U.S. arsenal. From their bases in West Germany these missiles could reach Soviet territory in only ten minutes. The Soviets have viewed the Pershing as the potential spearhead of a U.S. preemptive strike, posing the threat of a "decapitation" attack with little or no warning against Soviet command posts and political leadership. This fear, whether realistic or not, could have been a dangerous source of instability in the event of a serious crisis or conventional conflict in Europe, since it would have increased the Soviets' incentive to launch a preemptive attack of their own before the Pershings were used. By encouraging a hair-trigger Soviet posture, the Pershing deployment might also have increased the risks of accidental or inadvertent nuclear war.

Thus, the treaty serves NATO security not only by redressing the previous imbalance in I.N.F. missiles—eliminating an area of historic Soviet advantage—but also by strengthening crisis stability in Europe.

Although the Soviet Union has many nuclear delivery systems of adequate range, both missiles and aircraft, which it could use to attack western Europe, none of these now has the combination of assured penetration capacity, accuracy, and limited yield of the SS-20 missiles. Moreover, if an agreement reducing the number of strategic nuclear weapons is concluded, the number of alternative Soviet missile systems will be reduced, too, and there will be a greater need to dedicate the systems remaining to strategic targets. None of the longer-range missiles is yet equipped with conventional warheads, and there would be high costs in using these expensive vehicles to deliver a limited weight of conventional explosives.

In general, the alternative systems available to both alliances are either more dispersed, more distant, or less vulnerable than I.N.F. systems. This aspect strengthens the I.N.F. treaty and increases the gain in crisis stability already described.

The net military advantage to NATO of eliminating these Soviet missiles is considerably greater than the disadvantage to NATO brought about by the loss of Pershing IIs, ground-launched cruise missiles, and the German Pershing IAs. NATO has always considered itself a defensive alliance facing a numerically superior adversary which could initiate war by launching an aggressive attack. A Soviet first strike using highly destructive missiles equipped with nuclear, conventional, or chemical warheads could cripple NATO's nuclear and conventional forces and confer on the Soviets an enormous, perhaps decisive, advantage. This advantage would far outweigh the potential retaliatory effect of the few NATO I.N.F. missiles which might survive such a first strike. Consequently, the elimination of all of these Soviet weapons is clearly a benefit for NATO.

A further benefit of the I.N.F. treaty for NATO is the treaty's system of verification. Its precision is unprecedented and is making it possible to monitor compliance with a high degree of confidence. Initial experience with the verification provisions has been good. These verification measures will also have an important political dimension, breaking down traditional Soviet barriers of military secrecy, with considerable effect on Soviet and western views of the Soviet Union. To supplement satellite imaging and other national technical means, the treaty establishes new procedures for on-site inspections of missile-production plants, operating bases, and support facilities. Some eighty-four locations are designated for inspection on the Soviet side, including seven in eastern Europe; for the U.S., there are thirty-four locations, including twelve in western Europe.

Each side is carrying out several different types of inspections during the three-year elimination period and for ten years thereafter:

(1) Baseline inspections within ninety days of the treaty's start to verify the counts of missiles and launchers before destruction begins;

(2) Elimination inspections to supervise the destruction of missiles and launchers by burning, cutting, crushing, exploding, or firing;

(3) Close-out inspections to confirm elimination of the missiles and launchers;

(4) Periodic inspections of missile bases and support facilities to verify that they have been shut down. Teams of ten to thirty inspectors may carry out—on twenty-five hours notice—up to twenty inspections per year in the first three years of the agreement, fifteen per year during the next five years, and ten per year in the remaining five years;

(5) Continuous monitoring for thirteen years of the perimeter of one production plant in each country, to be carried out by teams in residence near the site. The U.S. plant is the Hercules Aerospace Company's facility in Magna, Utah, which manufactured motors for the Pershing II. The Soviet plant is the Votkinsk Machine Building Plant, an SS-20 production facility.

An additional verification measure of considerable benefit to the U.S. requires the Soviets to facilitate surveillance of the long-range SS-25 mobile missile, which is similar to the SS-20 but not covered by the treaty. For up to three years, the U.S.S.R. will be required, at U.S. request, to open the roofs covering SS-25 missile launchers and to keep them open for twelve hours. This will allow U.S. satellites to confirm that no banned SS-20s are being concealed at SS-25 sites.

The I.N.F. treaty also establishes a "special verification commission," which will meet at either side's request to resolve questions or complaints regarding compliance with the treaty.

I.N.F. AND FLEXIBLE RESPONSE

Despite the advantages of the I.N.F. treaty, NATO governments have viewed it with mixed feelings. Many conservative political leaders in the United Kingdom, Federal Germany, and France agreed with André

Giraud, defense minister in the conservative French government of Jacques Chirac, that the treaty was tantamount to a "nuclear Munich." Of greatest concern militarily to NATO governments is the treaty's impact on NATO's strategy of flexible response, because they had considered the Pershing II an irreplaceable component of that strategy. Many NATO governments would have much preferred retention of at least a hundred I.N.F. missiles to the zero–zero I.N.F. outcome, even if this had meant continued Soviet deployment of an equal number of missiles.

To understand this position, we must take a further short look at the evolution of nuclear deterrence in NATO strategy. Once the NATO countries had decided to compensate for Soviet and Warsaw Pact numerical superiority in conventional forces by deploying United States nuclear weapons, each major advance in Soviet nuclear weapons caused a revision of NATO's concept of deterrence.

As the Soviet Union developed aircraft and missiles capable of attacking American territory with nuclear weapons, the early idea that the United States would massively retaliate with nuclear weapons against Soviet aggression in Europe was discarded in favor of flexible response. The intention of most versions of the strategy of flexible response has been to make a decision by an American president to use nuclear weapons in the face of an overwhelming Pact attack on western Europe more plausible—and therefore more discouraging to the Soviets—by giving the president a wide range of choices. Thus the deployment of American nuclear weapons in Europe has been considered to "couple," or inextricably lock, the defense of Europe to the American strategic deterrent. We should bear in mind, however, that, for Europeans dependent for their defense on the decisions of a larger ally which they can influence but not control, no form of coupling can bring full or lasting confidence.

An early version of flexible response, developed by American and German theoreticians in the mid-1960s and based on American superiority over the U.S.S.R. in all types of nuclear weapons, held that the existence of a complete spectrum of nuclear weapons—building upwards from tactical nuclear artillery through short-range missiles like the Lance, through medium-range delivery systems and nuclear-capable aircraft—and then on to strategic-range missiles and bombers would create a "seamless web" of deterrence. In this view, the deployment in Europe of all but strategic-range weapons within this spectrum created the possibility of flexible response at a level selected by the U.S.

president, thus deterring use of the comparable delivery system by the Warsaw Pact. Deployment of a full spectrum of delivery systems would also make possible a graduated U.S. response at the next higher level of the escalation "ladder," achieving "escalation dominance" if the Soviets responded to an assault with short-range nuclear weapons by launching their own weapons of this kind.

Two developments put an end to this earlier version of flexible response. One was the Soviet Union's achievement in the late 1960s and early 1970s of parity with the United States in strategic-range nuclear weapons and its achievement of parity or even superiority in intermediate- and short-range systems deployed in Europe. The other was the improvement of Soviet air defenses over the same period.

The revised version of flexible response developed in the 1970s focused on the deployment of I.N.F. in Europe. Its adherents believed that, given nuclear parity between the United States and the Soviet Union, what could once again make the threat of American nuclear retaliation credible to the Soviet leadership—and to western Europeans, as well—was once more to add to the existing range of American nuclear weapons based in Europe missiles that could with assurance strike military targets on Soviet territory.

These missiles should be land-based, according to this version of the theory, so that they would physically stand in the way of Soviet ground attack, adding to the impression that they would in fact be used if needed. Strikes by these American weapons against targets inside the Soviet Union would demonstrate the utter determination of the American president to pursue the defense of Europe. If this action failed to stop a conflict, the next rung of escalation might then be an American preemptive strike on a portion of Soviet strategic systems. The Soviet leadership, faced from the outset by the certain prospect of strategic nuclear war, would be deterred from attacking NATO in the first place.

Yet the view that only the deployment in Europe of land-based American intermediate-range systems would really convince Soviet leaders that they risked strategic nuclear war if they decided to attack Europe, is flawed. Both objectively and in the eyes of Soviet leaders, the decision of an American president to use nuclear weapons in Europe would not depend on the availability of land-based American I.N.F. systems deployed in Europe, but on a hierarchy of more important values: among them, the situation of the 300,000-odd American servicemen in Europe, the president's assessment of the U.S./Soviet strategic balance at the time, the president's degree of conviction that the Soviet attack on Europe evidenced a parallel intention to attack the United States directly, and the president's own character and personality.

The presence or absence of land-based intermediate-range U.S. missiles deployed in Europe would be a secondary factor in this decision or, for that matter, in its execution. Many other American delivery systems are available for the purpose. As long as the United States maintains a strong troop contingent in Europe and rough parity with the U.S.S.R. in strategic weapons, including an assured capacity to retaliate in the event of a Soviet attack, prudent Soviet leaders will have to reckon with the probability that conflict in Europe would result in nuclear war.

But western critics of the I.N.F. treaty have advanced a further, more specialized argument against the elimination of American Pershing IIs, one which would apply only in the event that deterrence had failed and a war were in progress. In effect they have argued that in view of improvements in Soviet air defenses over past decades, the Pershing II is the only NATO weapon still capable of penetrating Soviet airspace to strike targets in the U.S.S.R. that will not result in automatic escalation to strategic nuclear war.

In rebuttal, let us consider first the size of the NATO nuclear arsenal in Europe. After I.N.F., NATO will have more than 4,000 nuclear warheads. Of these the U.S. will have 1,400 nuclear bombs for aircraft, 320 short-range Lance missiles, and 1,100 nuclear artillery shells deployed in Europe, as well as about 100 nuclear bombs on carrier-based aircraft normally stationed within range of Europe and 400 submarine-launched ballistic missile warheads assigned to NATO, subject to release by U.S. command authorities. European governments will hold a total of 300 nuclear bombs for aircraft, 380 Lance missiles, and 550 nuclear artillery shells.

In addition, the independent nuclear forces of the United Kingdom and France, not covered by the I.N.F. treaty, are significant and growing. These forces include bombers, land-based missiles, and submarine-launched missiles. Both countries are in the midst of major expansion and modernization programs; their combined nuclear warheads now total around 750, and large additional increases are planned for the 1990s. Behind these NATO-deployed systems, of course, stand the large strategic nuclear resources of the United States itself.

As regards penetration of Soviet airspace, some NATO air specialists believe that this can be accomplished by current or future NATO fighter-bombers, including the American F-111, B-1, and Stealth bombers. Penetration can undoubtedly be achieved by aircraft equipped with air-launched cruise missiles or stand-off missiles and by sea-launched ballistic and cruise missiles. Many of these armaments are in the hands of the United Kingdom and France as well as the United States.

So there is no shortage of penetration systems that can strike targets on Soviet territory. Nonetheless, critics of the I.N.F. treaty have argued that NATO should take steps to "compensate" for the loss of the alliance's penetration capacity brought about by the elimination of Pershing II. Among the possibilities raised have been stationing additional cruise missiles on surface vessels or submarines off NATO's Atlantic coast; forward stationing of B-52s equipped with conventional-warhead, air-launched cruise missiles; deployment in Europe of additional nuclear-capable American fighter-bombers like the F-111 or the F-15E; development of a new stand-off air-to-surface missile for NATO's present fighter-bombers; and replacement of the Lance missiles by a modernized version with increased range close to the maximum-permitted 500 kilometers.

In addition to arguing that NATO must have delivery systems capable of attacking Soviet territory itself, critics of the I.N.F. treaty stress the importance of the Pershing II as a weapon that can strike Soviet territory without making Soviet leaders believe they are under strategic attack; critics argue that this preserves the possibility of a negotiated outcome to conflict. There are flaws in this argument, too.

First, it assumes that Soviet leaders would be able to distinguish a limited nuclear attack by Pershings from a strategic attack by intercontinental ballistic missiles. But if indeed they can, they should also be able to distinguish a limited attack by any delivery means, including strategic missiles, from an all-out attack. The Pershing is not necessary for this mission.

Second, this argument assumes that the Soviets would respond to an attack by nuclear weapons other than I.C.B.M.s with restraint and refrain from all-out escalation to strategic nuclear war. But Soviet leaders have explicitly stated that they will treat any nuclear strike on their territory, limited or not, as a strategic attack and respond accordingly. Their repeated statements seem plausible and must be taken seriously. More to the point, it is simply improbable that escalation could be controlled once a nuclear war began, whatever the intentions of the initiator.

Our discussion of the relationship of I.N.F. to flexible response appears to justify some important conclusions:

(1) The I.N.F. treaty does not eliminate the possibility of nuclear strikes by the United States or other NATO states against targets on Soviet territory as part of flexible response against Pact attacks, nor does it alter whatever possibility may exist that a limited nuclear attack by the United States against Soviet territory will be perceived as limited.
(2) The I.N.F. treaty does not significantly affect the ability of an American president to use nuclear weapons in the defense of Europe. Choosing that option remains contingent on factors, described earlier, that are outside the I.N.F. domain and that will continue to be important in the thinking of Soviet leaders.
(3) The I.N.F. treaty does make an important reduction in Soviet capacity to launch a successful attack on western Europe and thus further reduces the risk of conflict in Europe.
(4) There is no strong military case for improving or modernizing American (or French or U.K.) nuclear weapons deployed in Europe. If there is a case to be made, it is a political and psychological one: to raise the confidence of a segment of European political opinion, important but not a majority, in the reliability of American nuclear support for Europe.

It is time to look in more detail at the politics of the treaty in the West.

THE POLITICAL LEGACY OF I.N.F.

Because it encapsulates so many of the unresolved—and probably unresolvable—issues of NATO defense, the I.N.F. treaty turned out to be as divisive in its effects on European/American relations as the dispute six years earlier over the deployment of American I.N.F. in Europe that led to the treaty. But this time, the negative effects focussed on European NATO governments, not on opposition parties and anti-nuclear groups.

Caught in a vise of pressure between their own domestic public opinion, which overwhelmingly favored the I.N.F. treaty, and their superpower ally, which also wanted the treaty, the governments of the European NATO countries had little choice but to support the treaty. Yet many leaders in several of these governments—in particular France, the United Kingdom, and the Federal Republic of Germany— were extremely upset both by the conduct and the outcome of the last phase of the I.N.F. talks and have made no secret of it. The conservative arms-control spokesman of Chancellor Kohl's Christian Democratic Bundestag caucus resigned in outrage. Senior British officials have stated that there must be no repetition of I.N.F.

This outcome was ironic. The Reagan administration had sought the closest possible consultation with the European NATO governments on common policy for the I.N.F. talks and had reported faithfully on the course of the talks. It was European NATO members who had insisted on the zero outcome in the first place; only later, when this approach had made no apparent progress, did they argue for low equal ceilings. Until the negotiations neared their end, consultation and cohesion with the European allies was exemplary, with the exception of the 1982 "walk-in-the-woods" episode, when the United States and Soviet negotiators discussed terms that had not been approved by their superiors (and that were subsequently thrown out). Even here, the annoyance of European NATO governments, and especially of Federal German Chancellor Schmidt, had nothing to do with the content of the potential agreement (that the Soviets would make a large reduction of their I.N.F. missiles if the U.S. did not deploy the Pershing IIs). Schmidt found that acceptable. He minded only that he had not been consulted before its rejection.

Despite closest consultations up to the end phase, for many senior officials of the French, British, and German governments, any benefits from Soviet concessions on the I.N.F. treaty were outweighed by the impressions they gained in that end phase of the unreliability of the American nuclear guarantees for Europe.

From the outset of the I.N.F. project, as we pointed out in Chapter 1, NATO governments had wanted a low equal number of Soviet and American I.N.F., because of their belief in the coupling theory and in the special value of the Pershing II. Despite the fact that they had, in 1981, rather cynically supported a zero–zero outcome as a sop to their anti-nuclear public opinion, the European governments retained this preference for low equal numbers.

But although they had placed these views on record with the Reagan administration not long before the 1986 Reykjavik summit and believed they had its agreement to adhere to this position, at Reykjavik President Reagan agreed to the double-zero outcome. The president and his delegation made an effort to argue for low equal ceilings with some missile deployment by both countries, but it proved difficult to press for the continuation of a mutual nuclear threat in the face of Soviet willingness to eliminate its intermediate-range missiles entirely.

This transaction put fear in the hearts of European officials with regard to the future of nuclear deterrence in Europe. The transaction could be repeated again and again, until western Europe was left without nuclear protection, face to face with Soviet conventional superiority. Indeed, at Reykjavik, President Reagan had also agreed in a general, unspecific way to the elimination of all nuclear weapons (a proposition which reappeared in the communiqué of the June, 1988, Moscow summit). This agreement was a direct blow to the insistent view of France and the United Kingdom that nuclear deterrence had to continue for the foreseeable future. It also cast serious doubt on the commitment of the United States to use nuclear weapons in the defense of Europe.

A further development at Reykjavik cast even more doubt on that commitment. One could write off President Reagan's agreement with General Secretary Gorbachev to eliminate all nuclear weapons as merely the expression of a distant dream. But when President Reagan himself took the initiative at Reykjavik to propose negotiation to eliminate all intercontinental ballistic missiles, the blow to the credibility of American nuclear support of Europe was heavy indeed.

Here was the president of the United States, the physical incorporation of the American nuclear guarantee, suddenly proposing the elimination of all strategic ballistic missiles, including the United States' intercontinental ballistic missiles, which were the final back-up weapon for extended nuclear deterrence and for NATO's strategy of flexible response, the anchor of all theories of coupling. If actually carried out, the suggestion that ballistic missiles be eliminated entirely would still leave the U.S. (and the U.S.S.R.) with a large force of nuclear weapons in the form of bombers and cruise missiles. Nevertheless, Europeans had grown accustomed to thinking of nuclear deterrence in terms of ballistic missiles. And although the Reagan administration had, prior to the Reykjavik summit, mentioned to its European allies that it was raising with the Soviets the idea of eliminating ballistic missiles, there had been no serious discussion.

So Reykjavik did far more damage to the credibility of NATO theories of coupling and flexible response than the prospective elimination of the Pershing alone would have. Reykjavik also placed the French and the British nuclear deterrent on shaky ground, by implying that sooner or later they, too, would become bargaining chips.

The furor among European conservatives following Reykjavik was at its peak in Federal Germany, an alliance member committed by treaty to have no nuclear weapons of its own and consequently in its own eyes completely dependent in its front-line position on the American nuclear guarantee. The uproar was greatest among members of the conservative wings of Chancellor Kohl's Christian Democratic Party and its sister party, the Bavarian Christian Social Union.

These groups had led the fight against majority opinion in the Federal Republic for deployment of the same Pershing II and ground-launched cruise missiles that would now be eliminated under the new treaty. They had been the chief spokesmen for the doctrine of flexible response and for the need to tighten the nuclear chain coupling Europe to the United States by means of I.N.F. This group of conservative politicians (called the "Stahlhelm faction," in an uncomplimentary reference to a right-wing veterans' organization of the Weimar period) strongly opposed the I.N.F. zero–zero outcome but did not consider it politic to do so openly. Instead, they retreated to the position that ground-based missiles with ranges of 500 to 1,000 kilometers be held at equal levels for the United States and the Soviet Union, a position that might have permitted the introduction of an improved Pershing IA by the United States.

But here, too, their efforts to prop up flexible response were frustrated. In early 1987, General Secretary Gorbachev offered to eliminate this category of missiles also. With Chancellor Kohl standing aside, there ensued a fracas between members of the Stahlhelm faction and Christian Democratic politicians who supported the second zero. After the United States accepted Gorbachev's offer, the holdouts were left with a last-ditch effort to block conclusion of the I.N.F. treaty by refusing to include the German Pershing IA in the bargain being struck.

The last straw was Chancellor Kohl's announcement, without warning or consultation, to his party supporters or his Free Democratic coalition partners, that he would destroy the German Pershing IAs if the U.S. and the U.S.S.R. scrapped their missiles of comparable range. The German conservatives were left without any substantive position, completely disillusioned in their own previous support of deterrence through American nuclear guarantees.

The position to which the German conservatives then moved is understandable, but it could not have been predicted. First, they turned with anger and disappointment from full dependence on the protection of the United States to the reluctant conclusion that Europeans were to be on their own for nuclear defense, and that a closer defense relationship among European countries and with nuclear France was the only available answer to their problem, if not a fully convincing one. Second, they concluded that since the United States (and the Federal Republic) was giving up its longer-range deterrent weapons, it made little sense to retain shorter-range ones—nuclear artillery and tactical missiles. The limitations of these weapons, they reasoned, would mean that most of the civilian casualties of a conflict involving the weapons would be in West or East Germany.

A remarkable shift of views had taken place. While they continued to attach weight to air- and sea-delivery means, the former advocates of nuclear deterrence had to some extent become advocates of nuclear disarmament, joining the rest of the German body politic. The former Atlanticists had become Gaullists. The conversion was not total, but it was startling.

The French and British governments observed these developments in Federal Germany with fascinated apprehension. In Germany they saw rampant public opinion, fuelled by continual Soviet proposals for nuclear disarmament, crush well-founded resistance to risky nuclear reductions. The same thing might happen in their own countries if the process were not stopped. Britain already had an active anti-nuclear opinion and France a strong incipient one, lacking only party leadership to make it troublesome.

With Gorbachev pressing for the elimination of all nuclear weapons worldwide, with his unwelcome flexibility in pushing for the elimination of I.N.F. between 500 and 5,000 kilometers, and with his clear desire to discuss reduction of tactical-range nuclear missiles and nuclear-capable aircraft in future East/West negotiation, two things seemed necessary. First, western European countries would have to form a tighter grouping on defense issues, something that would tie in the Germans and stop their descent into non-nuclear neutralism. Second, Europe would have to hold firm that it would tolerate no further nuclear disarmament until important conditions were met, including deep cuts in Warsaw Pact conventional forces and conclusion of a worldwide convention prohibiting chemical weapons. The latter condition was advanced with some cynicism, because France itself is a producer of chemical weapons and, along with the United States, has serious reservations about the verification of any ban on such weapons.

The ensuing French move to increase defense cooperation among the European members of NATO brought an enthusiastic response from Chancellor Kohl and ultimately took the form of a decision to establish a joint Franco-German brigade. It almost appeared that the I.N.F. treaty had brought France back to the integrated European army of the European Defense Community, a project that France itself had brought to a fall thirty years earlier because of concerns about an excessively close relationship with a new, postwar German army.

This European reaction to I.N.F. left one significant point of disagreement among the principal European NATO powers: the proposal to halt further nuclear reductions until after the U.S.S.R. makes stipulated concessions on conventional and other forces. Federal German leaders wanted negotiations to begin soon to reduce the numbers of nuclear artillery and tactical-range surface-to-surface missiles. France, Great Britain, and the United States wanted to postpone such talks for a considerable period and to introduce new nuclear armaments, among them a modernized, improved Lance tactical-range missile, to make good some of the losses they felt the I.N.F. treaty had incurred.

Because all NATO governments had formally welcomed the I.N.F. treaty as a gain in western security, the governments could not formally make the argument that nuclear modernization was needed in compensation. Instead, they insisted on faithful implementation of a decision that the NATO defense ministers had reached in 1983—five years before Gorbachev's surprising concessions on the I.N.F. treaty. But this still left the Federal German government of Chancellor Kohl caught between its loyalty to the NATO decision and Germany's increasingly anti-nuclear public opinion.

It seems fair to conclude that one aspect or another of the I.N.F. issue—deployment of the American missiles or the agreement to eliminate them—has provoked doubts across the entire spectrum of European political opinion over the value of Europe's defense alliance with the United States, and especially the nuclear connection, which for many has been the heart of that alliance.

The dispute of the early 1980s in western Europe over deploying American I.N.F. ruptured, probably permanently, the existing consensus among major western European political parties over the role of nuclear weapons in NATO strategy. Resistance to I.N.F. deployment was strongest in Social Democratic opposition parties, which have ever since questioned NATO strategy, American nuclear protection for Europe, the American leadership role in decision-making in the NATO alliance, and the gravity of the military threat posed by the Warsaw Treaty Organization. Outside the structure of political parties, millions of Europeans continue to concern themselves with issues of this kind, previously left to defense experts.

Then, in the second half of the 1980s, the circumstances under which the I.N.F. agreement was concluded alienated European conservatives and the right side of the political spectrum. This segment of European opinion comprises those most concerned by the military threat from the Warsaw Treaty Organization, and many of the original proponents of I.N.F. deployment and of the American nuclear deterrent. They also formed the group most committed to the NATO alliance with the United States and, in the past, the group most inclined to resist efforts to intensify intra-European defense cooperation as weakening the defense relationship with the United States.

The I.N.F. treaty brought the important military gains for European security we described earlier. But, as we have shown, it also brought a serious loss in United States influence in Europe. The deployment of American medium-range missiles was intended to bolster European confidence in the United States/Soviet defense relationship. Instead, the entire I.N.F. episode may have done more than any other single development of the past forty years to shake that confidence; to promote the belief that western European defense interests differ from those of the United States, to encourage western Europe to turn inward on defense matters; and to end the era of relatively unquestioning European acceptance of American primacy in defining strategy for the defense of Europe.

In many ways, the I.N.F. issue acted as a catalyst to consolidate a long-term decline in American prestige in Europe which had been under way since a postwar high in the 1950s. Like many Americans, Europeans were severely shaken by developments of the succeeding decades: the assassination of President John Kennedy; the unsuccessful American involvement in the Vietnam war; the Watergate affair and the resignation of President Nixon; and the failure of American society to make more progress in resolving the issues of race, poverty, crime, and drugs. Many Europeans considered the S.D.I. program an augury of American withdrawal from responsibility for the defense of Europe, and many disapproved of the use of American military power against Grenada and Libya. There were differences of evaluation and tactics between the United States and western Europe over the Soviet invasion of Afghanistan and the repression of the Solidarity movement in the early 1980s and over the consequences and treatment of the growing American national debt.

At the end of the 1980s, against the background of unprecedented levels of economic development in western Europe, the steady if slow rise of the European Community, and the emergence of a new Soviet leadership emphasizing conciliation with the West, American influence over decisions of the western European governments was by any rough calculation considerably less than half of what it had been at its peak following World War II. Only a real threat of war with the Soviet Union could restore the United States to its earlier level of primacy in the alliance.

It is important to realize these negative effects for the United States, but also not to exaggerate them. The political frictions between the United States and a wide spectrum of European leaders brought by the I.N.F. episode have had a positive aspect. Most of these European leaders have concluded that the only practical answer to the divergence they came to see during the I.N.F. dispute between U.S. and European security interests is intensified defense cooperation among western European countries. Indeed, at considerable cost in U.S. influence in Europe, I.N.F. has done a great deal to promote a European feeling of responsibility for their own defense and for intra-European defense cooperation. The costs here seem outweighed by the overall gain. At the same time, the NATO alliance as such is likely to continue indefinitely, in one form or another, together with its Warsaw Treaty counterpart, and the United States to play the leading role in it.

Despite this possible long-term gain, for the two European nuclear powers, Great Britain and France, the main result of their misgivings over I.N.F. was worry about the future security of Europe. France, in particular, now had serious doubts as to the reliability of two of its main defense partners, the United States and Federal Germany. These doubts brought worries about the coming Atlantic-to-the-Urals force reduction talks which were reflected in a number of extreme French positions during the preparation of a common western approach for those talks. British positions, too, were often negative, while the United States, fearful of intensifying European sensitivities following I.N.F., played a low-profile, mediating role in these preparations.

The diversity of views within NATO on the desirability of negotiating further force reductions with the U.S.S.R.—nuclear and conventional—which is one heritage of I.N.F., will directly affect the success of current efforts to build down the military confrontation in Europe. But before we deal with these intra-alliance differences, we should look at the NATO/Warsaw Pact relationship in conventional forces, which is the centerpiece of the current talks on force reductions.

3 Starting Point: The Current NATO/Warsaw Pact Force Relationship

The I.N.F. treaty has diminished the Warsaw Pact's capacity for sudden missile attack on NATO, nuclear or conventional, and has brought an increase in crisis stability. To this degree, war in Europe will be less likely after implementation of the treaty than before it. Also as a result of the treaty, the willingness of western European countries to cooperate with one another on defense has become stronger, for the reasons explained in the last chapter.

European NATO governments and strong majorities of public opinion endorse the I.N.F. treaty. Yet some European political leaders and defense experts continue to believe that it weakens NATO's nuclear defenses. They believe that even if Soviet leaders do not now wish to use their superior conventional forces to attack western Europe, their capacity to do so has grown and, with it, their capacity to intimidate the states of western Europe. This line of thought has once again focused attention on the balance of conventional forces between NATO and the Warsaw Pact. So too, of course, has the start of the new NATO/Warsaw Pact negotiations on reducing those forces in March, 1989.

In this chapter, we shall look hard at the current composition and capability of NATO and Warsaw Pact forces which are the subject of these new talks, and at the balance between those forces. This comparison will lead us to four main conclusions:

(1) A war of conquest in Europe as the result of a deliberate decision by the Soviet leadership to seize and hold the territory of western Europe by force in order to control its economic and human resources seems excluded as long as we posit a rational balancing of possible gains and losses by Soviet leaders. In their entirety, the forces of the NATO alliance are strong enough to deny the Soviet Union assured success in either a short preparation attack, even before implementation of the Soviet unilateral reductions announced by General Secretary Gorbachev in December, 1988, or a full mobilization attack. These are the main contingencies that

36

the NATO alliance was established to prevent and, in this, it must be regarded as a success.

(2) The force concentration in Europe is huge and war could start because of an irrational decision or act in a crisis situation inside the Soviet Union or between the alliances.

(3) If these two conclusions are correct, NATO's major military problem has changed. NATO is no longer confronted by a situation comparable to that of 1939 with an expansionist Hitler Reich, but by a situation like that of 1914, when a series of events triggered a conflict of dimensions not desired by any of the major participants. Today, an uneasy eastern Europe could be as much a crucible of war as the Balkans were in 1914.

(4) The military confrontation in Europe is increasingly obsolete, because the political disputes that were its origin have faded away. However, unless western governments can believe that the confrontation is a product of a world that no longer exists, they will be unwilling to accept that it should be their task to build down the confrontation. Instead they will devote themselves to more limited measures intended to make an on-going large confrontation somewhat less accident-prone, or as NATO governments often put it, more "stable."

These conclusions are not accepted by everyone and they deserve close examination.

NATO AND WARSAW PACT FORCES

The present concentration of military forces in Europe is the largest in peacetime history in size and destructive capability. In November, 1988, the NATO allies published aggregate totals of NATO and Warsaw Pact manpower and major armaments deployed in the area from the Atlantic to the Urals. In January, 1989, the Warsaw Pact published its own such figures. (A comparison of the two sets of data can be found in Appendix I.)

As we shall discuss later, the figures diverge. But if in each force category we use the higher estimate, the two alliances deploy a combined total of more than 7 million full-time, active-duty military personnel, 90,000 tanks, 125,000 armored vehicles, 128,000 artillery pieces, 62,000 anti-tank weapons, 8,000 helicopters, and 16,000 combat aircraft. Based on estimates of the U.S. Department of Defense (*Soviet*

Military Power, 1988), they deploy about 2,500 combatant naval vessels in the waters surrounding in Europe. In addition, the two alliances deploy a total of about 7,000 nuclear-armed surface-to-surface missiles in the Atlantic-to-Urals area and as many as 10,000 additional nuclear charges for artillery shells and aircraft weapons.

Where does the superiority between the alliances lie? The figures put forward by both the Warsaw Pact and NATO are open to question because of uncertainties of definition and what they include and exclude. But there can be no doubt that the Warsaw Pact is superior in tanks, artillery, and armored personnel carriers. Figures released by the Warsaw Pact itself point to a superiority of about 30,000 in tanks, 23,000 in other armored vehicles, and 15,000 in artillery pieces, as well as to a large superiority of about 1,500 in launchers for surface-to-surface missiles, and a smaller one of 750 in combat aircraft.

In most cases, NATO figures show a still larger Pact superiority: for tanks, 35,000; for armored vehicles, 44,000; for artillery, 29,000. NATO believes that it is faced by a total of 210 Pact divisions plus 43 independent brigades, against its own total of 72 divisions and 93 independent brigades. NATO's count of Pact divisions and formations is inflated, because NATO categorizes as "active" units some Pact units with 25 percent and some with only 5 percent of their wartime manpower, and the Pact has many more such low-manned units than NATO. In part, the discrepancies are explained by the fact that each alliance is counting something different. Nonetheless, these figures unambiguously attest to a very large numerical preponderance of Warsaw Pact forces, especially in armor and artillery.

Beyond this, the Warsaw Pact would have important geographic advantages in an attack on NATO. First, the shallowness of NATO territory. The Federal German border with East Germany is only 150 kilometers from Bremen, a major NATO port, and Hamburg is half that distance. Second, only 800 kilometers separate Federal Germany from Soviet territory—the Pact's major source of reinforcements. The United States, NATO's main source of reinforcements, is 5,000 kilometers distant.

Furthermore, NATO forces have some well-known weaknesses. These include shortfalls in stockpiles of ammunition and equipment to replace those put out of action in war; questions as to the capability of NATO's different national force components to fight together effectively; and above all, NATO's shortage of operational reserve forces to cope with possible breakthroughs of attacking Pact forces and doubts as to whether NATO's sixteen governments would be able to decide together to act rapidly in the face of multiple indications that the Pact was preparing to attack.

What would these disadvantages mean for NATO if the Pact decided to attack? Traditional military analysis of force capabilities seems too narrow to answer this question fully. It rigorously excludes from consideration non-quantifiable factors. Capabilities analysis is insistent on focusing on the adversary's finite military assets—the number of his divisions, tanks, and aircraft—and on excluding the intentions of the possible adversary on the ground that they cannot be reliably estimated. This particular exclusion is fully justified; what the adversary has in mind to do with his military capabilities tomorrow or in six months cannot be reliably measured.

But many military analysts are too comprehensive in excluding from analysis all non-quantifiable factors. They seem to feel that all intangible human thought processes which go on in the "black box" of the mind should be excluded. Yet we must posit the existence of rational interests on the part of the Soviet leadership—such interests as the survival of their political system and the improvement of their economy—and a rational capacity to weigh various strategies for furthering these interests in terms of their possible gains and losses. Estimates based on assessment of interests are made daily by foreign policy analysts but seldom factored into military analysis. Despite this, national interests, although they take the form of intangible beliefs and perceptions, do have important, measurable consequences, including military consequences, as we shall explore further in this chapter.

Capabilities analysis also deliberately excludes non-quantifiable military factors like the quality of leadership, troop morale, and familiarity with terrain, and sometimes even more measurable factors like the actual terrain on which combat takes place, the quality of equipment, the level of training, and the capacity for gathering intelligence on the battlefield and for mustering effective command and control. Although factors like these are difficult to measure, they account for the repeated victories of smaller forces over large ones, from the victory of the Greeks over far larger Persian forces in classical times to the repeated victories of Israeli forces over far larger Arab ones during the past forty years. They explain even the success of the *Wehrmacht* at the outset of Germany's attack on the Soviet Union in World War II, in which the *Wehrmacht*'s invading force, equipped with 3,000 tanks, was able to penetrate to the gates of Moscow against Soviet forces equipped with at least three times as many tanks—eight times as many according to some estimates.

The simplest form of capabilities analysis, merely tallying men and equipment on both sides—referred to pejoratively as "bean counting"—has the further shortcoming that it is static and does not take into account the interaction of armed forces in actual combat. Practitioners of dynamic analysis, aided by computers, attempt to measure this interaction, mainly by assessing the firepower or destructive capability of various armaments and measuring the rate of attrition or the number of casualties in men and equipment in this form of simulated combat.

There are significant variations in dynamic analyses of the NATO/Pact interaction, in part because analysts use different variables, whose significance becomes even greater in dynamic than in static analysis. But this form of analysis does point to the right question as regards the NATO/Pact balance: Can the Warsaw Pact's large and self-admitted superiority in numbers of combat units and armaments be converted into effectiveness in combat?

No one knows or can know the answer to that question with certainty. It is the central open question which analysts continue to dispute. Given a military confrontation as large and as complex as that between NATO and the Warsaw Pact, involving millions of active-duty personnel and hundreds of thousands of weapons systems of heavy firepower on both sides, it is unwise to be dogmatic about any aspect of the interaction of the forces of the two alliances in actual conflict. That caveat applies here.

Nonetheless, we can attempt some answer to the question of how the Pact's numerically superior forces would fare in combat against NATO's current forces. Even if the conclusions presented here are disputed, analysis of this kind is valuable for the design of arms-control approaches. If we can identify the types of armaments, military organization, and military operational doctrine for using those forces of greatest concern to each alliance, we can try to devise measures to cut back, restrict, or change these capabilities.

WAR IN EUROPE

A Warsaw Pact attack on NATO forces would presumably focus on NATO's Central Front in Federal Germany, which has 750 to 800 kilometers of common frontier with East Germany and Czechoslovakia. This is the area of greatest force concentration in Europe and the area which the Warsaw Pact would ultimately have to control for an attack to succeed, even if the attack began with strikes on NATO's northern flank in Norway or its southern flank in Greece and Turkey.

For the purpose of this analysis, we include in central Europe the forces stationed in France, Belgium, Luxembourg, the Netherlands, Denmark, and the Federal Republic of Germany, and those in East Germany, Czechoslovakia, Poland, Hungary, and the three Western Military Districts of the U.S.S.R. (the Baltic, Byelorussian, and Carpathian districts). Appendix II shows the deployment of these forces, which are the majority of those which would be involved in the early stages of a conflict in central Europe.

It is generally believed that a Warsaw Pact attack on NATO's Central Front would begin with a massive missile and air attack, presumably conventional, against NATO airfields, anti-aircraft and missile sites, weapons depots, and command installations, with the primary purpose of knocking out NATO's air and air-defense arsenals before they could be used effectively. As such an attack progressed, armored forces backed by very heavy artillery fire would attempt to break through NATO's forward defenses, followed by highly mobile operational units organized for the specific purpose of exploiting breakthrough, that would drive deep into NATO territory. Airborne commandos would be able to disrupt NATO's rear echelons, breaking the alliance's will to resist before a decision could be reached to use nuclear weapons.

Every NATO political leader is grimly familiar with this scenario, which comes in two main versions: an attack with minimum preparation using forces in place, rapidly reinforced by active-duty and reserve forces from the western U.S.S.R., or an attack following full mobilization, in which the Warsaw Pact mobilizes reserve divisions to bring its entire numerical preponderance to bear, at the cost of relinquishing the opportunity to catch NATO ill-prepared.

For years there has been vigorous dispute as to whether or how long NATO forces could hold against such an attack. The majority of western experts join General John Galvin, the American four-star general who is supreme commander of allied forces in Europe. General Galvin has said that if Pact forces attacked in central Europe, he would face defeat within ten days to two weeks and would have to request authorization to use nuclear weapons. General Galvin's predecessor, the much-respected General Bernard Rogers, concluded that NATO forces could hold out for only a week before he would have to request such authorization. Other experts—William Kaufmann, Joshua Epstein, Barry Posen, and John Mearsheimer—have made more opti-

Map 2 Warsaw Pact ground forces which may be involved in conflict in Central Europe

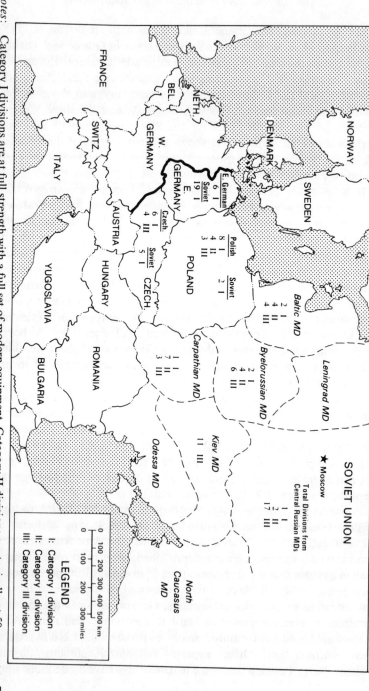

Notes: Category I divisions are at full strength with a full set of modern equipment. Category II divisions are typically at 50 percent to 75 percent strength with a full complement of fighting vehicles. Category III divisions are at 20 percent strength, might have a full set of combat equipment, but it would typically include older models.

Source: Congressional Budget Office study on *U.S. Ground Forces and the Conventional Balance in Europe*, Washington, D.C., June 1983.

MD = Military District.

mistic estimates. James Thomson of the Rand Corporation has produced a judicious summary of the controversy. He, too, concludes that the balance of forces in central Europe favors the Warsaw Pact and that NATO would be defeated in most circumstances.[1]

Even Thomson's reasoned assessment has weaknesses. He appears to underrate the significance of the air battle. He assigns a speed of mobilization and reinforcement to Soviet forces that exceeds all practical experience with questionable Soviet organizational capability in both military and civilian spheres, like the Chernobyl and Armenian earthquake disasters. Thomson and other commentators consider Pact victory on the Central Front tantamount to Pact victory in a European war. This judgment does not seem well-founded. A Pact attack on western Europe, whatever the outcome, would instead in all likelihood trigger a continuing world-wide war.

All of the analyses cited here were developed prior to General Secretary Gorbachev's announcement to the United Nations in December, 1988, of large unilateral reductions in Soviet forces, including reductions in forward-deployed Soviet forces in central Europe, which, when implemented, will significantly decrease the capability of Warsaw Pact forces to launch a successful attack on NATO.

In the remainder of this chapter, we shall review these issues. Doing so will give us valuable pointers as to the main threats that NATO sees in the Warsaw Pact's forces as well as other threats that the alliance has been less sensitive to.

THE AIR WAR IN EUROPE

The first phase of war in Europe could be decided in the first two or three days of combat. War would probably begin, as we have seen, with a massive air and missile attack by the Pact on NATO's airfields and ground-based air defenses. This attack could be nuclear, but current Pact strategy appears to be to try to keep the first phase of war conventional. The Pact's surface-to-surface missile forces, estimated at about 6,000 missiles, are numerically superior to NATO's at a ratio of about ten to one, and are gaining in conventional capability. There is now no practical defense against missile attack, although NATO countries are planning defenses. The Pact's attacking air forces would be numerically superior (although not qualitatively) to NATO's; the side that strikes first has great potential advantage in the air war.

If NATO's air forces were on the ground when the Pact's missiles and aircraft struck, the Pact could drastically reduce NATO's air capability. (NATO air forces would constitute up to half of NATO's firepower in the early phases of war.) Over the past decade NATO has spent a great deal on reinforced shelters for its aircraft, but considerable destruction would take place nonetheless and the runways of NATO's airfields could be broken up, preventing their use for some time in this crucial first period. Weapons loaded with persistent chemicals and delivered by aircraft or missiles would add to the disarray.

If NATO's aircraft were able to go into the air in time and NATO's ground-to-air defenses could shoot down enough of the attacking aircraft in time, then the outcome might be very different. Taking control of NATO's air space is essential to the success of a Pact attack. If NATO could maintain control of the air space over its territory (including much of the battle area itself), the chances of the Pact's success would be sharply diminished. NATO aircraft could be active in destroying the Pact's tanks, the impetus of attack could be slowed, and the Pact's forces might never achieve a decisive breakthrough. We can see such a situation in the failure of the U.S.S.R. to control the air in later phases of the war in Afghanistan after the arrival of American-made Stinger ground-to-air missiles.

For the first five days following a Soviet order to attack in Europe, NATO would be weaker than the Pact, with about 3,000 aircraft (these estimates include French aircraft) to the Pact's roughly 4,000. (See the statistics on the air forces of the Pact and NATO in Appendix III.) An additional 1,000 American planes are programmed to arrive within thirty days of an order to attack, however, and at that point attack aircraft deployed by the air forces would be numerically equal at about 4,000 on each side.

Some analysts argue[2] that even if the Pact made a concentrated air offensive against NATO's nuclear launchers, airfields, and lines of communication at the outset of a ground-forces attack, there would still be a better-than-even chance that NATO could penetrate the Pact's dense air defenses and take command of the air over central Europe. Even analysts who are more pessimistic believe that if NATO's air assets survived a first Pact attack, NATO would be able to prevent the Pact from taking control of NATO airspace and maintain "selective" control of the airspace over the battle area in order to give NATO forces close air support.[3] The crucial importance of NATO's air forces in war in Europe, together with the importance of aircraft as delivery systems for nuclear weapons, accounts for NATO 's reluctance to cut back on its aircraft in the current force-reduction talks.

THE WAR ON THE GROUND

As for the possibility of minimum-preparation short-warning attack using forces in place (what is often referred to as "surprise attack"), the Pact's ground-force commanders could, in fact, be ordered to attack from their garrisons in East Germany and Czechoslovakia within twenty-four hours, although they would doubtless object that they were being given insufficient time to prepare.

Most western military experts believe that the minimum period necessary for the Pact to mount an assault after "M-day"—the day on which a decision to attack is issued—is four to five days. At least that much time would be needed, they think, to load ammunition and supplies and to ready armaments for combat use. In repeated analyses over the years, United States intelligence agencies have expressed doubts as to the reality of this M + 5 scenario. They have argued that any Pact attack would be preceded by extensive political warning; that hasty initiation of hostilities does not conform with Soviet, or rather Russian, character and practice; that the Soviet Union would need more than four days to gear up; and that its preparations—for example, dispersing naval and strategic nuclear forces in case the United States made a nuclear response—would be detected and would signal the Soviets' intention.

These objections seem reasonable. Yet they have not laid to rest the worries of the NATO leadership. Let us look at the possibility of Pact attack with minimum preparation more closely.

ATTACK WITH MINIMUM PREPARATION

To mount an attack with less than a week's preparation, the Soviet Union could muster only an estimated thirty-five Soviet ground-force divisions from the ready units deployed in its "Western Theater of Military Operations" (see chart in Appendix IV). The Soviet Western Theater, which would be the staging area for an assault, includes East Germany, Poland, Czechoslovakia, and the Western Military Districts of the U.S.S.R.—the Baltic, Byelorussian, and Carpathian districts.

These thirty-five are the only divisions in the Soviet Western Theater classified by western defense analysts as "Category I"—that is, divisions with at least 75 percent of their manpower and all of their equipment on hand and capable of becoming fully combat-ready within four to five days.

Of the Category I Soviet divisions in the Western Theater, thirty are deployed in eastern Europe and five in the Western Military Districts— two ground-force and three airborne divisions. The two ground-force divisions are in the Byelorussian and Carpathian districts and would be of limited practical utility on four to five days' notice, because of the distance of more than 600 miles that they would have to travel to engage at the front. One or more of the three airborne divisions in the Baltic and Byelorussian Military Districts could be assigned special missions for the attack.[4]

Soviet ground forces in the Leningrad Military District to the north and the Odessa Military District to the south have missions directed not at the Central Front but at the NATO flank states and the neutrals (Norway, Sweden and Finland in the north; Greece and Turkey in the south). In any event, they could not be moved in time to participate at the outset of a short-preparation attack in central Europe.

Soviet divisions in the Kiev Military District, which some analysts include in the tally of forces that might be used for a short-preparation attack on NATO, are also too far away to be of immediate use; more to the point, they include no Category I or even Category II divisions. The four Soviet Category I divisions in Hungary, which are generally considered to be positioned against Italy, are also too far for an M + 5 attack. Movement of these divisions toward the Central Front through Austria is possible, but at best would probably take more than a week; such action would give unambiguous warning of pending attack before the attacker reached NATO forces in the hills near Salzburg. The two Soviet divisions in Poland would be needed in place to guard land communications with the Soviet Union and might well have to be reinforced if a conflict were lengthy.

So the Soviet Union might have available for quick attack only its nineteen divisions in East Germany and the two westernmost of its five divisions in Czechoslovakia, perhaps with two airborne divisions from the Western Military Districts for behind-the-lines attacks. In all, then, the Soviet force for a minimum-preparation attack using forces in place would probably number about twenty-three divisions.

What about non-Soviet Warsaw Pact forces? It is unclear both whether the Soviets would want to use these eastern European units of doubtful morale and political reliability for a minimum-preparation attack on the West and whether these divisions could be organized in time to participate in such an attack. But we will count some of them for a worst-case hypothesis. Whether or not East Germany's Category I divisions could be used is questionable. Their quality is high, but their loyalty doubtful in a fight against fellow Germans. But let us assume that four of the six East German Category I divisions could be used. (This total of East German Category I divisions predates the effects of unilateral reductions announced in late 1988, which will also affect Polish and Czechoslovak ready forces.)

Perhaps four of the eight Polish Category I divisions might make a weak push at Federal German and Danish forces in Schleswig-Holstein and Denmark to try to open the Baltic for the Soviet Navy, moving along the southern coast of the Baltic Sea and also making an amphibious attack on Denmark. Four of the six Czechoslovakian Category I divisions might try to push into Bavaria to tie down German and U.S. forces there. If we add these divisions to the twenty-three Soviet divisions already described, this would give us a Warsaw Pact force of some thirty-five divisions for a blitz attack on NATO's Central Front.

Analysis undertaken during the Mutual and Balanced Force Reduction talks in Vienna indicated that Category I Soviet divisions in eastern Europe are not generally 90–95 percent manned, as NATO intelligence had assumed, but more likely are 80 percent manned. Consequently, it could take as long as ten to fourteen days to bring in the specialists, including logistics troops, needed to push the divisions to maximum combat readiness. If these forces had to attack within four to five days, they could do so, but they would be correspondingly less effective.

At the outset of a Pact attack by thirty-five divisions with minimum preparation on the Central Front, NATO would have about twenty-two active-duty divisions to meet them. This count of NATO forces includes four American divisions in place in Germany plus two brigades from U.S.-based divisions and two regiments of armored cavalry—the rough equivalent of one more division. The Federal German force would consist of twelve divisions plus six home defense brigades to be filled up with reserve personnel within seventy-two hours, for a total of fourteen divisions. NATO would also have three British divisions in Germany.

This worst-case count includes only Federal German, American, and British forces in Germany. It excludes six German territorial mechanized brigades (which might within the next four to five years build up to the equivalent of two divisions but which might instead be restructured into smaller units), three French divisions already in Germany, and a total of three Belgian, Netherlands, and Danish divisions now pledged to be on line within three days. (See Appendix IV.) Crediting the fourteen German division-equivalents with 18,000 people each, which is low, the five U.S. divisions (including the brigades and cavalry regiments) with 18,000 each, and the three British divisions with 10,000 each, we find a total of more than 375,000 divisional personnel in these units. The thirty-five Warsaw Pact divisions have an average of 12,000 men each, or about 420,000 men in all. So NATO and the Pact would be nearly equal in divisional manpower.

If NATO's forces are ordered to readiness positions in time, they should be able to hold back an attack by the Pact. NATO has the upper hand when it comes to quality of armaments, training of troops, troop morale, and the advantages of the defender role (knowledge of terrain, informed leadership, and greater ease of command and control). The West's close observation of Pact forces since 1987 in the first years of implementing the Stockholm Document on confidence- and security-building measures (discussed in detail in Chapter 6) appears to bear out these qualitative assessments.

Especially in this short-warning scenario, western defense experts have been concerned about delays in NATO decision-making—correctly so, because if NATO's units in the Federal Republic fail to take their readiness positions rapidly, the Pact could succeed. But in practical terms, a decision to move into readiness positions does not have to be made by all NATO governments acting together in the NATO Council. Instead, it could be made by the U.S., the U.K., and Federal German authorities. Federal German leadership would be key.

THE NATO SCENARIO FOR M + 15

NATO analysts worry that the Warsaw Pact could mobilize and bring to bear less-ready units than its Category I divisions faster than NATO could and that the greatest danger to NATO would come at about M + 15. NATO analysts foresee a similar rate of buildup by the Pact whether in continuation of a conflict begun from a standing start or in preparation for a heavier Pact attack to start only when main forces were in place.

Many official estimates of the United States and NATO show that, by the end of ten to fifteen days, the Warsaw Pact could deploy about one hundred ground-force divisions on the Central Front. Such estimates usually include all twenty-six Soviet divisions in East Germany, Czechoslovakia, and Poland, up to thirty-one non-Soviet divisions from these three countries, and about thirty-three Soviet divisions from the three Western Military Districts of the U.S.S.R., including all Category I, II, and III divisions. (The higher the number, the less-readily mobilized the divisions.) Sometimes the four Soviet divisions in Hungary and six fully mobilized Hungarian divisions are added to this total, even though their mission is clearly to the south. Some analysts also would add the approximately thirty Category III Soviet divisions now stationed in the Kiev, Moscow, Ural, Volga, and Central Asia Military Districts of the U.S.S.R.

In this M + 15 time frame, NATO, if it decided early and moved rapidly, could, in addition to ready forces in Federal Germany described earlier, bring to bear two Belgian divisions, three Netherlands divisions, one U.K. division, two Danish divisions, eight French divisions (three in the Federal Republic and five in France—the participation of France being at least as likely as that of eastern Europe), and up to six American reinforcement divisions. The total would be twenty-two NATO divisions in addition to the twenty-two already listed (see the chart in Appendix IV).

Such a force buildup would give the Pact a roughly two-to-one ground-force advantage over NATO. The Pact would presumably try to use this advantage to defeat NATO quickly, by breaking through NATO's forward defenses and then developing a fast, penetrating attack by armored forces—first overpowering and then disrupting NATO's remaining defenses. However, an authoritative United States assessment made in 1979 to which we have already referred (see note 3) concluded that if NATO could maintain the integrity of its defense and block and channel the Pact's advance, it might control and eventually halt a forward advance of these dimensions, though NATO forces would then risk being worn down in sustained combat. In this case, the outcome would depend mainly on whether NATO could bring more reserves to bear.

SOME WEAKNESSES OF THIS ANALYSIS

The buildup of Pact forces described in this M + 15 scenario is frightening, but it is based on some faulty assumptions.

For many years, NATO has included in the tally of its combat-ready forces available for defense on the Central Front only the standing forces of Federal Germany, the United States, the U.K. and the Benelux countries (Belgium, the Netherlands, and Luxembourg), omitting all French forces and NATO reserve units. At the same time, many NATO descriptions of Pact forces, such as those given in various editions through the 1980s of *Soviet Military Power* and in Federal German Bundeswehr "White Books," make no distinction between combat-ready Warsaw Pact units and reserve units. Thus, in the M + 15 scenario just described, it is assumed that Warsaw Pact reserve forces, even the most unready, can be present in the forward area, ready to fight, within ten to fifteen days.

This assumption should be treated with deep skepticism. The traditional NATO system of dividing Pact units into three categories of readiness can be used to analyze it.

(1) Category I ground-force units are those with 75 to 100 percent of their personnel and equipment on hand and considered combat ready.
(2) Category II units have 50 to 75 percent of their equipment on hand and all of their weapons but need to requisition some transport from the civilian economy.
(3) Category III units are at 10 to 25 percent manning strength, with insufficient and inadequate combat equipment (mostly older models) and without much in the way of transport.[5]

Many NATO analyses assume that Category I Warsaw Pact units would be able to move in combat in twenty-four hours, Category II in five days, and Category III in fifteen days. But we have already pointed out that even Category I Soviet units might take ten to fourteen days to fill in with important specialists, though they could move sooner in emergencies. Category I East German units might be ready in two to four days. It is improbable that Category I Czechoslovak or Polish units could be committed to combat in under fourteen to twenty-one days unless they were under-manned, under-gunned, and under-organized to the point of limited effectiveness and high casualty rates. There are very few Category II divisions in the eastern European armies. Poland is credited with two mechanized infantry, one airborne division, and one amphibious assault division, and Hungary also with four divisions, for a total of eight. It stretches credibility to believe these units would be combat-ready in less than three weeks.

The Soviet Union is believed to have fifteen Category II units in the Western Military Districts at present. Detailed data exchange and future on-site inspections are likely to prove this number high but it will be accepted here; these units might be ready to move in ten days.

The most damaging flaw in the M + 15 scenario involves eastern European and Soviet Category III units. While NATO's M + 15, hundred-division Pact attack scenario places all these forces on the firing line, it is quite unlikely that the nine Czechoslovakian, Hungarian, and Polish Category III divisions could reach any serious level of combat efficiency in under sixty to ninety days, if indeed they ever saw action. Minimum analytical rigor would require deletion of these nine divisions from the M + 15 scenario.

What about the thirteen Soviet Category III divisions in the Western Military Districts, which are also counted in the M + 15 scenario, or the twenty-eight Category III units in the Kiev, Moscow, Ural, Volga and Central Asia Districts?

To argue that to assume that these divisions could be filled up with personnel and equipment, organized, given some rudimentary small-unit training, equipped with vehicles from the civilian economy, and moved forward to the combat area in less than thirty days is to assume a standard of performance by Soviet forces never before witnessed. Such speed would depend on a degree of management and organizational capability that does not exist in the Soviet Union. Observations from the 1968 Soviet invasion of Czechoslovakia, the 1979 invasion of Afghanistan, and the menacing Soviet exercises around Poland in 1981 are cited both by those western analysts who believe that the U.S.S.R. could muster its Category III divisions in fifteen days and by those who don't. However these episodes are interpreted, the Soviets have in the past taken between sixty and 120 days to ready their Category III divisions, randomly assigning reservists who have had no military training since their original conscript service. The Category III Soviet divisions probably could not meet even a thirty-day deadline.

Some members of Category III Soviet divisions might make it to the Central Front by M + 15, but they would arrive in much the same shape as the civilian-clad, bewildered Soviet reservists who in 1968 straggled into Prague two to three weeks after being called up. Thus, in a more realistic assessment, fifty Category III divisions that the Pact has been considered capable of deploying by M + 15 would be either dropped from western calculations of Pact forces in that time frame or one's assessment of their contributions cut back. Some western analysts worry that reservists in Soviet Category III units could be trained covertly and thus mobilized rapidly. In fact, some covert exercises could probably escape detection by the West. Consequently, NATO should seek safeguards against this possibility in the current round of talks in Vienna; some specific recommendations are in Chapters 10 and 11.

Just as NATO tends to overestimate the threat posed by the Pact in its M + 15 scenario, it tends to underestimate the defense that it could muster. For example, the Federal German Territorial Army could expand from its present active-duty strength of 80,000 to about 480,000 within a week. Many of these personnel would be used to fill up active-duty units or be assigned to the large manpower replacement pools attached to German divisions; others would be organized into the six home-defense brigades already mentioned, but also into six motorized regiments, fifteen home-defense infantry regiments, 150 independent security companies, and 300 platoons for rear-area security. Not counting the home-defense brigades (which would probably be committed to NATO command) and the independent security companies and platoons, the Territorial Army is roughly equivalent to three to four divisions of light infantry with no heavy weapons. Although some light-infantry regiments might be used in a forward position, the Federal Republic now plans to assign most to protect rear-area installations from sabotage and raids. However, a different pattern of organization and use could be devised to gain more combat units from German reserve personnel.

The Netherlands has eleven infantry, one commando, and two artillery battalions and Belgium twenty infantry and twelve reconnaissance battalions in their territorial forces; the U.K. has the equivalent of about a division. Under present plans, some of these reserve units would be used for behind-the-lines security and are usually disregarded in NATO estimates of the force balance.

However, although NATO usually considers only combat-ready forces when calculating its own troop strength, its M + 15 scenario assumes, as we have seen, that all Warsaw Pact Category I, II, and III units will be committed to combat. In their assessments of Pact forces, NATO analysts do not allocate any Pact units to provide security against commando or sabotage efforts by NATO or eastern Europeans or to guard lines of communication with the Soviet Union. True, the Pact has more heavily armed police units to perform this function than NATO has. Even so, the Soviet line of communication is so long that several divisions—most likely from four to eight Soviet divisions and as many non-Soviet Warsaw Pact divisions—would probably be held back to defend it. These divisions, too, would be deleted from a more realistic M + 15 assessment of Pact totals.

Also not considered in most western estimates of the M + 15 threat is the possibility that initial American reinforcements would in fact arrive within the time promised. NATO has moved toward completion of the program to pre-position equipment in Europe for the six American divisions scheduled to arrive within ten days of an order from NATO to mobilize. Moreover, in recent years the United States has expanded its airlift capacity; only a portion of the United States civilian air fleet could transport these American personnel rapidly.

The reinforcement practices of many NATO allies, especially the Federal Republic and the United States, also improve the odds for NATO in the M + 15 scenario. These countries replace people as needed—as noted, German divisions have big manpower pools standing by from which to draw replacements for wartime casualties. The Pact, in contrast, follows the practice of replacing not individuals but entire units once casualties become high enough. NATO analysts count the Pact's replacement divisions, but not NATO's individual replacements.[6]

Mobilization rates naturally influence the availability for combat of major armaments. If American reinforcements arrive as planned by M + 15 and break their tanks out of storage the NATO/Pact tank ratio will improve. The use of tanks held in reserve by NATO to replace tanks damaged in battle also will make the ratio more favorable. A recent analysis of the NATO/Pact tank balance suggests that at M + 10 this ratio might be no worse than 1:1.4.[7]

Admittedly, if Soviet forces trained on the northern or southern flanks of Europe were not deeply engaged, it is possible that the Soviet command would commit them to the Central Front. And of course, reinforcements sent in by both sides—particularly from the U.S. mainland and from inside the U.S.S.R.—will be vulnerable to interdiction. Air forces cannot fly if their landing fields and support facilities are destroyed. Reinforcement troops cannot travel without ships and aircraft to carry them, or ports and airfields to receive them. U.S. forces have a minimum of 3,000 miles to cover; Soviet forces from within the Soviet Union a much shorter distance of 600 miles or so. But forward movement of Soviet troops will largely be by road and rail and can be stopped by attacks on bridges and track.

Reinforcements supplied by European members of both alliances, having less distance to travel, will be less vulnerable to interdiction. An important point to keep in mind in any scenario of conflict on the

Central Front is that, of all combatants, Federal Germany would be least constrained by time and distance to succeed in calling up its 700,000 ground, air force and naval reservists within seven days. If an order came, they would be in place long before Pact reinforcements could arrive in East Germany or Czechoslovakia, no matter how rapidly the Soviet Union could call in, equip, and move forward its Category III divisions.

Terrain, as previously mentioned, will also be to NATO's advantage. As defenders, NATO forces will have the benefit of known positions and relatively favorable terrain. As defenders, they will be able to rapidly place obstacles, barriers and mines in the enemy's path—a strategy that isn't available to an attacker. This point is not merely of theoretical significance. During the past decade, there has been not only talk but cumulative effort on this strategy—effort which has added to the defensive capability of NATO forces but which the alliance has not generally factored into its calculations.

The most probable outcome of conflict described here is that both alliances would run out of ammunition and fuel after M + 30.

EFFECT OF PACT UNILATERAL REDUCTIONS

The foregoing analysis seeks to make the point that the numerical superiority of the Warsaw Pact's forces would not guarantee the success of a minimum-preparation attack on NATO's Central Front and that this uncertainty will continue to restrain Pact leaders from deciding to attack. This analysis assumes that NATO would prevail in the air and that the Pact is limited at the outset to using forces in place in eastern Europe. However, no amount of analysis can get around the hard fact of the Pact's numerical superiority. It is possible, given the present East/West balance of forces in the area that, especially if NATO failed to respond in time, a minimum-preparation Pact attack could succeed.

That will change once the unilateral Soviet reductions of forward-deployed forces in eastern Europe that General Secretary Gorbachev announced in December, 1988, are implemented. These will all but eliminate the chance of success for a standing-start attack by the Warsaw Pact in central Europe using forces in place. Scheduled for withdrawal are 240,000 Soviet active-duty personnel, 10,000 tanks, 8,500 artillery pieces and 800 combat aircraft now deployed from the Urals to central Europe. (A summary of the unilateral reductions announced by Gorbachev and other Pact leaders is in Appendix V.) Gorbachev's motives seem to be to save money and to have a positive impact on western—especially western European—opinion. If these are in fact his motives, then the reductions will be carried out in full. To fail to do so would be counterproductive for both aims.

The announced unilateral reductions of Soviet forces are of greatest importance for the Pact's surprise-attack capability. According to statements by Gorbachev and other Pact leaders, the Soviet withdrawals will include four Soviet armored divisions from East Germany and one each from Czechoslovakia and Hungary. Withdrawn units will be disbanded. Leaving aside the Soviet forces in Hungary as we did earlier in assessing chances for a successful attack using forces in place, this will reduce five armored divisions and about 50,000 men from the thirty-five division force we earlier reckoned the Pact could muster from forces in place for a standing-start attack on NATO's Central Front. This reduction would leave attacking Pact forces inferior to NATO forces in divisional manpower. Reductions from eastern Europe will also include a forward-deployed Soviet airborne brigade, which could have been used for behind-the-lines attack to disrupt NATO forces.

According to Gorbachev's announcement, Soviet unilateral withdrawals from eastern Europe will also include 5,000 tanks, the approximate tank holdings of more than fifteen Soviet divisions. Assuming that the six Soviet tank divisions to be withdrawn have a full complement of about 325 tanks per division, they will take with them about 2,000 tanks. According to authoritative Soviet statements, these tanks will be dismantled. This will leave 3,000 more Soviet tanks to be withdrawn from eastern Europe—the tank holdings of nine to ten further Soviet divisions. If half of the 8,500 artillery pieces to be unilaterally reduced are withdrawn from eastern Europe (and the remainder reduced from units in the U.S.S.R.), these 4,200 artillery pieces, at about 240 artillery pieces per division, will be the artillery complement of more than sixteen divisions. If after withdrawal of the six armored divisions the remaining unilateral reductions in Soviet tanks and artillery are spread among the twenty-four Soviet divisions still in East Germany, Czechoslovakia, and Hungary, a fundamental restructuring of these divisions into a new kind of infantry division will take place. As we shall see in the next chapter, it is the Soviet intention to carry out such a restructuring.

More important in the direct East/West context, these unilateral reductions will sharply reduce the tank and artillery holdings of the

Pact's active-duty units relative to those of NATO. The number of tanks in Category I and II units deployed in eastern Europe and in the Soviet Union west of the Urals will be cut from about 20,000 to about 15,000, as compared with NATO's holdings of more than 10,000. If the unilateral reductions by East Germany and Czechoslovakia of three active-duty divisions take the form of Category I units, then the number of divisions, tanks, and artillery available to the Pact for a standing-start attack will be further diminished. Under such circumstances Soviet leaders could have little confidence that a minimum-preparation attack using their remaining forward-deployed forces would succeed.

Some western defense analysts have argued that the ostensibly constructive intent of the unilateral Soviet withdrawals is spurious. They say that the withdrawals are based on military reforms introduced by the Soviet general staff after long preparation with the intention of making Soviet ground forces more effective and have little to do with a Soviet desire to move to a more defensive military posture. Some believe that the unilateral cuts will result in leaner, more dangerous Soviet ground forces, with greater attack capability, presenting an even greater threat to NATO.

The unilateral reductions Gorbachev announced in December, 1988, may in fact have their origin in recommendations of the Soviet general staff. The implication in much western commentary of this kind is that all the actions taken or proposed by Gorbachev with regard to the Soviet armed forces reflect planning by the general staff to make the whole of Soviet forces smaller but better equipped, with destructive power which exceeds their present capabilities. This seems much overdrawn. Gorbachev's proposal at the outset of the C.F.E. talks to reduce about 70 percent of Soviet armor and artillery west of the Urals, which we shall discuss in Chapter 7, is evidence of a political and economic objective imposed on the Soviet military, not of a scheme of force improvement drawn up by professional soldiers. Clearly, the Soviets' ability to attack Europe on short notice will be crippled by the withdrawals Gorbachev is making.

Having reached this conclusion we shift our attention to the prospects of success for a Pact attack following full mobilization.

FULL-MOBILIZATION ATTACK

In a situation of full mobilization the Warsaw Pact's lead in organized ground-force divisions would be at its greatest. If an attack took place following a ninety-day mobilization then NATO might have on hand a total of about seventy-two divisions in central Europe. The main NATO reinforcements not already noted in the description of the M + 15 situation would be the addition of as many as seventeen American divisions—mainly National Guard units, which receive a good deal more training than Soviet Category III divisions—and up to seven further French divisions. In a ninety-day period, the Pact would mobilize most of its Category III divisions for a total of about 110 divisions on this front (counting forces in Hungary).

When the fighting started, NATO's troops would have been in position for months preparing the terrain with obstacles. A tremendous war of attrition would ensue. Some conventional wisdom gives the Pact the upper hand, because NATO forces, although sufficient to block the Pact's first forward thrust, could be worn down. However, a good case can be made for the view that NATO's forces, equipped with operational reserves and with adequate time to prepare the terrain, could place the Pact's attack in stalemate. Such an outcome would be threatening enough to Soviet commanders to deter them from attacking.

PACT SUCCESS ON THE CENTRAL FRONT—DECISIVE FOR VICTORY?

In any event the M + 90 scenario (in which both alliances build up steadily to their maximum potential, both conventional and nuclear, for three to four months and the Pact attacks only then) is questionable for several reasons.

One is that neither side would be likely to hold still in such circumstances for three months. Another is that a decision to mobilize fully and visibly is implausible in a nuclear age. We shall look at possibilities of covert Pact mobilization in our chapters on reductions and verification, but they probably would not elicit the confidence of Soviet leaders in a period of great openness and broad person-to-person contacts with the U.S.S.R.

Even in the most pessimistic assessment of Soviet success in central Europe, some NATO forces would be able to retain a foothold in other parts of the continent. Pact forces would be enormously overextended in trying to control their angry conquests. As long as the war remained conventional, some form of western invasion along Europe's long coastline would remain a possibility and would have to be anticipated by Soviet planners from the outset. Soviet military planners would also have to reckon with the possibility that, in extended war, some or all of the European neutrals would throw their not inconsiderable military weight to the West; at a minimum, Soviet forces would have to be held back because of this danger, a point also not considered in NATO calculations of the number of attacking Pact divisions.

Even the defeat of western Europe would not end an East/West war. The United States, with all its formidable resources energized, would doubtless fight on. Despite appearances, this factor should be reassuring to western Europeans, because Soviet military planners would have to take this probability into account *before* deciding to attack western Europe. The fact is that conflict in Europe would not only spread to the whole of Europe but would sweep the world. Western naval superiority would play a role, as would chronic hostilities elsewhere on the Soviet periphery. There is the chance that Japan and even China would be drawn in. Particularly in an $M + 90$ scenario there would be the beginnings of serious war production, pitting the three leading industrial powers of the world—the U.S., the European Community, and Japan—against the fourth-ranking power, the Soviet Union. Not far in the background in a huge clash of this kind is the high probability of escalation to use of nuclear weapons.

It is difficult to believe that Soviet leaders would deliberately move toward attack in Europe against this background. Such an attack raises the prospect of a confrontation so vast that, whether it remained conventional or went nuclear, it would threaten the most vital Soviet interest, the continuation of the Soviet system.

The argument of the I.N.F. critics that NATO conventional forces have been so weak that only nuclear deterrence has prevented war and consequently that U.S. nuclear reductions under the I.N.F. treaty must be compensated for or restored in some way, does not hold water. The existence of nuclear parity between the United States and the Soviet Union doubtless increases the caution of both, especially since the Cuban missile crisis. But there are many other factors inhibiting a Soviet decision to attack western Europe.

Today, we consider the Soviet leadership rational enough to see that, given nuclear parity with the United States, strategic nuclear war should be avoided, because it might well bring destruction of the Soviet system. Why should Soviet leaders not be rational enough to make the same calculation regarding their central interests when exploring the potential consequences of a conventional attack on western Europe?

INTIMIDATION

Even the most worried critics of the I.N.F. treaty do not argue that a Soviet attack on western Europe is imminent. Instead they argue that the elimination of United States I.N.F. will leave western Europe more open than heretofore to Soviet political pressure and intimidation. It is quite true that, particularly in the 1950s and 1960s, the Soviet Union did not hesitate to threaten the European NATO countries if they did not desist from some step. For example, when Federal Germany entered NATO in 1955, the Soviets were so strongly opposed that they repeatedly threatened the country with nuclear obliteration. The most recent of these episodes occurred with the November, 1983, final vote of the Federal German Bundestag on deployment of American I.N.F., when the Soviets threatened to put inner-German relations in cold storage (an "ice age"), and moved SS-12s and SS-23s forward into East Germany and Czechoslovakia, promising to surround the Federal Republic with a "palisade" of missiles.

All these efforts at intimidation (including this most recent one, which did not cost Chancellor Kohl's coalition government a single negative vote or abstention) were unsuccessful. They failed in large part because close relations with the United States and confidence in American support have served as a counterbalance. Good relations between European and American leaders and the maintenance of parity in strategic nuclear weapons (it is hoped at reduced levels) are essential to shield Europe from Soviet pressure in the future.

In fact, experience indicates that, as long as the link with the United States is functioning more or less well, Soviet pressure is counterproductive, because it provokes militancy in European NATO governments and makes them more willing to spend on defense. The Soviet 1948 blockade of Berlin was the final impetus for the establishment of NATO. Effective Soviet intimidation of a demoralized Europe after a total falling-out between the United States and the western European allies is possible. But more likely than this is the continuation of understanding and cooperation between the United States and western Europe and the gradual growth over coming decades of western Europe's confidence in its own ability to cope with the Soviet Union. We examine this issue further later in the book.

EBBING OF THE COLD WAR

Long before Mikhail Gorbachev became general secretary of the Soviet communist party, the cold war political quarrel which was the source of the NATO/Warsaw Pact military confrontation began to dissipate.

The takeover of the eastern European states by local communist parties aided and controlled by the Soviets was a major cause of the cold war. The most dramatic and direct causes were the separation of Germany into two domains, the complete domination of East Germany by the Soviets, and the attempt by the Soviets to take Berlin by blockading the West's access to it from 1947 to 1948.

Under the impetus of these antagonisms, the rival alliances were formed. Both Soviet and western forces built up from their postwar lows. But it is important to note that in the years following, the West showed its reluctance to risk all-out war by challenging the status quo in Europe with force. It failed to intervene with arms in the Berlin blockade, the East Berlin riots of 1953, the 1961 construction of the Berlin wall, the Soviet invasion of Czechoslovakia in 1968, and the suppression of Solidarity in Poland in 1981. Though bitterly resented at the time, these decisions not to intervene were well founded. As it happened, most of these actions, though unrebuffed by the West militarily, cost the Soviet Union heavily in respect and authority.

However, the West's unwillingness to give political recognition to the status quo in eastern Europe remained high. Thirty years ago, NATO's official position was to refuse even to discuss the improvement of East/West relations or arms control in Europe until the Soviets agreed to reunify Germany. Indeed, in 1954 Chancellor Konrad Adenauer secured the dismissal of Harold Stassen, then the chief United States arms-control negotiator, because he seemed to have violated this rule.

But the West's refusal to accept the status quo in eastern Europe also eroded. In the early 1970s, the Federal Republic of Germany concluded treaties with the U.S.S.R., Poland, and East Germany, accepting the postwar incorporation of former German territories into the U.S.S.R. and Poland and the existence of East Germany as a separate state. The United States, France, and the United Kingdom, which, together with the U.S.S.R., had assumed responsibility for Germany as a whole after the war, endorsed this outcome, subject to the signing of a final peace treaty with Germany. All NATO states gave their endorsement when its members signed the Helsinki accords, in 1975.

The NATO countries continue to dispute the legitimacy of the communist governments of eastern Europe and the means by which they came to power, but not the borders of these states. The NATO allies, including Federal Germany, have relinquished any effort to change the borders of eastern Europe—or to reunify Germany—other than by the peaceful means of pressing for free self-determination by the populations of the eastern European countries of the Warsaw Pact. After these actions and the anti-nuclear demonstrations of the early 1980s, the Soviet's earlier concerns about the emergence of a militant irredentist Germany backed by American military power faded. Insofar as Soviet leaders had a real fear of the West in the postwar period, it was this.

Even more important to the ebbing away of the cold war than the West's acceptance of the territorial status quo in eastern Europe is the fact that the Soviet Union is no longer capable of challenging the status quo in western Europe. In the 1950s the Soviet Union, as the center of a powerful ideology and as a model for world revolutionary change, had great influence over the communist parties of the West. The great fear of NATO leaders then, one that surpassed their fear of the Soviet armed forces as such, was the strength of the West European communist parties under the domination of Moscow. It was the combination of the two that constituted the Soviet threat. Alone neither the European communist parties nor the Red Army wielded such a big stick. But together they seemed capable of taking over western Europe.

Today Marxist/Leninist ideology has lost its appeal and nearly the world over is regarded as an obstacle, not an aid, to political and economic development. The many weaknesses of the Soviet system have become evident, revealed as much by the statements of Soviet leaders as by outsiders. The appeal of the Soviet system as a model is negligible, both in western Europe and elsewhere. The Soviet Union has lost most of its authority over the western European parties, which are reduced to weakness. The once-powerful French communists received only about 10 percent of the vote in the 1988 elections. Only the Italian communists are strong, and they openly defy Moscow and declare their support for NATO. The help these parties could once have given the Soviets during an attack, by organizing uprisings, sabotage, and coups, is no longer available.

The Soviet Union has formally relinquished one persistent effort to change the status quo in the West. In the 1971 Berlin agreement it acknowledged the continuing rights of the United States, France, and the United Kingdom in the western sectors of Berlin. The Soviet Union and East Germany gave up their twenty-year effort to push the western allies out of Berlin—one which at least twice had brought East and

West to the verge of war—and accepted civilian access to Berlin regulated by treaty. And in 1988 CEMA, the economic organization of the Warsaw Pact countries, formally accepted the right of Federal Germany, set forth in the 1971 Berlin agreement but sometimes contested nevertheless, to represent the western sector of Berlin in international negotiations. (East Germany and the Soviet Union had independently recognized Federal Germany's claim in earlier cultural agreements.)

With the political confrontation in decline, the military confrontation to which it gave rise no longer makes much sense, at least on its present large scale. In 1987 the late Franz Josef Strauss, then the most conservative political leader in Federal Germany, stated after a trip to Moscow that the danger of war with the U.S.S.R. was negligible. Great Britain's prime minister Margaret Thatcher, who is famously conservative in her evaluations of the East/West military confrontation, has stated repeatedly that the cold war is over. If the likes of Strauss and Thatcher can be so optimistic, the rest of us may be certain that the East/West military confrontation is becoming superfluous.

What is true of the confrontation in the West is also true of the military confrontation in the Far East. Over the past decade, China, which was once highly concerned about the prospect of Soviet attack, has reduced its military budget and total armed forces by 25 percent. Although all major issues between the Soviet Union and China are not resolved, the leaders of the two countries, meeting in May, 1989, for the first Sino-Soviet summit in thirty years, registered real progress in improvement of their relations. Because China has been and continues to be open in criticizing the military activities of the Soviet Union, its assessment is important.

Most observers agree that war in Europe through deliberate Soviet attack is improbable. In this chapter we have reviewed some of the reasons why. We concluded that the cold war was in decline and that, on rational grounds, Soviet leaders would be foolish to risk war, which might entail the destruction of the entire Soviet system. Particularly if one of the Soviet objectives was to achieve access to western credits, technology, and managerial skills, these goals would be far more surely and safely achieved through trade and diplomacy.

Of course, there is no guarantee that the decisions of Soviet leaders—or western leaders—will always be rational. This would be a source of concern under any circumstances but all the more so in Europe, where the NATO/Pact military confrontation seems to have freed itself from its origins and to have developed a life of its own. A confrontation of these huge dimensions and destructive power can be set off by human error, new East/West tensions, a conflict outside Europe, or, most particularly, by unrest in eastern Europe, which has been rising with Gorbachev's restructuring campaign. The most effective insurance against these risks are measures to build down the military confrontation, to restrain the most dangerous activities, and to make surprise attack more difficult by burdening both sides with measures that would give early warning of a changed force posture.

We shall turn soon to a survey of these possible protections. But first we should look in more detail at some of the main criticisms of the present NATO force posture and some of the proposals made in recent years to reform it. From these we may get some helpful ideas about where to make cuts in the forces of both alliances and what changes could be made in their organization and operational strategy to reduce the chance of conflict, whether by intent or miscalculation. We shall also consider some measures other than cutbacks that can promote stability in the NATO/Pact confrontation.

4 The New Thinking about Armed Forces in West and East: Can It Help in East/West Negotiations?

The intense controversy of the early 1980s over deployment of new American intermediate-range nuclear missiles had important effects on thinking in western Europe about defense. It crystallized longstanding doubts and concerns about NATO's military posture into a sweeping and fundamental criticism of that posture. The result was the generation of an array of proposals to change the entire structure of western defense unilaterally. These proposals have been given many names: alternative defense, non-provocative defense, structural incapacity for attack, reactive defense. There is no standard designation. I prefer "non-offensive defense," because this term seems to me best to capture the intention of the theorizers.

The many and divergent blueprints for non-offensive defense have in common two general characteristics. First, they are aimed at reducing NATO's dependence on nuclear deterrence, as embodied in its strategy of flexible response: most non-offensive defense approaches eliminate NATO's land-based nuclear weapons and disperse concentrations of armor and centralized command and control to make them less attractive targets for Soviet nuclear weapons or for preemptive conventional attack. Second, these approaches identify certain types of weapons:— ground-attack aircraft, conventionally armed surface-to-surface missiles, artillery, tanks, and armed helicopters as the penetration weapons of conventional warfare, weapons especially suitable for deep-thrusting attack. They call for radical reorganization of NATO forces in which these armaments are cut back sharply or even eliminated in favor of high-firepower weapons of more limited range and mobility, with emphasis on high-tech munitions and sensors, in the effort to achieve "defense dominance."[1]

For years advocates of these reforms contended that even if they were carried out by NATO alone, the East/West military confrontation in Europe would be more stable as a result. There would be less incentive for either side to use nuclear weapons, fewer targets to strike, and thus less motivation for the NATO/Warsaw Pact arms race to continue. Moreover, advocates said, cutbacks by the West might motivate a response in kind by the Soviet Union and its allies.

Western professional military officers had no enthusiasm for non-offensive defense. Their criticism went to the heart of these strategies, to the deliberate relinquishment of the armored and air forces that had been put in place after World War II to drive a Warsaw Pact attacker from NATO territory. Although western forces began to adopt some recommendations of non-offensive defense on a piecemeal basis, the skepticism of the western military made it most unlikely that any of the new approaches would be unilaterally adopted by NATO as an overall strategy for western defense. But in a surprising and dramatic turn, civilian Soviet defense thinkers listened to western advocates of non-offensive defense and incorporated elements of the concept in their official proposals for the current force-reduction talks. Since then the concept found its way into the mandate for the talks that negotiators in Vienna from the West as well as the East agreed to in early 1989. Even NATO's own proposal for the talks, released shortly before they began, endorsed the concept.

In this chapter we shall review the development of non-offensive defense in the West and the way in which it has been adapted by Soviet experts. Finally, we shall analyze the new concepts to see to what extent they can provide useful goals or guidelines for both NATO and the Warsaw Pact in negotiating force reductions.

Inevitably, with its origin in groups opposed to the decision of the Federal Republic of Germany and other NATO governments to deploy American I.N.F. in Europe, non-offensive defense has been politicized from the outset. Most statements of support and many criticisms have been so politically charged that it has been difficult to obtain an objective reading of the advantages and disadvantages of specific suggestions. To complicate matters further, many western proponents of alternative defense have been civilians rather than professional soldiers—a point which also holds true for the Soviet Union. Some western advocates have offered simplistic formulations that fail to account sufficiently for the realities of combat. In dismissing these, professional soldiers have found it all too easy to dismiss other ideas from outside the traditional defense community that deserve serious consideration. Still, any suggestion for fundamental change of western defenses that have been in place for more than thirty peaceful years must bear a heavy burden of proof.

CRITICISMS OF THE NATO FORCE POSTURE

Advocates of non-offensive defense have focused on the fundamental issue of how NATO forces are organized and equipped rather than on how many forces there are or where they are located. As we saw in the last chapter, like Warsaw Pact forces, NATO ground forces deployed in the Federal Republic and adjoining countries are organized mainly in the form of mobile, heavily armored formations—main battle tanks, armored personnel carriers and armored self-propelled artillery and anti-aircraft weapons, backed by armed helicopters and ground-attack aircraft. This force organization is considered by a large majority of NATO's professional military officers to be the optimum method of organizing an all-purpose force with maximum flexibility of use. The mobility and armor of an armored force protects it against artillery or air attack at the outset of invasion and permits it to defend at points of actual enemy attack, to move to deal with possible enemy break-throughs, to engage enemy columns on their more vulnerable flanks, and to retaliate against invasion with at least a limited counterattack on enemy territory.

Anders Boserup, a professor of sociology at the University of Copenhagen and co-convener of the Pugwash group on conventional forces in Europe, is one of the major theoreticians of the criticism of this traditional NATO approach to force organization. Boserup attacks the basic concept of NATO defense—that peace is promoted by a balance of forces between NATO and the Warsaw Pact. He argues to the contrary that both NATO and Pact forces are similarly equipped with attack aircraft, tanks and mobile artillery and that the more closely armed forces of similar composition are in balance, the less stable the peace.

Efforts to maintain balance between similarly organized forces are destabilizing, Boserup contends, because they provoke an endless upward rachet of the arms race. What's more, they heighten the risk of a preemptive strike in a crisis and of preemptive escalation after a conflict begins. When one alliance (or both) has offensive capabilities stronger than the defensive forces of the other, there is an advantage in taking the initiative in crisis situations—for example, with preemptive air or missile attacks on the air defenses, airfields, missile sites, and command facilities of the opposing alliance.

The advocates of non-offensive defense appear to have borrowed from strategic nuclear analysis the concept of stability and to have taken longstanding western criticisms of the aggressive, armor-heavy stance of the Warsaw Pact and applied them also to the present organization of NATO forces. Both alliances are held responsible for maintaining an unnecessarily unstable force posture.

The response of supporters of NATO's present force organization is that the Warsaw Pact has much stronger armored forces than NATO and that NATO's armored forces have a short forward reach. Especially short, they say, is the reach of Federal German forces, whose installations for logistic and medical services are not mobile but fixed. To this Boserup and others point out that despite the Pact's overall numerical superiority, NATO and Pact forces are in fact organized around the same type of offensive armaments, both alliances emphasizing mobile armored formations that could be used for lightning strikes. They argue further that a short forward reach is not characteristic of American forces in the Federal Republic; that one undeniable area of NATO strength, at least qualitatively, is fighter-bombers; and that in its Follow-on Force Attack program, NATO is currently giving greater emphasis to deep defensive interdiction with weapons that could also be used for offense.

The proponents of non-offensive defense have made some specific criticisms of the current NATO force posture. These criticisms include the following assertions:

(1) The majority of NATO ground force officers are tank-centered, preoccupied by the central role of the tank in World War II Blitzkrieg tactics and unable to look objectively at other possibilities.
(2) NATO forces are too dependent on distant U.S. forces for rapid reinforcement. For political or military reasons, these forces may not arrive in time; Europe should be more reliant on its own capabilities.
(3) Owing in part to the close link to the United States, NATO forces on the Central Front are not structured for the specific mission they have there. They have support, logistics, command and control, and information systems designed for worldwide use that are cumbersome and ineffective at short range.
(4) Whatever their strength relative to that of the Pact, NATO forces are not set for a defensive role but for a penetrating counterattack.
(5) The NATO area is too shallow for a defensive force composed primarily of armored units. Such units should not be deployed as far forward on the Central Front as they now are. Because NATO, as a defensive alliance, has to await a first blow from the Pact, much

NATO armor would be destroyed or immobilized before it could be used. It would be better to interpose a tank-killing force of infantry, anti-tank weapons, and mines and to pull armored forces to the rear where they could then be used to meet the actual main thrust of an assault.

(6) The increasing cost of high-tech armaments (more than $2 million today for a tank and more than $40 million for a fighter-bomber) leads to "structural disarmament," in which certain weapons are cut back not because of strategy but because of finances. The resulting shortfall in armored forces creates a latter-day Maginot Line, weakened further by gaps resulting from maldeployment of NATO forces. (For example, heavier American forces are concentrated in the south, while Belgian and Netherlands formations deployed at plausible breakthrough points are not fully manned, with major components stationed to the rear on their own home territories.)

(7) The nuclear missions necessary to maintain flexible response divert scarce resources, especially aircraft, from NATO's conventional forces.

The main argument of proponents of non-offensive defense has been that stability and security depend not on a *balance of similar forces* but on the *superiority of the defensive forces* of either side over the offensive forces arrayed against them. Proponents want to create what they call "mutual defensive superiority" or "defense dominance." In such a scheme, the advantages that the attacker would receive from taking the initiative would not compensate for the advantage enjoyed by the defender.

The proponents of non-offensive defense contend that, although individual weapons systems can obviously be used for offensive or defensive purposes, it is possible to distinguish offensive configurations emphasizing mobility, range, and reach from defensive configurations emphasizing firepower with limited mobility and range. In other words, the organization of forces and the mix of equipment, together with the doctrine for use of these forces and their pattern of geographic deployment, can favor offense or defense.

Proponents of non-offensive defense want NATO to abandon its policy of responding to an attack by the Pact according to its severity and, if need be, making first-use of nuclear weapons. All prefer a policy of no-first-use of nuclear weapons. Most advocates would prefer to get rid of nuclear weapons completely, but they are sufficiently practical to realize that this will not occur in the foreseeable future. Therefore, they limit themselves to advocating the elimination of NATO's land-based nuclear weapons—artillery, surface-to-surface missiles, and fighter-bombers. Most current versions of such a strategy do envisage a sea-based American/French/British nuclear deterrent dedicated to European defense and also back-up deterrence through a United States strategic nuclear force of reduced size. Although these proposals also claim to present fewer big targets for nuclear attack, they are largely a recipe for conventional defense, on the assumption that, if conflict comes in Europe, each superpower will find it to its own advantage not to use nuclear weapons.

It is important that, for the most part, these approaches deliberately renounce not only nuclear retaliation as a deterrent but conventional retaliation as well. The objective is not to win a victory (decisive engagements are to be avoided, because they carry the risk of escalation) but to create a stalemate pause in which politics can take over. (This outcome is also the stated objective of NATO's flexible-response strategy.) To achieve such a pause, non-offensive defense relies on stationary forces or forces of limited mobility to gradually bring aggressive attack to a halt through attrition of the attacking force. In theory, the defending force is so organized that it cannot maneuver, concentrate, or accept a major battle. The guiding principle is *denial* of the territory sought by an attacker rather than *deterrence* through the threat of nuclear retaliation or, for that matter, conventional retaliation.

Proponents of non-offensive defense argue that a manifestly defensive system unsuited to attack will not be perceived as a threat by the Warsaw Pact, will reduce the risk of conflict, and will provide more effective resistance if conflict does break out.

In some practical respects, the proposals for non-offensive defense are not so different from a number of ideas generated in the past from within the international defense community. Over the years, more orthodox NATO military experts have proposed radical changes in the organization of NATO's forces for the sake of greater effectiveness. In the 1950s Sir John Slessor, marshall of the British Royal Air Force, proposed a highly trained home guard of limited mobility for Germany. In the 1960s B. H. Liddell Hart, the leading British authority of his time on military strategy, proposed a citizen militia on the Swiss model for Germany that would man a deep network of forward defense posts. In the early 1970s Kenneth Hunt of the International Institute for Strategic Studies proposed a three-layer structure for Germany composed of a forward belt of light formations along the dividing line, part active-duty units and part militia; a second belt composed of armored units; and a third rear-area belt of reserve units. The similarity of Hunt's idea to the alternative strategies being debated now is particularly strong.[2]

One of the earliest antecedents of today's non-offensive defense idea was put forward in the early 1950s, as Federal Germany negotiated with the western occupying powers on the reestablishment of German armed forces. Colonel Bogislaw von Bonin was the chief military planner of the Amt Blank, the precursor organization which in 1955 became the German defense ministry. Bonin proposed that the Federal Republic's contribution to NATO's defenses take the form of an eighty-kilometer belt of anti-tank weapons, minefields, and defensive positions manned by light infantry and local militia.[3] Bonin was dismissed and his ideas never carried out. German forces organized as he had proposed could not have interlocked with American forces heavily armored as they had been during and since World War II. And Chancellor Konrad Adenauer and his government considered it essential that the new German forces be able to mesh with American and other allied forces so that the defense of Germany would fully involve all of NATO.

The reason for Germany's rejection of Bonin's plan helps to explain NATO's dismissive response to subsequent ideas for the reorganization of German defense. NATO is predicated on the idea that the allies must participate in defense in a forward position that would involve each ally in war with Warsaw Pact attackers from the very outset of conflict. Yet to a large extent, non-offensive defense, like Bonin's strategy, is based on the divergent idea that individual western European countries can and should rely more on themselves for defense and correspondingly less on the alliance and its dominant member, the United States. Underlying this nationalist objective is a new assessment of the Soviet threat: the belief that Soviet attack on western Europe for the purpose of conquest and holding territory to exploit its productive resources is highly unlikely. The more likely cause of war in Europe, many believe, would be a war originating in eastern Europe or outside Europe entirely. Consequently, advocates of alternatives to flexible response argue that what Europe needs now are mechanisms to preserve stability in a crisis and to decrease the inducement for either side to make a preemptive attack.

MODELS OF NON-OFFENSIVE DEFENSE

The Federal German experts Horst Afheldt and Norbert Hannig proposed the classic models of non-offensive defense. In Afheldt's concept armored units and attack aircraft are replaced by small units dispersed throughout the Federal Republic of Germany. These units would be either stationary or of limited mobility, concealed in protected positions, and backed by a large number of electronic sensors and rocket artillery designed for anti-aircraft and anti-tank missions. Hannig, in contrast, has suggested the creation of a "defensive wall," in which defenses are concentrated in a forward position and emphasize rocket artillery. In effect, Hannig substitutes heavy firepower with a capacity to shift target areas along the front for the mobility of NATO's present tanks and artillery.[4]

The successors to these early models favor an eclectic approach. Generally, they retain armored forces similar to the present formations of the Bundeswehr and other NATO allies but shrink their numbers and interpose a stationary barrier of high-tech or light-infantry defenses along the dividing line to take the initial impact of a Pact attack. Such models represent an effort to reconcile components or elements of non-offensive defense, including high-tech weapons, with the present NATO or Bundeswehr force organization.

The stated objective of most of these mixed approaches is to improve conventional defense, reduce reliance on nuclear weapons, improve crisis stability, increase political support, reduce costs, and introduce a degree of defensive specialization among NATO countries. Advocates of this mixed approach would do away with NATO's Follow-on Forces Attack strategy, which calls for deep strikes using conventional weapons at the outset of a conflict in Europe. Such a focus, they say, implies a developed capacity to initiate offensive warfare. Most versions place far greater reliance than now exists on reserve forces, including local reserves to man border areas of the Federal Republic. Many also foresee a much diminished role for the forces of NATO allies in the ground defense of Germany.

This group of proposals is the subject of current debate about non-offensive defense, because it lays a stronger claim to replace the current NATO force posture than the more radical alternatives of Afheldt or Hannig. (Afheldt, in fact, has modified his own model to include some armored forces.)

The proposals put forward by the Federal German defense expert Lutz Unterseher and the Study Group on Alternative Security Policy, a group close to the German Social Democrats, are a useful example of this second school. In one model Unterseher and his colleagues have called for a defensive system of three belts or zones (such belts are a characteristic feature of this group of approaches):

(1) A thirty-kilometer "Containment Net" manned by decentralized infantry detachments—partly active duty, partly reserves;

(2) A fifty-kilometer zone manned by what Unterseher and his colleagues call the "fire department"—mechanized forces including anti-tank infantry, some tanks, and helicopters that could be brought to bear quickly. These forces would have operational mobility and their effectiveness would depend largely on the use of obstacles, prepared shelters, and heavy firepower rockets;

(3) A rear-area force designed to protect against sabotage and invasion by air.

In a different, more recent model, Unterseher has advocated a belt of sensors and mines at the Federal German border. Behind this would be a "web" of 450 Federal German infantry battalions deployed in dispersed, prepared, and hardened positions. Behind this would be a "spider" component of 150 mobile combat battalions, some of them provided by NATO allies, and equipped with light-armored infantry vehicles, mobile anti-tank weapons, and some tanks. Finally, there would be a rear echelon to defend the country from sabotage and invasion by air. The scheme features decentralized ammunition and fuel depots, small units, and light interceptor aircraft and ground-to-air missiles, but no fighter-bombers. It also foresees a diminished role for allied ground forces in Germany, whose number would shrink from about 400,000 in peacetime to 100,000. In addition to providing some ground forces, the allies would be expected to specialize in aircraft and naval forces. The total mobilization strength of the Bundeswehr in wartime would be cut from 1.3 million to 680,000.[5]

Another proponent of the compromise approach, Albrecht A. C. von Mueller, director of the newly founded European Center for International Security at Starnberg, Bavaria, has made a determined effort to mesh non-offensive defense concepts with current defense strategy and organization. His approach, which he calls the "integrated defense model" or "integrated forward defense," takes the form of four zones:

(1) A five-kilometer belt at the border, with firepower from artillery rockets, attack drones, and mines of all kinds;

(2) A "hook" or "net" zone twenty-five to fifty kilometers deep and manned by light infantry "techno-Kommandos" equipped with "third generation" precision-guided munitions, mortars, and scatter mines;
(3) A sixty-kilometer-deep "maneuver zone" with heavily armored units to cope with breakthroughs and to expel a weakened invader from German territory;
(4) A rear-defense zone consisting of a network of mobile defense units to deal with sabotage and air landings and provide logistic support.

In this scheme interceptor aircraft would specialize in maintaining air superiority over Federal German territory. There would be no fighter-bombers.

Von Mueller considers his approach an advanced form of flexible response. However, like other adherents of non-offensive defense, he foresees a policy of no-first-use of nuclear weapons. He would deploy them only at sea, as a deterrent against their use by the Warsaw Pact. He is silent as to the role of NATO forces in his concept.[6]

CRITICISM OF NON-OFFENSIVE DEFENSE

NATO commanders and defense experts scorned the first wave of non-offensive defense models proposed by Afheldt and others. They argued that these models were excessively oriented to current Warsaw Pact attack options, which could change. They said that models relying largely on high-tech weapons would fix NATO's defenses in one mode and deprive them of the flexibility of a mobile armored force. Because the non-offensive concept relied so heavily on stationary equipment and positions, they said, Warsaw Pact forces would be able to drive a corridor through Federal Germany, by using chemical or nuclear weapons (although proponents do allow NATO a nuclear deterrent) or by mounting an air attack from an altitude above the range of ground-based anti-aircraft weapons. The Pact could also bomb population centers and grapple with NATO's forces at the front later. In probably the most telling criticism, NATO officers argued that the absence of an armored counter-attack capability would make it impossible for NATO to push an attacker out of its territory and would make the attacker's own territory a sanctuary, free of any threat of retaliation, from which it could launch further attacks.

These criticisms were taken seriously by the authors of the second wave of non-offensive defense approaches—the syncretic models like those of Von Mueller. Most of these newer approaches are variations on the existing NATO defense organization rather than proposing its elimination. All depend to some extent on nuclear deterrence and all envisage some use of traditional armored forces; most would use interceptor aircraft against Pact bomber attack. Indeed, one American commentator, Steven Canby, has criticized these new versions as circling back to NATO orthodoxy. His point has some justification. However, it overlooks the conceptual underpinnings of the non-offensive defense concept, which diverge widely from those of the current NATO approach in their rejection of flexible nuclear response, in their preference for preponderance of defensive over offensive force elements, and in their advocacy of attrition rather than retaliation as the goal of NATO defense.

Notwithstanding the efforts of the originators of this second wave to design a robust defense, the proposals do have some clear military drawbacks. Many, like those of Unterseher or Social Democratic Bundestag Deputy Andreas von Buelow, would cut back the number of active-duty soldiers of the Bundeswehr by a disturbingly sharp margin—by far more, indeed, than the demographic contraction of the conscript age group will necessitate. (Federal Germany expects a shortfall of some 100,000 draft-age men per year beginning in 1994.) They propose spending less rather than more on conventional defense, and would make defense still more dependent than it is now on the mobilization of reserves—an option that may be difficult to choose in a time of crisis.

Most non-offensive defense proposals posit the total elimination of land-based nuclear weapons from Federal Germany. In the past, NATO commanders criticized this aspect as "decoupling" and seriously undercutting the American nuclear guarantee. However, as we saw in Chapter 2, the U.S./Soviet agreement to eliminate intermediate-range missiles has broadened support for reducing or eliminating land-based nuclear weapons in the Federal Republic. Now a large majority would support the view of non-offensive defense and choose to rely mainly on sea- or air-based nuclear weapons.

Non-offensive defense models place infantry and combat engineer units in permanent forward positions on the German border. Proponents argue that such deployments are needed to buttress NATO's defenses, which are especially vulnerable on the Central Front. These forward zones have been criticized, however, on the grounds that they may not be as strong against a conventional attack by the Pact as

NATO's mobile armored forces. Many alternative models deploy reservists along the border in the area of first impact, where they may not perform well. Further criticisms are that the new scatter mines are extremely costly and a very large number would be needed for coverage even of the most penetrable areas of the Federal German border region. Others point out that, with so many NATO forces permanently committed to do battle against tanks, the Pact could change its tactics and go in for airborne assault or simply send infantry in ahead of its tanks. (Non-offensive defense advocates claim their proposals provide for sufficient air defense and variable firepower as well as armored forces to cope with both possibilities.) Critics contend that a defense strategy emphasizing fixed installations and only a small retaliatory force would make it relatively easy for the Warsaw Pact to calculate the risks of mounting an attack, thus weakening deterrence.

NATO experts say that the less mobile the alliance's defenses are, the more inviting they become as targets for chemical weapons or tactical nuclear weapons. This point is debatable. NATO commanders are concerned about the vulnerability of their own fixed targets—anti-aircraft, airfields, ammunition depots—in rear areas of the Federal Republic to chemical, nuclear, and conventional weapons. Most non-offensive defense models disperse these potential targets. Moreover, it is unclear which would have a lower casualty rate in the face of concentrated conventional artillery fire or air bombardment: the mobile armored units with accompanying infantry in armored personnel carriers now deployed by NATO on the Central Front or the troops manning dug-in firing platforms or protected by rapidly installable prefabricated shelters that the alternative models would deploy.

A central difficulty with the ideas of the non-offensive defense group has to do with money. The defense funds of the Federal Republic and other NATO countries have stopped growing and are likely to decrease. Non-offensive defense adherents want to spend less on ground forces and more on "shield" forces of limited mobility. Those who want to concentrate scarce resources on armored forces as the most flexible and therefore most rational defense investment have as justification the offensive and defensive experience of World War II and of warfare in the Middle East.

NATO force planners may see the theoretical benefit of shield assets as a supplement of existing forces. They do not now have enough money to field at an adequate level the basic armored force on which they rely, however, and they do not want to subtract from these funds to invest in any defenses of limited mobility. (If money were available, as Karsten Voigt, defense expert of the German Social Democrats, suggests in an excellent survey of non-offensive defense, there would still be a problem of transition: if the new posture were added on to NATO's force structure, it would augment NATO's capacity to attack behind the new shield; if NATO's forces were cut back before the new posture was assumed, NATO would be more vulnerable than it now is to Pact attack.)[7]

The criticism of even these modified models of non-offensive defense that NATO experts hold most firmly is directed against the programmatic reduction of dual-use, offensive–defensive weapons like fighter-bombers, surface-to-surface missiles, and armored units in the interest of defense dominance and structural incapacity for attack. Most NATO military commanders would not wish to unilaterally give up or curtail their means of dealing with a Soviet breakthrough, of pushing an invading force out of the Federal Republic, or of mounting at least some retaliation on the attacking force in its own territory. We will return to this issue of counterattack capability later in this chapter and in our chapters on reductions and on actions that could be taken by NATO and the Pact early in the new talks.

What most worries many American and West European observers is the attenuated relationship between the Federal Republic and its NATO allies (and the United States in particular) posited by most but not all non-offensive defense programs. They either exclude the allies from the defense process (the first Afheldt plan, for example), reduce the allied presence (as in the Unterseher approach), or indicate an intention to dispense with the allies at some future point. Reduction of the allied, especially American, troop presence in Germany may be a long-term possibility, but despite mounting frictions over activities of allied forces in Germany, including low-level air force training flights and weekend artillery practice in training areas, most Germans would not wish to encourage it, especially not unilaterally. As we have sought to show, despite their antipathy to the stationing of short-range nuclear weapons on German soil, most Germans still adhere to nuclear deterrence as useful insurance against Soviet attack. Without a considerable American military presence in the Federal Republic, the threat by the U.S. to use nuclear weapons in defense of a beleaguered Germany would lose further credibility.

ASSESSMENT

The vocabulary of non-offensive defense has been adopted by President Richard Von Weizaecker and by Chancellor Helmut Kohl to explain Federal Germany's long-term defense objectives; in late 1988 a working group of Chancellor Kohl's Christian Democratic Party went so far as to commend many of its concepts as general guidelines for Federal German forces. As we shall discuss, the basic idea has even been incorporated by NATO into its program for the current force-reduction talks.

But we must distinguish between acceptance of some of the concepts of non-offensive defense by political leaders in the West and the prospects for actual implementation of this strategy by NATO as a comprehensive unilateral substitute for its current force organization. Here the response has been far less positive.

As a practical matter non-offensive defense in Europe could only be put into practice if the government of the Federal Republic of Germany so decided: the Federal Republic's eastern border is the line of confrontation between the main ground forces of NATO and the Pact and it is along this border that non-offensive defense would have to be installed. The Federal Republic has held hearings on non-offensive defense in its Bundestag, or parliament, and senior officers of the German armed forces have held several roundtable discussions with proponents. But there it has ended. There is no chance of formal adoption of the non-provocative approach by Chancellor Kohl's government as a unilateral strategy. The opposition Social Democrats have accepted some aspects of alternative defense, but their current prospects of coming to power are uncertain. And if they did participate in the German government, it is probable that they would not make radical changes in defense but instead would build further elements of the alternative models into Federal Germany's existing military posture.

Indeed, that is happening now. In its program for restructuring the Bundeswehr—*The Bundeswehr in the Year 2000*—the Federal German defense ministry is placing more emphasis on deployment of infantry instead of armor near the border with East Germany and more emphasis on scatter mines and obstacles. The U.S. Army in Germany has shown increased interest recently in terrain-contouring and obstacles. Measures like these have been proposed by advocates of non-offensive defense, but they have also long been advocated by more conservative critics of the NATO-force posture. Their piecemeal adoption by NATO forces will probably continue over the years.

THE NON-OFFENSIVE DEFENSE CONCEPT IN THE U.S.S.R.

The main defect of a unilateral western shift to non-offensive defense has been that it would radically alter the organization of NATO forces but would leave Warsaw Pact forces with their present force organization, deployment, and doctrine. It would also leave them with their large numerical superiority in most major armaments, free to use these assets in different ways to overcome a defensively restructured NATO. However, parallel actions by the Soviet Union and other Warsaw Pact states to restructure their own armed forces along the lines of non-offensive defense could change this critical view.

The prospect of parallel action seemed more real—and any chance that the West would adopt non-offensive defense unilaterally was ended—when Mikhail Gorbachev was designated General Secretary of the Soviet Communist party and the Soviet Union began a deliberate campaign to achieve arms control agreements with the West. At that point it no longer seemed reasonable to argue for unilateral changes in the NATO force posture but rather for negotiated reduction of the NATO/Pact confrontation.

Despite East/West discussion of the possibility of new force-reduction talks, a minority of advocates of non-offensive defense (Unterseher and members of his group, for example) stuck with the unilateral approach, at least for a time. But the majority took the discussion as an opportunity to argue that negotiated force reductions should be shaped to reflect the goals of non-offensive defense. In October, 1987, four prominent western alternative-defense thinkers—Anders Boserup, Frank Von Hippel, Robert Neild, and Albrecht von Mueller—wrote to General Secretary Gorbachev urging that negotiated reductions focus on "offense-capable" components of the forces of both alliances and lead to a situation of "mutual defensive sufficiency." Gorbachev replied a month later endorsing this approach.[8] In early 1988, in what was presented as the first joint East/West proposal on non-offensive defense, Albrecht von Mueller and the Polish expert Andrzej Karkoszka suggested a negotiated reduction of tanks and aircraft down to 50 percent of the weaker side.[9]

Six months later, at the May/June, 1988, Moscow summit with President Reagan, General Secretary Gorbachev proposed a three-step program for reducing the number of NATO and Pact forces in Europe, beginning with the elimination of asymmetries between the two alliances in their holdings of major armaments and ending with the dismantling of the "offensive core" of the forces of both alliances. In a remarkable example of West/East communication, the vocabulary of non-offensive defense had been picked up by the leaders of the Warsaw Pact states and their ideas advanced at the highest level in an official Soviet proposal.

How did this come about?

In the mid-1980s, the Soviet Union and the Warsaw Pact, having already endorsed a plan for the complete denuclearization of central Europe, began to endorse, as well, the concept of exclusionary or thin-out zones along the dividing line between the two alliances in central Europe. Such zones are relevant to non-offensive defense concepts, many of which posit one or more zones along the dividing line between the two alliances where static defenses could be deployed but not armored or other heavy, mobile arms. As we shall discuss later, they are thus a way for the alliances to contractualize an agreement to move into a non-offensive defense posture covering at least a portion of their forces.

The Soviet Union has not only urged exclusionary zones and corridors in central Europe; it also moved gradually toward full endorsement of the general concept underlying non-offensive defense proposals—the idea that NATO and Pact forces should be configured for defense and not for offense. This is a marked departure from earlier treatment of this subject by Soviet officials and academicians. Traditionally, both groups have expressed great skepticism as to the value and practicality of the non-offensive defense approach, and they have insisted that priority be given to negotiated reductions of armed forces. However, in a February, 1987, speech to the Moscow "International Forum," General Secretary Gorbachev said that the number of NATO and Pact armed forces should be reduced in a way that would exclude the possibility of surprise attack and remove the most dangerous offensive arms from the zone of contact. There should be a balance of reasonable sufficiency, he said, in constantly declining forces. He added, "Quite naturally, military doctrines must be of a defensive nature."

Soviet defense experts first applied their own concept of "reasonable sufficiency" (the phrase was introduced by President Dwight D. Eisenhower in the late 1950s) to the strategic nuclear balance. They argued that national security depends more on a political approach to other countries than on an effort to have stronger military forces than all possible opponents combined; that for effective retaliation against a nuclear attack, the defender would need only a relatively small number of weapons; and that it is mistaken to respond to each improvement of U.S. nuclear forces with a Soviet move of the same type. The Soviets then turned to apply this theory to conventional forces, with the idea of adopting doctrine, deployment, and organization of the forces to favor defense over offense. With this shift, reasonable sufficiency became a mirror image of the concept of non-offensive defense developed by western thinkers.[10]

The theme of defensive force postures is more fully developed in the May, 1987, communiqué of the Political Consultative Committee of the Warsaw Pact, which urges "reduction of the armed forces and conventional armaments in Europe to a level where neither side maintaining its defense capacity would have the means to stage a surprise attack against the other side or offensive operations in general." The document ends with an invitation to NATO states to join with the Pact to compare the military doctrines of the two alliances in order to reduce mutual suspicion, ensure a better perception of each other's intentions, "and to guarantee that the military concepts and doctrines of the two military blocs and their members are based on defensive principles."

During 1987 and 1988, conferences of the German Social Democrats with East German, Hungarian, Polish, and Czechoslovak Communist parties resulted in strong endorsements of the principles of non-offensive defense. The statement of the July, 1988, meeting of the Pact's Political Consultative Committee picked up Gorbachev's summit proposal of May, 1988, including in the Pact's proposed approach for the current force-reduction talks a final stage of East/West reductions in which "the armed forces of both sides would acquire a strictly defensive nature."

Western defense experts have raised the question of whether these endorsements have substance or are merely designed to make the Soviet Union and its allies appear cooperative to western publics. In August, 1988, Frank Carlucci, secretary of defense under President Reagan, toured the Soviet Union—the first such visit ever made by a holder of that office. He said he saw no evidence of a letup in Soviet military production, deployments of Pact forces, or Warsaw Pact maneuvers to indicate that a change was occurring. What's more, western defense experts have pointed out, the production of Soviet tanks and aircraft continues at a high rate.

Under repeated questioning from westerners soon after these interesting new Soviet pronouncements, Soviet and Warsaw Pact officials and academicians were unable to specify what a posture of non-offensive defense would mean for the Warsaw Pact in specific terms. They did say that application of the non-offensive approach would mean large Soviet and Warsaw Pact reductions of tanks, artillery, and heavy mobile armaments, and said shifts in Soviet doctrine had already been introduced into the curriculum of leadership courses for Soviet officers and in the pattern of Soviet exercises in the field. Yet they were unable to be more explicit and to say, for example, how Pact forces in East Germany would look given such cutbacks.

One reason for this lack of specificity soon became clear: the Soviet military itself was deeply divided on this subject and not yet prepared to commit itself in practical support for non-offensive defense. In Soviet practice, the political leadership decides on strategy and the professional military works out its implementation. Yet in this case, it was evident that the process was not coordinated and that the Gorbachev leadership had taken the Soviet military by surprise. Senior Soviet officers published articles in which they argued that Soviet forces were already defensively oriented; "reasonable sufficiency" for ground forces, they argued, means a force posture like the one the Soviet Union already had, capable of decisive counterattack against NATO aggression. Soviet defense minister D. T. Yazov wrote in early 1988 that "it is impossible to rout an aggressor with defense alone—after an attack has been repulsed, the troops and naval forces must be able to conduct a decisive offensive."[11] The criticism Minister Yazov was raising against Soviet statements on non-offensive defense was precisely the main criticism raised by NATO professional officers against the views of western theorists: the deliberate relinquishment of reduction of capability for counterattack.

Those supporting the new concepts did not give up. Dr. Andrei Kokoshin of the Moscow-based Institute of the USA and Canada has published articles seeking to find precedents for the defensive concept in early Soviet military practice. Among his examples is the crucial battle of Kursk in World War II, in which Soviet military leaders deliberately adopted a reactive defense against a predicted *Wehrmacht* tank attack (but then made a massive counterattack with their own tanks). In an important follow-on article (June, 1988) in the journal of the Institute of World Economy and International Relations, Kokoshin and his co-author, General V. V. Larionov, presented four basic variants of defensive strategy used by Soviet forces in the past, including Kursk. Variant three, used by Soviet forces against the Japanese army in Mongolia at the battle of Khalkin-Gol, in 1939, is a strategy in which "the defending side defeats the invader without transition to counterattack beyond its borders." In the fourth variant, for which no historical example is given, each side, as in the non-offensive defense approach, deliberately abstains from having the means of counterattack.[12] Thus, like western advocates (and western critics) of non-offensive defense, these Soviet experts have also identified one specific area for future East/West investigation and discussion: counterattack capability.

A leading western expert on Soviet military strategy, David Holloway, traces the source of the surprising Soviet shift to "reasonable sufficiency" to Leonid Brezhnev's foreign and military policies. These did not move toward world dominance of socialism or make the Soviet Union more secure but instead yielded a record of failure, *inter alia* in Afghanistan, and with a more heavily armed United States and a hostile China and Japan.

Holloway sees further sources of the "new thinking" in the determination of Gorbachev and his reform-minded colleagues to overcome the poor performance of the Soviet economy and their related efforts to control the economic costs of defense, a motive that seems directly to underlie Soviet efforts to create a more benign international environment for internal reform of the Soviet system and that is likely to endure.[13]

The proof of serious adherence to the concepts of non-offensive defense that western officials were asking for appears to have been furnished by General Secretary Gorbachev in his December 7, 1988, announcement of Soviet unilateral reductions to be carried out in 1989 and 1990. Gorbachev announced that, after the withdrawal of six Soviet armored divisions from East Germany, Czechoslovakia, and Hungary, the remaining Soviet forces in eastern Europe would be reorganized. "After a major cutback of their tanks," he said, their structure "will become clearly defensive."

Subsequently, Foreign Minister Shevardnadze in his March 6, 1989, speech at the opening of the C.F.E. talks (text in Appendix VII) stated that the number of tanks in Soviet forward-deployed tank divisions will be reduced by 20 percent, bringing the divisions from a standard holding of 328 each to about 260 each; that the tank holdings of Soviet forward-deployed motorized rifle divisions, now about 270 per division, will be reduced by 40 percent to 160 each. Another Soviet official informed Phillip Karber, a leading American defense expert, that the tank holdings of some Soviet motorized rifle divisions in the western U.S.S.R. will be cut even more radically, down to forty tanks per division, resulting in the establishment of defensive infantry divisions similar to some the Red Army had in the past. This changed organization of Soviet ground forces might contain some useful ideas for the future organization of NATO forces.

OPTIONS FOR THE C.F.E. TALKS

Not only have Soviet leaders made non-offensive defense a priority in their own approach to the new Vienna force-reduction talks. The concept is also reflected in the mandate for the talks worked out by Pact and NATO negotiators in January, 1989. The mandate specifies as one main goal of the new talks, in addition to eliminating the capacity for surprise attack, the elimination "of the capacity for initiating large-scale offensive action." In suggesting this language, NATO negotiators clearly had in mind the Warsaw Pact's conventional superiorities in tanks and artillery, creating in the Pact what NATO calls invasion capability. But East/West agreement on this concept gives it general status. Logically, the capability for large-scale offensive action must mean force organization with a heavy mix of penetration weapons— not only tanks, artillery, and armored troop carriers, but also surface-to-surface missiles, aircraft, and helicopters.

Going beyond this, the NATO ministerial communiqué of December 8, 1988, which contains the outlines of NATO's negotiating program for the Atlantic-to-the-Urals talks, ends with a statement that is surprising for NATO, given the rejection by NATO commanders of non-offensive defense theory. It is that if NATO's reduction proposals can be accepted and implemented, NATO would wish to consider as a means of enhancing stability in Europe "the restructuring of armed forces to enhance defensive capabilities and further reduce offensive capabilities." Although this statement, repeated in NATO's March 6, 1989, position paper for the talks, may have more to do with the NATO leadership's reading of western European political opinion than with a commitment to non-offensive defense, it nonetheless marks remarkable progress toward acceptance of this concept in both East and West.

The question now becomes, how can this conceptual agreement be put in practice in the Atlantic-to-the-Ural talks?

We can agree with the adherents of non-offensive defense that the organization of forces—the mix and amount of weapons with which forces are equipped, the geographic deployment of the forces so equipped, and the operational–tactical strategy that lays out how these weapons and forces should be used—can favor either offense or defense. This gives us three components of the military confrontation in Europe that could be discussed on an East/West basis in conjunction with the Atlantic-to-the-Urals talks. Let us look more closely at each one.

Responding to NATO's charges that the Warsaw Pact's military doctrine is an important element of a generally aggressive military posture, from 1986 on the Warsaw Pact has repeatedly offered to discuss the military doctrines of both alliances. NATO has been apprehensive that the discussion would focus on such topics as NATO's strategy of flexible response, whose credibility and public support are, as we have seen, already somewhat shaky.

But a discussion of doctrine need not be propagandistic and unproductive. It could instead take as its point of departure the mandate for the force-reduction talks. As we have seen, the mandate specifies as one main goal of the talks the elimination of the capacity for initiating large-scale offensive action. This is a central issue of military doctrine, in very practical form.

How should we go about measuring the capacity for initiating large-scale offensive action? Each alliance, NATO and the Warsaw Treaty Organization, insists that it is purely defensive and would not deliberately attack the other. Given the huge potential costs of war in Europe, we may take these statements seriously as regards present intentions. But, as we have seen in our earlier discussion in this chapter of criticisms of the organization of both alliances, the problems of measuring which alliance has more invasion or attack capability, or of measuring each alliance's capability for counterattack are, in practice, the same: even if we concede for purposes of discussion that both alliances, the Warsaw Pact as well as NATO, are defensive, the force elements needed for effective attack and for counterattack are the same.

How strong should counterattack capability be? Each alliance would surely wish to have sufficient military capability to halt an aggressor and to deny him success. But should each strive for the additional capacity needed to push an invader off its territory, recognizing that, in theory, greater capacity can be used for offensive purposes? Or, going beyond that, should each alliance have the capacity to retaliate against the aggressor, to punish him for the attack through achieving military victory over his forces? The issue of measuring and limiting capacity for counterattack and of defining the acceptable objectives of counterattack is one approach to defining a defensive posture for each alliance.

Another possible application of non-offensive defense concepts to the C.F.E. talks is in the selection of armaments for reductions, a theme which, under present circumstances, is likely to be a focus of East/West dispute in the talks. We would argue here that, although individual weapons systems, like tanks, can be used for either offensive or defensive purposes, the advocates of non-offensive defense are right in holding that it is possible to distinguish between offensive force configurations emphasizing mobility, range, and reach, and defensive forces emphasizing firepower with limited mobility and range. Thus, the organization of forces and the mix and amount of equipment can favor either offense or defense. Certain weapons like tanks, surface-to-surface missiles, ground attack aircraft and armed helicopters, which can be classed as penetration weapons, seem more indispensable for attack than for defense. In attack, there is no real substitute for weapons like these, whereas in defense, substitutes, adequate if sometimes not as effective, can be found.

If this view is accepted, a major objective of negotiated reductions should be to select precisely these penetration weapons for reduction while maintaining current deployments of more defensive armaments or even increasing them. In addition, non-offensive defense concepts can of course be helpful in providing ideas for the organization of post-reduction forces. Some possibilities have emerged in our discussion of the planned reorganization of Soviet forces following unilateral reductions.

The third area in which non-offensive defense proposals may have relevance is in geographic restrictions on force deployment. Here, ideas of pulling back or otherwise constraining deployment of those armaments identified as most valuable for the offensive from forward positions could be considered. We will take up this possibility further in Chapter 9.

ASSESSMENT

The major achievement of the proponents of non-offensive defense is to have added important dimensions to our understanding of the nature of the East/West military confrontation in Europe. It is probable that, in the C.F.E. talks, each side will to a greater or lesser degree use the vocabulary and analysis of non-offensive defense in criticizing each other's reduction proposals and in describing its own long-term objectives.

That many of the general concepts of the non-offensive defense analysis have been adopted both by NATO and Warsaw Pact governments is a remarkable endorsement of them and a considerable vindication for the theorizers, given the criticism they have endured in their own countries in the past.

We have suggested roughly how some of these ideas could become the subject of discussion in the Atlantic-to-the-Urals talks. What remains is to try to work out in more detail whether they can be incorporated into specific measures for East/West negotiation. We will turn to this possibility later, but first we must analyze the difficulties that hindered the unsuccessful M.B.F.R. talks. Some understanding of the reasons for the failure of those talks can be a corrective to keep the new talks on course.

5 Lessons from Failure: Vienna One and What We Can Learn from It

After fifteen years of fruitless negotiation, the NATO/Warsaw Pact talks on the "Mutual Reduction of Forces and Armaments and Associated Measures in Central Europe," referred to in the West as the "Mutual and Balanced Force Reduction" or M.B.F.R. talks, were closed down quietly and without recrimination on February 2, 1989, to make way for the expanded C.F.E. force-reduction talks, which began the following month. The M.B.F.R. talks will probably come to be considered the most resounding failure in the history of postwar arms control.

What caused this sorry outcome, and what lessons does it hold for the current talks? Did the M.B.F.R. talks contain built-in obstacles that will doom the successor talks to failure? Or did they founder on errors that can be corrected? Over the dragging years of M.B.F.R., a number of hindrances large and small became clear. Here we shall analyze both the impact they had on the M.B.F.R. effort and the impact they may have on its sequel.

WAS THE WESTERN NEGOTIATION APPROACH BADLY DESIGNED?

Twelve members of NATO participated in the M.B.F.R. talks: Canada, the United States, the United Kingdom, Norway, Denmark, the Benelux countries (Belgium, the Netherlands, and Luxembourg), the Federal Republic of Germany, Italy, Greece, and Turkey. As for other NATO countries, France refused to participate; Iceland has no armed forces; Portugal was in the throes of political upheaval; and Spain had not yet joined the alliance.

By mutual agreement among NATO participants, the West's ultimate goal for M.B.F.R. was to reduce the full-time active-duty ground- and air-force military personnel of each alliance to an equal level of 700,000 men in ground-force manpower and of 900,000 men for ground- and air-force manpower combined. Critics charge that this goal was shortsighted. They point out that the greatest threat presented by the Warsaw Pact is not that it has more soldiers but that it has more arms. Indeed, as we saw in Chapter 3, the Pact's superiority in numbers of ground-force armaments, tanks, artillery, armored personnel carriers, and armed helicopters is wide and it has grown steadily over the years. Instead of trying to cut back military personnel, critics contend, the M.B.F.R. talks should have focused on cutting back the Soviet "invasion capability"—the increasingly heavily armed forward-deployed ground-force divisions in East Germany and Czechoslovakia.

The short reply to this criticism is that cutting back on Soviet armor is what NATO proposed from the outset of the negotiations in October, 1973, and for many years thereafter.

The NATO alliance's original proposal for a first-phase reduction, augmented in 1975 by a proposal to withdraw fifty-four nuclear-capable American F-4 aircraft, thirty-six Pershing I missile launchers, and 1,000 nuclear warheads, was to withdraw 29,000 United States soldiers in return for the withdrawal of a Soviet tank "army"—a tank corps, in western terminology—consisting of five divisions, 1,700 tanks, and 68,000 men. Only in a second phase was there to be reduction of manpower to a common ceiling. Paradoxically, in 1988, General Secretary Gorbachev announced the unilateral withdrawal of more Soviet divisions from eastern Europe than the West had asked for in the M.B.F.R. talks. But in M.B.F.R. the Soviets had rejected the West's reduction offers and in 1979 NATO, having decided to deploy American Pershing IIs and ground-launched cruise missiles in Europe, rescinded its nuclear reduction proposal. Only then did NATO make the proposal critics today question for a small reduction solely in Soviet and American manpower, while asking the Soviets to withdraw three complete divisions.

The West was timid in this first East/West effort to cut back forces in Europe. NATO decided to aim for an equal ceiling on manpower because that was as much as seemed feasible. At the time NATO made this decision, its own estimates of Pact manpower showed that the Pact had a superiority of only 35,000 men in central Europe, the region to which negotiations were limited. NATO thought it could obtain the Pact's agreement to eliminate this modest superiority. (Only after NATO had decided on an equal ceiling on manpower as a longer-term goal did member countries learn that the alliance's intelligence agencies, having reviewed with extreme care the information available on Pact forces, were increasing their previous estimate by more than 100,000 men.) Because the Pact's superiority in most major armaments was estimated to be very large, NATO doubted that the Pact could be persuaded to eliminate its superiority there. Only later, with Gorbachev's concessions in the I.N.F. negotiations, did the West come to a bolder view of what it could reasonably ask the Soviets to do in negotiating armament reductions.

Moreover, in M.B.F.R., western European participants were adamant in their refusal to reduce any of their own armaments. The modest reduction in United States aircraft and nuclear armaments that NATO offered to the Soviets was only barely acceptable to European NATO members. And when NATO negotiators proposed these reductions to the Warsaw Pact, they were instructed to inform the Pact at the same time that the proposal was in no sense a precedent for armament reductions by West European NATO states. Those states, the Pact was told, would never reduce their own armaments.

The West European NATO governments were motivated to take this position by the fact that the Soviet Union could fulfil a pledge to reduce its arms by withdrawing them to Soviet territory, only 600 miles or so from the line of confrontation between the two alliances on the Federal German border with East Germany and Czechoslovakia. The M.B.F.R. talks were limited to the territory of the Federal Republic and the Benelux countries in the West and East Germany, Poland, and Czechoslovakia in the East. Inside the Soviet Union—territory not covered by the talks—arms withdrawn from Europe by the Soviets could be added to a vast stockpile whose size would not be restricted and could even be increased.

And while withdrawn Soviet arms could be stockpiled, arms reduced by western European states would have to be destroyed and a residual ceiling placed on whatever armaments of that type remained. Western Europe would be in a position of enduring treaty-mandated inferiority to the Soviet Union and the Warsaw Pact. And the European NATO commanders themselves did not wish to take the irrevocable step of destroying weapons that had been so expensive to acquire. An alternative to destruction—secured storage subject to verification by on-site inspection—was not considered then, although it should be in the current force-reduction talks.

For its part, the Warsaw Pact proposed an initial, "symbolic" reduction by each side of 20,000 troops with their armaments, to be followed by reductions of 15 percent in manpower and armaments by both alliances, to be taken in large units. This proposal accorded with the Pact's longstanding contention that there was rough equality in the threat posed by each alliance even though there was not a one-for-one numerical equality in all types of arms. As seen by NATO, the proposal's adoption would have preserved the Pact's numerical superiority in men and armaments and run directly counter to NATO's refusal to contractualize this superiority.

As the M.B.F.R. talks began, the U.S.S.R. strongly rejected any thought of asymmetrical reductions. It insisted on equal treatment and equal security in U.S./Soviet nuclear talks and considered the maintenance of the existing East/West balance in conventional forces, if at a lower level, as the only effective way to assure its undiminished security under arms control. Soviet negotiators rejected the western designation for the new talks—"Mutual and Balanced Force Reductions"— because they knew from statements of the NATO governments that, to NATO, "balanced" meant asymmetrical Warsaw Pact reductions larger than those of NATO. (How far the Pact has come since then is evidenced by the Warsaw Pact position paper of July, 1988, for the current force-reduction talks, which calls for "balanced" reductions.)

The Warsaw Pact made a tactical mistake when it incorporated this equal-percentage position in the draft of a formal reduction agreement, which it presented to western negotiators in Vienna only a few days after the M.B.F.R. talks began, in October, 1973. NATO negotiators rushed to counter the move by presenting the outline of an agreement of their own. With that, each alliance became barricaded behind its draft. To change any aspect of these proposals once they were on the table was regarded by both sides as a major concession and as demonstrating softness toward the adversary. What followed were fifteen years of diplomatic trench warfare. It would have been far better to have started the M.B.F.R. talks with an exploratory phase of general discussion and only later to have put specific proposals on the table. The error has been repeated in the current talks, but the starting positions of the two alliances were closer to one another.

THE DATA ISSUE IN M.B.F.R.

Carrying out the Warsaw Pact's reduction proposal would have required agreement on total manpower figures for each alliance, so that percentage reductions could be calculated. For their part, NATO participants proposed an equal ceiling for each alliance of 700,000 men for ground forces and 900,000 men for ground- and air-force manpower combined. Pact representatives responded that this would require them to reduce more personnel than NATO, to the detriment of the Pact's security: apparently Pact representatives were admitting a manpower superiority for their alliance.

To move the negotiations to a more concrete phase, NATO representatives then challenged the Pact to produce data on its own forces. In 1975, after a year's urging, the Pact produced figures showing approximate equality with NATO. NATO representatives disputed them, and in so doing began an argument about the reliability of data that persisted for a decade.[1]

Was it necessary for NATO representatives to insist on resolving the data issue before taking up other questions? In the mid-1970s NATO representatives felt they had little choice in the matter. NATO intelligence agencies believed that the Pact had deliberately cut back its figures. The Pact's truthfulness, and thus its good faith in honoring whatever treaty might be negotiated, was in question.

The dispute between East and West over the total number of Warsaw Pact ground- and air-force personnel in eastern Europe brought into focus a major problem area of negotiated force reductions—the difficulty of verifying manpower ceilings. For any negotiated reduction to be meaningful, it must be accompanied by a ceiling to restrain future buildups. Manpower is the most mobile and easily concealed of military assets; it can fade into forests or villages without a trace. Monitoring an agreement on manpower is possible, but it is contingent on a large number of intrusive sampling inspections. In 1988 General Secretary Gorbachev suggested on-site inspections to verify data and settle disputes. But during the M.B.F.R. talks the Soviets, true to their tradition of secrecy in military matters, refused to agree to any form of inspection whatsoever.

Resistance to inspection was not the only problem complicating verification. From the beginning of the talks, Warsaw Pact participants had proposed that reductions be carried out by units with their equipment. But NATO opposed this approach. Although the United States and Federal Germany wanted Soviet withdrawals to be made by units, they wanted to reduce their own manpower by thin-out. Both countries insisted on preserving the freedom to restructure and reorganize their forces, perhaps in more numerous units with fewer personnel, in the interest of military effectiveness.

From the verification point of view, one clear lesson of the M.B.F.R. talks is that reductions should be undertaken in units, with ceilings imposed as appropriate on the various types of units restricted. To reduce by thin-out makes verification so difficult that the problem could undermine the successful negotiation of a treaty.

Another lesson of M.B.F.R. is that cutbacks in armaments alone, without simultaneous cutbacks in total manpower as well as units, would also create large technical obstacles to verification. How can one effectively verify, say, a reduction in the number of Soviet tanks if there is no change in the number of units to which the tanks are assigned and no change in the number of troops assigned to operate the tanks? And how much military significance would a cutback in armaments alone have? Combat capability is the combination of men and armaments organized into units. Serious reduction proposals will find some way to reduce all three together. Moreover, if negotiated reductions are to reduce costs, as they should, they should include cuts in manpower which in the West accounts for more than 50 percent of defense budgets.

In December, 1985, NATO tried to break the impasse in M.B.F.R. over troop strength and the verification of negotiated cutbacks. Picking up informal Soviet suggestions, it proposed U.S. and Soviet reductions of a specified size, with residual ceilings heavily verified, and gave up its insistence that both alliances come to specific agreement on the total manpower of each before reductions could proceed.

Should NATO have taken this step sooner? Perhaps. Yet, if the figures of both alliances for a given force component are contested, as we have shown in Chapter 3 is still very much the case in the C.F.E. talks, it may be difficult to agree which side has a numerical superiority in a given armament or on new common levels to which both should reduce.

True, both sides could reduce to some agreed "arbitrary" level and the outcome could be verified. But a major reason for seeking detailed data exchange in the first place is to make verification possible. We must keep in mind that verifying that the large number of units, armaments, and manpower permitted by a treaty does not exceed agreed ceilings cannot be accomplished in a single act. Rather than a complete census, it necessarily must take the form of on-site sampling of a large number of units over time. To form a clear picture of how the Pact puts its data on forces in the field together, western intelligence agencies will have to compare the Pact's figures with their own estimates. Differences that emerge can then be clarified by discussion. In this way, when the time for verification comes, the western monitors will have a clear idea of what to look for.

Let us summarize the main points of this close interaction between data and verification as background for our further discussion: (1) It will be impossible after reductions are made to inspect every single

Warsaw Pact unit simultaneously to assure that ceilings are not being violated. For the Pact's ground forces alone, even if in the course of time there were a very large reduction of, say, fifty divisions, about 150 active-duty and reserve divisions with thousands of subordinated units would remain to be checked. Consequently, the verification process will have to include sampling inspection of some units. (2) For effective sampling to take place, NATO verifiers will need to know what to expect from each of the units they monitor—how many arms and men these units should have. Commanders of units inspected will have to provide up-to-date data on unit strength in men and armaments, but NATO inspectors will have to have their own dossiers for each Pact unit before verification inspections begin. (3) Because of the Pact's policy of secrecy in the past, NATO verifiers do not now have that information for every Pact unit; in some cases they have had to extrapolate from what information they do have. (4) So that NATO can be confident of its data on all Pact units before reductions begin and verification starts, the Pact will have to supply its own figures on all its units early in the C.F.E. talks.

For each side this data exchange should consist of a presentation of the geographic location, official designation, and strength in men and major armaments of all units, active duty and reserve, down to the brigade/regiment level, as of some given date (say January 1, 1989, or January 1, 1990). NATO can then compare its estimates with the Pact's figures, unit by unit, and begin to work out discrepancies through discussion and on-site data evaluation inspections.

Data exchange limited to aggregate figures, like those published by both NATO in late 1988 and the Pact in late 1989, which give only total holdings of certain armaments and do not identify specific units and their strength, do not provide a basis for finding out what causes differences in totals.

The process of compiling updated, possibly revised, NATO data on all major Pact units will have to be completed in advance of on-site inspection and verification of reductions and it will be time-consuming. Without advance clarification of data, the NATO agencies called on to verify an East/West reduction agreement are likely to balk at taking on the responsibility. This could cause severe difficulties when the ratification of a reduction agreement comes up in the United States Congress and in the parliaments of other NATO countries.

These lessons from the M.B.F.R. experience seem clear. Unfortunately, NATO may be in danger of overreacting to the failure of the M.B.F.R. talks and drawing the wrong conclusions from it. When in late 1987 and early 1988 the Soviets offered an exchange of detailed data, to be accompanied by on-site inspection in disputed cases, NATO backed away on the grounds that negotiations that began with a discussion of data would inevitably end as the M.B.F.R. talks had. Like generals re-fighting the last war, the officials of western governments sometimes seem so intent on avoiding repetition of the last crisis that they fail to take new developments into account. What is new in this case is the willingness of the U.S.S.R. and its allies to exchange detailed figures and to permit on-site verification to resolve differences. Another change is agreement in principle by the Soviets and NATO alike that reduction to a negotiated level can, if necessary, substitute for a pre-reduction acceptance of data.

Could the data controversy have been resolved during the M.B.F.R. talks themselves? The answer is a probable yes, if the Pact had been willing to do then what it is apparently willing to do today. For example, discussion during M.B.F.R. indicated that some conscript Polish units used mainly for construction of buildings for civilian purposes had not been included in the Polish count although they were technically military personnel, had received military training and could, in theory, have fulfilled a combat function in the event of conflict. Nonetheless, omission of these units from Polish figures had some rational basis and the issue might have been resolved by discussion.

In hindsight it also appears that NATO, which had to assemble its estimates of Pact forces for M.B.F.R. against the barrier of tight Pact military security, may have overestimated the manning level of Soviet divisions in eastern Europe. This issue, too, could have been clarified by further exchange of data, but there were barriers on both sides to doing so. Up to the late 1980s, the Soviet military was the sole custodian of data on Soviet armed forces, and has generally allowed no civilian access to this information, even by officials of the Soviet government. In M.B.F.R., the Pact was grudgingly brought to exchange data in 1975, providing national totals for ground- and air-force manpower, and again in 1980, dividing its total ground-force manpower into two categories: those "subordinate to corps" and "others." But then the Soviet military in effect went on strike, claiming that to divulge more data, including data on actual manning levels of Soviet forces in eastern Europe, would mean releasing information of military value to an adversary, something which it could not do without a clear indication that an East/West agreement to reduce forces was in the offing.

Officials in the Soviet foreign ministry had reason to press the military for the release of more data, because western charges that the

Soviet Union had deliberately falsified the data and had pressured its allies to do so were damaging Soviet diplomacy beyond the confines of the M.B.F.R. talks. Moved by similar considerations, the Poles gained agreement from Moscow and their other Warsaw Pact allies to present more information on their construction corps. It would have been advantageous to NATO to discuss the new Polish figures, because to do so would have pressured the Soviet military to relent. But NATO, in the grip of reaction to the Soviet invasion of Afghanistan, refused to move on a piecemeal basis. It insisted that it would not take up the Polish issue in detail until the Soviets produced more data on their forces. The Soviet political authorities failed to intervene to resolve the issue in Moscow.

General Secretary Leonid I. Brezhnev had the authority to compel the Soviet armed forces to relax their opposition to releasing more data on Soviet and Pact troops. But bringing this pressure to bear would have cost Brezhnev something in political terms, and he was not sufficiently interested in the goals of the M.B.F.R. talks to pay the price.

Even on the western side there were problems of secrecy. If the NATO participants had taken the initiative to present their own information on Pact forces, they might have induced Soviet authorities to release more information themselves. But NATO intelligence agencies were apprehensive that handing over their hard-won figures would reveal the gaps in their knowledge. They also feared that presenting some data that was more accurate than others might reveal intelligence sources. So here NATO, too, declined to proceed. This reticence continues, as we shall see later.

The data problem in the M.B.F.R. talks was solvable. The failure to solve it was a failure of will on the part of participating governments, especially the Soviets, to make the decisions necessary to clear the way.

THE COLLECTIVITY ISSUE

Whether residual ceilings after reductions should be imposed nation by nation or alliance-wide was a source of trouble during M.B.F.R. that negotiators never shook off. The Pact, worried about the possible revival of German militarism, wanted national ceilings imposed on all M.B.F.R. participants in order to restrain German forces, and said so more than once. After two world wars with Germany, the Soviet Union and its allies had high respect for German military potential. Once the

1975 Helsinki accords had confirmed the post-World War II borders of Europe, the Soviets wanted to use the M.B.F.R. talks to complete the job of a peace treaty, by placing restrictions on the Federal German military; they were satisfied as to their control over East German forces, which they had kept small.

NATO pressed instead for collective, alliance-wide manpower ceilings. The European members of NATO were worried that if an M.B.F.R. agreement limited the national strength of each NATO country, and the United States or some other ally then cut back its forces unilaterally, NATO's aggregate strength would fall below the 900,000-man limit NATO had proposed. This fear was not baseless: the European NATO states were especially worried that the United States might someday withdraw forces from NATO, either to use them elsewhere in the world in pursuit of national objectives or to bring them home, owing to domestic political or economic pressures. They had seen American withdrawals from Europe in 1967 because of a disadvantageous balance of payments and further draw-downs to meet the requirements of the war in Vietnam. And they had observed how close Senator Mike Mansfield had come in the early 1970s to pulling all American forces out of Europe, partly in retaliation for the refusal of NATO countries to take a more active role in the Vietnam war.

The European NATO countries felt that the Soviets were free of any such concern. The Soviets, they reasoned, would always be able effectively to pressure their allies to maintain their forces, and thus their strength would never fall below the permitted level. A unilateral withdrawal by a NATO member would then give the Pact a military superiority that was entirely legal.

In its frontline position, Federal Germany was especially sensitive to the threat of "desertion" by the United States or by other allies with forces in Germany. The painful memory of the strict controls placed on German national forces after World War I by the Versailles peace treaty strengthened the Federal Republic's opposition to national ceilings—all the more so because those ceilings would be administered by a country whose victory over Germany in World War II was attended by fierce retribution.

Yet at the same time that the NATO allies called for an alliance-wide ceiling for themselves, they wanted a separate national ceiling for the U.S.S.R. The forces of the Soviet Union represented the main threat to NATO. NATO considered the forces of the other Warsaw Pact participants—East Germany, Poland, and Czechoslovakia—a lesser threat. It wanted an M.B.F.R. agreement that would maximize Soviet reductions and place strict limits on the Soviet forces remaining after reductions. It feared that, given a collective ceiling, the Soviet Union could readily circumvent this goal, by obliging the Pact to cut back and making up the difference with better trained and equipped Soviet forces.

NATO's concern was probably not realistic even at the time. Like the United States, the Soviet Union had for years been urging its allies to do more for their own defenses—to such an extent, in fact, that non-Soviet Warsaw Pact members not only wanted national ceilings on Federal German forces but also on their own forces, as a way of protecting themselves from Soviet pressures to build up. It was unlikely, then, in the event of negotiated reductions, that relative national shares of Warsaw Pact forces would greatly change. As in NATO, those shares were the product of a long bargaining process. The Soviet Union undeniably possessed the political muscle to oblige its allies to reduce their forces and make room for Soviet increases. But to do so would have gone against a well-established pattern.

Parallel to NATO's claims that unless the U.S.S.R. were restricted it could end up by expanding its forces, the Pact argued that NATO could make changes in its own ground forces by internal agreement, so that Federal Germany would end up with the lion's share of NATO ground-force manpower while other NATO allies shifted their manpower to the air force or navy. The *Wehrmacht* would be reborn. That Federal Germany's NATO allies would themselves wish to prevent such an outcome was clear, but the Pact's negotiators did not allow themselves to be convinced by this argument.

In the interest of reciprocity, NATO was willing to apply a separate ceiling on United States forces in NATO, thus balancing the proposed national ceiling on Soviet forces. But this concept had a flaw, because United States ground forces made up only about 25 percent of total NATO manpower, while the Soviet Union's forces made up 50 percent of the Warsaw Pact's manpower. Warsaw Pact negotiators asked, rhetorically, how the Pact could maintain its own permitted level of forces if a non-Soviet participant made unilateral cuts and the Soviet Union were prevented by a national ceiling from making them up.

Federal German Chancellor Schmidt courageously tried to break the deadlock by proposing in a Bundestag speech in 1975 that no single country in either alliance be permitted to have more than 50 percent of the alliance's total active-duty ground-force personnel. Such a rule, without singling out either the Soviet Union or the Federal Republic of Germany, would in practice have imposed limits only on the U.S.S.R.

while giving Federal German forces, which then composed 40 percent of NATO's total, 10 percent "room at the top" for future growth. But the German Christian Democrats, then in opposition, resisted this idea and Federal German Foreign Minister Hans Dietrich Genscher adamantly opposed it.

As the collective-ceiling/national-ceiling impasse continued, Warsaw Pact negotiators contributed potentially useful formulas to end it. One was that members of an alliance could be allowed to compensate for a unilateral cut by another member by taking a share of needed increases proportional to their own share of alliance manpower at the time. (The Pact did not deal directly with the possibility that some NATO members might be unwilling or unable to meet their share of the shortfall; it suggested "intra-alliance consultation" for this contingency.)

The collectivity issue was one M.B.F.R. problem which had a productive outcome, at least in part. We earlier referred to the July, 1988, document of the Political Consultative Committee of the Warsaw Pact, which presented the Pact's general approach to the C.F.E. talks. The document stated that the goal of the first phase of the talks should be to achieve roughly equal "collective" levels of military personnel and conventional armaments. Yet the national-ceilings issue has nevertheless again emerged in the C.F.E. talks, in the form of the demand by NATO participants for specific ceilings on the number of armaments that can be held by individual participants or by stationed forces. The demand was clearly issued with the Soviet Union in mind.

THE PROBLEM OF GEOGRAPHIC COVERAGE

In its preparations for the M.B.F.R. talks NATO had decided to focus on central Europe, the area of greatest concentration in the forces of East and West and militarily the vital area of the alliance. If the Warsaw Pact were to break through NATO's defenses in central Europe, it would have a relatively easy path to the Atlantic coast and military victory. Successful attacks by the Pact on NATO's northern and southern flanks are less likely and in any case would not be nearly so devastating. To control Europe, the Soviet Union would have to win in central Europe.

Properly, these considerations gave a key role in the M.B.F.R. talks to the Federal Republic of Germany. But as we have pointed out, the Federal Republic is sensitive to any implication of Soviet control over its armed forces and to any suggestion that those forces are separable from the NATO alliance.

Accordingly, in 1972, when NATO was deciding to delineate the area of coverage for the current talks, Belgium, the Netherlands, and Luxembourg agreed to include their own national territories, in order to circumvent the isolation of the Federal Republic that could occur as a result of restrictions and limitations that might be included in an M.B.F.R. agreement. Even so, as a reason for its own opposition to the M.B.F.R. talks, France voiced concern that a successful agreement would render Federal Germany a "special zone," isolating the country from its allies. With the passage of years this risk gained importance in the eyes of some European governments—especially the Federal Republic itself—and deterred them from pressing for a positive outcome to the talks. Although NATO wanted to include portions of the western U.S.S.R. in the area to be covered by the talks, the Soviets refused, and in September, 1972, a year before the M.B.F.R. talks began, Secretary of State Kissinger conceded the point to the Soviets.

East Germany, Poland, and Czechoslovakia and the national and Soviet forces stationed in these countries were encompassed by the eastern portion of the area of coverage. NATO tried to add Hungary, with its own forces and the Soviet forces stationed there, but backed down when the Soviet Union insisted that if Hungary were included, then Italy, against which Soviet forces in Hungary were ranged, would have to be included, too.

Despite the willingness of the Benelux countries to allow their forces to be covered, Federal Germany's fear of isolation from its allies caused it to repeatedly urge France to participate in the M.B.F.R. negotiations. The F.R.G. was also motivated by its desire to avoid a status inferior to that of other members of the European Community—France, in particular. If France, too, could be subject to any limitations and restrictions contained in an M.B.F.R. agreement, this situation could be avoided. The Federal Republic, the United States, and other NATO allies made many efforts to persuade France to join in. So did the Soviet Union, which wanted coverage in the new talks of French military potential.

But France adamantly refused. Like Federal Germany, it was apprehensive of Soviet controls over its military forces. It argued further that the whole M.B.F.R. enterprise was defective. In the French view, the failure to cover Soviet territory made the Soviet Union a "sanctuary" in which forces withdrawn from eastern Europe could be maintained or even grow. And whereas those forces could be as close as

600 miles from the dividing line in Germany, American forces withdrawn from Europe would have to return to the United States, more than 3,000 miles away across the Atlantic.

Even more important, France seemed to fear—though it never said so outright—that inclusion of both parts of divided Germany under a central European arms-control regime might ultimately move the German states to reunify under conditions of neutrality. France could have reduced the possibility of this unfavorable outcome and also perhaps have persuaded the Soviet Union to include some of its own territory in the talks if it had agreed to participate in M.B.F.R. But France was still under the strong influence of Charles de Gaulle's rejection of arms control. This did not change until the late 1970s, when support for arms control became an issue in French domestic politics.

Then, too, France was worried about submitting itself to the tight discipline desired by European NATO members for the M.B.F.R. talks (a desire provoked by the concern of European NATO members that the United States and the Soviet Union might strike some deals independent of their allies, moving towards a "condominium" over Europe). France did not want to re-enter the NATO integrated military command, which it had left in 1966 under de Gaulle, through the back door of tight NATO discipline in arms-control negotiations. Its concern, as we shall see, shaped France's positions in the Conference on Disarmament in Europe—which brought thirty-five countries together in Stockholm from 1984 to 1986 to discuss ways to reduce the risk of war—and continued to shape its positions as NATO prepared for the current force-reduction talks. But France's refusal to join M.B.F.R. was a serious obstacle to the success of the talks, not least because it diminished Federal German enthusiasm for a positive outcome.

The West's dissatisfactions over the restricted geographic scope of the M.B.F.R. talks were partially addressed in February, 1981. That year General Secretary Brezhnev agreed to extend the coverage of the pending Stockholm conference to the Ural mountains in the U.S.S.R., 1,200 miles inside the Soviet Union's western border. They were met further in April, 1986, when General Secretary Gorbachev made a further unilateral concession by proposing that the same area of coverage be used for new talks on force reductions in Europe. The "Atlantic-to-the-Urals" area is, in fact, the area covered by the C.F.E. talks.

In 1986, too, France agreed to participate in a properly articulated force-reduction negotiation. Since 1978 it had been emerging from the isolation from arms control imposed by Charles de Gaulle and had in fact pressed for a Europe-wide conference on force reductions. With Gorbachev's concession of territory and France's participation, the "special zone" difficulty was apparently overcome. Yet, as we shall see when we consider NATO's preparations for the C.F.E. talks in Chapter 7, France's underlying concerns—the risk that Federal Germany's ties to NATO will be weakened by a treaty and France's unwillingness to be seen as reversing past policy and accepting closer ties to NATO—continue to plague the alliance.

TRAIN WITHOUT A LOCOMOTIVE

Throughout the M.B.F.R. talks NATO was very slow to resolve the issues that arose. It took the alliance ten years to put a full draft of an agreement on the table. Each of the West's major moves in the talks took about two years to progress from discussion among NATO negotiators to discussion in NATO capitals, then by the NATO Council in Brussels, and finally back to Vienna for presentation to the Pact. In part, this slowness stemmed from NATO's character as a coalition of sovereign states with diverse views. In part, it stemmed from the fact that although NATO had agreed to a specific objective in the talks—a common East/West ceiling on military manpower—it had not agreed to any general long-term goals. The lack of such goals, which could have served as criteria for resolving individual issues, still hampers the alliance in the C.F.E. talks.

The most serious shortcoming in the M.B.F.R. talks was attributable to both sides: lack of sustained interest in an outcome.

The Federal German Social Democrats had pushed the NATO alliance toward force-reduction negotiations with the Warsaw Pact as soon as Willi Brandt became Foreign Minister in 1966, in a broad coalition with the Christian Democrats. But most of the NATO allies approached the opening of the M.B.F.R. talks with mixed feelings. The Nixon and Ford administrations in Washington were preoccupied with Watergate and Vietnam. In arms control they gave priority to negotiations with the Soviet Union over nuclear weapons, which the American public continues to consider a far more direct threat to its security than the NATO/Pact confrontation in Europe, although the NATO/Pact confrontation could also trigger a world-wide nuclear holocaust. The Nixon administration's main interest in M.B.F.R. was to use the prospect of the negotiations to block passage of Senator Mansfield's resolution calling for the unilateral withdrawal of American forces from Europe. After the resolution was defeated in 1971 and again in 1972, the Nixon administration lost interest in M.B.F.R.

Most officials of the administrations that succeeded Nixon's considered that the Vienna negotiations were mainly a project of the European allies, that the talks were not going anywhere, and that the main U.S. objective should be to avoid problems among Washington agencies and with the allies. The Department of Defense and the Joint Chiefs of Staff were preeminent among the Washington agencies, but their enthusiasm for results was limited by the concern that if American forces were withdrawn pursuant to an M.B.F.R. agreement, Congress might mandate that the forces be disbanded. During the Carter administration, the United States position on M.B.F.R. was at a stalemate because of differences between Secretary of State Cyrus Vance and National Security Adviser Zbigniew Brzezinski, who gave his staff orders to maintain consensus on M.B.F.R. in Washington and the alliance and to avoid problems, including unscheduled movement in the talks.

In 1979, as NATO got ready to deploy new American medium-range missiles in Europe, Washington showed the low priority it attached to the M.B.F.R. talks. It proposed that NATO annul its 1975 offer to withdraw 1,000 United States nuclear warheads; that the U.S. withdraw the warheads unilaterally (in order to make a decision to deploy I.N.F. more palatable to European opinion) and that NATO declare the M.B.F.R. talks over. The European NATO states, for their part, were willing to accept the first part of Washington's proposal but not the second, reasoning that for NATO to take the initiative to close down the M.B.F.R. talks would cause adverse public opinion reaction and add unnecessarily to the problems of gaining acceptance of I.N.F. deployment. M.B.F.R. limped on.

Washington was content throughout the M.B.F.R. talks to leave the burden of taking the initiative with the European members of NATO. But Chancellor Willi Brandt left office in 1974 in connection with a scandal involving the presence of an East German spy on his staff. His easy-going, confident Foreign Minister Walter Scheel, later to be elected Federal President, was replaced by Hans Dietrich Genscher, an official of great energy and devotion to detail, but then holding a decidedly pessimistic view of the merits of arms control agreements with the Soviet Union. A refugee from East Germany with bitter experience of Soviet occupation and domination, Genscher resisted any hint of Soviet control over Federal Germany.

Because Genscher's small Free Democratic Party was essential to the existence of the Schmidt coalition, Schmidt was unable to override Genscher's distaste for M.B.F.R. Genscher adopted as his own the French argument that M.B.F.R. agreement would create a "special zone" around the Federal Republic. And he fiercely resisted Chancellor Helmut Schmidt's useful suggestion that no participant have more than 50 percent of its alliance's manpower.

The Free Democratic Party has kept itself alive in German politics by acting as a counterbalance or governor on the larger parties with which it shares power. Consequently, when the Free Democrats are members of a coalition with the Social Democrats, they lean to the right on foreign policy and defense issues. When they are in a coalition with the more conservative Christian Democrats, as has been the case since 1982, they lean to the left. Given the party's swing left in recent years and the significant change in the arms control policies of the U.S.S.R. since the emergence in 1985 of General Secretary Gorbachev, Genscher's views toward East/West arms control agreements have become far more positive. But he has never dropped his sensitivity to the "special zone" question.

When Schmidt was in power and blocked by Genscher, a stalemate occurred in German arms-control policies. Federal Germany no longer played a leadership role in NATO's considerations of M.B.F.R. but a static, defensive one. Conservative British governments have generally had a negative view of the M.B.F.R. talks, and the Labour government leaders Harold Wilson and James Callahan were too weak to take the helm for Europe. With France determinedly remaining on the sidelines shouting criticisms at the NATO players, there was no major western European state that could give political impetus to the M.B.F.R. talks. On M.B.F.R. the NATO alliance was a train without a locomotive.

The Soviet attitude toward the M.B.F.R. talks had always been unenthusiastic. True, Leonid Brezhnev had urged their prompt beginning in a speech he gave in May, 1971, pulling the rug out from under Senator Mansfield and his supporters, whose resolution to withdraw forces from Europe came up for Senate vote only a few days later. At that time, Brezhnev and his advisers were apparently worried about the effects of abrupt American withdrawal from Europe—in particular the possibility of large compensatory increases in the Federal German armed forces, a prospect which Brezhnev and men of his generation understandably viewed from the perspective of the German threat they had known in World War II. Brezhnev was less interested in M.B.F.R. than in his project for more general East/West talks on security and economic cooperation in the Conference on Security and Cooperation in Europe (C.S.C.E), which began at the same time as M.B.F.R. and in the endorsement of Europe's postwar boundaries that he sought there.

The NATO states, acting through Secretary of State Henry Kissinger, told the Soviet Union in September, 1972, that their willingness to participate in the C.S.C.E. talks would be contingent on Soviet participation in M.B.F.R. The Soviet Union complied, although at this point it clearly was not ready for serious force-reduction negotiations. In the aftermath of the invasion of Czechoslovakia, Soviet leaders feared the impact of reducing the Soviet military presence in eastern Europe on the region's political stability. This concern remains important for the Soviet Union, because few of the eastern European governments could long sustain themselves in power in the absence of Soviet troops in their territory or at their borders.

Only after the Soviet Union decided to make four-to-one reductions of Soviet nuclear warheads to American warheads and two-to-one reductions in missiles in the I.N.F. talks did the Soviet Union's deep-seated opposition to asymmetrical conventional reductions change. By then the M.B.F.R. talks had lost all momentum.

As we have shown here, the M.B.F.R. train broke down over the data issue, over the question of reduction of armaments, and over the size of the M.B.F.R. reduction area. But neither the Soviet Union nor the United States nor any West European government took the initiative to get the train moving. The essential ingredient for a successful outcome—strong political interest by at least some of the participants—did not exist.

Many things were wrong in this first set of Vienna force reduction talks. But one thing that was not wrong was the recognition on both sides, however halting and imperfect, that the time had come to begin to cope through East/West agreements with the military confrontation in Europe. The next step in that direction, the Stockholm Conference on Disarmament in Europe, was far more successful. We shall examine why in the following chapter.

6 The C.D.E. Parallel Track: Success of the Stockholm Conference

While the M.B.F.R. talks floundered, the negotiations of the thirty-five-country Conference on Security and Cooperation in Europe, or C.S.C.E., prospered. The C.S.C.E. negotiations also began in 1973, as part of an East/West package deal to start M.B.F.R. They culminated in August, 1975, in the Helsinki Final Act, a generally worded document that endorsed the postwar boundaries of Europe as subject to change only by peaceful means and called on participants voluntarily to notify major military exercises in advance. The participants at Helsinki and in ensuing C.S.C.E. activities include the sixteen members of the NATO alliance, the seven members of the Warsaw Treaty Organization, and twelve European neutral and non-aligned states.[1]

While M.B.F.R. plodded on, a series of increasingly successful specialized conferences took place on the three Helsinki "baskets" or chief agenda items: (1) security and human rights; (2) cooperation in economics, science and environment; and (3) facilitating human contacts, including cultural and educational exchanges. From one to three meetings took place each year from 1978 to 1989, and at least three a year are planned in coming years. "Follow-on conferences" to review and encourage progress in the Helsinki agenda and to amplify it were held in Belgrade (October, 1977, March, 1978), Madrid (November, 1980, September, 1983), and Vienna (November, 1986, January, 1989).

Referred to collectively as "the C.S.C.E. process," these recurrent East/West conferences are likely to continue indefinitely, because the three major groups of participants—NATO, the Warsaw Pact, and the neutral states—want them to. Western Europe views the C.S.C.E. process primarily as a means of promoting more open government in eastern Europe; the European neutrals as a means to play an active role in defusing the East/West military confrontation; eastern European members of the Warsaw Pact as a means of building linkages with western Europe and of gaining further latitude for internal change; and the Soviet Union as a forum in which to improve its relations with western Europe and to influence the policies of western European countries.

Initially, the United States was a reluctant participant in the Helsinki negotiations. It doubted that the Soviet Union was sincere in pursuing detente in Europe and feared that rhetorical statements of principle in Helsinki would undermine the more substantial and far-reaching arms-control objectives of the M.B.F.R. talks in Vienna. As the Helsinki process has itself yielded significant advances in human rights and military security over the years, American interest has increased. Indeed, one of the major concerns of recent administrations has been that the Helsinki review conferences be as productive in the realm of human rights—for example, by easing restrictions on emigration in the Warsaw Pact states—as they have been in the realm of military security.

It would seem that, unobtrusive as the conferences of the C.S.C.E. process have been—this is one reason for their success—they may provide the slowly emerging institutional framework for a future European order that would have as its components the two alliances and the European Community, with the U.S. and the U.S.S.R. as co-guarantors. We will discuss this possibility further in coming chapters.

Today, two parallel negotiations are taking place in Vienna under the aegis of the C.S.C.E. process: the negotiations on Conventional Armed Forces in Europe (that is, the C.F.E. talks), and the continuation of the conference on Confidence- and Security-Building Measures and Disarmament in Europe (C.D.E.), whose first session concluded successfully in Stockholm in September, 1986. That there are two parallel conferences dealing with two closely related aspects of the East/West military confrontation in Europe, force reductions and confidence-building measures, rather than a single integrated conference, is owing chiefly to certain concerns of the United States about the security aspects of the C.S.C.E. process, which we shall discuss in the next chapter.

The most recent C.S.C.E. review conference, which ended in Vienna in January, 1989, set the agendas for both negotiations (see Appendix VI). Indeed, both of the new Vienna negotiations stem from western and eastern initiatives at the 1978 Belgrade review conference and they will continue to be jointly managed by future C.S.C.E. follow-on conferences. The next one will be held in Helsinki in March, 1992. For these reasons we cannot make an accurate forecast of future efforts to deal with the East/West military confrontation without looking hard at the Conference on Disarmament in Europe.

The Conference on Confidence- and Security-Building Measures and Disarmament in Europe began in Stockholm in January, 1984. Often

Map 3 Participants in the C.D.E. negotiations on confidence-and security-building measures in Europe

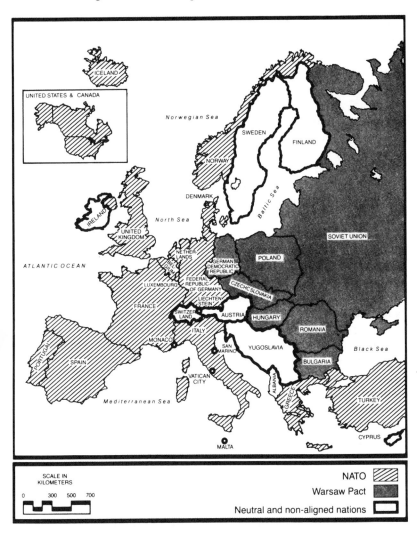

Source: Reprinted by permission of the publisher, from *Watershed in Europe* by Jonathan Dean (Lexington, Mass.: Lexington Books, D. C. Heath & Company, copyright © 1987 Union of Concerned Scientists).

called "Conference on Disarmament in Europe," or C.D.E., it culminated in September, 1986, with an agreement called the "Stockholm Document." For reasons partly having to do with the reluctance of western participants formally to accept the division of Germany and the incorporation of the Baltic states of Latvia, Estonia, and Lithuania in the U.S.S.R., the Helsinki Final Act itself and the results of C.S.C.E. deliberations have hitherto not been considered as treaties but rather as a kind of international executive agreement.

With the Stockholm Document, the signers sought to reduce the risk of miscalculation and misperception in the huge concentration of armed forces in Europe through a system of advance notification and observation of military activities that goes far beyond what was set forth in the parent Helsinki accords. A further, unstated objective of western participants was to make it harder for the U.S.S.R. to use force movements to intimidate its neighbors. Since the Stockholm Document took effect in January, 1987, experience with it has been generally positive. Observers on both sides have been able to witness military exercises, and many satisfactory on-site inspections in Warsaw Pact and NATO countries have taken place; there had been eighteen of these by the end of 1988.

What did the Stockholm conference achieve and why did it succeed where the M.B.F.R. conference failed?

The opening of the Stockholm conference on January 17, 1984, was at an inauspicious time. Many European NATO and Warsaw Treaty states looked on the conference as a lifeline by means of which East/West arms control might be rescued from dangerous seas. Only two months before, in mid-November, the Soviet Union had walked out of the U.S./Soviet negotiations at Geneva on I.N.F. and strategic nuclear armaments in response to NATO's decision to proceed with deployment of new American medium-range missiles after the I.N.F. talks had failed to bring results. General Secretary Andropov had died after a rule of only a little over a year and had been succeeded by Konstantin Chernenko, a Brezhnev crony who seemed likely to continue Brezhnev's policies. The second C.S.C.E. review conference in Madrid, which had set the mandate for the Stockholm talks, had dragged on for nearly three years of rancorous debate over the 1979 Soviet invasion of Afghanistan and the 1981 suppression of the Solidarity movement in Poland.

Despite these tensions—perhaps, in part, because of them—the Soviet Union and its allies had accepted most of NATO's proposals at Madrid on the mandate or agenda for the Stockholm talks. The objective of those talks, it was decided, would be to agree on confidence- and security-building measures to reduce the risks of military confrontation in Europe—measures that would be militarily significant, politically binding, and adequately verified. And while Brezhnev was still alive, he had made a significant concession, included in the Stockholm mandate. He had agreed in February, 1981, that the talks would cover the whole of Europe, from the Atlantic to the Ural Mountains—800 miles to the east of Moscow and the traditional geographic division between Europe and Asia. (The NATO allies, led by the French—earlier, President Charles de Gaulle had made the concept of "Europe to the Urals" a familiar slogan—tried in vain in the original C.S.C.E. talks in Helsinki to get the Soviets to extend the area of coverage to the Urals. The Soviets allowed only a 250-kilometer-wide strip of Soviet territory to be covered by the Helsinki accords. NATO again vainly tried to win this concession at the Belgrade review conference.)

Notwithstanding this important Soviet move extending the area and a usefully formulated mandate bearing the strong impression of western views, East and West were far apart as the Stockholm talks opened. NATO participants wanted a program of specific measures to enhance military security. The Warsaw Pact seemed more interested in establishing general limitations on the use of force, including nuclear and chemical weapons, and in covering naval forces with agreed confidence-building measures. However, as the negotiation moved on, Warsaw Pact participants accepted most of NATO's specific proposals.

The negotiations through which these differences were reconciled need not concern us here. Our main interest is in analyzing their outcome from the perspective of our central theme in this book: building down the NATO/Pact confrontation.[2]

In essence the Stockholm Document obligated its signatories: (1) to provide an annual calendar forecasting most major activities of ground forces taking place in the area from the Atlantic to the Urals, including amphibious and airborne activities; (2) to provide even more detailed information on the nature of these activities forty-two days in advance; (3) to invite observers from all signatory countries to watch force activities of a specified size; and (4) to permit up to three inspections per year of its forces by ground or by air to prove its compliance.

The result of these requirements is an extensive and unprecedented exchange of information between the two alliances on the activities of their ground forces.

The Stockholm Document is an important advance over the Helsinki accords. The Helsinki document on "Confidence-Building Measures and Certain Aspects of Security and Disarmament," contains a voluntary commitment, not an obligation, to give twenty-one days' notice of maneuvers involving more than 25,000 troops and also to provide (unspecified) details on the designation, purpose, and nationality of the forces involved, the type and numerical strength of the forces, and the area and duration of the maneuver. At the host country's option, observers may be invited to witness exercises taking place anywhere within an area from the Atlantic to a line 250 kilometers inside the western border of the U.S.S.R.

From 1975 to 1986 notice of about one hundred exercises in the East and the West was given under this accord. The Soviet Union failed to give full notification of one major exercise, Zapad 81, which took place on the borders of Poland at the time of the suppression of the Solidarity movement and was clearly intended to intimidate pro-Solidarity Poles. The United States invited Warsaw Pact observers to ten exercises during this period. The Warsaw Pact invited the United States to only two exercises; the Pact's invitations ceased after 1979, when relations between the two powers became strained because of the Soviet invasion of Afghanistan.

The Stockholm Document is stronger than the Helsinki accords in a number of ways. Although the Document, like the accords, is not a treaty, it is characterized as "politically binding." Its area of coverage is wider, with the inclusion of Soviet territory east to the Urals. Notice must be given of major military "activities," not just maneuvers. Signatories must give not less than forty-two days' notice (up from twenty-one days in the accords) for any activity involving 13,000 troops or more (the notification level is down from 25,000 in the accords). It is expected, though not required, that signatories will report such activities a year in advance.

The Stockholm Document adds an element not contained in the Helsinki accords: it prohibits exercises involving 40,000 to 75,000 troops unless a year's notice is given and prohibits exercises of more than 75,000 men without two years' notice. This measure is a "constraint"—an agreed limitation on military activity—and it is the first such measure approved by East and West. (It made its way into the Document at the behest of the Irish, with backing from the other neutral and non-aligned participants in the conference—just one of many useful contributions made by this group in the Stockholm talks.) Observers now must be invited to all ground-force activities involving more than 17,000 men and to all airborne or amphibious exercises involving more than 5,000 men. And the Soviet Union and other Warsaw Pact countries agreed to submit to a limited quota of on-site inspections without reserving a right of refusal.

The Document contains a general provision renouncing the threat or use of force. During the Stockholm conference the Warsaw Pact pushed energetically for a treaty binding the signers not to use force to resolve conflicts. The ten-paragraph declaration on this subject at the beginning of the Document represents the West's major concession to the Warsaw Pact at Stockholm, but it does not add much to obligations already imposed by the United Nations Charter or the Helsinki accords. And in fact the West was able to turn even this concession to its advantage. The Document obliges the signers to resist using force against any state regardless of its social system and whether or not it is an ally. This language implicitly disallows "the Brezhnev doctrine": the proposition (asserted by the U.S.S.R. to justify its invasion of Czechoslovakia, in 1968) that the socialist commonwealth has corporate interests that override the individual interests of its component states. The Document also includes commitments proposed by the West to respect human rights and to act against terrorism.

DETAILS OF THE DOCUMENT

The Stockholm Document requires participants and host countries to give forty-two days' notice of "military activities" involving at least 13,000 troops under a single operational command, or at least 300 tanks (if organized as a division), or at least two brigades (or regiments—the Warsaw Pact equivalent). Airborne or amphibious activities involving 3,000 men or more are also subject to notice, in deference to the specific interests of the neutral and non-aligned states, as well as of NATO states like Denmark, Norway, and Turkey, who are sensitive to the threat of a Warsaw Pact amphibious attack. The criterion for pre-notification is based on participation by force components—two or more brigades and a large number of tanks—rather than on manpower alone; and because these components are more visible to NATO's information-gathering means, it is easier to verify.

However, the reference to a single operational command in this measure is potentially ambiguous, because compliance will depend in part on the statements of a deploying country, which could evade reporting requirements with the claim that forces engaged in a field activity are operating under two or more independent commands. The phrase "military activities" in the Document is a considerable improvement over the reference to "maneuvers" in the Helsinki accords, because it is broader and more comprehensive. But NATO could not gain agreement to the term it preferred—"out-of-garrison" force movements. This term would have covered military activities like change-of-station, which are not covered by the Document as worded. Both Pact and neutral participants were unwilling to identify and locate the installations where their forces are garrisoned. The West should seek to redress this flaw at the current C.D.E. conference.

Air forces are subject to the rules of notice if they participate in reportable ground-force activities and if more than 200 sorties by fixed-wing aircraft are involved. (Helicopters are excluded.) Naval forces are subject to the rules of notice only if they participate in amphibious exercises involving ship-to-shore gunfire. The coverage is scanty. According to statements of Warsaw Pact officials, NATO's naval and air forces are the Warsaw Pact's biggest concern in the East/West confrontation. These provisions are as much of a concession to that concern as the Pact has managed to elicit from a resistant NATO to date.

The Stockholm Document provides that notice be given before forces brought into an area to participate in a notifiable activity arrive or are concentrated outside of garrisons. This measure will cover the transport of large numbers of American troops for NATO's large annual exercises. It does not cover American or Soviet forces that merely pass through Europe on their way to exercises or an engagement elsewhere in the world and that remain at airfields, garrisons, or ports.

Each participant's calendar of activities subject to the requirements of notice must be submitted, along with considerable information on the character and scope of the activities reported, by November 15th each year. Much more extensive information—more than thirty-five items—is required when the 42-day advance notice of an activity is given. This ranges from the general purpose of each such activity to the number of artillery pieces to be used.

It should be emphasized that participants are exempt from any obligation to give notice of alert exercises, regardless of scale. Word of such activities must be given only as the exercises begin and observers need not be invited for the first seventy-two hours. We will comment later on this major loophole of the Stockholm agreement.

Observers must be invited to all ground-force activities involving 17,000 personnel or more or to amphibious exercises involving 5,000 personnel or more. Each signer of the Stockholm Document may send two observers, military or civilian, to such activities. The observers have diplomatic immunity. The host country is charged with developing a general program for the observers—to take care of their lodging, transportation, and daily briefings. Wherever possible, observers are to be allowed to talk directly to officers and troops participating in an exercise—a potentially important, though not foolproof, means of obtaining information on the actual character of an activity. The observations that have been made since 1987 have been generally satisfactory and an improvement over practices under the auspices of the Helsinki accords.

Any signatory of the Stockholm Document may request an opportunity to inspect the activities in the area of any other signatory to confirm compliance with these notification requirements. No explicit reason need be given. Many inspections have already been carried out to ascertain whether field activities conform to the information given or whether undeclared activities were in fact large enough that notice should have been given.

However, individual signatories are not required to accept more than one inspection a year from any one signatory or more than three a year in all. This low figure was set to make on-site inspection acceptable to the Soviet Union, which might otherwise have been subject to multiple inspections by each of the sixteen NATO allies. Nonetheless, the quota is low and should be increased. In asking for an inspection, the requesting state has to designate a specific area where it believes a notifiable activity may be taking place. The size of the area is not supposed to exceed that typical for a corps-level exercise (the Warsaw Pact equivalent is an "army")—perhaps thirty square kilometers. Approval is to be given within twenty-four hours. Inspection must take place within thirty-six hours. It may be from the ground or by air or both.

Host country ground and air transport is used—a sore point with NATO participants, who originally wanted to use aircraft of the requesting state. When the Pact rejected this, NATO suggested that aircraft of the neutral states be used for all inspections. NATO felt that relying on the Pact's aircraft to inspect the Pact's forces could lend itself to misuse—for example, by failing to overfly the requested area. In practice, officers of the requesting countries have been permitted to check the navigation of the aircraft during flight. Moreover, with use of the aircraft of the host country, there is less risk of misunderstandings or problems with air-traffic control.

Inspections may not last more than forty-eight hours. Inspectors may use their own maps, binoculars, and cameras and must be permitted to be in continuous communication with their headquarters, using communications equipment provided by the host country. This is another sore point, for obvious reasons, but has worked well in practice. Obviously, failure to communicate would be a signal of trouble. Inspection teams can be composed of four people and can be divided into two groups for wider coverage. The inspecting personnel have diplomatic immunity. Experience with on-site inspection in the Soviet Union and eastern Europe since the Document went into effect in January, 1987, has been good, with inspectors brought to the place to be inspected in time and given good access to the area and to the activity concerned.

LOOPHOLES IN THE DOCUMENT

The Stockholm Document has considerable significance as a means of mutual reassurance and for its important innovations: the insistence on long-term calendars; the prohibition of large-scale activities unless included on these calendars; the obligation to invite observers; and the first agreement on East/West on-site inspection.

The Stockholm Document is not an arms-control agreement in the usual sense of that term but a confidence-building one. It neither reduces nor limits the size of NATO or Warsaw Pact armed forces. It does nothing to discourage the NATO/Pact competition in weaponry. Its only constraint on military activities, though a useful precedent, is the prohibition of large-scale activities undertaken without substantial notice.

The Stockholm Document is flawed by some ambiguous wording: "under single command," "military activities." It is also flawed by several deliberate omissions. These include:

(1) the failure to prohibit activities involving between 13,000 and 40,000 troops if a country has not given notice of those activities on its annual calendar;
(2) the fact that alert activities of any size are permitted without any notice;
(3) the lack of rules to cover mobilization in place or force increases within garrisons; and
(4) the lack of rules to cover troops in transit, whatever their number, if the troops stay in garrisons or at airfields.

Because alert exercises and mobilization activities are excluded from coverage, the Stockholm Document has only limited value as a means of assuring early warning of preparations for attack or even as a means of preventing activities intended to intimidate.

Disappointingly, the Stockholm Document does not provide for the mutual exchange of information down to the battalion level, as NATO participants had asked. This is one of the two NATO proposals at Stockholm that failed to win the agreement of the Pact, and also of other participants like Yugoslavia and Turkey. (The other western proposal not acted on at Stockholm provided for the intensification of bilateral military contacts among participants.)

For the most part, Soviet and Warsaw Pact negotiators were still bound by their tradition of secrecy during the Stockholm talks and were not willing to move on exchange of information. The real breakthrough from previous Soviet views on verification and on-site inspection did not take place until the spring of 1987 in the I.N.F. talks, when United States negotiators put forward specific proposals on I.N.F. verification. Moreover, NATO countries at Stockholm did not press for the exchange of information with as much vigor as they should have. They were hampered by disagreement on the matter within their own ranks. For example, Turkey took the position that detailed information on forces below the division level should not be made available. Instead of pressing for an exchange of data on at least that level, NATO fell into a deadlock of internal dispute over how far such an exchange should go.

ASSESSING STOCKHOLM

In the light of its achievements and its shortcomings, how should we evaluate the Stockholm conference? Our general assessment must be positive. Stockholm demonstrated that the Helsinki accords forum could achieve important results in security (just as the Vienna review conference, which ended in January, 1989, achieved important progress in human rights), and, consequently, that the C.S.C.E. process has strong potential for the future. Although overshadowed by the more substantial achievements of the I.N.F. treaty, the Stockholm Document was the first East/West arms-control agreement to have been implemented since SALT I and the A.B.M. treaty limiting defenses against ballistic missiles took effect in 1972. In its provision for on-site inspection of Soviet territory, the Document was a breakthrough. It established the principle of coverage of Soviet territory to the Urals, which is a prerequisite for the success of the C.F.E. talks on force reductions and which will be the minimum standard for any other negotiations on the East/West confrontation in Europe. And it introduced the first constraints on military activities in Europe, a concept with much promise for future efforts to stabilize the confrontation.

One successful objective of the Document is to familiarize participants with the pattern of normal peacetime activities of the forces of potential opponents, the better to notice immediately major departures from those patterns. A second equally important achievement is that the Document is allowing observation of previously secret Warsaw Pact military activities and contributing to a better-founded, more accurate assessment of the equipment, training, leadership, morale, and readiness of the forces of both alliances. It is replacing with sober realism some of the exaggeration and mythology that have characterized the public appraisals of the two alliances.

Why did the Stockholm conference succeed when the M.B.F.R. talks failed? The conference was helped by its modest scope. And it was helped by the requirements of the Helsinki process. The scheduling of the new C.S.C.E. review conference to start in Vienna in November, 1986, had the effect of creating a deadline for the negotiators in Stockholm. In fact, Stockholm participants did stop the clock to buy time, but the approach of the deadline clearly moved the talks forward. After the Stockholm conference ended, some American officials regretted that there had been a deadline and resolved to prevent one from being imposed on the next force-reduction talks. This fear of deadlines is mistaken. As demonstrated by the Stockholm conference, by the I.N.F. talks, and other arms-control negotiations, as long as deadlines apply to both sides, they are productive and help governments accelerate the tempo of decision-making.

The chief reason for the success of the Stockholm talks was also the reason for the later success of the I.N.F. talks: a demanding and rather rigid western position toward which the Soviet Union and its allies were willing to move, making many changes from their starting position. Such a formula can work only if one side really wants an agreement.

The Soviet Union's concessions to the West at Stockholm include its willingness to cover the Soviet Union to the Urals; dropping its demand for specific coverage of naval forces; acceptance of the substance of western measures on notification and observers; acceptance of on-site inspection; and dropping cherished Soviet negotiating themes like no first use of nuclear weapons and the establishment of nuclear-free zones.

What NATO had to do for its part to achieve agreement with the East—to commit itself to present information on military exercises in advance, to invite Pact observers to these exercises, and to permit limited on-site inspections by Pact officers—does not represent much of a sacrifice. Most of the information that NATO must give the Pact is available already either in publications, in the records of parliamentary inquiry, or through the extensive information-collecting espionage efforts of the Pact, which have been facilitated by the open societies of the West. The Pact, in contrast, must relinquish some of the secrecy that has surrounded even its more innocuous peacetime military activities. The Pact's leaders have in the past considered secrecy a valuable military asset and advantage over the openness of the NATO alliance.

Throughout the Stockholm talks, the neutral and non-aligned group pressed both alliances toward compromise. As mentioned, this grouping was responsible for the document's constraint on the holding of large-scale activities without notice. Some NATO officials, including some Americans, felt that the pressures of the neutral and non-aligned block were an inconvenience, particularly when brought to bear on NATO. But seen objectively, the weight of those pressures fell largely on the Warsaw Pact. The countries belonging to this group—prominently, Finland, Sweden, Switzerland, Austria, and Yugoslavia—have a strong continuing interest in the possible consequences for them of the NATO-Pact confrontation. Their influence is by and large constructive.

C.D.E.-2—ITS CONTENT AND PROSPECTS

The most immediate task for negotiators in the present phase of C.D.E. talks, which began in Vienna on March 9, 1989, on the same day as the C.F.E. force-reduction talks, is to fill in the gaps of C.D.E.-1. Negotiators call these new talks "C.D.E. 1B," instead of C.D.E.-2, because they are reserving the term C.D.E.-2 for a future negotiation that will amalgamate both confidence-building and force reduction. Despite the somewhat theological differences among western participants that underlie this nomenclature, here we can use the term C.D.E.-2 for the continuation of the Stockholm talks.

First, at C.D.E.-2, ambiguities in wording of the Stockholm Document must be resolved—among them the definition of "military activities." It should now be possible to obtain agreement to use the "out-of-garrison" definition that NATO advanced at C.D.E.-1 and thus to cover force movements from garrison to garrison or to do so in some other way. Second, there should be an exchange of detailed data on the forces, not to preclude an even more detailed exchange of NATO and Pact data in the C.F.E. talks. Third, the C.D.E.-2 negotiators should again explore the possibility of writing rules to cover mobilization activity. Because of the sensitivity of neutrals and non-aligneds like the Swedes, the Swiss, and the Yugoslavs, whose defenses are more dependent on mobilization than on active-duty formations, it may not be possible to go very far on this subject. Still, the mobilization and reinforcement capacity of the Soviets is a major concern of NATO military commanders. The logical answer is to seek constraints and restrictions on reserves in the NATO/Pact C.F.E. force-reduction talks, which do not include the neutral and non-aligned block.

Fourth, the problem of alert exercises, whose omission from the Stockholm Document is a major weakness, must be tackled. NATO commanders quite properly see alerting troops without warning as an essential part of their training. If this were the only problem with alerts, it could probably be resolved by notifying C.D.E. governments of the timing of alert exercises confidentially while keeping this information from the troops whose readiness is to be tested. However, NATO also views alerts as a way to move its forces into readiness positions in crisis without having to wait for a formal decision by the NATO Council, which might be hard to achieve. As we saw in Chapter 3, the movement of NATO forces into readiness positions before a Pact attack begins can mean the difference between defeat and repulsing the attack. The insistence of NATO commanders on retaining the right to call an alert at will reflects an essential difference between the political systems of East and West. The exemption for alerts, therefore, cannot be eliminated.

The best way to tackle the alert problem may be through some combination of a numerical restriction on alerts in C.D.E.-2 and early-warning measures and constraints on the activities of reserve forces in the NATO/Pact force-reduction talks. In C.D.E.-2 NATO could permit each alliance an unlimited number of training alerts on notification but give each alliance a limited quota of alerts for undeclared purposes involving more than 17,000 troops from national forces, perhaps four per year, and consider placing limits on the duration of alerts held under this quota. This should be adequate for situations of genuine crisis but would hamper the ability of any government to use repeated large-scale alerts as a means of intimidation.

In the Stockholm conference NATO rejected Warsaw Pact proposals to restrict the size of out-of-garrison activities. The idea of limiting the concentration of forces that would be likely to precede an attack is attractive, however. To violate such a limitation would be a clear warning signal of aggressive intent helpful to decision-making in NATO. Rules on the concentration of forces would also inhibit the use of large-scale military exercises for intimidation. Early in the M.B.F.R. talks the NATO countries themselves proposed such a measure for U.S. and Soviet forces but then dropped it. The Soviet Union in turn pressed for the measure both in the M.B.F.R. talks and in the Stockholm conference; NATO rejected it in both cases.

The underlying problem is the same as that which vexes the issue of restrictions on alert exercises: in a real crisis a restriction on the number of NATO personnel allowed to move forward to readiness positions could be serious. Numerical constraints on the size of out-of-garrison activities could also hobble the large annual exercises that NATO commanders consider essential for the training of a coalition army. NATO may have found a useful solution for this problem. In its proposals for C.D.E.-2, NATO suggested that the level at which participants would have to give two-year notice of large-scale military activities be lowered to 50,000 men in place of the 75,000 specified in the Stockholm Document. This measure if agreed upon would place some practical limits on force concentration while permitting NATO to conduct its large exercises involving force components of several allies; these have to be planned several years in advance because of their complexity and cost.

CONFIDENCE-BUILDING MEASURES FOR AIR AND NAVAL FORCES

Besides filling the gaps of the Stockholm conference it will fall to C.D.E.-2 negotiators to discuss expanding the Document's coverage to include the independent activities of air and naval forces not related to ground-force exercises. In theory, it does not make sense to draw a tightening circle around ground-force activities in Europe and to omit air and naval forces.

Constraints on air forces have been considered since the SALT I negotiation, when the United States proposed a limitation on the number of bombers allowed in the air at any given time. Now that both alliances have deployed in Europe aircraft equipped with radar sensors which can monitor aircraft activity in the sky, a limit on the number of military aircraft permitted over the East and the West seems practicable. However, such limitations are not foolproof, because a sudden cessation of aircraft activity in the air could mean that they are loading munitions and fuel in preparation for attack. Given the importance of attack aircraft at the outset of a NATO/Pact conflict, measures affecting aircraft have to be weighed very carefully to assure that no advantage is inadvertently given an attacker. Negotiators in Stockholm might, however, consider requiring that participants report the entry of single aircraft into the Atlantic-to-Urals area covered by force reductions and that they give notice in advance of the entry of more than one aircraft, with a numerical threshold to be agreed.

Since World War II naval forces have been largely exempt from arms control. The exception is the May, 1972, U.S./Soviet agreement on the "Prevention of Incidents On and Over the High Seas," which established rules to require surface naval vessels and naval aircraft of the two countries to keep their distance from one another and to refrain from simulating attack. In C.D.E.-1, the Soviet Union and its allies failed to gain coverage of navies in confidence-building measures. In the interim between the end of C.D.E.-1 in September, 1986, and the beginning of C.D.E.-2 in March, 1989, the Soviet Union was active in promoting the concept of naval arms control in a series of unofficial conferences. There are indications of growing public interest in the Scandinavian countries, Great Britain, Federal Germany and in Turkey and Greece on NATO's southern flank. It is clear that there will be a major Warsaw Pact push on this subject in C.D.E.-2.

The Pact has envisaged restrictive zones within which major naval activity would be limited or would not take place. This idea should be studied, but at first sight it seems to serve the Pact's interests more than NATO's. Recently, Soviet officials and academicians have begun to talk of keep-out zones which only one designated power would refrain from entering, like Soviet ships near Atlantic reinforcement routes. This approach may be more promising. Schedules far in advance might be unworkably restrictive for naval forces continually in training and continually on the move. One possibility for discussion might be to require that notice of large-scale naval activity be given thirty days in advance.

Protection of the sea reinforcement route to Europe by NATO

navies will be essential as long as any sizeable East/West military confrontation in Europe continues. At the same time, with further negotiated reductions in U.S. and Soviet nuclear forces in prospect and negotiations on reduction of conventional land-based forces starting in a new expanded format, some coverage of naval forces in negotiated arms control is logically inescapable. Whether naval confidence-building measures in the European context are the right point of entry to this complex problem is, however, an open question.

Another subject that negotiators could take up in Stockholm is the exchange of information on military budgets. The Warsaw Pact proposed such an exchange at the first conference and called for mutual restrictions on these budgets. Up to now the United States has opposed discussion of military spending at the Stockholm conference, because American territory is excluded from that conference's mandate and because of the difficulty in precisely attributing to defense of Europe portions of the overall United States defense budget. It has preferred to pursue the matter of budgets from within the United Nations where total military budgets can be examined once the Soviet Union, under the impact of *glasnost*, has finally pulled data together and submitted it.

There is much to be said for that position. Even so, the C.D.E.-2 conference might be a more manageable arena for a focused consideration of military spending on forces in the area from the Atlantic to the Urals, and one in which the subject could be explored with more interest and better follow-through, in parallel with consideration of the subject at the United Nations. A disclaimer stating that military forces on United States territory remain exempt from C.D.E.-2 agreements notwithstanding any agreements specifically concerning American military spending could clear up confusion about the document's geographic coverage.

GOALS OF THE TWO ALLIANCES IN C.D.E.-2

In late 1988, both alliances published their general goals for C.D.E.-2. (The text of the NATO communiqué is in Appendix VIII, that of the Warsaw Pact in Appendix VII.) A short comparison of the two documents can show us where these goals coincide and where they diverge.

The NATO statement, issued following the ministerial session on December 8–9, 1988, makes the achievement of greater transparency on military forces, described as "an essential requirement for real stability," the main NATO goal in C.D.E.-2. To this end, NATO has proposed at C.D.E.-2 a number of improvements on the Stockholm Document. These include a broad exchange of information "concerning military organization, manpower and equipment as well as major weapons deployment," to be evaluated through sampling inspections. This is the data-exchange item on which NATO failed to gain agreement in C.D.E.-1. To achieve greater transparency of military activities, NATO is proposing that more detailed information be required when notice of military exercises is given, that the arrangements for observers be improved, and that the regime of verification and inspection be strengthened. NATO is also proposing measures to improve contacts and communications between military staffs of participating states—the second NATO proposal at the Stockholm conference that was rejected. Finally, NATO has agreed to the Warsaw Pact's proposal for an exchange of views on military doctrine and has suggested that this discussion be held in C.D.E.-2. NATO emphasizes that the discussion must not be purely theoretical, but tied to actual force posture.

The Warsaw Pact's program for C.D.E.-2, adopted at the meeting of Pact foreign ministers at Budapest on October 28–29, 1988, and repeated in a position paper submitted on March 9, 1989, at the outset of C.D.E.-2, is more ambitious. The Pact ministers consider that the aim of further agreements on confidence- and security-building measures should be to promote progress toward force reductions. Characteristically, the NATO ministers emphasized "stability" in their proposals for C.D.E.-2; Pact ministers emphasized reductions.

As we have seen, the NATO program focuses essentially on improvement of the C.D.E.-1 regime as contained in the Stockholm Document. But the Pact program seeks to expand the focus of the Document to cover "all elements of the forces—ground, air, and naval forces" of the participating states. It urges that "confidence- and security-building measures should be applied to all the military activities of the participating states that affect European security or constitute part of military actions taking place within the boundaries of Europe." There is an implication here not only that air and naval forces should be fully covered by agreed measures but also that the geographic scope of C.D.E.-2 measures should be extended to cover all the territories of all participating states, not just the area from the Atlantic to the Urals.

Specifically the Pact proposes:

(1) A program of constraints—agreed restrictions—on the size and

frequency of military exercises, including alert exercises, and on military activities near borders of participating states. The suggested limit is 40,000 men.

(2) Extension of the C.D.E.-1 regime to air and naval forces, with a detailed program for pre-notification of activities of air and naval forces, annual calendars of such activities, the invitation of observers, and inspections. Eleven specific measures are proposed for naval forces alone.

(3) Establishment of a common European risk-reduction center to exchange information and to deal with military incidents.

(4) Measures to increase predictability and openness, to include the regular exchange of data on armed forces down to the brigade or regiment level, the establishment of fixed observation posts, including some in central Europe, and exchanges of military personnel.

PROSPECTS FOR C.D.E.-2

After reviewing the outcome of the Stockholm talks and the programs of the two alliances for a second round of these talks in Vienna, we have a basis for predicting developments at C.D.E.-2. Both alliances agree on improvements in the existing C.D.E. regime to improve pre-notification, arrangements for observers, and verification. There is also general agreement by the alliances on data exchange and on the intensification of bilateral military contacts. Some progress in these three areas at C.D.E.-2 seems assured.

The Pact is proposing a European risk-reduction center in which all C.D.E. states would participate. Many NATO governments object to such a center on the grounds that it would give the Soviet Union a contractual right of oversight over NATO defense decisions. Nevertheless, public opinion in western Europe supports establishing such a center and, in the long run, agreement on it appears possible. The pros and cons of such a center are discussed in Chapter 9 of this book.

The real struggle at C.D.E.-2 will be over two subjects: constraints on military activities, and coverage of air and naval forces in confidence- and security-building measures. By and large, as we shall discuss in a later chapter, NATO governments and NATO military commanders do not like constraints on the activities or deployments of NATO military forces. The main reason for their objection goes back to an issue that was central to our earlier discussion of the force balance in Europe: the unwieldiness of NATO in making decisions in comparison with the authoritarian, Soviet-dominated Warsaw Pact. NATO officers fear a situation in which the Pact might violate agreed restrictions but NATO could not promptly decide to suspend parallel restrictions on NATO forces. In general, military commanders prefer full freedom to dispose over their own forces even if the adversary is numerically stronger to a fallible regime of mutual restrictions. NATO will resist most of these Pact proposals.

The most difficult issue at C.D.E.-2 is the Pact's proposals to expand the coverage of confidence-building measures to air and naval forces. We have already given some indication of the complexity of this problem. Most NATO governments will join the United States in opposing air and naval coverage. But this time, the Warsaw Pact is likely to be far more tenacious than it was at Stockholm in pushing its proposals for air and naval measures and it has considerable public support in western Europe. No easy solution can be foreseen, and the issue seems likely to delay and possibly block agreement in C.D.E.-2. The East/West debate will at least educate western publics on the pros and cons of air and naval confidence-building measures.

One possible compromise might be for NATO to accept the Pact's proposal for extension to the naval forces of the two alliances the United States/Soviet Incidents at Sea agreement to which we referred earlier in this chapter. The United States could not strongly oppose the extension of this very limited agreement in which it is itself a participant. In return, the Soviet Union would gain expansion of the scope of C.D.E. to cover naval forces—of interest for future C.D.E. conferences—but would have to relinquish most of the substance of its present proposals on naval forces.

THE RELATIONSHIP BETWEEN THE STOCKHOLM CONFERENCE AND NATO/PACT FORCE-REDUCTION TALKS

In the past, NATO has not given much attention to the relationship between the Helsinki and Stockholm conferences and the M.B.F.R. talks, but damage has been minor, because the M.B.F.R. talks did not yield any agreements to get in the way of the proceedings in Stockholm. Now the stakes are higher, because there is a real chance that both sets of talks at Vienna, C.F.E. and C.D.E.-2, will be productive. Consequently, NATO needs to give careful thought to the relationship between the two, both in terms of content and procedures.

As for content, all negotiation of reductions should—and probably will—take place in the C.F.E. talks. The European neutral and non-aligned countries made it clear during the first Stockholm conference that they have little interest in making cutbacks, given the small size of their active-duty forces to begin with. Scaling down NATO and Pact forces belongs in an alliance-to-alliance framework.

Given the opposition of the neutral and non-aligned countries to limitations on their reserve forces and NATO's goal of obtaining restrictions on Soviet reserves, that matter, too, should be discussed in C.F.E., not C.D.E. Certain other constraints, such as pulling back armaments or ammunition from the line of confrontation between the two alliances in the interests of disengagement, are by their nature more applicable to an alliance-to-alliance confrontation than to thirty-five separate states, and so should also be the province of the force-reduction talks. However, if NATO and the Pact agree in Vienna to pull back their armored forces from the dividing line between the two alliances, it would be appropriate and useful for the Stockholm conference to adopt a measure prohibiting armored-force maneuvers within fifty kilometers of national borders. Such a measure would be in the interests not just of the alliances but also of countries outside the alliances that have sensitive borders—Finland and Yugoslavia, for example, which share frontiers with Pact countries.

What about the procedural and political links between the C.D.E. and C.F.E. talks? After all, each conference has received its agenda from the same source—the Vienna C.S.C.E. review conference. Here the picture has been clouded by controversy within NATO over how closely the two sets of negotiations should be connected. We shall review that debate in the next chapter.

7 The Two Alliances Ready Themselves

A major paradox of the current Vienna force reduction talks is that the West has a chance to gain major concessions from the Soviet Union that it may not be prepared to accept. In recent years the Soviet Union has become more and more committed to holding talks with the West on force reductions in Europe and apparently more and more willing to meet the West's terms for such talks. But at the same time NATO has remained unconvinced that deep force reductions will enhance its security and less flexible than the Pact in its prerequisites for reductions. The reasons for the divergence are worth examining here, for they are obstacles that must be resolved in order to make real progress in Vienna.

The best way to understand why and how the two alliances are at odds is to review the positions they have taken over the two years of active preparation leading to the opening of the C.F.E. negotiations, in March, 1989. Let us begin with the Soviets.

THE APRIL, 1986, SOVIET PROPOSAL

On April 18, 1986, six months before the Stockholm talks on confidence-building measures ended, Soviet General Secretary Mikhail S. Gorbachev proposed new negotiations within the Helsinki process for substantial reductions in all components of ground forces and tactical air forces—both conventional and nuclear—stationed from the Atlantic to the Urals. Initially, Gorbachev proposed, reductions should be made in the forces of the NATO and Warsaw Treaty alliances. Subsequently, the forces of the neutral and non-aligned European states would also be cut back.

As confirmed and amplified by the Warsaw Pact Political Consultative Committee—the Warsaw Pact equivalent to NATO meetings of heads of government—which met in Budapest in June, 1986, this new Soviet proposal called for reductions by "equivalent" units together with their arms. Armaments would either be destroyed or stored in accordance with agreed procedures.

The reductions, which would "maintain the present military

balance," would proceed on schedules worked out by the alliances. The first would take place within one to two years and consist of 100,000 to 150,000 men from each alliance—a cutback roughly equal to that anticipated by negotiators in the M.B.F.R. talks. By the early 1990s the alliances would cut another 25 percent of their forces. At that point, according to the Warsaw Pact, the total reduction would come to 500,000 men for each alliance. In a third phase, NATO and the Warsaw Pact would make still more cutbacks, at which time the neutral and nonaligned countries of Europe would also reduce their forces.

The Pact suggested that reductions be configured to reduce the risk of surprise attack. Forces would be thinned out in a zone spanning the line of confrontation. Bringing additional forces into that zone would be controlled. The size and number of military exercises would be limited. There would be procedures for the exchange of information and other confidence-building measures. Zones free of nuclear and chemical weapons would be established. There would be provisions for "reliable and effective" verification, to include national technical means and on-site inspections, the exchange of data, and oversight by a commission composed of representatives from all participating states. This commission would conduct on-site inspections, supervise the destruction or storage of armaments, and staff checkpoints at railway junctions, airfields, and ports.[1] (The concept of checkpoints, originally a Soviet idea dating from the mid-fifties, had already been agreed to in principle by M.B.F.R. negotiators.)

Gorbachev's proposal for the new talks was the final blow to the already moribund M.B.F.R. negotiations. Designed to be attractive to the Western allies, it addressed France's interest in discussing force reductions in a second phase of the Stockholm Conference on Disarmament in Europe, which France had helped to initiate. It addressed the interest of many NATO countries in including Soviet territory in the area subject to force reductions, thus overcoming a serious shortcoming of the M.B.F.R. talks. It addressed Federal Germany's abiding interest in bringing France into negotiations on European forces. Finally, it provided NATO as well as Warsaw Pact governments with an opportunity to close down the M.B.F.R. talks without recrimination. The fear of being accused by the other side of lack of interest in building down the military confrontation had held both alliances at the negotiating table in Vienna long after they had given up on the talks. Aware of public support in western Europe for the new talks, the NATO Council responded favorably to the Pact's proposal.

Why this new Soviet proposal? One reason was that the Soviet Union had always favored the Helsinki forum over the M.B.F.R. forum, among other reasons because the Helsinki process includes the whole of NATO, including France and the United Kingdom, and also the neutral European states, whose forces the Soviet general staff usually ranges with those of NATO in its scenarios of conflict. Moreover, the M.B.F.R. talks were too deep in the mire of deadlock to fit well into Gorbachev's activist approach to arms control. As such they were unlikely to evoke new interest from the West European public, whose favor the Soviets were ardently courting as part of a larger campaign to improve relations with Europe. Nor were the M.B.F.R. talks an effective vehicle if, as became increasingly plausible, the Soviet Union wanted for its own reasons to cut back the NATO/Pact confrontation.

For all their advantages to the West, the Soviet proposals of 1986 had a formidable defect. They reflected the longstanding Soviet approach of protecting and preserving the status quo in arms control in Europe. Here, as in the M.B.F.R. talks, the Soviets were asking for reductions in equal numbers and by equal percentages. NATO's acceptance of this approach would "contractualize"—give formal acceptance in treaty form to—the Warsaw Pact's numerical superiorities in most major armaments and would obligate NATO to renounce increasing its own holdings of these weapons. NATO participants had categorically refused to accept this arrangement in the M.B.F.R. talks; they vigorously criticized the new Pact proposals on the same grounds.

Meanwhile, new Soviet proposals called for the Soviet Union and the United States to exchange data bilaterally while the mandate for the C.F.E. talks was being negotiated. NATO officials fended off this suggestion, arguing that such an exchange would be premature and an inappropriate prelude to a negotiation that would be multilateral. Both these criticisms were justified. Moreover, the Warsaw Pact failed to suggest any real link between an exchange of data and force reductions as such. And although Pact officials begin to talk about eliminating asymmetries in the armaments of both alliances, and also about reducing conventional forces to "reasonable sufficiency" or to a capability for non-offensive defense only, they also had not established any connection between those two goals.

THE MAY, 1988, SOVIET POSITION

The components of a coherent Soviet position on reductions were brought together in the proposal which General Secretary Gorbachev presented to President Reagan at their Moscow summit meeting in May of 1988. In essence, Gorbachev proposed tying an exchange of data to reductions, using such an exchange to document the existence of "imbalances" between the alliances in major weapons, and then negotiating to eliminate these imbalances. As Gorbachev's suggestions were described by Soviet foreign minister Eduard A. Shevardnadze, in a June, 1988, speech to the United Nations, the U.S.S.R. was proposing a four-step program:

(1) Reciprocal exchange of data, backed by on-site inspections to check the data and to resolve differences on specific issues;
(2) Negotiation of ways to eliminate the imbalances and asymmetries revealed by the data exchange;
(3) After the elimination of imbalances a further cutback by each alliance of 500,000 military personnel together with armaments; and
(4) Further cuts in forces and armaments. By means of these third-stage reductions, Shevardnadze said, "the armed forces on both sides would be given a defensive character and their offensive core would be dismantled."[2]

A detailed exposition of the May, 1988, Soviet position on force reductions appeared in a position paper adopted by the Warsaw Pact Political Consultative Committee in July, 1988. (Pertinent sections are in Appendix VII of this book.) In their position paper the Warsaw Pact leaders urged early East/West agreement to bring about "the elimination of the existing asymmetries and imbalances," by means of substantial reductions designed to preclude surprise attacks and offensive operations. They proposed separate East/West talks to build down the number of tactical nuclear weapons in Europe eventually to zero.

For the first phase of conventional reductions, the Pact proposed establishing "roughly equal, (balanced) collective levels" of manpower and armaments, lower than present levels, through "eliminating imbalances and asymmetries in individual types of conventional arms" and disbanding units holding these arms. The Pact proposal was noteworthy not only for the concept of eliminating numerical superiorities. It also accepted the term "balanced"—to refer to elimination of superiorities—that it had rejected in the M.B.F.R. talks, and accepted the idea that residual ceilings should be "collective," covering all forces of each alliance in a single total. This too, as we saw in Chapter 5, was a major western interest in the M.B.F.R. talks.

Confirming the remaining Gorbachev proposals, the Pact suggested that initial reductions be followed by a second phase in which the two sides would make cutbacks of 500,000 men each in units, together with their armaments. Reductions would be continued in a third phase in which "the armed forces of both sides would acquire a strictly defensive nature."

The Pact proposed that, in order to reduce the risk of surprise attack, a zone should be established along the dividing line between the alliances in which the number of armaments allowed would be limited. Few or none of the more dangerous, destabilizing types of conventional armaments would be permitted in this zone. The depth of the zone on either side of the dividing line could be decided on the basis of "geostrategic factors," the Pact said (thus perhaps implying some willingness to accept deeper zones on the Pact than the NATO side). In the zone, troop movements and the size and number of military exercises would also be restricted.

The Pact also urged verification measures, to include onsite inspection without right of refusal and the use of checkpoints. A standing international verification commission would coordinate the effort and deal with problems of compliance.

Did the Soviets mean the new proposal to be taken seriously? Were they opening up some prospect of real agreement after the frustrations of M.B.F.R.? The proposal had been sketched with a broad brush and might contain some deliberate traps and ambiguities. In general, however, it was the right approach to begin building down the NATO/Pact confrontation. It accepted NATO's conceptual approach in the M.B.F.R. talks, by combining the exchange of data that NATO had been seeking in M.B.F.R. for more than fifteen years with the goal of eliminating the superiorities in individual armaments or force types that such an exchange might reveal. Potentially, this move was of central importance for negotiated reduction of the European confrontation. True, the proposal retained the longstanding Pact call for reductions in equal numbers in a second phase, but there could be no quarrel with this, because the proposal provided first for the elimination of asymmetries. Finally, it gave the official stamp of approval to the concept of non-offensive defense, although reserving implementation to a distant third phase of reductions and providing no details on how that concept would be put into practice.

Despite all of these concessions NATO was wary. One reason for doubt has been the evident resistance of the Soviet military described in Chapter 4 to the new emphasis of the Soviet leadership on non-offensive defense. Another reason has been the continued high rate of production of the same armaments whose number the Soviets have proposed to reduce. Yet another reason has been the probable resistance of the Soviet military to large-scale eliminations of officer billets, an issue that had turned the Soviet military against Khrushchev in the 1960s when he made big cuts in ground forces in order to build up the arsenal of ICBMs.

A compelling source of western doubts has been the possible impact on political stability in eastern Europe of major Soviet troop withdrawals. Western leaders themselves are nervous about that impact and the possibility of widespread public unrest followed by repressive Soviet military intervention, perhaps even in East Germany with its common border with the Federal Republic of Germany. The potential in such a situation for serious miscalculation on both sides would be great. Western leaders doubted that Soviet leaders would wish to take actions through large withdrawals that could turn the region into a powder keg.

In the spring of 1986, as eastern European officials came to terms with Gorbachev's initial proposal for new force-reduction talks, they were clearly moved by similar concerns. During the fifteen years of the M.B.F.R. talks, the stability of eastern Europe had become less and less secure. Gorbachev's *glasnost* campaign was being energetically invoked by pro- and anti-communist elements of the public in Poland and Hungary and to a lesser extent in East Germany. Hungary had made an apparently successful change from the leadership of the aging Janos Kadar, who had kept the Hungarian system together since the 1956 uprising. The leadership of Czechoslovakia had also changed uneventfully, if minimally. However, leadership changes were overdue in East Germany and Bulgaria. Romania appeared ripe for a coup to decide the Ceausescu succession. Discontent in Poland had grown, with workers, intellectuals, young people, and the Church creating continuing difficulties for the Jaruzelski government.

What would happen in this ferment if the conclusion of an East/West force-reduction agreement brought the highly publicized withdrawal of thousands of Soviet troops and a verification and early-warning regime that scattered hundreds of roving NATO military personnel over the countryside of eastern Europe? What would happen to governments incapable of sustaining themselves without the visible prop of Soviet forces inside their countries or on their borders? The relaxation of East/West tensions had already brought spats between Hungary and Romania about the treatment of the Hungarian minority in Romania reminiscent of the Balkan disputes before World War I.

In informal conversations with westerners immediately following Gorbachev's 1986 proposal, eastern European officials expressed decided preference that American and Soviet troop reductions be kept small and symbolic. Since then, however, they have become bolder, and will say now that large Soviet reductions are acceptable, because the armies of the Pact states are loyal and capable of maintaining public order on their own. The statements may or may not be true as far as the loyalty of professional officers is concerned, but they do not seem at all descriptive of the probable reliability of conscript manpower. Significantly, Polish military units were not used to maintain public order in the Solidarity unrest of 1980 to 1981. Instead, the government called out heavily-armed riot police. Units of this sort, which are relatively numerous in most Pact countries, are loyal to existing regimes, because their own survival depends on the survival of the system.

Soviet academicians have claimed that the issue of complete Soviet withdrawal from eastern Europe under conditions of complete American withdrawal from western Europe is under study in Moscow. That study is not likely to be seriously pursued under present circumstances, but the fact that it is spoken of at all is significant. Some Warsaw Pact academicians appear to believe that the Soviet Union could maintain political stability in eastern Europe with only a third of its forces now deployed there. The calculation is probably correct. Even so, worries about the impact of reductions on political stability haunt the discussion in Vienna now as they haunted it in the past.

The West's reasons for doubting the seriousness of the Soviet Union's intentions in the sphere of force reductions became a good deal less compelling on December 7, 1988. On that day General Secretary Gorbachev announced to the United Nations surprisingly large force cuts that the Soviets had decided to make unilaterally. As described in Chapter 3, these include the withdrawal and disbandment by the end of 1990 of four Soviet tank divisions and a total of nearly 4,000 tanks from East Germany. Among these units withdrawn will be the only Soviet air-assault brigade in East Germany (one of the key components of the Soviet capacity to mount a surprise attack), and a forward-deployed military bridging unit. Two more tank divisions will be withdrawn from Czechoslovakia and Hungary by 1990. (See Appendix V for details.) Ironically, the number of divisions that the Soviets will withdraw is about what the West sought in M.B.F.R.; the tank reductions come to three times what the West sought.

The Soviet Union's capacity to use its forward-deployed forces to attack NATO's Central Front without warning will be considerably weakened by these reductions. NATO will have nearly as many divisions on the Central Front as the Soviets will have in eastern Europe—and more tanks. Any attack would then require the dispatch of reinforcements from the U.S.S.R., a process both time-consuming and visible to the West. A further cutback that Gorbachev announced to the U.N.—5,000 tanks from the western part of the Soviet Union, a number equivalent to the holdings of sixteen more Soviet tank divisions—will leave the Soviets with fewer reinforcements to send.

The effect of the Soviet decision to make unilateral reductions on the Soviet negotiating position in the pending C.F.E. force-reduction talks was unclear at the time of Gorbachev's announcement. But it looked as though Soviet leaders, aware of divided opinion on the talks within NATO, had discounted the possibility of making early progress in the talks. Moved by the desire to achieve early economic savings and to win political credit in the West, the Soviets apparently decided to make the cutbacks whether they could be used as bargaining chips or not.

As the NATO countries were quick to point out, even with these unilateral cuts, Soviet and Warsaw Pact forces will still have a large numerical superiority in major armaments. But after Gorbachev's announcement, there could no longer be any reasonable doubt of the seriousness of the desire of the Soviet leadership to participate in a long-term build-down of the NATO/Pact military confrontation in Europe.

However, there was a question of timing. The Soviet Union, having demonstrated its good faith through the unilateral cuts, could now afford to wait if the current talks got stuck. More specifically, the worry was that the Soviet Union might be content with the impact on western European public opinion of its unilateral withdrawals beginning in April, 1989, each segment of which could be heavily publicized. In this way, the Soviet Union could wait it out at the Vienna negotiating table with some generally-worded reduction proposal until NATO made some specific moves of its own, whether unilaterally or in negotiation. Given the cautious attitude of the NATO governments, this would have been a recipe for protracted inaction at Vienna.

This possibility was dispelled and Soviet determination to push for a real build-down in the European confrontation convincingly demonstrated when the Soviet Union came out with a forcing bid at the opening of the C.F.E. talks. Speaking for the Warsaw Pact on March 6, 1989, in Vienna, Foreign Minister Shevardnadze in practice accepted and went beyond NATO's opening proposal for huge Warsaw Pact reductions in tanks, artillery and armored vehicles to an equal level 5 to

10 percent below NATO's current holdings of these armaments. (The Shevardnadze text is in Appendix VII.)

Shevardnadze called for a three-phase reduction. In the first phase, to be implemented within two to three years of acceptance, the two alliances would reduce their "attack combat airplanes of tactical aviation, tanks, combat helicopters, combat armored vehicles, armored personnel carriers and artillery, including multiple-rocket launcher systems and mortars" and their active-duty military personnel, to a level 10 to 15 percent below the present holdings of the numerically weaker alliance. Shevardnadze proposed that separate negotiations on reducing or eliminating tactical-range nuclear weapons be started "as soon as possible."

The Soviet Foreign Minister proposed that, in a second stage of conventional reductions, whose implementation would also last two to three years, each alliance would reduce its forces by another 25 percent, about 500,000 men in units with their armaments. In the third phase of reductions, the armed forces of each alliance would be given "a strictly defensive character." As in earlier Pact programs, Shevardnadze proposed establishing zones of lower levels of military armaments along the line of confrontation and pulling back nuclear weapons on each side far enough that they would be out of range of the opposing alliance's territory.

The significance of the Soviet proposals was that they had presented a fleshed-out plan for reductions in a first phase which in major aspects came close to NATO's proposals for initial reductions (discussed below) and provided for huge, asymmetrical cuts of Pact armor and artillery. For example, even if calculated on the basis of NATO's more modest proposals, the Pact's reduction of tanks to a new equal level of 20,000 per alliance would cause the Pact to reduce 37,000 tanks—65 percent of its entire tank force west of the Urals. NATO in contrast, would withdraw only about 2,000. For artillery, reduction to the level proposed by NATO would mean a Pact reduction of about 30,000 artillery pieces to the proposed NATO parity level of 16,500 (again 65 percent of the Pact total west of the Urals), as compared with NATO reductions of only about 830 artillery pieces (5 percent of NATO's current holdings). The Soviet Union would reduce its own holdings of tanks and artillery west of the Urals by about 70 percent. (Figures are in Appendix IX; it is harder to calculate reductions in armored personnel carriers, because the two alliances have been using conflicting definitions.)

As the C.F.E. talks opened in Vienna, this smash service by the

Warsaw Pact put the ball very much in NATO's court. But how were NATO's own preparations for the talks progressing?

NATO PREPARES FOR THE RETURN TO VIENNA

If, despite some obvious drawbacks, the Soviets showed a highly positive attitude in preparing for the C.F.E. talks and took actions deliberately designed to build up momentum there, NATO did not reciprocate. Just as NATO did not like the I.N.F. zero outcome, it has been suspicious of the Soviets' openhandedness in offering conventional reductions. The NATO countries did not react with pleasure to Gorbachev's Moscow summit proposals, even though they offered the NATO countries what they had been asking for for years in M.B.F.R.—an exchange of detailed data and the elimination of asymmetries to a level below that of the numerically weaker side. At the Moscow summit, President Reagan fended off Gorbachev's overtures instead of welcoming them. Shortly thereafter, the State Department reacted by accusing the Soviet Union of dragging its feet in setting the mandate for the force-reduction talks. NATO responded to the Soviet and Pact announcement of unilateral reductions by pointing to the large numerical superiorities that the Pact would still have after the unilateral reductions were carried out.

NATO's skittishness was explained by some continuing basic disagreements within the alliance which persist even after President Bush took the initiative at the May, 1989, NATO summit to make some proposals of his own. These are:

- whether NATO should seek further nuclear reductions;
- whether NATO can really afford to make any reductions in the number of its tactical aircraft even to obtain asymmetrical reductions in Pact armor;
- whether NATO can afford deep cutbacks of its own ground forces without giving up forward defense in Germany; and, most important,
- in the light of uncertainties about the continuation of the Gorbachev policy in the U.S.S.R., what the basic goals of the C.F.E. negotiations should be.

We saw in earlier chapters how the conclusion of the I.N.F. treaty left most European NATO governments shaken and worried about the proven capacity of the new Soviet leadership to play on the desire of European publics to reduce the risks and costs of the NATO/Pact confrontation. Many NATO governments, especially those of France and the U.K., which, as nuclear powers, feel a special long-term responsibility for European defense, remain apprehensive that they are being drawn into a negotiating process that could ultimately lead to the wholesale withdrawal of American forces from Europe, the end of American nuclear protection, and the collapse of the entire postwar system that has provided the framework for an unprecedented era of peace and prosperity in western Europe, and this in the face of continuing uncertainty about the long-term course of the Soviet Union.

Understandable as it is, this defensive attitude has not been a good frame of mind in which to take on the challenge of negotiations to stabilize and build down the NATO/Pact confrontation. And these general worries have motivated a broad range of disagreements among the European allies on the substantive issues of the talks. These differences are so numerous, run so deep, and cover so many specific aspects of the talks that they cast real doubt on NATO's capacity to unite in a productive negotiating stance and to accept and build on the concessions which the Warsaw Pact is offering. Moreover, most of these issues are so important that they will continue, even if a first agreement is achieved in Vienna, to shape NATO attitudes toward a build-down of forces in Europe. Let us consider one by one the more important issues that have divided NATO members. Then we shall be prepared to interpret the proposals for the talks that NATO advanced in Vienna.

WHAT, IF ANY, NATO FORCES SHOULD BE REDUCED?

Divergence in the views of NATO states begins with the fundamental question of whether NATO should envisage sizeable reductions of its own forces in the C.F.E. negotiations.

France, which is perhaps more apprehensive about the post-I.N.F. future of NATO's defenses than any other country, argued at the outset of the intra-alliance consultations on the new talks that their primary objective should be the reduction of Warsaw Pact superiorities in major armaments. If the Soviet Union was intent on a changed policy toward the West, France maintained, then it should demonstrate its serious-ness by unilaterally eliminating the Warsaw Pact's numerical superiori-ties in major armaments. Even in that event, reductions in NATO forces were inadvisable—especially American conventional and nuclear forces. NATO had too few forces as it was, and needed them all to face the Soviets if they ever returned to militancy.

At the other end of the spectrum of opinion within NATO was Federal Germany. The I.N.F. negotiations had convinced the German public that the Soviet Union under Gorbachev had become less aggressive. Germans wanted the Pact's superiorities in major weapons to be eliminated and expected NATO to make cutbacks in return. Even in a climate of such optimism, however, the Federal German government was willing to urge in NATO only a token reduction in NATO's forces of about 5 percent—only half what NATO itself had called for during the M.B.F.R. talks more than a decade earlier. As the NATO country sharing a common border with the largest concentration of Pact forces, the German government felt strongly that NATO could not make any larger reduction without compromising its strategy of forward defense.

Most members of NATO lined up behind Federal Germany in favor of negotiating a minimal reduction in NATO's armaments as opposed to a larger reduction or none at all. So it was this position that prevailed when NATO formally announced its negotiating points for the current talks, in Brussels, in December, 1988. The main element of NATO's starting proposal was that both alliances should cut back the number of their main battle tanks, artillery, and armored troop carriers to a new equal level, slightly below NATO's current holdings.

We discuss details of NATO's plan later in this chapter. However, an important aspect of NATO's starting position should be mentioned now: The NATO governments accepted as valid Federal Germany's worries about forward defense, worries shared by most NATO senior commanders. Accordingly, the governments accepted the advice of their military staffs that the NATO reductions should be limited to 5 to 10 percent of NATO's holdings of tanks, artillery, and armored troop carriers, and that NATO could not afford further reductions without damage to its strategy of forward defense on its Central Front in Germany. Such damage could not be risked, it was argued, given uncertainties about the future policy of the Soviet Union. The problem is that, if NATO continues to adhere to this reasoning, it could block deeper cuts in the NATO/Pact military confrontation.

SHOULD NATO'S NUCLEAR WEAPONS BE FURTHER REDUCED?

Aware of friction within NATO on the subject of nuclear reductions and anxious to reach agreement so new talks could begin, the Soviet Union did not insist in the Vienna discussions of the mandate for the C.F.E. talks that its coverage extend to nuclear weapons. It dropped a proposal that reductions in nuclear-armed, surface-to-surface missiles of tactical range be included. The Soviets also dropped their insistence that the language of the mandate explicitly cover aircraft capable of delivering both nuclear and conventional warheads. However, the Soviet Union has maintained its public pressures for continuing the I.N.F. process. Its stated aim, dating from January, 1986, is to eliminate nuclear weapons from Europe. Foreign Minister Shevardnadze restated this proposal at the opening of the C.F.E. talks.

As we saw in Chapter 2, western Europe's nuclear powers, the U.K. and France, would have preferred an I.N.F. treaty that left some U.S. I.N.F. in place, even at the cost of continued deployment of Soviet I.N.F. With mounting concern, they observed how public opinion overran the resistance of like-minded political conservatives in the Federal Republic of Germany and pushed the Federal German government not only into agreeing to the proposed cutback of American and Soviet I.N.F. to zero but also to the elimination of ground-based missiles with a shorter range, including the German Pershing IAs, the "second zero." They feared that, if there were new talks on reducing tactical-nuclear armaments, the Soviet Union might appeal again to anti-nuclear majorities in Europe (including France, where there is a high degree of anti-nuclear sentiment in the general public outside the political parties) to bring effective pressure on their governments for further deep cuts in nuclear arms.

In a worst-case world, such a campaign might ultimately sweep the American nuclear weapons remaining in Europe away and place unendurable pressure on the U.K. and France to cut back the number of their own nuclear weapons sharply or eliminate them altogether. Western Europe would be left to face a Soviet Union that would be a major nuclear power even after having cut the number of its strategic-range nuclear warheads in a START agreement with the United States.

This is why the U.K. called for a freeze on further NATO nuclear reductions as soon as the conclusion of the I.N.F. treaty seemed probable. And it is why France made clear to its allies that it would withdraw from preparations for new force-reduction talks if they insisted on including in the talks further reduction of NATO's nuclear weapons. The two governments were joined by a United States administration apprehensive after the I.N.F. episode of doing more damage to the credibility of American nuclear protection for Europe.

The three NATO nuclear powers pressed hard for the fulfillment of the agreement reached in 1983 by NATO defense ministers meeting at Montebello in Canada. As we saw in Chapter 2, that agreement, leaving aside the question of whether the I.N.F. talks would succeed, had called for NATO's other nuclear forces to be modernized and strengthened. NATO defense ministers decided that this was to be done by replacing the aging United States-made surface-to-surface Lance missile, whose production line was scheduled to close down in the 1990s, with a nuclear-armed missile having a range four times greater than Lance's seventy miles; by developing new air-to-surface standoff nuclear missiles which could be fired from aircraft 500 to 600 miles from their targets; and possibly by reinforcing American nuclear-capable aircraft deployed to Europe and adding nuclear-tipped sea-launched cruise missiles to United States naval vessels assigned to NATO. Some NATO officials injudiciously suggested that these augmentations of NATO nuclear forces were needed to "compensate" for the elimination of American missiles in the I.N.F. Treaty, thereby contradicting NATO's official assessment of the treaty as a gain for NATO security, but accurately revealing their true assessment of the treaty.

The three NATO nuclear powers set themselves against making further reductions in NATO's nuclear forces until those forces were modernized, until an agreement eliminating the Warsaw Pact's conventional superiorities had been implemented, and until a treaty prohibiting the production and stockpiling of chemical weapons anywhere in the world had been concluded. Responding to these pressures, the other NATO states agreed with some reluctance to exclude reduction of nuclear armaments from the mandate of the forthcoming Vienna reductions.

But this decision left open the NATO response to the Soviet proposal for separate talks on cutting tactical-range nuclear arms in Europe. The negative attitude of the nuclear powers toward cutting back nuclear arsenals in Europe is not the only one in NATO. Norway, Denmark, Greece, and Spain maintain with varying stringency their declared opposition to peacetime deployment of American nuclear weapons on their territory. And the countries of NATO's northern tier—Norway, Denmark, the Benelux countries, and especially Federal Germany—

were and are not happy with the position on cutbacks that NATO's nuclear powers have taken.

Even German conservatives, as we showed in Chapter 2, have joined in a nearly unanimous demand by Federal Germany's major political parties for the elimination of, or at least deep cuts in, tactical-range nuclear weapons through East/West negotiation. Now that United States I.N.F. and the German Pershings were going, there would be no seamless web of deterrence stretching from nuclear artillery to American strategic nuclear missiles. With this justification gone, tactical nuclear weapons stood in isolation as weapons whose short range, if they were used, could mean heavy civilian casualties in both German states.

In a political trial balloon loosed during a visit to Washington in November, 1988, Chancellor Kohl let it be known that his coalition government might ultimately be ready to accept deployment of modernized Lance missiles of greater range if nuclear artillery were eliminated by negotiation. But the opposition Social Democrats and Green Party continued to vigorously oppose both nuclear artillery and deployment in Federal Germany of modernized Lance missiles. Their emphasis on the subject elicited increasing public support. At the beginning of 1989, polls showed that 80 percent of the German public wanted all nuclear weapons deployed in Germany to be eliminated. Only a few months later, Chancellor Kohl, facing Federal elections in 1990, shifted to a position calling for postponing a decision on whether to deploy a modernized Lance and for reaching an alliance decision on an early start for East/West talks on reducing tactical nuclear armaments; the Chancellor's representatives urged that these talks should take place simultaneously with the new talks on reducing conventional armaments.

NATO's struggles to reconcile these divergent views have been only partially successful. Despite high-level efforts—a NATO foreign ministers' meeting at Reykjavik in January, 1988, and a NATO summit of heads of government at Brussels in March, 1988—wide disagreement among NATO countries over the role of nuclear weapons in NATO defense continued. Even the compromise reached at the NATO summit of May, 1989, which we will discuss in the next chapter, did not seem likely to hold; it provided for new U.S./Soviet negotiations on reducing tactical-range surface-to-surface missiles (not nuclear artillery) to begin when a NATO/Warsaw Pact agreement on reducing conventional armaments had been concluded and its implementation had begun.

In early 1989, as the NATO states prepared for the new talks on conventional arms and for the meeting of the heads of government to commemorate NATO's fortieth anniversary, there was a wide gap among the positions of the NATO governments on the nuclear issue. Federal Germany wanted the United States and the Soviet Union to start negotiating soon to reduce the number of their tactical-range, surface-to-surface missiles to an equal and low level. Yet, with its Free Democratic coalition partners once again fighting for political survival as the 1990 general elections neared, there were doubts whether Chancellor Kohl's Christian Democratic party would resist Free Democratic pressures for complete elimination of these armaments. France and the United Kingdom wanted to postpone such negotiation as long as possible, at least until after the conclusion of an East/West agreement on reductions in conventional forces. And to block the creeping infection of nuclear reductions, France continued to oppose inclusion of its own delivery systems in any negotiations on reductions. In the late 1980s, the United States appeared intent on gaining agreement of NATO countries to deploy a modernized Lance missile on their territories in order to gain Congressional approval to fund the new missile. A new dispute over deployment of United States nuclear weapons in Europe, frustratingly similar to the initial stages of the I.N.F. dispute over the deployment of American Pershings and ground-launched cruise missiles, but under even more adverse political conditions as concerned European political opinion, was again in the making.

The Federal German public has been especially insistent that "nuclear" artillery be reduced in number or eliminated. These weapons have a fifteen- to twenty-five mile range that would mean high civilian casualties if they were ever used. In its preparations for the C.F.E. talks, NATO agreed to make a limited reduction in its own holdings of artillery to accompany the Warsaw Pact's elimination of its large numerical superiority in artillery pieces. Some of NATO's nuclear-certified artillery pieces might be cut back in this connection.

But getting rid of artillery pieces, as the German public will realize sooner or later, does not go to the heart of the matter. Nearly all artillery pieces of large caliber are "nuclear capable"; the nuclear capability is in the artillery rounds—called "artillery-fired atomic projectiles"—not the cannon. A reduction in nuclear artillery, if it is to be pursued seriously, means a reduction in the number of nuclear rounds.

Eventually, NATO may unilaterally withdraw nuclear artillery rounds and challenge the Pact to reciprocate. But the United States,

backed by France and the U.K., resisted German proposals to negotiate with the Soviets reciprocal reductions in the stockpile of nuclear
artillery rounds. The rounds are relatively small, easy to conceal, and
relatively easy to transport into the Atlantic-to-Urals area from outside
it. Followed to its logical conclusion, enforcing compliance with the
reduction of nuclear artillery rounds would require intensive verification, including identification of storage sites and access to them, and,
no doubt, ultimately, control of their production. In rejecting this
difficult assignment, NATO may find itself in the inconsistent position
of insisting on detailed verification for reductions of conventional arms
while depending only on the Soviets' good faith to follow through with
reductions in nuclear artillery rounds.

As we have mentioned, other aspects of NATO plans to modernize
its nuclear forces include the development of a new standoff nuclear
warhead missile for aircraft and increasing the number of United States
nuclear-capable aircraft deployed in Europe. Anti-nuclear opinion in
Federal Germany is less opposed to nuclear-armed aircraft than it is to
nuclear artillery and surface-to-surface missiles—in part, because they
are longer-range weapons and in part because they are stationed in
other NATO countries in addition to Germany and thus do not single
out Germany as a base for nuclear weapons.

But there are the seeds of a future East/West controversy over
nuclear arms here, too. Should NATO augment its nuclear forces with
new airborne nuclear delivery systems at a time when the Pact forces
against which they are directed may be dramatically reduced? For its
part, the Soviet Union is likely to react vigorously against the prospective deployment of a new air-launched standoff missile on highly
mobile NATO aircraft which could attack Soviet territory from many
directions.

In the context of the run-up to the C.F.E. negotiations, the Warsaw
Pact emphatically and repeatedly stated that if there was to be a deal
obliging it to reduce the number of its tanks and artillery, then NATO
must reduce the number of its fighter-bombers. However, NATO
military commanders were reluctant to do this, given the increased
importance of aircraft as delivery systems for nuclear weapons following the I.N.F. treaty's elimination of all but short-range nuclear
missiles. Once again, it is France that was the most stubborn.

In consequence, NATO agreed internally not to include aircraft in
the first phase of reductions. Yet some NATO officials said privately
early in the preparations for the talks that if agreement to reduce forces
is to be achieved in Vienna, aircraft would have to be involved, if not

directly through reductions, then through constraints on ground-based infrastructure, including ammunition stocks. And in negotiating with the Warsaw Pact the mandate or terms of reference for C.F.E., NATO agreed to include aircraft in the general coverage of the new talks without promising any specific reduction. This is reflected in the wording of the C.F.E. mandate which, in a gesture to the Soviet position, says that no weapons system may be excluded from reductions because it possesses capabilities "in addition to conventional ones".

President Bush's surprise proposal at the May 29–30, 1989, Brussels NATO summit short-circuited what was sure to be a long and tenaciously fought debate among NATO members, especially France and Germany, over the timing of NATO agreement in principle to reduce aircraft in the C.F.E. talks. But, as we will see in the next chapter, some complex problems remain: How can the number of aircraft be cut back with confidence, given their great mobility? How should the Pact's large numerical superiority in interceptor aircraft be handled? Should an agreement require the destruction of any aircraft that are withdrawn, and should controls be placed on production?

GROUND-FORCE REDUCTIONS AND THE FORCE-TO-SPACE RATIO

The force-to-space issue plays a major role among controversial issues which complicated NATO's preparations for the C.F.E. talks and which are likely to continue to have important effects on NATO policy. NATO active-duty ground-force divisions are strung out along the 750 kilometers of Federal Germany's border with East Germany and Czechoslovakia where they face a larger number of Warsaw Pact divisions. Most NATO officers argue that, depending on terrain, a modern division can cover a maximum width of thirty kilometers of defensive line. They consider that NATO's sparse quota of ground-force divisions is already stretched to a minimum. In hilly areas some divisions must cover as many as ninety kilometers. These officers point out that NATO's strategy of forward defense, intended to give maximum protection to Federal Germany's dense population, requires defending the line of potential attack along its entire length, because Pact forces could pick their point of attack anywhere along that line. If there were too few NATO divisions, then even with the stepped-up firepower of modern divisions, the forward line could be breached easily. Hence, NATO officers argue, even if the Pact offered to withdraw a very large number of its own forward-deployed divisions, NATO still could not afford to make deep cuts of its own without relinquishing the concept of forward defense at the border.

To maintain Federal German adherence to the NATO alliance, it is necessary that Germany be defended on its eastern border if conflict comes in Europe. However, as we saw in Chapter 4, other force postures that can provide effective forward defense exist. One is to use rapidly movable armored divisions as an operational reserve behind a belt of infantry, minefields, and obstacles. However, discussion of alternatives has been hindered by Federal Germany's understandable fear of damaging forward defense, and by the insistence of many NATO commanders as a matter of doctrine that armored forces, especially tanks, are the most effective and flexible component of defensive forces. The force-to-space issue is a major reason why many NATO governments entered the C.F.E. talks viewing them as a trap rather than an opportunity, and why they have been determined to hold NATO reductions to a minimum. As the talks got under way, NATO appeared to be locked by its own forward defense strategy, or at least its own current interpretation of that strategy, into continuing the East/West military confrontation at a high level.

RESIDUAL CEILINGS

Effective residual ceilings—commitments to limit the level of Pact and NATO forces after reductions—are essential to a reduction agreement. But can NATO's members agree on any?

NATO wants the negotiations in Vienna to emphasize armaments rather than manpower. It would be best to make cutbacks by units (perhaps by battalions, since these are the largest units equipped with a single major weapon), to disband or place in reserve status the units withdrawn, and to impose strict ceilings on the number of active-duty and reserve units allowed each alliance once the cutbacks are made. As we discussed in Chapter 5, cutbacks and ceilings imposed by units will be easier to verify and are a more effective way to diminish each alliance's combat potential. Unfortunately, both the United States and Federal Germany have resisted residual ceilings so that they can be free to restructure their forces after the cutbacks. If they persist in this position, the Soviet Union too may claim this right.

CAN NATO AGREE TO EXCHANGE DATA WITH THE PACT?

In the M.B.F.R. talks, NATO pressed the Warsaw Pact for a decade to enter into more detailed exchanges of data on military forces. At the Moscow summit conference in May of 1988, General Secretary Gorbachev declared the Pact's willingness to do so, and to agree to on-site verification to settle disputes. Most important, he proposed that the data exchange be used to reveal superiorities on both sides so that they can be eliminated.

As discussed in Chapter 3, at the end of 1988 and in early 1989, the two alliances published total figures on their own forces and on those of the opposing alliance. These aggregate figures revealed many differences between the estimates of the two alliances. But aggregate totals are of no value in resolving such differences. For that purpose, each alliance must lay out its own complete force deployment, unit by unit, giving the current strength of each unit in men and major weapons. By comparing the detailed figures provided by the Pact with their own holdings on the same Pact units, NATO intelligence agencies can identify the areas of major discrepancy for further discussion and possible on-site inspection.

In late 1988, after arduous discussion, NATO's members at last reached an agreement on the data they would be willing to exchange in Vienna. But they decided not to carry out a general data exchange in the conventional force-reduction talks but rather in the parallel C.D.E.-2 talks on confidence-building measures. Data would be exchanged in the force-reduction talks, but only for those armaments to be reduced after participants had agreed on them. Immobilized by fears that disputes over data would derail the new force-reduction talks as they derailed the old—not a repugnant outcome to some NATO governments, but one that could be politically costly—NATO seemed unable to capitalize on the important changes in the Soviet and Pact position. Indeed, France and other NATO countries objected to exchanging data on aircraft with the Pact in any forum, arguing that to do so could imply that NATO has changed its mind about making cutbacks of aircraft.

Moreover, as the C.F.E. talks began, NATO diplomats were in the midst of controversy with NATO intelligence experts, who resisted being drawn into a data-exchange process that either could obligate them to reveal intelligence methods and sources or make their work appear inadequate to western publics. The resulting hesitation and indecisiveness on the data issue has tarnished NATO's prestige and may tarnish it still more.

VERIFICATION

Verifying compliance with the force-reduction agreements made in Vienna will probably be harder than verifying compliance with the I.N.F. treaty or even a START treaty. After the weapons that will be subject to cutbacks are withdrawn, tens of thousands of weapons just like them, most of them highly mobile, will remain in service. Making sure that they do not exceed the limits set for them will require intensive, intrusive inspection, both on-site and from airplanes and helicopters. Yet many NATO governments seem more apprehensive of opening their territory to the Pact for purposes of verification than interested in having the Pact open its territory to them. Already, France and Turkey, both with relatively limited experience in arms control and with a tradition of maintaining close hold on military information, have shown concern about intrusive verification by the Pact. The United States, with no territory of its own in the reduction area, tends to be more eager for tough verification measures as applied to the Soviets than many of its allies. Despite the need for intensive verification, NATO seems to want to exempt many sensitive sites from inspection, a problem that is also plaguing American and Soviet negotiators in the talks on strategic nuclear reductions. The debate within NATO on verification also promises to be long and difficult.

ONE REDUCTION AREA OR SUB-REGIONS?

The members of NATO had great difficulty in deciding among themselves whether the talks should deal with the area from the Atlantic to the Urals as a single region or divide it into sub-regions. Looked at superficially this is a trivial question. But in reality it is not. Any division of the Atlantic-to-the-Urals area will probably require extended East/West negotiation, because the division has a direct bearing on the ratio of East/West reductions and the question of which forces are cut back most.

Setting up sub-regions is a good way of focussing reductions on Soviet forward-deployed forces in eastern Europe, and for preventing excessive concentration of forces once reduced. Sub-regions could also be a means of breaking up the C.F.E. talks into more easily negotiated phases or segments. For example, the Soviets might agree more readily to scale down their superiority in tanks if the first reduction can be limited to their Western Theater of Military Operations—eastern Europe plus the adjoining Western Military Districts of the U.S.S.R.— than if they are asked to agree to pull tanks out in the whole of their territory west of the Urals in a single very large cut.

There are other reasons for subdividing the area from the Atlantic to the Urals. The security problems of NATO's Central Front are different from those of the northern and southern flanks. On the Central Front NATO is primarily interested in cutting back the Pact's superiority in forward-deployed ground forces, especially armored forces. But Norway, to the north, cares less about Soviet tanks—which do not immediately threaten it—than about the large number of armed helicopters deployed by the Soviets on the Kola Peninsula. Denmark is most concerned about the Pact's amphibious forces. Turkey, on the southern flank, feels threatened both by the Pact's air forces and its amphibious forces. Yet at the urging of the United States, NATO had agreed to eliminate naval and amphibious forces from the scope of negotiation and to withhold any action on aircraft reductions until a later stage of negotiation. This conflict in interests might be settled if NATO could more flexibly negotiate different reduction programs for different sub-regions.

How sub-regions should be drawn also raises conflicts of political interest among NATO member states. Consider Federal Germany, for example. It has two main national goals in the current talks. The first is to decrease the capacity of the Soviets to attack the Central Front using forces deployed from eastern Europe or the Western Military Districts of the U.S.S.R. The second is to avoid being saddled with treaty restrictions not shared by at least one other major member of the European Community. This is the "special-zone" or "singularity" objection that NATO heard from Federal Germany in the M.B.F.R. talks, on the question of deploying American I.N.F. in western Europe, on the question of deploying American binary chemical weapons in Europe, and also on the need for eliminating tactical-range nuclear weapons or reducing their number.

During NATO's preparations for the C.F.E. talks, Federal Germany urged establishing a central sub-region inside the Atlantic-to-the-Urals area, to be composed of France, the Federal Republic, the Benelux countries, East Germany, Czechoslovakia, Poland, and the three Western Military Districts of the U.S.S.R. Intrinsically, it was a reasonable proposal. As we have seen, this area contains the bulk of forces on each side that would be involved in at least the early stages of war in the vital central European region.

But France would not agree to become part of such a zone. Just as Federal Germany resisted being treated differently from France, France did not want to be treated differently from the United Kingdom, the other major member of the European Community. So France suggested a sub-region to be composed of France, the U.K., the Federal Republic, Italy, the Benelux countries, Spain, Portugal, and Denmark in the West and most of the U.S.S.R. to the Urals in the East. With the exception of Denmark, the NATO portion of this sub-region would consist of the membership of the Western European Union, the defense grouping of western European countries that was the precursor of NATO. (France has been pressing its European allies to revive the Union as they integrate their defense activities—ultimately perhaps, if the effort is successful, as a substitute for all or part of NATO.)

NATO wavered over France's suggestion. Some NATO countries, like Italy, resisted France's plan to bolster the Western European Union. Norway and Iceland objected to being isolated from the remainder of NATO. Turkey in the south was especially unhappy about being excluded.

American officials wanted no formal sub-region in the Atlantic-to-the-Urals area. They urged that the alliance press for parity with the Warsaw Pact in tanks, artillery, and armored troop carriers in the entire Atlantic-to-the-Urals area and that it seek to restrict Soviet deployments in eastern Europe by negotiating additional ceilings on foreign forces stationed in the territory of their allies.

In particular, the United States wished to avoid establishing sub-regions for NATO's northern and southern flank countries. Establishing sub-regions might lead to separate reduction programs for them. The United States feared that separate programs for the northern and southern flanks would intensify the desires of Norway and Turkey to insist on cutbacks in naval, amphibious, and air forces—cutbacks already strongly urged by the Soviet Union and its allies and determinedly resisted by the United States and some other NATO members.

But strong resistance to treating the Atlantic-to-Urals area as a single unit came from France. Top French leaders viewed the goal of seeking alliance-to-alliance parity in a single Atlantic-to-the-Urals reduction area as implying that the C.F.E. talks are being conducted bloc-to-bloc. They wished to avoid any hint that France was reentering NATO's integrated command through the back door of integrated negotiation.

French leaders have feared that such an implication could shake the delicate right/center/left defense consensus in France and make the French military posture the subject of intense domestic argument, as has occurred in Federal Germany.

For these reasons, France has insisted that, contrary to all appearances, the C.F.E. negotiations are not being conducted between the two military alliances but rather among twenty-three individual countries who happen to be members of the two alliances—sixteen NATO countries and seven Warsaw Pact countries. Therefore, France also insisted in the preparations for C.F.E. that NATO refrain from proposals establishing overall parity between NATO and the Pact in reduced armaments. Instead, France argued, NATO should speak in terms of reducing forces to limits expressed in terms of percentages of the total armament holdings of the two alliances combined together.

Some French officials also argued that parity in conventional forces between the two alliances was undesirable, because it might undermine the rationale for NATO's nuclear deterrent forces. This rationale, they said, is stronger for western publics when it is clear that the Pact possesses conventional superiority. It is evident that when this French argument against parity is combined with French insistence that further reductions of NATO's nuclear forces should not take place until the Pact makes deep conventional reductions, the result can only be a vicious circle of inaction.

NATO DISCIPLINE OR NATIONAL SOVEREIGNTY—HOW THE WEST IS CONDUCTING THE C.F.E. TALKS

An important reason why France refused to join the M.B.F.R. talks was its unwillingness to subject itself to the tight internal discipline that the twelve NATO states participating had imposed on themselves. The "Ad Hoc Group" of NATO M.B.F.R. negotiators in Vienna closely followed instructions agreed by the NATO Council, reported to the NATO Council, and coordinated the full text of each statement they made to Warsaw Pact negotiators on the basis of complete consensus.

This procedure effectively assured the alliance's unity during fifteen years of M.B.F.R. negotiations, but it was slow and cumbersome, and it wholly excluded individual national initiative vis-à-vis the Warsaw Pact. France, observing the conduct of the M.B.F.R. negotiations from the vantage point of its continuing membership in the NATO Council, found this NATO lockstep repugnant and felt that submitting to it would be tantamount to reentering NATO's integrated structure.

Moreover, as we saw in the last chapter, France was a moving force behind convening the first Stockholm C.D.E. conference, the forum for discussion of confidence-building measures in Europe organized within the framework of the Helsinki C.S.C.E. process. And it was France who led the successful effort by western European countries and the United States to persuade General Secretary Brezhnev to include Soviet territory as far east as the Urals within the scope of the Stockholm C.D.E. conference.

France again had its way on methods of coordinating the positions of the NATO states participating in the C.D.E. conference. This coordination was left to a group of officials from national capitals. Although this group met, to be sure, at NATO headquarters in Brussels, it took the place of the NATO Council in working out the terms of western policy for the talks. Instead of the formal directives that the NATO Council had sent to M.B.F.R. negotiators, representatives of the NATO countries at the Stockholm conference received their instructions from their home capitals, based on guidelines developed by this special group. And rather than plan each western statement to the last word, the representatives at the Stockholm talks met in a NATO caucus for a loose coordination of positions that did not preclude the presentation of divergent national views.

At the outset of the C.D.E. talks, the United States, which saw advantages in more flexible procedures and wished to assure French participation in these new negotiations, went along. For the most part, the procedures were successful. But toward the end of the Stockholm conference, the United States became dissatisfied with the pressures that the nonaligned countries brought to bear on representatives of both alliances to compromise. And it was irritated by France's actions on a number of issues. One was France's refusal to permit explicit reference in the negotiations to the NATO alliance and to NATO positions. Another was France's refusal, which eventually won out, to back a position favored by the United States and most NATO members to use the aircraft and pilots of European neutral countries rather than of host countries in carrying out on-site inspections of Warsaw Pact countries as well as of NATO countries.

Nonetheless, at the outset of NATO's preparations for the C.F.E. talks, France insisted as a precondition for its participation in these new talks that the procedures of the Stockholm conference govern NATO's conduct at C.F.E. Accordingly, a "High Level Task Force" of officials from national capitals was formed to work out negotiating strategy for the allies. At that point the United States asked for changes. One of its proposals—for tightened discipline among NATO participants in the C.F.E. talks based on the M.B.F.R. model—was only partially successful. The United States also argued that the new talks were potentially more far-reaching, with more direct consequences for the alliance's security, than the Stockholm conference, which had focussed on the exchange of information. Therefore it insisted that the force-reduction talks be conducted between the two alliances, without participation of the neutral and nonaligned countries, and in a forum wholly separate from the Helsinki process, whose requirement of periodic review could impose artificial negotiating deadlines.

France did not agree. In making its original proposal for what became the Stockholm Conference on Security- and Confidence-building Measures in Europe (C.D.E.), France had proposed a second phase of negotiations within the framework of the Helsinki process to deal with force reductions. Moreover, France rejected a separate alliance-to-alliance forum as creating the unacceptable and inaccurate impression that France was moving back to NATO's integrated command. In the French view, the new force reduction conference should be subordinate to and under the authority of the Helsinki process. Even more, the new conference should be directed by consensus among the participants of the C.D.E. talks on confidence-building measures—which would also continue, although in Vienna—including their neutral and non-aligned members.

The stage was set for a two-year debate between French and United States representatives in national capitals, at Brussels, and also in the third C.S.C.E. review conference in Vienna. In time, the United States conceded that the agenda for the new force-reduction talks could be set by the C.S.C.E. review conference. But it continued to argue that the force-reduction talks be separate and distinct from the conference on confidence-building measures and that they exclude the neutrals and non-aligned countries. For its part, France agreed that the participants in the force-reduction talks could be limited to the members of NATO and the Warsaw Pact. But it prevailed in its insistence that the new talks not be referred to as alliance-to-alliance negotiations and that the participants should simply be listed alphabetically—"Belgium, Bulgaria," etc.—and spoken of collectively as "the group of twenty-three."

Over time the Franco–American dispute narrowed to the issue of the organizational connection between the C.F.E. force-reduction talks, the C.D.E. confidence-building talks, and the C.S.C.E. process of continuing negotiations on security, economics, and human contacts. It was finally decided that the C.F.E. negotiators in Vienna should report to the C.S.C.E. review conference, rather than to C.D.E.-2, as their supervisory organization, and that the nonaligned and neutral participants in C.D.E.-2 could inform themselves of the course of the force-reduction negotiations and have their views heard there.

Those familiar with the record of past NATO differences will not be surprised by these struggles. Although they lasted longer than many comparable disputes, the NATO alliance has survived far worse ones, including the traumas of France's withdrawal from NATO's integrated command, the shift of NATO headquarters from Paris to Brussels, and the ongoing debate over flexible response. It was able, too, to overcome these difficulties in preparing for the force-reduction talks. But the effort to find a common denominator between American and French positions on the proper forum for the talks absorbed a great deal of time and energy of NATO officials throughout the system—time that might have been better spent working out NATO's position.

In September of 1988 François Mitterrand, having been reelected president of France six months earlier, declared his intention of focussing his second six-year term on arms control and implied that France might relax its opposition to the reduction in American (but not French) tactical-range nuclear weapons in Europe in exchange for similar Soviet reductions. A slight relaxation of some of the more extreme French positions on the force-reduction talks followed. However, concerns that the United States might be withdrawing from responsibility for Europe's defense and that Federal Germany might be drifting toward neutrality remain central in French thinking and will result in France's continued balkiness in the C.F.E. talks unless the United States finds ways to reassure its ally, at least as regards the first of these worries.

The NATO states were well aware at the outset that bringing France into European arms-control efforts would be difficult and would entail costs, and this has certainly been the case. But at least the process has been started. And, fortunately, it has been started in a period of decreased East/West tensions. Moreover, France has been right to support the Helsinki C.S.C.E. process so ardently, and the United States wrong to oppose it, although France has been right for the wrong reasons.

In actuality, France has been striving to preserve the appearance of sovereignty free of excessive dependence on the American superpower in NATO. In part, it has sought to make sure that the force-reduction talks would have no risky outcome—meaning, given France's hyper-caution, no outcome at all. In part, France has tried to keep the force-reduction talks within the framework of the Helsinki C.S.C.E. process out of pride of authorship. It has clung to its original vision of the C.D.E. conference as a two-stage negotiation, first of confidence-building measures and second of disarmament.

The right reason for fitting the new force-reduction talks into the C.S.C.E. process is over time to build that process of continuing East/West discussion into enduring institutions. If present trends in East/West relations continue, the C.S.C.E. structure is likely to provide a useful basis on which to construct a rudimentary pan-European security system. If the C.F.E. force-reduction talks and the C.D.E.-2 conference on confidence-building measures are successful, they will lead to yet more negotiations on building down the NATO/Pact confrontation. There will be a practical need for common East/West institutions to handle notices of upcoming military activities, coordinate visits by observers, deal with matters of verification and compliance, and help reduce the risk of conflict, by keeping crises from developing.

In the still longer term, the patterns of cooperation arising from working together on the three "baskets" of the Helsinki process—security and human rights in Europe; cooperation on economics, science, and the environment; and humanitarian issues (personal and group contacts, culture, and education)—can provide the skeleton for common East/West institutions. In this process the countries of Europe, East and West, can have a greater say than they would in military alliances dominated by two superpowers, although these alliances will, in all probability, also continue and the superpowers themselves participate in the C.S.C.E. process.

The disagreement within NATO over the appropriateness of the Helsinki process as a framework for the new force-reduction talks, over the acceptability of East/West parity as a conceptual basis for the talks, and over the use of the Western European Union as a basis for subregions inside the Atlantic-to-the-Urals area, as well as over further reductions in nuclear weapons, is also symptomatic of disagreement over a much larger issue, the future shape of defense cooperation in the West. The struggle, less unequal than it may appear at first sight, is between a renascent France pressing for a European defense grouping and a United States somewhat diminished in prestige and authority pressing for the preservation of NATO in its traditional form. Later in this book we shall suggest measures to deal with these frictions.

Such evident and protracted internecine debate in NATO would plausibly be a fruitful target for Soviet exploitation. But aside from occasional displays of amusement at the squabbling by NATO negotiators in Vienna over the terms of the mandates for the C.F.E. and C.D.E.-2 talks, the Soviet Union and its Warsaw Pact allies largely showed restraint. Apparently, as in the case of their relative flexibility on the issue of exclusion of nuclear weapons from the C.F.E. mandate, the Soviets were more interested in an end to the squabbling so that the talks could begin.

NATO DECIDES

In December of 1988 the NATO countries announced the general approach that they planned to advance when the C.F.E. talks started the following March. That approach was made more specific and many details added in the position paper for the C.F.E. talks published by NATO on March 6, 1989, the eve of the talks' formal opening on March 9. (Texts are in Appendix VIII.)

NATO proposed reduction in the number of main battle tanks, artillery, and armored troop carriers of both alliances to a level about 10 percent below NATO's current holdings for tanks and 5 percent for artillery. ("Armored troop carriers" are a new category combining more heavily armed infantry-fighting vehicles with armored personnel carriers. Until NATO and the Pact work out their existing differences in defining this category of armaments, specific reduction percentages cannot be calculated, but the proposed NATO reduction here, too, appears under 5 percent of present holdings.) NATO did not include in its reduction proposals the attack aircraft, combat helicopters, or tactical-range surface-to-surface missiles whose reduction was proposed by the Pact, nor did NATO's reduction approach provide for cuts in active-duty military manpower as proposed by the Pact. The initial phase of the new negotiations revolved around these differences.

For main battle tanks, NATO proposed cutbacks to 20,000 for each alliance. Artillery would be reduced to an equal ceiling of 16,500 and armored troop carriers to an equal ceiling of about 33,000 per alliance with a sub-limit of 12,000 for the armored infantry-fighting vehicles of each alliance. NATO's approach is complicated in its details. It is made somewhat harder to understand by a residue of French efforts to structure the NATO approach so that it would minimize impressions of alliance-to-alliance negotiation or of parity between the alliances. Here we set forth the NATO position in a way that seems most clear.

In the Atlantic-to-the-Urals area taken as a whole, NATO proposed parity between the two alliances at a level of 20,000 for tanks; 16,500 for artillery; and 28,000 for armored troop carriers, plus a limit of 12,000 for armored infantry-fighting vehicles. (This proposal for over-all parity is listed as Limit 4(1) in NATO's proposal; in it, France finally conceded in practice that the NATO allies could explicitly ask for equality with the Pact in reduced armaments.)

NATO also proposed six separate sub-limits on tanks, artillery, and armored troop carriers in addition to these overall parity ceilings. Each of these sub-limits is described in the next chapter, but two in particular are mentioned here.

The first was a "sufficiency limit," whereby no single country in either alliance could have more than 60 percent of its alliance's permitted total of tanks, artillery, or armored troop carriers. The specific limits were 12,000 tanks; 10,000 artillery pieces; and 16,800 armored troop carriers. This is Rule 2 of the NATO position paper. (In deference to the French position, NATO stated the single-country ceiling on tanks, artillery, and armored troop carriers as 30 percent of the total armament holdings of the two alliances combined. This translates to 60 percent of the total quota to be held by each of the alliances after reductions.) The purpose of this restriction is to hold down the U.S.S.R.'s portion of the total number of reduced armaments permitted to the Warsaw Pact. It would amount, in practice, to a national sub-limit on Soviet forces without any NATO country under-taking a comparable obligation.

The second sub-limit would apply to the armaments deployed by alliance members on the territory of other alliance states (tanks, 3,200; artillery, 1,700; and armored troop carriers, 6,000). This limitation would serve to hold down Soviet forward deployments in eastern Europe.

The NATO proposal also contained a provision for annual data exchange on holdings of reduced armaments—main battle tanks, artillery pieces, and armored troop carriers—down to the battalion level and on personnel in combat and combat-support units. "Combat support" is a category that includes combat engineers, signals, commu-nications, and so on. The position paper also provided that notice be given of changes in unit structures above the battalion level and of increases in the personnel of such units. This notification provision substitutes for a residual ceiling on units of the type reduced.

This was the only data-exchange proposal that NATO made for the C.F.E. talks. (As noted, NATO proposed a more general exchange of data for the C.D.E.-2 talks on confidence- and security-building measures.) The NATO position paper stated that there would be a need for verification arrangements, to include the exchange of detailed data about forces and deployments, the right to conduct on-site inspection, and other measures designed to assure compliance. But the position paper gave no details of these measures.

The NATO paper also stated that there would be a need for stabilizing measures, to include measures of transparency, notification, and constraint, applied to the deployment, movement, storage, and levels of readiness of conventional forces, including their armaments and equipment. Again, the paper gave no details. As with verification, NATO had not yet developed specific proposals when the C.F.E. talks opened.

NATO's position paper suggested that there would be a need for non-circumvention provisions, *inter alia*, to ensure that the manpower and equipment withdrawn from any one area would not have adverse security implications for any participant. This measure echoed an M.B.F.R. measure introduced at the request of the NATO flank states, which continue to wish to prevent an increase in Soviet forces on their own borders as the result of negotiated withdrawals.

NATO's March, 1989, position paper ended with the same generally worded points as the December, 1988, NATO communiqué. It stated that if NATO's proposals were implemented, NATO would "be willing to contemplate" further reductions in conventional armaments and, as we discussed in Chapter 4, "the restructuring of armed forces to enhance defensive capabilities and further to reduce offensive capabilities." Given NATO's internal agreement to limit its own reductions, the position paper made no reference beyond this generally worded one to further reductions in the NATO/Warsaw Pact confrontation.

In the remainder of this chapter we shall consider NATO's position on reductions. In Chapter 8 we shall take a harder look at other elements of the NATO program.

NATO'S AIMS IN THE NEW NEGOTIATIONS

Looking at the formidable array of differences among NATO countries described in this chapter, many of which were only superficially laid to rest in NATO's March, 1989, position paper, it is possible to conclude that NATO cannot unite to negotiate effectively and that the force-reduction talks will not be successful. Such a conclusion would go too far. Nonetheless, the description of allied differences presented in this chapter does appear to justify the conclusion that NATO will find it difficult to take the initiative at C.F.E. If the talks are to move forward, they will probably have to follow the pattern of the Stockholm C.D.E. conference and of the I.N.F. negotiations, in which the West took a demanding and rigid position and the Soviet Union moved toward that position, in the long run accepting most of it.

In practice, NATO members settled on four main objectives for the C.F.E. talks: to reduce the Pact's capacity to launch a surprise attack; to reduce the Pact's capacity to initiate any large-scale offensive action; to avoid any negotiated outcome that diminishes NATO's present degree of security; and, specifically, to eliminate the Pact's superiorities in tanks, artillery, and armored troop carriers.

As we have seen, NATO in effect proposed parity between the two alliances in tanks, artillery, and armored troop carriers, by urging that the numbers of these armaments be cut back by both alliances to a new equal level 5 to 10 percent less than NATO's current holdings.

The concept of parity between East and West has unassailable status in the West's approach to arms control. As the term was developed in nuclear arms control, "parity" is not exact equality, which would imply identically organized and equipped forces on both sides, but rough equality between forces that are somewhat differently constituted. In the SALT talks and in the START negotiations, in M.B.F.R. and in I.N.F., the United States and its NATO allies have pressed the concept of parity as a major western goal. As regards the C.F.E. talks, they have done so with considerable success. The reduction approach for C.F.E. outlined by General Secretary Gorbachev at the 1988 Moscow summit—data exchange followed by the elimination of asymmetries or imbalances—is an implicit acceptance of the idea of parity at the level of the numerically weaker state, and Soviet acceptance of this idea became more explicit in the early stages of C.F.E.

Parity with the Pact should certainly be one of NATO's main negotiating requirements in the C.F.E. talks. If Warsaw Pact numerical superiorities in tanks, artillery, and armored troop carriers can be eliminated and the holdings of both alliances brought into balance at a new level after a small NATO reduction, this would be an enormous stride forward. Given the Pact's forthcoming proposal for Phase I reductions, the prospects for reaching agreement on initial reductions of this kind seem quite good.

But if parity in these three armaments is a highly desirable goal for NATO in the C.F.E. talks, is it a sufficient goal? Early in this book, we suggested that it is not, and there are strong reasons for that conclusion. We have already mentioned France's concerns over the implications of parity for the position of France in the alliance. NATO military commanders also have tacit objections to parity, but different ones. They see in parity once achieved a slippery slope toward further reductions that could undermine NATO's forward-defense strategy, by leaving the alliance with too few divisions to cover NATO's long frontier with the Pact, especially in central Europe. We have sought to show that there are ways to cope with this concern by restructuring forces. That parity provides a useful basis for further reductions in the East/West military confrontation in Europe after initial cutbacks should be regarded as a considerable advantage, rather than as a drawback.

A major reason why NATO's starting position in the C.F.E. force-reduction talks was inadequate was that the achievement of parity in tanks, artillery, and armored troop carriers will not by itself decisively reduce the risks of the East/West military confrontation in Europe. Parity in these three armaments alone, leaving untouched the Pact's superiority in surface-to-surface missiles, combat aircraft, and armed helicopters and without making provision for early-warning measures and constraints on deployments, would not of itself eliminate the risk of surprise attack by Pact forces or necessarily bring increased stability to the confrontation.

Even if these remaining Pact armament superiorities could be dealt with, rough equality between the two alliances could, in some circumstances, create more, rather than fewer, dangers: Warsaw Pact forces only as strong as those of NATO could still launch a surprise attack, choosing their point of concentration and entry along NATO's thin defensive line. However, parity between the forces of the alliances in selected armaments would for the first time create the possibility of successful NATO attack on the Warsaw Pact. In future crises, Pact commanders could be as uneasy as NATO commanders now are over unexplained activities of forces of the opposing alliance. The gains and the inducements for preemptive action would increase for both sides, and there might be less rather than more stability. With the still very large forces of both sides similarly equipped with heavy armor, mobile artillery, armed helicopters, fighter-bombers, and missiles, the European confrontation might even more easily than at present be triggered into explosive conflict by human error or miscalculation or the pressure of outside events—events outside Europe or widespread unrest in eastern Europe.

Moreover, in a situation of parity, each alliance would be even more sensitive to force improvements in the other than it now is, and arms-race competition might intensify. And there would be no reduction in the enormous costs of the confrontation, at least not for NATO, after the minimum reduction in NATO forces that NATO now envisages.

Thus parity could be a recipe for indefinite continuation of the East/West confrontation without real diminishment of its risks and costs. In this sense, parity should be supplemented with broader reductions of further types of force components, with early-warning measures, and with negotiated restrictions on deployments—and by mutual commitments to make deeper cuts.

To summarize, as matters stood when the NATO countries entered the C.F.E. talks, the NATO position had several weaknesses:

1. NATO was placing a low limit of about 5 to 10 percent on reduction of its own forward-deployed tanks, artillery, and armored personnel carriers. This could be an internal floor on NATO reductions, without relationship to how many forces the Warsaw Pact was prepared to reduce.

2. Even if it could be negotiated with the Pact, the NATO position would not decisively reduce the possibility of conflict between the alliances by miscalculation or through the impact of outside events. For this purpose, early-warning and constraint measures are needed. But the NATO approach presented at the outset of the C.F.E. talks contained no proposals for early-warning measures or for constraints on forward Pact deployment of especially threatening armaments, munitions, or equipment.

3. At the outset, NATO was refusing to reduce the number of tactical-range surface-to-surface missiles, where the Pact has a ten-to-one advantage over NATO, or combat aircraft, where the Pact also has numerical superiority, although the Pact itself had proposed such reductions. These are precisely the armaments which the Pact would use with decisive effect at the outset of an attack against NATO.

4. The initial NATO approach did not provide for residual ceilings on reduced units or for manpower reductions, or for controls on continued production in the reduction area of armaments of the type reduced. Pact forces could build up after initial cuts. Other

      than a cut of armaments, there were no controls on Soviet reserve
      or mobilization capacity.

5. The NATO approach at the outset of C.F.E. did not provide for
      full and detailed data exchange early in the C.F.E. talks or for
      other measures to monitor the unilateral reductions announced
      by Gorbachev, to assure against the non-return of these forces
      and to develop more precise knowledge of remaining Pact forces
      and, above all, to make joint preparations from the outset for the
      arduous task of verification.

Just as important as any one of these faults of design, by setting a
high floor on its own reductions and rejecting manpower reductions,
the initial NATO approach in C.F.E. would do little or nothing to
reduce the costs of the NATO/Pact confrontation.

THE NEED FOR NATO GOALS

For the new C.F.E. talks to succeed, the countries of the western
coalition will have to have some more general vision of a long-range
outcome. They need a formula that can be understood by western
political and public opinion—one that will exploit to the full the
opportunity created by the reform movement in the Soviet Union
during the possibly limited period while that reform movement remains
at its peak. They need a negotiating objective that can sustain for a
considerable period the commitment of the public and national leaders
alike and provide the continuity of political interest needed to cut
through tough negotiating problems and bring the whole unwieldy
negotiating enterprise to a fruitful result. NATO leaders need a
negotiating concept that will compel them to go beyond the tendency of
many of them to view their task as merely to manage a continuing East/
West military confrontation in Europe. It is necessary to have such a
concept to proceed rationally and effectively even with first-stage
reductions.

Earlier in this book, we gave reasons why the East/West military
confrontation has become obsolete as the cold-war political conflicts
that gave rise to it have seeped away. The confrontation is overdue for
dismantling. The emergence of a reform-minded Soviet leadership has
provided the opportunity to do so.

We can conclude that the overriding NATO objective for the C.F.E.
talks should be to build down an increasingly nonfunctional NATO/

Warsaw Pact military confrontation in a controlled, safe way, assuring undiminished security and diminished risk for NATO as the reductions are made.

How far should a build-down be expected to go? It does not seem productive now to think of the ultimate shape of the East/West military relationship in Europe and of minimum force deployments under that concept. Neither side is ready to move toward a completely disarmed Europe. The Soviets themselves are not proposing a demilitarized Europe, but cuts which would leave them with something more than half of their current forces. There is still too much mutual suspicion and too much justifiable doubt whether the positive changes in the Soviet Union will continue. Instead, we have to think of some intermediate position between the present levels of confrontation and a disarmed state of assured peace and stability in Europe. We can define this intermediate position as an equal plateau of reduced military effort that western countries can comfortably occupy for a decade or more with less stress, risk and cost as they observe the evolution of the Soviet system and Soviet policy toward the West.

If there is to be such a plateau, at what level should it be set? NATO entered the C.F.E. talks proposing a 5 to 10 percent reduction in its current deployment of tanks, artillery, and armored troop carriers. NATO cuts of this limited size are certainly acceptable for a first phase of cuts eliminating large Pact numerical superiorities and bringing the Pact down to equality with NATO at the new levels. But they are not adequate if the objective is a serious build-down of the NATO/Pact confrontation in Europe. Post stage-one armed forces of nearly three million men on a side, armed with 20,000 tanks and four thousand aircraft of the most modern design after destruction of old models and with thousands of nuclear weapons, are not yet a recipe for stability. The Pact has been suggesting a 25 percent reduction of manpower and armaments after elimination of asymmetries through initial cuts of 10 to 15 percent, for a total reduction of its forces of 35 to 40 percent from their own current levels. That, too, is not enough. On the analogy of the strategic arms talks (START), a 50 percent reduction by NATO, with Pact forces cut back to the new NATO levels, would be a reasonable level for that plateau.

A further major objective for NATO (and for the Pact) that would give the entire enterprise more impetus would be to make deep cuts in the current costs of the confrontation. A reasonable goal for the West would be to achieve by the year 2000, through negotiated reductions and other savings, a drop in current western expenditures for the defense of Europe of at least 30 percent. Engaging public and political interest on both sides in the prospect of real savings from negotiated force-reductions will generate pressures on the leadership of both sides to achieve results. This would also help to avoid the main shortcoming of the unsuccessful M.B.F.R. talks: the absence of sustained interest of political leaders in achieving results.

Briefly stated, the long-term objective for the new talks proposed here is to create over the next decade a safer, less costly plateau for the military confrontation in Europe, by making a 50 percent cutback in major NATO weapons and military manpower, with Pact forces reduced to the new NATO level, and by cutting NATO's expenditures by 30 percent.

Because deep cuts to equal levels are not by themselves an adequate assurance of increased stability, yet another major objective of the talks should be to insulate the NATO/Pact confrontation against the shocks of external events and human error, and to reduce incentives to preemptive action in crises. A system of early-warning measures and force constraints would help to achieve this.

Applying the conclusions of our review in Chapter 4 of the organization of Pact and NATO forces, the talks should also move the alliances, as they appear to agree should be the case, toward a more defensive configuration of their forces. This can be accomplished by designing reductions so that they will cut most deeply into offensive armaments and so that they will compel the alliances to restructure their remaining forces in ways that favor defensive over offensive elements. The outcome of 50 percent reductions should be a situation where neither alliance has enough offensive strength to prevail over the defensive strength of the other.

Both alliances have agreed to include among the agreed objectives of C.F.E. the elimination of capacity for large-scale offensive action. Moreover, as we have reported here, both alliances have explicitly adopted as a long-term goal restructuring their forces to a more defensive mode. If the alliances are serious about these aims, they should seek to implement them from the outset of negotiated reductions rather than at their end.

Doing so would mean not only cutting deployments of tanks, artillery, and armored troop carriers, but also cutting three other weapons systems that are also more valuable for offense than defense and in which the Pact has numerical superiority which it is apparently willing to reduce: combat helicopters, surface-to-surface missiles, and aircraft used to attack ground targets. And it would mean making no reduction in deployments of defensive armaments such as anti-tank and anti-aircraft weapons.

Thus we can add to our concise statement of the goal NATO should pursue in the talks. The equal plateau sought after deep cuts should be one on which the forces of both sides are restructured in a defensive mode.

It is not the job of the NATO countries to become deeply involved in Soviet domestic reform. But it is to their clear advantage to seek to consolidate trends in Soviet foreign policy that ease the strain on western defense and decrease the military threat the Soviets pose to the West. In the C.F.E. talks the West has a chance both to reinforce positive trends in the U.S.S.R. and to build delays involving long periods of time to any renewal of negative trends.

Earlier in this chapter, we discussed the rapidly changing situation in eastern Europe as one reason for possible Soviet caution in agreeing to deep negotiated cuts in forward-deployed Soviet forces. Under the impact of the Gorbachev reform movement, the whole of eastern Europe is today in ferment. Over the next decade, the most likely trigger for war in Europe is widespread, uncontrollable unrest in one or more eastern European countries. Suitably designed arms-control agreements will decrease the possibility of East/West conflict arising from unrest, from a crisis mentality, and from misperception of the military activities of the adversary alliance. Arms control is not part of the problem in eastern Europe, but part of the solution. This is a major reason for western interest in concluding such agreements and doing so soon.

The instability in eastern Europe is already there. The West has no interest in maintaining the internal status quo in eastern European countries; rather, it is interested in promoting change in that status quo. But East and West do share a common interest in assuring that the process of change in eastern Europe does not spill over into East/West conflict.

A well-designed arms-control regime for Europe—early-warning measures, verification, and the shift of each alliance to a more defensive posture through selective armament reductions—would decrease the likelihood of a situation in which the huge military confrontation in Europe is triggered into conflict during a crisis in eastern Europe by misperception of the military activities of the other alliance. This is, in part, what happened prior to August, 1914. The arms-control regime should provide additional treaty barriers to Soviet intervention to repress unrest in eastern Europe. It should also provide reciprocal restraints on western military activities to reduce possible fears by a nervous Soviet leadership at moments of crisis that the NATO alliance was seeking to take military advantage of the unrest; such fears could result in preemptive military actions and the beginning of war. The regime should include early-warning and observation measures for both alliances to reduce the risk of misunderstandings.

The East as well as the West can share most of the objectives just described. But NATO should also have a series of objectives of its own in the new talks.

Mikhail Gorbachev is making a real effort fundamentally to reform the Soviet system, a process which will last for decades. Moreover, he has consolidated his personal power position. Nonetheless, the question persists: how long will Gorbachev last—in good health, successfully withstanding efforts to supplant him, and without himself making important changes in his own approach in the face of failure? No one can answer these questions. It would appear that most of the plausible successors of General Secretary Gorbachev would continue the main lines of the current Gorbachev policy, motivated by continuation of the same economic problems which underlie the present policy. Nevertheless, the Soviet situation is volatile. Seizure of power by a group intent on reversion to confrontation and expansion cannot be excluded. Successful or not, an effort to reestablish a complete totalitarian regime would take considerable time after an initial coup. The western countries would receive long political warning, not least through the thousands of new personal contacts established in recent years.

Some in the West are urging that NATO deal with its uncertainties about the Soviet future by holding back on force reductions or waiting for some final outcome of the Soviet ferment. Rather than doing this, the western countries should actively use the flexibility now being shown by the Gorbachev leadership to cut back Soviet forces to such an extent and in such a way as to interpose a long period of time before a less conciliatory successor could build up his forces sufficiently to be confident about the outcome of any conflict. We should try to build maximum delay into a program of reductions and restructuring of Soviet forces, time for the western countries to react to adverse developments.

To meet these objectives, NATO should provide safeguards and insurance against negative change in Soviet policy through reductions, early-warning measures and constraints, and through a functioning NATO reserve structure and a continuing NATO nuclear deterrent. Reductions can eliminate any real possibility for successful standing-start attack by forward-deployed Soviet forces in eastern Europe. But NATO also needs an additional program of reductions and controls over Soviet reserve and mobilization capacity in the Soviet Union. Because NATO is still thinking exclusively in terms of limited cuts in its own forces and not of a more comprehensive reduction approach, it has not yet concerned itself with this issue. A successful NATO program will also decrease the ability of the Soviet Union to intimidate western Europe militarily; well-designed measures will reassure those in the west who might otherwise be apprehensive that the Soviet Union could at some point use its remaining armed forces for aggression and will increase their determination to resist possible political pressures.

In the next chapter, we will look at some initial moves by both sides which considerably increased the possibility of an early first agreement in the C.F.E. talks. We will also look at some of the remaining problems faced by C.F.E. negotiators that we have only touched on here. Applying the NATO objectives just discussed to those problems can help western negotiators solve them.

8 Negotiators' Headaches: Substantive Problems of Force Reductions

The closeness of the Warsaw Pact's opening position at the start of the C.F.E. negotiations to NATO's own position meant that the new negotiations were off to a promising start. A rapid series of moves in May, 1989, first by the Soviet Union and then by the United States, made startling progress in resolving the main issues of principle for a first C.F.E. agreement. After only three months of negotiation, participants in the C.F.E. talks had progressed about as far as the U.S. and U.S.S.R. had moved in the I.N.F. negotiations in 1986 after four full years of negotiation. As a result, an early first agreement in Vienna appeared within reach.

In the first part of this chapter, we will review the fast-moving initial stage of the C.F.E. to set the framework for a treatment of the negotiating issues which still have to be resolved before a comprehensive first agreement can be completed. Progress toward settling some of these issues is likely to be achieved in coming months, but many of them will remain topical for subsequent phases of negotiation.

The Soviet moves came first, followed by President Bush's moves at the NATO summit at the end of May, 1989.[1] Gorbachev's first substantive discussion of the C.F.E. subject matter with senior officials of the Bush administration took place during the May 10–11 visit of Secretary of State James Baker to Moscow. Foreign Minister Shevardnadze had, at the opening of the Vienna talks, indicated readiness in principle to make Soviet and Pact reductions of tanks, artillery, and armored troop carriers of at least the same general dimensions as those proposed by NATO. But in Moscow, Gorbachev presented actual figures which substantiated this agreement and made it concrete. He said the Warsaw Pact was willing to reduce its overall holdings to 20,000 tanks and 28,000 armored troop carriers, precisely the equal levels proposed by NATO for holdings of these armaments by each alliance. He said the Pact would reduce to 24,000 artillery pieces. This was more than the 16,500 proposed by NATO, but a large part of the difference might be accounted for by definitional discrepancies, as the

166

Pact had included many more weapons than NATO in its artillery total, including small caliber mortars.

Using NATO data, this would mean Warsaw Pact reductions (including unilateral cuts already announced) of 37,000 tanks, 42,000 armored troop carriers, and perhaps 30,000 artillery pieces as compared to NATO reductions of 2,200 tanks, 830 artillery pieces, and fewer than 1,000 troop carriers. These would be very large, even huge, asymmetrical cuts by the Pact. Gorbachev also proposed reducing the "strike" aircraft of both alliances to 1,500, combat helicopters to 1,700 and military personnel to 1.3 million. These force components were not then in the NATO reduction program.

The figures presented by General Secretary Gorbachev appeared to represent total reductions for both the first and the second stages of reduction proposed by Foreign Minister Shevardnadze at the beginning of March—described in the last chapter and in Appendix VII—rather than proposals for a first stage of reductions. Most of the ceilings proposed represented cuts of about 60 percent in Pact forces west of the Urals (40 percent below NATO levels, using the Pact's data for NATO forces), the total reduction for both stages of cuts proposed by the Soviets. It remained to be seen how this approach could be made to square with NATO's call for elimination of Pact superiorities in a first stage of reductions.

Gorbachev also informed Secretary Baker that the Soviet Union was ready to move on NATO's proposals, described in the last chapter, for a "sufficiency" national ceiling on Soviet forces within the Warsaw Pact total and for a limit on Soviet forces stationed in eastern Europe. Less than two weeks later, Soviet negotiators in Vienna gave specific proposed figures for these two limits. For the "sufficiency" limit (60 percent of its alliance total for any single member country) they were: 14,000 tanks, 17,000 artillery pieces, and 18,000 troop carriers, as compared with the 12,000 tanks, 10,000 artillery pieces, and 16,800 armored troop carriers proposed by NATO. The totals represented a higher percentage of the overall total permitted each alliance; for example, Moscow's proposed 14,000 tanks were 70 percent of the 20,000 tank limit, not 60 percent, but were clearly within negotiating distance of each other. For the limit on armaments stationed on the territory of other allies, the Soviets proposed a limit of 4,500 tanks, 4,000 artillery pieces, and 7,500 armored troop carriers, again quite close to NATO's proposals of 3,200 tanks, 1,700 artillery pieces, and 6,000 troop carriers.

Viewed from the perspective of the M.B.F.R. talks, where the Soviets had, as described in Chapter 5, resolutely fought off every effort to impose national limits on their forces, these Soviet concessions were remarkable. A "stationed forces" limit on Soviet forces deployed in eastern Europe would interpose a contractual barrier to reinforcing these forces either for force buildup prior to attack or to suppress local opposition in eastern Europe. The sufficiency limit would keep the total of Soviet forces deployed west of the Urals approximately equal to total NATO forces on the Central Front, making a successful full mobilization attack improbable.

Taken together, these specific Soviet proposals regarding the reductions and ceilings proposed by NATO were unambiguous evidence of a serious Soviet intention to conclude an agreement in Vienna. The tempo of these moves indicated that there was more to come and that the Soviets were aiming for an early agreement as well. Initially, NATO followed its habit of playing down Soviet moves. The White House press spokesman ill-advisedly called Gorbachev "a drugstore cowboy", a term implying flashiness and phoniness. But senior officials of the Bush administration grasped the actual significance of the Gorbachev moves and were impressed.

In fact, these Soviet moves added to the many discomforting pressures on the Bush administration, still new in office in the spring of 1989, to act more decisively on East/West issues. The administration faced a disaster at the pending NATO summit of heads of government, a meeting convened to celebrate the fortieth anniversary of a vigorous NATO alliance. NATO officials had not been able to agree on a formula to be included in the communiqué document defining long-term NATO policy which would describe when and under what conditions a possible U.S./Soviet negotiation on reducing tactical-range nuclear missiles could be held.

Unaccountably, the Bush administration had taken over without review an ill-advised effort launched in the late Reagan administration to obtain advance deployment commitments from European NATO allies for a new, extended-range Lance missile in order to assist in gaining Congressional approval to fund the new missile. What both the Reagan and Bush administrations inexplicably overlooked was that, although the other NATO nuclear powers, France and Britain, were demanding that the U.S. "compensate" for the elimination of U.S. intermediate-range missiles in the I.N.F. treaty, the situation was far different in the main NATO country which would be involved in deployment of a new Lance missile, the Federal Republic of Germany.

The I.N.F. treaty, as we saw earlier, had the effect of bringing German conservatives to a common front with the opposition Social Democrats and Greens in favor of sharply reducing tactical nuclear armaments in Germany and perhaps eliminating them. Washington overlooked this development, together with the fact that it had been these same Christian Democratic political leaders who earlier had both demanded the American I.N.F. missiles and had made possible their deployment against very strong domestic opposition. After they had shifted their position, relinquishing the view that deployment of American nuclear armaments in Germany was a necessary reassurance, there was no longer any leadership support in Federal Germany for deployment of a new Lance. In this vacuum, the opposition to deployment gained headway by leaps and bounds until Chancellor Kohl, in an isolated and much weakened position, had to signal Washington that a deployment commitment was, for a time at least, no longer possible.

The Bush administration showed good political sense in pulling back from its effort to obtain a deployment commitment and in agreeing in NATO to postpone it until 1992. But, irritated by criticism of this action from American conservatives and by a month-long silence on the subject from the Federal German government, itself caught in a deep turmoil with its Free Democratic coalition partner over the same issue, the Bush administration injudiciously allowed itself to take what appeared to be a categorical position against any negotiation on reducing tactical-range missiles, no matter at what point or stage.

The Federal German government was now immobilized over the question of whether U.S./Soviet negotiations on reducing tactical-range missiles should take place parallel with the C.F.E. talks or begin only after C.F.E. was concluded. There was agreement between the Christian Democrats and their Free Democratic coalition partners that negotiation should take place as soon as possible. Instead, the Kohl coalition was transfixed by a dispute between Christian Democrats and Free Democrats as to the goals of such a negotiation: reduction of the huge Pact numerical superiority to low equal ceilings, as with conventional armaments, or elimination of these armaments, as the Soviets and the German opposition parties were demanding. Earlier, there had been a clear Christian Democrat/Free Democrat understanding that the goal should be an equal ceiling somewhat below NATO's present level. But with the approach of the 1990 elections and the renewed possibility of their failure to qualify for representation in the Bundestag through obtaining 5 percent of the popular vote, Free Democrats, led by Foreign Minister Genscher, were having second thoughts in the direction of missile elimination.

Negotiated elimination of the missiles was supported by a large majority of the German public. But it was completely unacceptable to the NATO nuclear powers, who viewed possible failure to retain and modernize tactical missiles as a potentially decisive threshold for the elimination of all NATO nuclear armaments. (In actuality, as we will discuss in the final chapter, that threshold may turn out to be the fate of the air-launched standoff missile now planned by NATO.) As the NATO summit approached, France maintained its position opposing negotiation on tactical-range missiles but remained diplomatically silent, allowing the United States and United Kingdom to take the burden of the unpopular position of opposing early negotiation.

A pending political disaster over nuclear deployments and reductions was not the only problem of the Bush administration as the NATO summit neared. Conservative and cautious by nature, President Bush and his principal advisers were also being criticized by American and European media for a slow lackluster start of the Bush administration, especially in comparison with Gorbachev's action-packed drive toward an improved East/West relationship. All the President's advisers had been able to come up with after an intensive five-month policy review was a revival of President Eisenhower's Open Skies proposal—actually a useful move by the administration, as we will discuss in Chapter 9, but one which suffered from an absence of plans as to how the idea could be applied in practice, thus adding to the criticism of the administration for inactivity.

But at the Brussels meeting itself, aided by highly skillful handling of the media and sustained by the desire of all other NATO heads of government to make the meeting appear a success, President Bush was able to make a sudden and highly successful recovery, a recovery which converted the May 29–30 NATO summit from a likely disaster to a remarkable demonstration of renewed American leadership of the alliance.

In a surprise move, he took the initiative to put forward three suggestions for the NATO–Warsaw Pact negotiations on reducing conventional forces in Europe. NATO governments were informed of President Bush's proposals in the week before the summit and formally accepted them at the summit meeting itself, so that they are now alliance policy.

In essence, the three proposals were:

1. Land-based combat aircraft and helicopters should be included in

negotiated reductions and cut to an equal level 15 percent below current NATO levels.

2. United States and Soviet ground and air force personnel should be reduced to an equal level of 275,000 men in the Central European sub-region.

3. The timetable for reaching a NATO-Pact agreement on force reductions should be accelerated in order to achieve agreement within six to twelve months.

Of these moves, the President's proposal to reduce combat aircraft and helicopters is the most important. As we have seen, since the outset of C.F.E., the Soviets had insisted that combat aircraft be reduced as part of an overall agreement eliminating the Warsaw Pact's large superiorities in tanks, artillery, and armored troop carriers. It is likely that they would have made inclusion of aircraft reductions a requirement for any C.F.E. agreement. Moreover, given that the agreed aim of the new Vienna talks is to reduce the capacity of either side to attack, it is wholly logical to include in reductions aircraft and helicopters, which are essential to the success of any offensive operation.

President Bush's aircraft reduction proposal has eliminated an estimated two years of debate within NATO about when to move on this subject and thus brought closer an early East/West agreement. The President's suggestion that the aircraft cut be 15 percent of current levels corresponds to the dimensions of the first-stage cut proposed by the Pact and should be acceptable to it.

But a 15 percent cut of what? As the initial phase of negotiation closed, there was no East/West agreement on which aircraft will be reduced by both sides. The Soviet Union has counted ground-attack aircraft and fighter-bombers on both sides but excluded its own medium bombers and the very large number of Warsaw Pact interceptor aircraft deployed in the Atlantic-to-Urals area. It claims NATO has about 4,000 such "attack" aircraft and the Pact about 2,800. (For Pact figures, see Appendix I.) If in a first-stage reduction, the Pact cut 500 aircraft to a common ceiling for each alliance of 2,380, NATO would have to reduce over 1,500.

For its part, NATO was counting in its data on Pact aircraft all interceptor aircraft, land-based naval bombers, and training aircraft in addition to ground-attack aircraft, fighter-bombers, and medium bombers, for a Pact total of over 14,000 aircraft to NATO's roughly 6,600. Using this reduction base, a 15 percent reduction of 750 NATO aircraft to a common ceiling of 5,700 aircraft per alliance would oblige the Pact to reduce about 8,000 aircraft. That was a lot of airplanes, many of them defensive interceptor aircraft, even in a situation where the Soviets have already indicated willingness to make much larger reductions of ground force armaments than NATO.

President Bush's proposal that United States and Soviet manpower in Central Europe be reduced was valuable because it cut through NATO's previous reluctance, based on the difficulty of verification, to include military personnel in reductions. This action, too, partially met the Pact proposal that negotiated reductions should cover military personnel as well as armaments. The Bush proposal foresaw a 10 percent reduction of about 30,000 U.S. personnel deployed in Central Europe to 300,000 forward-deployed Soviet personnel. Once again, the asymmetry was high despite demonstrated Soviet flexibility. The proposal was inconsistent with earlier NATO proposals in C.F.E.: it omits the personnel of French, British, Canadian, Netherlands and Belgian units stationed in Federal Germany, well over 100,000 men for ground forces alone, despite the fact that NATO has included the armaments of these forces in its proposals for equality in the armaments held by stationed forces of both alliances deployed in Central Europe. Moreover, the Bush proposal does not cover Soviet military personnel deployed in the Soviet Union west of the Urals. These personnel should be reduced or limited to give NATO some control over Soviet mobilization potential and to preclude circumvention through increasing the personnel of permitted units. The Soviets in turn will be interested in gaining some hold, even if indirect, over the future size of the Federal German forces. And without negotiated manpower reductions for all NATO countries, it will be very difficult for NATO countries other than the United States to realize savings from force cuts.

We will discuss aircraft and personnel reductions in more detail later in the chapter. But these points suggest that it will be very difficult to achieve an agreement complete in all details within the six- to twelve-month period President Bush suggested. A two- to three-year timetable seems more realistic for a completed agreement. A partial agreement on some individual aspects, such as manpower reduction in central Europe, would be possible in a shorter time and, under some circumstances, a desirable encouragement to the reduction process. In addition, NATO has yet to agree internally on a verification approach to propose to the Pact and this will be time-consuming to negotiate, whatever the degree of Pact flexibility.

However, the President's commitment to seek an early agreement was significant in two respects. By suggesting the possibility of early conclusion of an agreement on conventional forces cuts, the Bush proposal made possible a temporary compromise in the divisive dispute in NATO over the timing of U.S.-Soviet negotiations on tactical-range nuclear missiles.

The compromise reached was to postpone starting new talks on reducing tactical-range missiles until after work on an East-West agreement on reducing conventional forces has been completed, the agreement has been ratified by all NATO parliaments—possibly a lengthy process—and has entered into force and its implementation begun. An earlier beginning of missile talks would have made sense from the viewpoint of building down the most dangerous elements of the NATO-Pact confrontation and eliminating perhaps the most dangerous area of Pact superiority—about 1,400 missile launchers which could be used with conventional or chemical or possibly nuclear warheads at the outset of a conflict. But the NATO nuclear powers were apprehensive that an early negotiation could result in the elimination of NATO's tactical nuclear weapons before Pact conventional superiority was cut. Continuing the dispute over this subject within NATO would have seriously damaged alliance relationships and could have led to delay and slowdowns in both the talks on conventional reductions and in talks on reducing tactical nuclear armaments—it can still do so.

Second, President Bush's proposals represented his personal engagement in favor of early agreement in the C.F.E. talks. This engagement reduced the inclination in NATO to maintain the military status quo in Europe as insurance against a new Soviet policy which many NATO officials have feared was not genuine. The President's commitment evidenced his administration's belief that the Gorbachev policy did represent a genuine opportunity to eliminate the Pact's numerical superiorities.

NEGOTIATORS' HEADACHES

East/West arms-control negotiation is deadly serious business. Reducing a huge military confrontation of enormously destructive capacity is a ticklish and sensitive task, something like defusing a giant bomb. So far the East/West confrontation in Europe has not erupted into war. But removing some of the device's components in the wrong way could bring it closer to detonation. In the current Vienna force-reduction talks, NATO participants—whatever their current assessment of the possibility of war in Europe—are testing every step of the path they are mapping in collaboration with the Pact before entrusting even a small portion of their security to it. Although they may show more flexibility than in past negotiations, Pact negotiators are just as wary.

Given these characteristics, arms-control negotiation often resembles an attempt to press through a dense thicket of thorn bushes. In the remainder of this chapter, we shall describe some of the remaining substantive issues with which negotiators on both sides are having to contend as they push their way through the C.F.E. force-reduction talks. Doing so will give readers a feel for the nature and the difficulty of the negotiation task.

In some cases, the principles developed in the last chapter will point to a solution. (And where possible solutions are clear they will be presented in some detail in coming chapters.) But it should be kept firmly in mind that many of the issues before the negotiators in Vienna have no single solution that is fully satisfactory to both sides or that is satisfactory when measured against a criterion of effectiveness in building down the NATO/Pact confrontation. For these, the negotiators will have to make hard trade-offs between conflicting values.

After the spurt of Soviet activity in the first three months of the Vienna talks and the American response to it which we have just described, many of the main issues of principle whose solution was needed to conclude a first reduction agreement in Vienna had already been dealt with. The two alliances had agreed on the force components to be reduced: tanks, artillery, armored troop carriers, combat aircraft, armed helicopters, and active-duty ground and air force personnel. They had also agreed on a reduction method which essentially involved a percentage cut from the current holdings of the numerically weaker side, depending on definition of the reduction base, probably NATO in all these cases, with the Warsaw Pact coming down to the new NATO levels. In an impressive number of cases, they had either agreed on the actual numerical levels or the proposals of the two sides were close enough to justify a prediction that they would ultimately be agreed. But many difficult problems remained to be tackled, including the issue of verification, to be treated in a later chapter.

Included among the specific negotiating problems we shall be discussing here are: (1) whether and how to divide the Atlantic-to-the Urals area into sub-regions; (2) how to go about reducing aircraft and also the issue of reducing surface-to-surface missiles; (3) what disposal should be made of reduced armaments and what should be done about continuing production of these armaments in the reduction area;

(4) the problem of modernization of reduced arms; (5) whether reductions should be carried out by disbanding complete units, with a prohibition against increasing the number of remaining units of this type; and (6) whether military manpower should be more broadly reduced than President Bush has proposed. Negotiators at Vienna will have to find some solution for all of these issues before a first reduction agreement can be concluded and many will have to be tackled repeatedly in the process of negotiated build-down.

THE C.F.E. MANDATE—WHAT IS AGREED AND WHAT IS NOT AGREED

To introduce this range of problems, let's first look more closely at the "Mandate for Negotiation on Conventional Armed Forces in Europe," agreed to by representatives of the NATO and Warsaw Pact states in Vienna on January 10, 1989. This mandate (text in Appendix VI) provides the C.F.E. talks with an agenda and defines their subject-matter.

The mandate provides that:

> The objectives of the negotiations shall be to strengthen stability and security in Europe through the establishment of a stable and secure balance of conventional armed forces, which include conventional armaments and equipment, at lower levels; the elimination of disparities prejudicial to stability and security; and the elimination, as a matter of priority, of the capability for launching surprise attack and for initiating large-scale offensive action.

> These objectives shall be achieved by the application of militarily significant measures such as reductions, limitation, redeployment provisions, equal ceilings, and related measures, among others.

The language of the mandate represents an important achievement for the NATO participants, because the Soviet Union and its Warsaw Pact allies accepted many central concepts contained in the NATO draft for this negotiating agenda. These include "the elimination of disparities prejudicial to stability," a point that covers in language accepted by both alliances NATO's longstanding demand for the elimination of the Pact's numerical superiorities. The mandate also includes the NATO objective, discussed in Chapter 4, of "eliminating, as a matter of priority . . . the capability for launching surprise attack and for initiating large-scale offensive action." NATO also had its way on the selection of armaments to be covered. The Warsaw Pact conceded that nuclear and chemical weapons and naval forces would not be addressed directly in the C.F.E. talks.

Thus, extracting the essence of the mandate, the agreed objective of the C.F.E. talks is to strengthen security in Europe through agreed reductions, equal ceilings, deployment restrictions, and other measures covering all land-based non-nuclear armed forces of the participants stationed in the area from the Atlantic to the Urals. NATO deflected Soviet insistence that specific mention be made of nuclear-capable aircraft by agreeing that no land-based armaments will be excluded from negotiation merely because they have nuclear as well as conventional capability. This provision of the mandate places both aircraft and surface-to-surface missiles under the scope of the negotiations.

The content of the C.F.E. mandate is much broader than the mandate for the M.B.F.R. talks, which was merely "the mutual reduction of forces and armaments and associated measures in Central Europe." Much more was agreed at the outset of the C.F.E. talks than was ever agreed in M.B.F.R. and this is an important gain.

WHAT'S IN; WHAT'S OUT: PROBLEMS OF DELINEATING THE REDUCTION AREA

The C.F.E. mandate specifies that: "The area of application shall be the entire land territory of the participants in Europe from the Atlantic to the Urals, which includes all the European island territories of the participants. In the case of the Soviet Union, the area of application includes all the territory lying west of the Ural River and the Caspian Sea." The mandate also excludes a portion of southeastern Turkey along its border with Iraq, Syria, and Iran.

An area stipulated for coverage by arms-control negotiations is one in which the forces deployed by both alliances can be subject to reporting requirements, reduction, or restrictions. The main question posed by the designation of such an area is which forces will be included by its delineation and which left out. In our chapter on the M.B.F.R. talks, we discussed the reasons for NATO's dissatisfaction with the relatively small reduction area covered by M.B.F.R.: Federal Germany's feelings of being "singled out" for control; the absence of coverage of French forces; and, above all, the absence of coverage of Soviet forces on Soviet territory.

The much larger Atlantic-to-the-Urals area of the new talks meets these particular problems. But it creates other problems of inclusion and exclusion. In the last chapter, we discussed NATO's long and difficult efforts to divide the larger Atlantic-to-the-Urals area into subregions. These difficulties within NATO were resolved at the last minute, just as the C.F.E. talks got under way. Nonetheless, it is likely that the question of subregions will be reopened, both because the Warsaw Pact has its own divergent ideas on the subject and because of the intrinsic difficulties of the problem itself.

Let us look first at some potential problems in defining the Atlantic-to-the-Urals area of coverage as such and then turn to the issue of dividing this area into subregions.

Two-thirds of the territory of the Soviet Union and the entire territories of the United States and Canada are not included in the Atlantic-to-the-Urals reduction area. But, with the exception of a small portion of Turkey, the entire territory of all remaining NATO and Warsaw Pact members is included. This means that armed forces stationed in the eastern U.S.S.R. and in the United States and Canada would not be subject to any reductions, restrictions, or constraints that might be negotiated in the C.F.E. talks unless there is some special agreement to do so, and that these outside forces could grow or shrink as their governments see fit. On the other hand, nearly the entire forces of countries whose territory is inside the Atlantic-to-the-Urals area except for a small number stationed outside Europe will be subject to restrictions. This distinction unavoidably creates two classes of participants in the talks, with the possibility of invidious political differentiation. One important example is the potential inequity of limiting production in the Atlantic-to-the-Urals area of armaments of the types reduced by agreement without limiting production of the same types of armaments outside the area.

The exclusion of large portions of Soviet territory from coverage in the C.F.E. talks could have important consequences for NATO in addition to the possibility that the number of forces already stationed there might grow. If the Soviet Union were to cut back its forces west of the Urals by simply shifting them east of the Urals, NATO could be at a severe disadvantage. NATO's forces in western Europe would be disbanded and U.S. forces withdrawn far away to the United States. But so long as the withdrawn Soviet units remained outside the reduction area, beyond the reach of negotiated restrictions, the Soviet Union could station them as close to the Urals as it liked, ready for rapid movement westward, maintain them in combat condition, and even build them up and strengthen them.

It would clearly be in NATO's interest to require the U.S.S.R. to disband the units that it will have to reduce by agreement and to destroy their equipment. Indeed, the Warsaw Pact itself offered to do this in its June, 1986, Budapest proposal for new force-reduction talks—and subsequently. Disbanding withdrawn Soviet forces cut under an agreement or at least preventing them from being stationed east of the Urals would also deter political tensions with Japan and China, which would be in the interest of both NATO and the Soviet Union. Such a measure would also relieve the Soviets of the expense of constructing new installations east of the Urals to receive a massive influx of redeployed forces.

There's a catch, however. If NATO asks the Soviets to disband the units they cut back, will the Soviet Union insist that American and Canadian forces withdrawn from the reduction area by agreement also be disbanded and not replaced? It is not clear that both countries will be willing to do so as a matter of agreement because this action would by implication place a ceiling on the forces of both countries on their home territories. The United States has already rejected one alternative suggestion made by the Pact in its 1986 Budapest proposal: a freeze on all American, Canadian, and Soviet forces that would otherwise be geographically exempt from an agreement. (That idea, perhaps articulated in a different way, deserves more consideration.) If NATO instead asks that reduced Soviet units be converted to reserve status and kept together with their armaments in a specified area west of the Urals but close to them, as far back as possible, would the Soviet Union accept such restrictions without asking that similar limits be placed on the location of reduced forces of NATO countries located inside the Atlantic-to-the-Urals area, that, for example, reduced French forces be taken out of Federal Germany, converted to reserves, and confined to French territory? Would NATO find this acceptable?

Whether the area from the Atlantic to the Urals is treated in an agreement as a single unit or divided into subregions will also have consequences. As we saw in the last chapter, opinions in NATO have diverged widely on this topic.

We have already discussed France's unhappiness with the idea of establishing parity in classes of weapons between East and West if the reduction area is treated as a whole. France has been apprehensive lest such an outcome give French citizens the impression that their government is realigning itself with the NATO alliance and rejoining NATO's integrated military command.

A further objection to treating the reduction area as a whole is the flexibility this could give the Soviets in organizing their reductions, to the disadvantage of the West. If the Soviets could make their cutbacks wherever they wished, they might choose to disband reserve units deployed in Soviet territory and leave intact their best combat-ready active-duty units, which are deployed forward in eastern Europe and equipped with the Soviets' most modern armaments.

One way to oblige the Soviets to focus their reductions on these forward-deployed units, as Federal Germany and other European NATO states wish, is to create a subregion for central Europe and to cut the forces of both alliances to equality within that area. But that is not the only way. As we saw earlier, another option, proposed by the United States, is to restrict the armaments of forces stationed by one member of NATO or the Pact on the territory of an ally. Applying this stationed-forces approach would capture the forces deployed by the Soviet Union in other Warsaw Pact countries (East Germany, Poland, Czechoslovakia, and Hungary), as well as the forces of NATO allies deployed on foreign soil—primarily in the Federal Republic of Germany.

Although the issue of how to define these sublimits was discussed heatedly within NATO up until the very day the C.F.E. talks opened, NATO finally decided to propose limits on stationed forces as well as subregions.

In practice, NATO proposed a system of seven separate restrictions on forces: In the Atlantic-to-the-Urals area as a whole NATO is proposing overall common ceilings of 20,000 tanks for each alliance; 16,500 artillery pieces each; 28,000 armored troop carriers each; and 12,000 armored infantry-fighting vehicles (a sub-category of armored troop carriers) each. This is NATO's Limit 4.1.

In addition to these overall parity ceilings, NATO proposed six different sub-limits on tanks, artillery, and armored troop carriers:

1. Neither alliance may deploy more than 11,300 main battle tanks, 9,000 artillery pieces, and 20,000 armored troop carriers in the area consisting of, for NATO, the territory of Belgium, Denmark, the Federal Republic of Germany, France, Italy, Luxembourg, the Netherlands, Portugal, Spain, and the United Kingdom (namely, the W.E.U. countries plus Denmark); and, for the Pact, the territory of Czechoslovakia, the German Democratic Republic, Hungary, Poland, and the territory of the Soviet Union west of the Urals, including the Baltic, Byelorussian, Carpathian, Moscow, Volga, and Urals Military Districts. This area (Limit 4.3) is formed by deleting from the overall Atlantic-to-the-Urals

area the northern and southern flanks—Norway, Iceland, and the Leningrad Military District of the U.S.S.R. in the north and Greece, Turkey, Bulgaria, Romania, and the Odessa, Kiev, Trans-Caucasus, and North Caucasus Military Districts in the south.

2. Neither alliance may deploy more than 10,300 tanks, 7,600 artillery pieces, and 18,000 armored troop carriers in the area consisting of Belgium, Denmark, the Federal Republic of Germany, France, Italy, Luxembourg, the Netherlands, and the United Kingdom in the west and Czechoslovakia, the German Democratic Republic, Hungary, Poland, and the Baltic, Byelorussian, and Carpathian Military Districts of the U.S.S.R. in the east (Limit 4.3). This is the area pressed for by the Federal Republic of Germany, with the addition of the United Kingdom and Italy. This subregion is formed by deleting from the preceding one Portugal and Spain as well as the Moscow, Volga, and Urals Military Districts of the U.S.S.R.

3. Neither alliance may deploy more than 8,000 tanks, 4,500 artillery pieces, and 11,000 armored troop carriers in an area consisting of Belgium, the Federal Republic of Germany, Luxembourg, the Netherlands, Czechoslovakia, the German Democratic Republic, and Poland. This area (Limit 4.4) is formed by deleting from the previous one Denmark, France, Italy, and the United Kingdom for NATO and, for the Pact, Hungary, and the Baltic, Byelorussian, and Carpathian Military Districts of the U.S.S.R. This area is the same as that covered by the M.B.F.R. talks.

4. Delineating these geographic sublimits reveals what amounts to a fourth sublimit, not specified in the NATO proposal: neither alliance should deploy more than 18,700 tanks, 7,500 artillery pieces, and 8,000 armored troop carriers in the territory deleted from the Atlantic-to-the-Urals area to form the first subregion—namely Norway, Iceland, Greece, and Turkey for NATO, and Bulgaria, Romania, and the Leningrad, Odessa, Kiev, Trans-Caucasus, and North Caucasus Military Districts of the U.S.S.R. for the Pact.

5. As discussed earlier in this chapter, NATO also proposed a "sufficiency limit" (Rule 2) whereby no single country in either alliance can hold more than 60 percent of an alliance's total quota of tanks, artillery, or armored troop carriers. (In deference to France's opposition to parity, this figure is expressed as 30 percent of the combined total for both alliances. For ease of understand-

ing, we instead present this limit as 60 percent of the total permitted to each alliance.) The specific limits are 12,000 tanks, 10,000 artillery pieces, and 16,800 armored troop carriers. The purpose of this restriction is to hold down the Soviet Union's portion of the total number of reduced armaments permitted to the Warsaw Pact.

6. The final sub-limit NATO proposed under the overall parity ceiling was the stationed-forces limit (Rule 3) on the armaments deployed by alliance members on the territory of other alliance states (tanks, 3,200; artillery, 1,700; and armored troop carriers, 6,000). The purpose of this limitation is to hold down Soviet deployments in eastern Europe by making them equal to the combined holdings in the three armaments of the United States, France, the United Kingdom, Belgium, and the Netherlands in Federal Germany, as well as United States deployments in the Benelux countries. (See Appendix IX for comparison of NATO and Pact zonal proposals.)

Other than the equal overall limits or common ceilings NATO suggested for each alliance, the last two—the limit on the total armament holdings of any single country and the limit on armaments of one ally stationed on the territory of another—are the most significant of these ceilings. As we have explained, the first would in effect impose a national ceiling on the forces of the U.S.S.R., the only country in either alliance that has approached, and in fact now exceeds, a 60 percent limit on total holdings. The second would also impose a sharply reduced ceiling on the number of forces that the Soviets could deploy in eastern Europe. Surprisingly, the Soviet Union has indicated its willingness to accept both ceilings.

From the western viewpoint, the sufficiency ceiling on Soviet forces is intrinsically desirable. Its formulation in the current NATO proposal represents an improvement over the western position in M.B.F.R. There, as we saw earlier, disagreement between Chancellor Helmut Schmidt and Foreign Minister Hans Dietrich Genscher prevented the use of Schmidt's proposal to break the M.B.F.R. deadlock over national ceilings. (Schmidt had proposed that no single country in either alliance be permitted to hold more than half of an alliance's total quota of active-duty ground and air force military personnel.) The present NATO proposal, although setting the level at a higher figure, vindicates the approach he suggested.

We have already noted that the relationship of forces within the Pact is likely to remain fairly stable for political and economic reasons. Despite this, given the Soviet Union's dominant position in the Pact and the desire of all eastern European members of the Warsaw Pact to reduce their defense budgets, the proportion of Soviet forces could increase. However, despite Soviet agreement in principle to the sufficiency limit, negotiation on this subject has not been completed and difficult issues may yet arise. Indeed, the Soviet Union may make the same objection to national sub-limits that the NATO countries made on their own behalf in M.B.F.R. Under the restrictions, a national sub-ceiling, the Soviet Union may complain, it would be unable to make up for unilateral reductions that might be made by other Pact members after agreed reductions take effect to restore the Pact total holdings of arms and men to the level permitted by agreement. The right answer to this objection now—and one very much in the spirit of this book—is for the NATO countries to offer to meet this contingency by reducing their forces further themselves.

In theory the sufficiency limit would also apply to NATO countries. But in practice the numerically largest NATO ally, the Federal Republic of Germany, holds only about 35 percent of NATO's tank holdings. The Soviet Union may argue, as it did in the M.B.F.R. talks, that a ceiling of this kind would in theory permit very large increases in Federal German forces, or for that matter, United States forces, within the 60 percent limit. Such increases are unlikely. However, if the Soviet Union persists with this objection, the NATO allies might consider recasting the sufficiency limit so that, rather than referring to a single country, no two countries on either side could hold more than 65 percent of their alliance's quota. (The result would be a continuing limit of 60 percent on Soviet forces. Czechoslovakia, the next largest Pact country, holds only 5 percent of the Pact's tank total. In the West, the two strongest participants in terms of armaments, the Federal Republic of Germany and the United States, have only about 50 percent of NATO's tanks, including the stored tanks of both forces.)

A related problem stems from NATO's determination to reserve for decision within the alliance the allocation to individual NATO states of the overall reduction quotas worked out with the Pact. This position is motivated by a desire to avoid national ceilings on the forces of individual NATO participants and is an inheritance from the collectivity issue that we discussed in our M.B.F.R. chapter. It can create problems with the Pact. These problems include the not unnatural desire of the Pact to know how many reductions each NATO participant will make and the not unnatural desire of NATO participants to avoid contractual national limits on the forces of individual NATO participants which negotiating individual reduction quotas with the Pact could entail. Yet in the interim, as we have pointed out, the Pact has agreed both to collective residual ceilings and the sufficiency and stationed forces units. NATO can now afford to inform the Pact directly of individual reduction quotas and to relinquish going to the extreme, as in M.B.F.R., of suggesting that the Pact would be informed of them only through publication in the western press.

The NATO proposal for equal limits on arms held by the stationed forces of both alliances was an improvement over its M.B.F.R. predecessor. In M.B.F.R. the NATO countries proposed that ceilings be placed only on the stationed forces of the U.S.S.R. and the U.S.A. (as they have now done for manpower). The forces were of unequal size and the M.B.F.R. formula also omitted the U.K., French, Belgian, and Netherlands forces stationed in Germany.

The limit on stationed forces that NATO has proposed in C.F.E. would restrict the capacity of the Soviet Union to reinforce its forces in eastern Europe in the event of political crisis. The suggested ceiling of 3,200 tanks on stationed forces would mean, in terms of the current average tank holdings of Soviet armored and motorized rifle divisions in eastern Europe, reduction from thirty divisions to only ten. However, perhaps up to fifteen divisions would be possible under the lower division holdings of tanks announced by Foreign Minister Shevardnadze at the outset of the C.F.E. negotiations (a cut of 20 percent in the number of tanks assigned to tank divisions and of 40 percent in the number of tanks assigned to motorized rifle divisions).

The configuration of the remaining four subregions or sublimits that NATO foresees for the Atlantic-to-the-Urals area bears the marks of the internal political struggles in the alliance that produced these limits. In particular, what we here call Zone 2, the Atlantic-to-the-Urals area minus the northern and southern flanks, does not appear to have much logic except as a device to exclude the flanks while avoiding setting up separate programs for them. Italy, Spain, and Portugal have little to do with the Central Front. The inclusion of nearly all of the Soviet Union up to the Urals in the eastern portion of the central zone yields extreme asymmetries that could be hard to negotiate. The combination of northern and southern flank countries of NATO to form one group— Sub-Region 4 in our numbering—also does not appear to have much logic. It might in fact have been better to go ahead and devise separate programs for the northern and southern flanks.

For its part, the Warsaw Pact had its own ideas on the subject of how sub-regions should be delineated. As we pointed out earlier, at the outset of the C.F.E. talks, it accepted equal overall common ceilings for each alliance in armaments designated (and also in ground and air force personnel). In May, 1989, it also presented its own proposal for three concentric bands or sub-regions. In an ascending order of size, the smallest zone, the Central European Zone, was composed on the western side of the territories of Denmark, the Benelux countries, and the Federal Republic of Germany; on the eastern side, East Germany, Czechoslovakia, Poland, and Hungary—this is the so-called "Jaruzelski Zone" suggested by the Poles. In this zone, the Soviets suggested a limit for each alliance of 8,700 tanks, 7,600 artillery pieces, 14,500 armored troop carriers, 400 attack aircraft, and 570,000 servicemen. NATO limits for the nearly comparable Central European Zone 3 above, proposed under Rule 4.4, which omits Denmark and Hungary, were 8,000 tanks, 4,500 artillery pieces, and 11,000 armored troop carriers, plus 400 attack aircraft and 570,000 military personnel. The two proposals were again within negotiating range.

The second concentric zone or band proposed by the Pact, the Forward Zone, added to central Europe Norway, Italy, Greece, and Turkey for NATO and in the east, the Leningrad, Baltic, Odessa, North Caucasus and Transcaucasus Military Districts, Romania, and Bulgaria. The proposed limits were: tanks, 16,000; artillery, 16,500; armored troop carriers, 20,500; attack aircraft, 1,100; helicopters, 1,300; and servicemen, one million.

Zone 3 includes all remaining territory of the Atlantic-to-the-Urals area—in the west, Iceland, the U.K., France, Spain, and Portugal; in the east, the Byelorussian, Carpathian, Kiev, Moscow, Volga, and Urals Military Districts. Here, the proposed ceilings are: for tanks, 7,500; armored troop carriers, 7,500; attack aircraft, 400; and 350,000 servicemen.

When NATO negotiators objected that the Pact's "Forward Zone" did not include the Soviet Union's Byelorussian and Carpathian Military Districts, the major source of rapid reinforcements for an attack on NATO's Central Front, Warsaw Pact negotiators indicated at the end of June, 1989, that they were prepared to be flexible on this subject, too, and to design new zones more acceptable to NATO.[1]

Summing up, we can say to this entire subject of subdividing the Atlantic-to-the-Urals area what readers may already have concluded: as long as NATO can effectively insist on overall sufficiency limits on Soviet forces and on Soviet stationed forces, the exact configuration of the remaining sub-limits is a secondary matter, even though one destined to be much debated between the alliances because it involves the size of the forces of individual NATO states. The original United States proposal on this subject in NATO captured the essentials.

HOW SHOULD REDUCTIONS BE COMPUTED?

For the moment leaving aside discussion of which armaments the two alliances should agree to reduce in the C.F.E. talks, let's look at the question of how reductions of one alliance should be balanced against reductions by the other: in other words, the terms of trade.

We have noted that the two alliances have already agreed on a reduction method. But to understand it better, let's compare it with some alternative approaches. Several have been suggested. In what became known as the "Jaruzelski Plan," the Polish government in the spring of 1987 proposed a trade-off of most feared elements: reduction of Pact tanks in return for reduction of NATO aircraft. Some western experts have developed this idea further, suggesting specific trade-off ratios. Others, like Senator Sam Nunn, the influential chairman of the Armed Services Committee of the U.S. Senate, have suggested reduction by cutting division-size units. In the spring of 1987 Senator Nunn proposed a reduction by 50 percent in United States divisions deployed in Germany against a cut of the same proportions in Soviet divisions deployed in eastern Europe—a cut, he said, of two United States divisions and twelve or thirteen Soviet divisions.

Others have suggested using Armored Division Equivalents, or ADEs, as a criterion for deciding on the size of reductions by both alliances. As we saw earlier, ADEs are a firepower measurement using as their standard the firepower of a United States armored division. Other experts are seeking to use dynamic analysis to develop a table of equivalents for Pact and NATO units. Some Soviet academicians and military officers and some western experts have suggested working out a detailed, specific system of comparison between Warsaw Pact and NATO armaments in which the latest model United States tank might get ninety or a hundred points and a thirty-year-old Pact tank twenty to thirty points, surely a procedure that would take many years to negotiate.

Many of these approaches have positive aspects. Some may still be introduced into East/West talks at some stage. But in practice, the two alliances seem to have agreed on a reduction method, at least for the time being.

That method emphasizes reduction of selected armaments. At the outset of C.F.E., there was dispute over which armaments. But there seems to be agreement that the number of types of armaments to be reduced should be limited. Reductions would occur by setting a new equal level below the holdings of the weaker side in a given armament, with both alliances scaling their holdings down to reach it. In the event of a dispute over data the new agreed level can be set arbitrarily somewhere close to the holdings of the numerically weaker side, but without specific reference to it.

This is the reduction method the NATO allies vainly promoted in the M.B.F.R. talks. It is, in effect, based on the traditional "bean counting" method, one that equates all heavy tanks—what NATO calls main battle tanks—without regard to quality or age. It is rough-hewn but far less complicated than developing a single agreed standard for tank and aircraft reductions, a single scale of ADEs for Federal German and Romanian or Hungarian divisions, or even a system to equate Soviet and American divisions alone. The percentage reduction approach is relatively simple and easily understood. Above all, it has the advantage that the two alliances have in practice agreed on it. It should be maintained.

WHAT ARMAMENTS SHOULD BE SUBJECT TO REDUCTIONS?

At the outset of the C.F.E. talks the Warsaw Pact indicated that it was prepared to reduce tanks, artillery, and armored troop carriers as proposed by NATO. Many definitional differences remained to be solved, like the Pact's inclusion of light mortars under artillery and its inclusion of light tanks together with the thirty- or forty-ton, heavily armed main battle tank. But from the outset, it seemed agreed in principle between the alliances that reductions should include at least these three main armament types, as NATO had advocated from the beginning of its preparations for the C.F.E. talks.

But should further force elements be included in reductions? In its proposals for C.F.E., the Warsaw Pact urged reduction of "attack combat aircraft," "combat helicopters," and, in separate negotiations, "reducing and eliminating tactical nuclear weapons." It has also proposed the reduction of military manpower, a topic we deal with later in this chapter. As it entered the C.F.E. talks, NATO had reservations of varying intensity about reducing all of these force components. As we have seen, President Bush's proposals at the NATO summit resolved some of these issues, at least in principle.

But what about reducing further armaments? Are there general standards whose application could help in reaching agreed solutions? Perhaps there are two: first, the requirement to hold down the additional complications which bringing in more weapons systems will unavoidably load on an already highly complex negotiation. This means that certain less important categories of equipment like small arms, machine guns, and vehicles without armor should be omitted. Second, given their objective of seeking to eliminate the capability for surprise attack and for initiating large-scale offensive action, the alliances should consider the importance of a given weapons system in an attack, as well as its relative significance for defense. Logically, weapons that are primarily defensive like anti-aircraft weapons—at least the less mobile ones for area defense—and anti-tank weapons, should be omitted from reductions.

On that basis, there is a good case for including armed helicopters in reductions as the Pact has proposed and as NATO has agreed following the Bush proposal. Armed helicopters, with their relatively long range, speed, heavy firepower, and capacity for rapid forward movement, are essential weapons for surprise attack. Like tanks they are valuable for anti-tank defense, but they can be replaced by other weapons for this defensive purpose, whereas for the offense they have no equivalent.

Transport helicopters can be converted to armed helicopters by adding a pod of weapons and armor plate to protect the pilot from ground fire. The United States did so in the Vietnam war and the Soviets in Afghanistan. However, the absence of weapons mounts and armor plate is a verifiable distinction. Moreover, it would take a considerable amount of time to convert a large number of transport helicopters to armed helicopters, a fact that would minimize the role they could play in a surprise attack.

In NATO's view the Pact has more helicopters of all types than NATO in the Atlantic-to-the-Urals area. But Pact sources, including Soviet defense minister Yazov, claim that NATO has the edge in number of armed helicopters (and this may in fact be the case for the central European area—see Appendices I and II). This divergence may rest on different definitions of what models should be counted on both sides, but that is an argument to be resolved by a discussion of data and does not make any less compelling the need to reduce the number of helicopters poised for combat in Europe.

Ammunition, not proposed by either alliance thus far, is another promising category for reduction. In any event it would be helpful for the two alliances to exchange data on their ammunition stocks. Forward deployment of large stocks of ammunition would be necessary for effective attack in central Europe. NATO officials believe that the Soviet Union has built up large new stocks in East Germany over the past decade and some think that the Warsaw Pact is storing far more ammunition in central Europe than NATO is. If data exchange and on-site verification confirms this, NATO would have a case for proposing that the Pact reduce its superiority in ammunition to the NATO level in weight and volume. Even more than with other armaments, the practicality of such a measure would depend on how sub-regions of the Atlantic-to-the-Urals area are defined. A stricter rule could be applied to the central European region and a less strict rule to rear areas.

If reduction of ammunition stocks proves too cumbersome on a practical level, the alliances might consider constraints instead, like placing major ammunition stocks in secured storage—a fenced area monitored by sensors and inspectors. A further constraint, if secured storage could be agreed, would be to restrict the amount of ammunition that could be removed from storage in a given period. A more far-reaching measure would be to pull back major ammunition storage sites a fixed distance from the line of confrontation and to require that forward transport go through fixed checkpoints. Munitions for aircraft as well as ground forces should be considered when looking at ammunition control measures.

THE NEED TO NEGOTIATE NUCLEAR REDUCTIONS IN VIENNA

We have described the intense controversy within NATO over whether the alliance should improve or cut its arsenal of tactical-range nuclear weapons remaining after the elimination of American medium-range missiles under the I.N.F. treaty or both. At the beginning of this chapter, we described the compromise reached at the 1989 NATO summit: to postpone a decision on Lance modernization until 1992 and to postpone opening East/West talks on reduction of tactical missiles until after implementation of an agreement to reduce conventional arms has begun.

In accordance with the 1983 decision of NATO defense ministers meeting at Montebello, Canada, the United States is moving toward replacing the Lance missile, scheduled to go out of production in the mid-1990s, with a new nuclear-capable missile with a range four times the seventy miles of the Lance. The new missile would fall just below the lower limit of the I.N.F. treaty's prohibition of land-based missiles with ranges between 500 and 5,500 kilometers. It would be launched by the Multiple Launch Rocket System, a twelve-tube artillery rocket launcher now in wide use in NATO; about 600 of these M.L.R.S.s are scheduled for deployment.

Much has happened in East/West relations since the Montebello decision—not only the conclusion of the I.N.F. treaty but also Soviet moves in the START talks and the Soviet announcement of unilateral reductions in Europe: enough, indeed, to call that decision into question. Originally, the NATO nuclear powers—the U.S., the U.K., and France—wished to avoid another negotiation with the Soviets like I.N.F. and hoped to carry out the entire transaction of deploying a new Lance missile as a unilateral modernization of NATO nuclear forces. But, as we have seen, it proved impossible to carry out this approach and the alliance is now committed to negotiation to reduce tactical-range missiles.

Indeed, it would have avoided lasting scars and the possible eruption of further disputes within NATO over the timing of U.S./Soviet talks on missile reductions if NATO had planned from the outset to carry out Lance modernization within the framework of an East/West agreement to reduce tactical-range missiles to an equal level somewhat below that of current NATO holdings. At the time, this was the only basis on which European public opinion was likely to accept deployment of a modernized Lance. Given the ensuing controversy and intensification of public opposition to deployment, that opportunity may have been lost. The NATO nuclear countries were unwilling to follow the I.N.F. precedent because of their fears that, through the interaction of Soviet policy and western European public opinion, the result would not be modernization of tactical-range missiles, but their elimination. With regard to the timing of East/West negotiations on reducing missiles, they also feared that if these talks were held parallel to C.F.E., they could be pushed to a conclusion before C.F.E., leaving NATO without tactical missiles but with continuing Pact conventional superiority.

There was a possible way out of this dilemma, direct discussion with the Soviet leadership, which had other more important objectives in the West than implementing in the immediate future its long-range aim of eliminating nuclear armaments from Europe. In early 1989, the United States was unwilling to trust itself on this path.

Yet it is probable that the determination of the Federal German public sharply to reduce or eliminate nuclear artillery and tactical-range surface-to-surface missiles, and public sympathy for this view in the Benelux countries, Norway, Denmark, the U.K., Greece, Spain, and Italy will persist. Public pressure by the Soviet Union and Warsaw Pact countries for the elimination of nuclear weapons from Europe will also continue. Before the NATO summit, Gorbachev announced the unilateral withdrawal of 500 Soviet warheads, a gesture without much effect. After the summit, on a visit to France in early July, 1989, he offered still more unilateral reductions in return for an early start of East/West negotiations on reducing tactical nuclear weapons. This public campaign would doubtless continue unless the Soviet leadership saw reasons to stop it. As a consequence of these factors, the NATO compromise on timing of negotiations on reducing tactical nuclear missiles may be reopened in connection with the German elections of 1990 or after them when a new German government is formed. Sooner or later, it will be necessary to have a clarifying discussion with the Soviets.

We have tried to make clear throughout this book that the NATO governments will have to make a choice: Either they must play an active role in shaping the process of building down the NATO/Pact confrontation, including nuclear armaments, and present ways to meet the interests of western publics and the Soviet leadership without compromising the security requirements of NATO, or they can stand pat and watch the Soviets try to sell western publics on some still more radical version. In that event, NATO would be damaged whether the Soviet model for a build-down were finally accepted or rejected.

Looking at the issue in practical terms, we see that the mandate for the new Vienna talks adopted by East and West already covers the possibility of negotiating reductions in the major systems for delivering nuclear weapons now deployed on the ground in Europe: artillery, aircraft, and surface-to-surface missiles. Some reduction in the number of nuclear-capable artillery held by both alliances will be inevitable if artillery pieces are cut under the heading of conventional armaments. Yet such a reduction would not have any effect on the numbers of surface-to-surface missiles and nuclear-capable aircraft in Europe nor long deflect the interest of the Federal German public in a cutback of tactical-range missiles. Let us look at the possibilities for cutbacks of each in turn.

PROBLEMS OF MISSILE REDUCTIONS

As regards missiles, the Warsaw Pact deploys a total of more than 6,000 tactical-range nuclear missiles (Frog, SS-21, and Scud-B) in central Europe, as compared with NATO's deployment of from 600 to 700 nuclear Lance missiles (plus about 300 conventional warhead Lance missiles and 100 French PLUTON nuclear missiles), for a Pact superiority of nearly ten to one.

A NATO/Pact force reduction that did not touch this very large Pact superiority and left most northern European countries within range of the Pact missiles could not be considered a gain in security. An agreed objective of the C.F.E. talks reductions is to cut back on weapons that might be used in surprise attack or to initiate large-scale offensive actions. Tactical missiles are a prime candidate. We have pointed out in discussing the East/West force balance in Europe that the first phase of Pact attack on NATO would consist of attack by surface-to-surface missiles armed with conventional warheads. It would make sense for NATO to seek to eliminate this Pact superiority along with Pact superiority in ground-force armaments.

When negotiations on the reduction of the number of tactical-range missiles take place, how should they be carried out? As we shall discuss in more detail in Chapter 10, perhaps the best way would be in a U.S./Soviet forum separate from, but coordinated with, the force-reduction talks.

An alternative approach would be to negotiate this subject in the group of twenty-three itself. The mandate for the force-reduction talks would permit such a discussion so long as it focussed only on delivery systems and, at least initially, ignored nuclear warheads. However, a separate forum, whose writ would be confined to reductions in American and Soviet missiles, might better reassure France that its own nuclear missiles would be exempt from reductions. In addition, the United States could promise France that it would oppose any Soviet efforts to secure the inclusion of French missiles. (The U.K. has no surface-to-surface missiles of its own but mans some American Lance missiles.) Given the Soviets' willingness to exclude U.K. and French nuclear armaments from the I.N.F. treaty, they might be willing to exclude French missiles from a tactical-range missile agreement also.

Negotiations to reduce American and Soviet arsenals of tactical-range missiles would cover the holdings of all NATO countries deploying the American-built Lance missiles (Belgium, the Federal Republic, Italy, the Netherlands, and the U.K.), with the U.S. advised

192 Meeting Gorbachev's Challenge

by a steering committee of representatives of these allies. For the East, all of the Soviet-built missiles held by all Warsaw Pact countries would be covered. Alternatively, it might be wise if all countries in which Soviet and United States missiles are deployed participated directly in such talks, rather than the U.S. and the U.S.S.R. only. The I.N.F. talks were not open to the NATO deployment countries, and their absence from the negotiating table was a source of friction between the United States and its European allies whose lasting effects greatly exceeded the convenience of holding the talks bilaterally.

Regardless of the forum in which East/West talks on reducing the number of tactical-range missiles are held, NATO should, before such talks are held, seek an advance commitment from the Soviets not to force discussion of the elimination of these missiles.

Although a case can be made on military grounds for eliminating tactical-range missiles, it is doubtful for political and psychological reasons that important groups in the West would be prepared to accept such an outcome even after large Soviet reductions of conventional forces. The conviction of the NATO defense community that continuing nuclear deterrence through deploying tactical-range missiles is essential is very strong. True, these attitudes may change if there is a C.F.E. agreement providing for large cuts in conventional Soviet forces. Many opposition political leaders in Europe would favor the elimination of tactical missiles and will press for that. But for the British, French, and United States governments, with their post-I.N.F. concerns about NATO's nuclear deterrence, it is another story. Even the present Federal German government, which leads those NATO states calling for negotiating reductions in tactical-range missiles, has for the most part favored low equal ceilings to be imposed so that NATO could retain a small quota. Consequently, reducing the Pact missile superiority to an equal level somewhat below NATO holdings may well be the only point of agreement which can be achieved between the two conflicting viewpoints in NATO, one favoring no missile reductions, the other favoring their elimination.

While the long-term Soviet objective apparently remains the elimination of tactical as well as strategic nuclear weapons, Soviet diplomacy showed considerable flexibility and restraint in not pressing its nuclear demands during the long preparatory talks for C.F.E. The Soviet leadership might be willing to settle for a low equal ceiling on surface-to-surface missiles in order to avoid an extended deadlock in NATO which could block conclusion of an agreement on reducing conventional arms and cause difficulties in the START talks and in other aspects of its relations with the United States, and to adhere to a relevant commitment for the same reason. Indeed, on his visit to France in mid-1989, General Secretary Gorbachev spoke of a "minimum deterrent," thus indicating Soviet willingness to reduce tactical-range missiles to a low equal level instead of eliminating them. U.S./Soviet talks on this subject, perhaps at the summit level, in which the U.S. also discusses its plans for deploying a limited number of modernized delivery systems, including Lance and stand-off missiles for aircraft, in a minimal deterrent force for Europe, might be a means of reducing and controlling frictions over this subject. Such frictions could block an orderly build-down of the confrontation and increase instability in both eastern and western Europe and would not be in the interest of either side.

If East/West talks on reducing tactical-range missiles are held, should they cover all U.S. and Soviet-built missiles below the I.N.F. range limit of 500 kilometers, whether missiles of these ranges are intended for use with nuclear, conventional, or chemical warheads?

It was agreed in the I.N.F. treaty to cover all medium-range ground-based missiles, because distinguishing between those armed with conventional and those with nuclear warheads would have made verification far more difficult. Reducing only nuclear-capable missiles of less than 500-kilometer range might be possible if such missiles had a distinctive appearance or used distinctive types of launching systems. This is not the case with the Lance, which can be equipped with either conventional or nuclear warheads, or apparently with the main candidate for the Lance follow-on which, as currently intended, will use the same launcher (the Multiple Launch Rocket System) as the conventionally armed Army Tactical Missile (or A.T.A.C.M.) now in development in the United States. The Lance follow-on missile and the Army Tactical Missile will apparently also not vary widely in size; both will be small and relatively easily concealed. (A further verification problem, especially as regards Soviet systems, may be to distinguish between missiles and launchers designed for surface-to-surface fire and those designed for anti-aircraft purposes. Moreover, some anti-aircraft launchers can be used in a surface-to-surface mode.)

It thus seems logical to apply the I.N.F. solution of covering all missiles, whether nuclear- or conventionally armed, in negotiated reductions and in residual ceilings on tactical-range missiles. Moreover, in talks on reducing tactical-range missiles, NATO would be seeking a low equal ceiling on armaments of this type, not their elimination as in

I.N.F. Both types of missiles would continue to be deployed, intensifying verification problems.

Parity at a low level in tactical nuclear missiles would be militarily advantageous for NATO. It would eliminate the Pact's superiority in these weapons systems, which the Pact might use preemptively at the start of a conflict. For its part, NATO would be sacrificing little by agreeing to a low equal ceiling. A small number of tactical nuclear missiles would be adequate to deter the use of such weapons by an opponent, thus fulfilling one major requirement of flexible response. And NATO's political chances of deploying a larger arsenal of these weapons look poor for the foreseeable future. Western European publics might be persuaded to accept the deployment of a modernized Lance missile but only if it could take place in the framework of a U.S./Soviet agreement providing for negotiated reductions and would thus not lead to renewed East/West frictions.

There is a further reason beyond verification and political acceptability for covering all tactical-range missiles, whether armed with nuclear or conventional warheads, with a low equal ceiling. The United States has in advanced development the conventionally armed A.T.A.C.M., which has a range of up to 200 kilometers. Like the nuclear-armed Lance follow-on missile, the A.T.A.C.M. would be launched by the Multiple Rocket Launching System, which NATO forces in Europe are deploying in large numbers, currently for use with shorter-range conventional precision-guided munitions. NATO officers believe that the A.T.A.C.M. will be extremely valuable for interdicting Warsaw Pact logistics and reinforcements. The missile is the cutting edge of NATO's strategy of Follow-on Forces Attack (or F.O.F.A.—the strategy of responding at the outset of a conflict with strikes in enemy territory against forward-moving Soviet tanks and other reinforcements). NATO officers also see a highly important role for the A.T.A.C.M. in countering an armored breakthrough of NATO's forward defense: its range and accuracy would make possible its use for cross-corps support.

The potential merits of the A.T.A.C.M. have already elicited critical comment from the Warsaw Pact. As for Pact missiles, some NATO officers believe that the Pact's large stock of tactical-range missiles is already capable of delivering chemical or conventional warheads as well as nuclear warheads. Others believe that the Pact's missiles are still too inaccurate to effectively use conventional warheads, which are far less powerful than nuclear ones. Some NATO experts also believe that the Pact is behind in the design and development of highly destructive conventional warheads. However, the Pact's Soviet-built missiles already have sufficient range to reach most NATO airfields, command posts, and ports on the Central Front, and improvement of both destructive capacity and accuracy is merely a matter of time.

In short, the West may still be ahead in conventional missile design. But one of the biggest mistakes of western publics in looking at new military applications of the West's technological lead is to believe that any given improvement on the NATO side will create an enduring gain in the NATO/Pact force competition. NATO officials sometimes contribute to this misapprehension when supporting new weapons for funding by Congress and European parliaments. But these officials know something that they do not tell: that at best new NATO weapons systems represent a gain over less advanced Pact weapons of a similar type for a period of only six to ten years and that a technological lead is valuable only as part of a process of innovation that continues indefinitely. Today's advantage can be maintained only if it is followed by another one tomorrow. Western publics would be less enthusiastic about new weapons systems if they realized that they are merely milestones in a long-term competition rather than enduring improvements in NATO's defense.

The second main reason, then, for a ceiling on both conventionally and nuclear-armed tactical missiles is that what is now in the offing, as the next act of the NATO/Pact competition in "force improvements," is large-scale deployment by both alliances of tactical missiles equipped with conventional warheads. A recent study by the Congressional Budget Office of possible improvements in NATO conventional forces in Europe estimated that NATO might wish to deploy up to 20,000 A.T.A.C.M. conventional warhead missiles.[2] This number appears high given the expense of these missiles, but the deployment of several thousand is plausible. Presumably, the Pact would deploy an equal or greater number of its own tactical missiles with conventional warheads.

Such a development would be highly destabilizing. Defense against these short-flight missiles would be very difficult. There would be strong pressures for rapid preemptive use of these weapons at the outset of a conflict, because of the advantage of knocking out the opponent's air defense, air fields, missile installations, and command installations before the other side attacked one's own installations of this kind first. The new missiles could be fired without the inhibitions and delays that restrain the use of nuclear weapons. Widespread deployment of these weapons will place the NATO/Pact confrontation on hair trigger, more sensitive than at present to the jarring effects of human error and outside events.

For these reasons it would be greatly to NATO's advantage to seek to place all surface-to-surface missiles, both nuclear and conventional, under a single low equal ceiling. NATO's willingness to place restrictions on its superior missile and warhead technology might induce the Pact to reduce its much larger number of missiles.

As we saw in Chapter 7, if U.S./Soviet negotiations on the reduction of tactical-range nuclear-tipped missiles are undertaken, they will eventually have to turn to the question of reducing stocks of nuclear artillery rounds and warheads for aircraft bombs and missiles. Verifying reductions in these armaments would be even more difficult than verifying the level of missiles. These nuclear explosives can be easily concealed inside the reduction area or rapidly brought into it. If this issue is to be dealt with effectively, the supervised destruction of warheads and controls on new production by the Soviet Union and the United States seems unavoidable. This also applies to warheads for strategic delivery systems if the arsenals of strategic armaments are cut back. But, given the complexity of the problem, finding a way to deal with nuclear artillery shells and bombs deployed in the Atlantic-to-the-Urals area should probably await a second stage of East/West talks.

PROBLEMS OF AIRCRAFT REDUCTIONS

We have referred to some of the problems of reducing aircraft in connection with the NATO May, 1989, summit decision to proceed with reductions. But there are many other problems. NATO's original unwillingness to cut its modern fighter-bombers was both because these aircraft are essential for NATO in conventional war and because the elimination of medium-range American missiles by the I.N.F. treaty has increased the significance of NATO aircraft for nuclear deterrence. For NATO, aircraft have the additional importance that their mobility provides flexible firepower which can be brought to bear in weak corps sectors of the NATO front like the undermanned Belgian and Netherlands sectors. Air power is the one area of NATO forces over which NATO commanders have some pre-delegated authority, thus countering possible NATO slowness in reaching political decisions in a crisis.

For their part, Soviet and Pact leaders repeatedly insisted that aircraft must be included in reductions negotiated in C.F.E. Gorbachev called for reductions in tactical aircraft when he proposed the talks, in

April, 1986. In every major statement on C.F.E. since then, the Warsaw Pact's leaders emphasized that aircraft must be included.

Soviet officials have made three main arguments with regard to reductions in ground-attack aircraft:

1. The importance and value of these aircraft in any large-scale attack (Nazi Germany's use of Stuka dive bombers to attack the Soviet Union and France early in World War II is cited as an example).
2. NATO's numerical and qualitative superiority in this category of aircraft. (We have pointed out that definitional difficulties in aircraft reductions are acute. Both the Department of Defense's *Soviet Military Power* and the International Institute of Strategic Studies' *Military Balance* [1988 editions] acknowledge some NATO numerical superiority, but its size and even its existence vary directly with the counting rules used.)
3. The political argument that if the Soviet Union is to be expected to make large asymmetrical reductions in ground-force weapons, then the West must make some quid pro quo. Civilian Soviet officials often make the additional point that if the Soviet military is to be persuaded to make massive cuts in its forces, then it, too, will expect a commensurate concession by the West.

As we saw in our discussion of the I.N.F. treaty, the Soviets have consistently and repeatedly attempted, since the U.S. moved its first B-29s to the U.K. in the late 1940s, to negotiate the reduction or elimination of American systems capable of delivering nuclear weapons to Soviet territory from bases in Europe or Asia. These are the so-called forward-based systems, or F.B.S.s. This long-term Soviet motive continues strong and may drive the Soviets' proposals for reductions in aircraft. If NATO should agree to reduce the number of its ground-attack aircraft, the U.S. would finally make the cutback in its forward-based systems that the Soviets have sought so long.

The possibly exaggerated repute of the Stealth bomber has probably intensified this Soviet interest. The Soviets' fear of western air power runs deep and thus it is likely, despite the flexibility which the Warsaw Pact showed early in the C.F.E. talks, that Pact negotiators would have made aircraft reductions an essential precondition for asymmetrical reductions in ground-force weapons. There is some element of equity here, too. If NATO expects the Pact to reduce the force elements

NATO most fears, then there is a case for NATO to reduce its armaments most feared by the Pact.

Aircraft reductions also make sense for NATO in terms of its own security interests. As we noted in Chapter 3, if the Warsaw Pact decided to make war on NATO, the first phase of attack would probably be a massive assault by fighter-bombers to knock out NATO's aircraft and missiles, to gain control of the air over NATO territory, and then to attack points of NATO resistance on the ground. Theoretically, if NATO felt sufficiently threatened by the Pact in a crisis situation, it, too, might mount a preemptive attack, and again the first phase would be an air assault on the Pact's air bases. Given their speed, range, and firepower, aircraft are an essential armament for invasion and forward advance, replaceable only to a certain degree by missiles and fully by no other weapons system. NATO's fighter-bombers can also aid defense by attacking offensive weapons on the ground, but their tank-busting role can be taken over by less mobile short-range armaments, including rocket artillery.

NATO's ground-attack aircraft provide about half its total firepower and NATO should be stingy with aircraft cuts, since it stands to gain the most leverage from them. But now that the Pact has given detailed evidence of its already declared readiness to make large reductions in ground-force armaments, NATO should be prepared to actually move on aircraft reductions.

As with nuclear reductions, it may be necessary, in order to gain a consensus favoring aircraft reductions in NATO, to assure France and possibly the U.K. that their own nuclear-capable aircraft will not be cut. For this a solution attempted during the M.B.F.R. talks, where France refused to participate or to permit inclusion of its own forces in negotiating cuts, could be useful. What NATO then intended was to count French forces in the total for the alliance, to compute from that figure the NATO reduction that would have to be made to get down to the maximum number of ground forces allowed, and then to let members of the alliance make up the French shortfall among themselves. This is only the most salient example of a further problem which will plague NATO as the C.F.E. talks advance—how to distribute agreed overall cuts among the NATO member states.

The case for eliminating some NATO—and some Warsaw Pact—fighter-bombers is strong, but the practical difficulties of agreeing on air reductions are so numerous that aircraft reduction may become the equivalent in the C.F.E. talks of the sea-launched cruise missile in START—intrinsically the most difficult problem to negotiate.

We have already mentioned one central issue: what type of aircraft should be covered in reductions and included in the so-called "reduction base" from which reductions will be calculated? It would be logical to count aircraft designed specifically for ground attack, like the short-range, tank-busting United States A-10 and its Soviet-made equivalent, the SU-25 Frogfoot aircraft. Like armed helicopters, these aircraft are useful for defense but even more so for attack. But what about other types? Longer-range aircraft capable of attacking ground targets with either conventional or nuclear armaments, like the American F-111 fighter-bomber, as well as Soviet medium-range bombers stationed in the area covered by the talks, should also be candidates for reduction. A rigorous definition would also cover reductions in multi-role aircraft capable of functioning both as ground-attack aircraft and as air-to-air fighters, like the American F-16 and the Soviet MiG-21.

The International Institute of Strategic Studies' *Military Balance 1988–89* credits NATO with about 2,800 ground-attack aircraft and the Pact with about 2,300, a NATO superiority of about 500 for aircraft deployed in the area covered by the C.F.E. talks (Appendix II). But if all aircraft in the Atlantic-to-the-Urals area falling under the reduction base defined in the previous paragraph are included in the count (like the medium bombers of the Smolensk air command), the Warsaw Pact would have numerical superiority. (See the chart in Appendix X.)

It would be reasonable to omit from the reduction base reconnaissance aircraft, most of which are light and not heavily armed, as well as aircraft equipped with electronic jamming equipment or special radar sensors, as well as light training aircraft used for primary training. If sea-based naval aircraft are to be omitted, there is some case for omitting land-based aircraft from reductions although a ceiling would have to be placed on them to prevent circumvention. But what about interceptors and air-to-air fighters? The Pact admits to superiority in interceptor aircraft and there is no dispute over this fact, even though definitional difficulties persist. The Warsaw Pact data published in January, 1989, credits the Pact with more than 1,800 interceptors and NATO with only fifty (Appendix I) while the International Institute for Strategic Studies' *Military Balance, 1988–89* credits the Pact with about 4,400 interceptor aircraft as compared with fewer than 1,200 for NATO.

Interceptor aircraft can also be used to attack ground targets. Many aircraft configured solely as air-to-air interceptors can be equipped with air-to-ground missiles and air-to-ground radar, which makes them usable, if not highly effective, for ground attack. (Low load capacity and lack of pilot training are further limitations on their ground-attack capability.) Moreover, if the fighter-bombers allowed each alliance were reduced to an equally low number but one side had a larger number of interceptors, this advantage could be useful in helping the fighter-bombers break through to their targets in the battle area or deeper in the territory of the adversary and interceptors can be used to gain control of the air over the battle area.

Therefore, if the number of ground-attack aircraft is to be reduced, some way will have to be found to deal with the Pact's advantages in interceptor aircraft—perhaps by reduction, perhaps by permitting an increase in the number of interceptors allowed NATO, or by giving each side a single maximum total that would cover all combat aircraft. In the latter case, the overall level might be cut and each alliance would have "freedom to mix"—it would be left to each alliance to decide how many aircraft to devote to air defense and how many to ground attack. Another way of dealing with Pact superiority in interceptors would be to freeze their level and to levy a kind of surcharge, say 10 percent, to be included in computing the number of attack aircraft to be reduced by the Pact.

The Warsaw Pact's superiority over NATO in ground-based air defenses could also complicate negotiating cutbacks in aircraft, because the better the Pact's air defenses, the less the penetration capacity of NATO's ground-attack aircraft. The Pact also has many more airfields at its disposal than are available in the constricted NATO area and perhaps this factor should also be taken into consideration in figuring reduction totals. To some degree offsetting these advantages of the Pact, NATO's material and human ground-based air force infrastructure seems numerically larger than that of the Pact and is probably qualitatively superior as well. For this reason, NATO aircraft could probably make more sorties per day in a conflict than Pact aircraft could.

Then there is the difficult question of whether reductions in the number of aircraft should encompass reinforcement aircraft earmarked for the European theater in the event of war—which can arrive at their destinations rapidly—or whether reductions should cover only aircraft already deployed in the Atlantic-to-the-Urals area. The United States has about 1,000 aircraft in the United States earmarked for European defense and could in theory send a further thousand if Europe were the sole site of East/West conflict. And the Department of Defense calculates in *Soviet Military Power, 1988* that the Soviet Union could theoretically send at least 800 more ground-attack aircraft and a thousand more interceptors under the same conditions.

In Chapter 10, which contains proposals on reductions, we shall suggest some specific solutions to these difficulties of how to calculate air reductions once it is decided to proceed with them.

But if the scope of air reductions can be agreed, what should be done with the aircraft pulled from service? The prime characteristic of aircraft—their speed—makes disposal a special problem. The United States and the Soviet Union have the biggest air forces in Europe. Reduction of these aircraft by withdrawal from the Atlantic-to-the-Urals area would have little military impact, because in the event the agreement were violated or conflict broke out, the aircraft withdrawn could return to the reduction area in a very short time, possibly within hours. If aircraft are ultimately to be reduced by agreement in Vienna, simply withdrawing them outside the Atlantic-to-the-Urals area would not make much sense unless ground units for servicing, fuelling, and arming them were also withdrawn—a difficult enterprise if the number of planes in question were limited, and one which would be resisted by commanders anxious that their remaining aircraft be combat-ready.

Would the destruction of reduced aircraft or secured storage under surveillance of the opposing alliance be better alternatives than withdrawal? NATO may be reluctant to destroy modern fighter-bombers, which cost more than $40 million apiece in the West. The Pact too may be reluctant to do so. Secured storage in hangars or enclosures subject to inspection by the opposing alliance seems the best of the alternatives. But secured storage might have its own shortcomings: how valuable would reductions in Soviet aircraft deployed inside the reduction area be if the U.S.S.R. were unrestricted outside the area and could fly in reinforcements in minutes? And how reassuring would United States air reductions under similar circumstances be to the Warsaw Pact? Given these problems, reduction by withdrawal, which is not preferable if our objective is to cut back the confrontation, may turn out to be politically the most acceptable approach for both sides. Therefore, it cannot be discarded as a reduction method.

Aircraft reductions raise in acute form a general problem associated with the reduction of armaments of all kinds: how to deal with the continuing production of restricted armaments at plants located inside the reduction area. Several issues are involved: On the one hand, western European countries attach high economic, military, and political value to their production of armaments, and especially of modern aircraft. Sovereignty and prestige considerations play a role. On the other hand, from NATO's point of view, Warsaw Pact reductions in aircraft, tanks, artillery, helicopters, and armored personnel carriers would not make sense if the Pact could continue to produce these armaments without restriction inside the reduction area. Hence controls of some kind will have to be placed on production. But, of course, such restrictions will have to be reciprocal.

Both the Soviet Union and western Europe export considerable quantities of their armaments abroad. France has indicated that it would not welcome restrictions on its production of tanks or aircraft if these restrictions were not applied to United States home territory or to the entire U.S.S.R. Nor would France welcome Soviet inspectors in its tank or aircraft factories, giving them the chance to pry out both military and trade secrets. In the context of American relations with the western European NATO states who are seeking to develop their own military and civilian aircraft industries in competition with the United States, proposals to place western European production of military aircraft under some form of Warsaw Pact control while leaving American production wholly unencumbered would not be at all attractive.

The best answer for production inside the Atlantic-to-the-Urals area of aircraft and other armaments reduced by agreement may be to place new production in secured storage at production plants subject to inspection by the opposing alliance. Signers of the agreement would have to give notice of shipments from their plants, and shipments within the reduction area would be allowed only to replace obsolete equipment on a one-for-one basis. Limits on production totals and inspection inside plants probably should not be attempted at the outset. They pose too many problems, especially in terms of equal treatment for all participants.

Even a modest system of controls like this would set up an inequity between the U.S., the U.S.S.R., and Canada, most or all of whose aircraft production facilities would be exempt from controls, and all other participants, whose plants producing reducible arms would be regulated. All American and Canadian military plants and all Soviet military plants east of the Urals would be free to step up the production and deployment of aircraft and weapons whose production and deployment by countries within the reduction area would be hobbled by rules. For this reason, some form of controls, especially on aircraft, may ultimately have to be extended to the remainder of Soviet territory and to American and Canadian territory. At the least a reporting requirement may be needed for the U.S., Canada, and the U.S.S.R., and perhaps even a ceiling on field deployments by these countries. Such a ceiling would, in turn, call into question the worldwide military roles of both the U.S. and the U.S.S.R. However, as we shall seek to show in the last chapter, this may be advantageous rather than disadvantageous.

Given the special difficulties of negotiating reductions in aircraft, some experts have suggested that cutting back on aircraft munitions and support personnel and equipment might be more practical. These restrictions could lower the sortie rate of each alliance, diminishing the capacity of the alliances to send individual aircraft on missions. Such measures would not be easy to verify. Nor would they be easy to negotiate, because NATO generally assigns more ground-support personnel to aircraft than the Pact does and thus would have to make a larger cutback. Cutting back on airfields available for military purposes and "demobilizing" them by placing obstacles or buildings on the airstrips is at first view attractive, but NATO has far fewer airfields than the Pact, while many attack aircraft can land in fields and on roads. And by itself, paring down the infrastructure of the alliance's air forces would not have the psychological and material advantages for a build-down of the NATO/Pact confrontation that actually reducing fleets of aircraft would have.

DISPOSING OF REDUCED GROUND-FORCE ARMAMENTS

If the M.B.F.R. talks had succeeded, given the opposition of the western European NATO states to reducing their own armaments, armament reductions would have been limited to the holdings of the United States and the Soviet Union. In 1975, NATO offered to pull back United States nuclear-capable F-4 aircraft, Pershing IA missiles, and nuclear warheads to bases in the United States in return for reduction of a Soviet tank corps with its tanks. (Gorbachev's announced unilateral withdrawal of Soviet tanks from eastern Europe would result in three times the Soviet tank withdrawals the West was seeking in the M.B.F.R. talks.) The Soviet tanks and other armaments of Soviet ground-force divisions would have been pulled back to bases in the Soviet Union.

In distinction to NATO's willingness to pull back to the United States reduced United States nuclear armaments, NATO argued in M.B.F.R. that withdrawing the heavy equipment of reduced American ground forces to United States territory 3,000 miles away across the Atlantic Ocean would place NATO at a serious disadvantage in comparison with the Pact because of the close proximity of Soviet bases in the U.S.S.R. to the Central Front. Thus NATO argued that the

United States should have the right to store in the Federal Republic of Germany the ground-force equipment it pulled from service. At some points in the M.B.F.R. talks the Warsaw Pact countries appeared ready to concede this point; at other times, they opposed it. The issue was never resolved definitively. Consequently, the issue of how reduction by storage would be monitored was not discussed in detail either.

A change from the M.B.F.R. talks is that all participants in the C.F.E. talks, including the western Europeans, are committed by the agreed mandate to participate in armament reductions—to some extent. But with the possible exception of aircraft, disposal by withdrawal may not be practical.

As for Soviet reductions, NATO will understandably do its best when negotiating the disposal of reduced armaments to insure against reversion by the Soviets to a more aggressive policy. We pointed out earlier that the withdrawal of Soviet arms outside the reduction area beyond the Urals could leave them in the hands of active-duty units. Although it would take these units a considerable amount of time to move into combat position, their military capability would remain intact.

Withdrawing heavy American equipment 3,000 miles across the Atlantic would make it unavailable in the early stages of a war in Europe. In the current talks the United States, joined by Canada and also the United Kingdom (separated as it is by the English Channel from continental Europe) are taking a dual position. On the one hand, they are suggesting that reduced armaments be destroyed as the best way of securing a lasting decrease in Soviet combat power. On the other hand, they are trying to protect their own capacity to store tanks and other armaments by applying sub-limit restrictions, such as those on stationed forces, only to those armaments held in units. Doing this would permit each alliance, within the overall limit, to store other tanks in the various subzones. NATO has about 6,000 stored tanks in central Europe; the Soviet Union is believed to have a considerable number in the U.S.S.R., but estimates vary widely. To monitor the stored armaments, NATO and the Pact are proposing some form of secured storage—placing arms in a fenced area monitored by the opposing alliance—as a means for doing so.

For those NATO and Warsaw Pact countries whose entire territory and armed forces, with minor exceptions, are inside the Atlantic-to-the-Urals reduction area, withdrawal as a means of disposing of reduced armaments is not feasible. Withdrawal of these arms beyond the Urals or to North America is theoretically possible but would be highly impractical. So for these countries, disposal will have to mean either secured storage or some form of destruction.

Supervised destruction is the most effective method of disposing of armaments reduced by agreement. It is the option that negotiators chose for disposing of American and Soviet I.N.F. missiles, and it would be the logical means for disposing of tactical-range surface-to-surface missiles, if cutbacks in these armaments can be worked out. The Warsaw Pact suggested destruction or dismantling as the preferred means of disposal for reduced arms when it proposed new force reduction talks in 1986; it also proposed supervised storage as an option. President Bush proposed destruction at the May, 1989, Brussels summit. Clearly, destruction is preferable if the objective is to build down the NATO/Pact confrontation.

But would either alliance wish to destroy its most modern, effective, and costly tanks and artillery, which are typically deployed forward in active units, while retaining older models in its reserve units or in storage? The Soviet Union has said it would dismantle some armaments of units unilaterally withdrawn from central Europe. Yet the tendency on both sides may well be to transfer the most modern armaments to reserve units and to destroy older equipment in their place. Similarly, there probably will be a desire to avoid destruction of armed helicopters if they are included in reductions and to convert them instead to transport functions. United States officials have already suggested to Congress that United States tank reductions would be drawn from war reserve stocks stored in Europe rather than from front-line tanks, and Soviet officials, too, have backed off from earlier pledges to destroy the equipment of unilaterally withdrawn units.

Destruction of reduced armaments would, of course, preclude the storage in Federal Germany of American, Canadian, or U.K. equipment in order to hold it for use in forces airlifted in during a crisis. The destruction of armaments reduced in the C.F.E. talks will also not cover similar armaments in the larger eastern part of the U.S.S.R. outside the Atlantic-to-the-Urals area or United States and Canadian equipment deployed in North America or elsewhere in the world. The number of these armaments could increase. It would be a matter of concern for NATO if the U.S.S.R. made large increases in its tank holdings east of the Urals.

As with aircraft, the destruction of reduced ground-force armaments will have political as well as military implications: The United States, Canada, and the U.S.S.R. would be free to increase their holdings of reduced armaments deployed outside the Atlantic-to-the-Urals area. But their respective allies, with substantially all their forces inside the reduction area, would not. This distinction between the military situation of the two superpowers and their allies might grate on the sensitivities of some allies. The distinction might be somewhat more acceptable if NATO acts, as it did in M.B.F.R., to exclude some possible future European Defense Union from the restrictions that might be included in a possible C.F.E. agreement.

Regardless of the means of disposal of reduced armaments finally agreed to, the production of reduction-category armaments inside the reduction area will be a problem. Inside the reduction area several countries of each alliance produce such armaments: tanks, armored personnel carriers, artillery, and helicopters, as well as aircraft. A major Soviet tank-production plant is west of the Urals. A Soviet tank reduction will not be meaningful if some Soviet tanks are destroyed or stored in the Atlantic-to-the-Urals area but Soviet production plants in the area produce still more tanks and perhaps store them near units of the Soviet ground forces, where they could be used to increase combat power in a sudden breakout from an agreement or as replacements for tanks lost in combat. Although NATO was unable to agree in its opening position in the C.F.E. talks to address this issue, some control over production in the Atlantic-to-the-Urals area of reduced items will have to be applied.

But will it be necessary actually to limit production of these plants? Many are used not only to supply material for alliance forces but also for overseas sales. Not only the Soviet Union but its allies and also France, the U.K., and Federal Germany make large sales of tanks, helicopters, artillery, and armored personnel carriers to Third World countries. Should production of these arms be restricted and if so, should there be inspection of the production process in both alliances to enforce the restrictions? That would surely be a sensitive issue. It seems unnecessary to go so far. Yet, as with aircraft production, it probably will be necessary to place the entire production of such plants located in the reduction area in secured storage subject to inspection by the opposing alliance and to give notice both of the amounts produced and of all withdrawals of equipment, whether for overseas sales or for replacement of worn-out equipment in the field.

In its initial position NATO chose the simpler alternative of limiting reductions only to the armaments held by organized units of the armed forces of the two alliances, whether active duty or reserve, and of ignoring the issue of continuing production of reducible arms in the reduction area.

Disposal of reduced armaments entails many problems. Withdrawal seems out of the question. Both storage and destruction raise difficult issues. Consequently, it is probable that the two alliances will in the long term agree on some combination of destruction and secured storage rather than choosing one method over the other.

THE PROBLEM OF MODERNIZATION

It is evident from past arms-control negotiations that professional military officers in both alliances will insist on the right to modernize and improve remaining armaments permitted them by an agreement and that governments, too, will seek to protect this right in concluding agreements. In a simpler age, it might have been possible to limit the number of spears and longbows and to leave it at that. Today, technology, and technological innovation, is the problem. It is a known dynamic of arms-control agreements, especially those concluded in periods of continuing tension, that both sides seek, as NATO seems to be doing after I.N.F., to upgrade the armaments that are exempt from any agreement in an effort to make up for the lost capability of the armaments they are obliged to cut. Thus for example, if tanks were reduced by a C.F.E. agreement, but armored personnel carriers were not, both alliances would be sure to focus their research and development efforts on bringing armored personnel carriers ever closer to the destructive power and armor of tanks.

To some extent, C.F.E. negotiators will deal with this problem when they work out the details of residual ceilings for reduced armaments. These ceilings will specify some performance characteristics of reduced weapons, like their range, and seek to assure that modernized follow-on versions with these characteristics are covered by the ceiling. For example, the unsuccessful 1975 western proposal in M.B.F.R. for reduction of Pershing I would have covered all follow-on models with ranges over 500 kilometers, including Pershing II. Non-circumvention provisions that forbid actions which circumvent the purpose of agreed reductions are also relevant to this issue. But if artillery and tanks are reduced, will the alliances be permitted to introduce armaments that operate on other principles, like electromagnetic rail guns? We have seen the same problem emerge in the context of the controversy over the extent to which new space-based technology is covered by the prohibition in the A.B.M. treaty against testing or deployment of missile defense systems other than the ground-based systems permitted under the treaty.

Historically, competition to improve armaments has sometimes been intensified by arms-control restrictions, as is demonstrated by the history of pre-World War II naval arms-control negotiations, which produced the heavily armed, compact German pocket battleship. The main practical constraints on this type of competition are economic. A satisfactorily implemented build-down of the military confrontation in Europe would eventually reduce military budgets on both sides and both the resources and the motivation for a high level of technological innovation.

In the meanwhile, it is a genuine dilemma. If there is a need for armed forces, then they should be as effective as possible. But force improvements do generate a competitive reaction. The theoreticians of non-offensive defense whose ideas we reviewed in Chapter 4 seem to have part of the answer: change the character of the forces and shift the main focus of competition to defensive forces.

In practical terms, we may have to leave the modernization issue at that. But it would be logical if our aim is to build down the NATO/Pact confrontation also to explore whether some agreed measures designed to slow the rate of technological innovation might be feasible in the interests of stability between the reduced forces of the two alliances. As the weaker of the superpowers in technological innovation, the Soviet Union has repeatedly proposed negotiation to explore restrictions on new technology. The United States, for the most part in the lead technologically, has not been enthusiastic about pursuing this subject, although it did agree in the SALT II talks to do so in the SALT III negotiations, which never took place, and may again agree to do so in a START treaty. The A.B.M. treaty itself is a generally successful, if much assailed, effort to limit the deployment of new technology. Effective control of the entire process of technological innovation would mean opening up the research laboratories on both sides, a far-reaching step.

However, if in the context of the European confrontation the Soviet Union acts to eliminate numerical superiorities in various armament categories, it may be worthwhile to attempt to deal more seriously with the matter of technological competition through practical measures. It has been suggested by some experts that, at a minimum, each alliance could inform the other at least a year in advance, and longer if feasible, of modernized equipment and new models it intended to deploy, thereby reducing some of the negative impact such deployments often have. Accordingly, in C.F.E.-2, NATO has proposed an information exchange on major conventional weapons deployment programs. (See Appendix VIII.) Some degree of mutual transparency for weapons systems in field trials might also be considered.

Whether it will be possible for the alliances to go beyond this and work out some effective restrictions on modernization or innovation remains open. This whole subject, which is a microcosm of the East/West military confrontation, calls for much more intellectual effort and research than it has received.

PROBLEMS OF REDUCING MILITARY MANPOWER

President Bush has proposed a mutual reduction of Soviet and American ground and air force manpower in Central Europe. Should NATO seek negotiated reductions in military manpower of all participants in the Vienna force-reduction talks? This may seem a strange question. After all, if NATO ultimately decides that the western objective in the C.F.E. talks should be to build down the military confrontation in Europe, thus reducing the risks and costs, then the reduction of military manpower would seem a logical part of the process. The mandate for the C.F.E. talks, which refers to reduction of armed forces including their armaments, permits manpower reductions. Across-the-board manpower reductions form part of the Warsaw Treaty reduction proposals in the negotiations. But the initial NATO reduction position did not provide for manpower reductions or manpower ceilings, in part because of the difficulty of verifying manpower ceilings.

In theory, at least, reducing armaments but not manpower would have some advantages. In that case, there would be no overall manpower ceiling on the full-time, active-duty military personnel of either alliance and no limits on the number of units they could deploy, whether active-duty or reserve. The two alliances would be free to decide for themselves whether they wanted to discharge the personnel manning the armaments being cut from service or instead to shift these personnel to new military assignments, including building up units of a more defensive type, like infantry or combat engineers. In this context, the Soviet leadership announced that it would restructure remaining forces in a more defensive mode when making its unilateral cutbacks in eastern Europe.

From the Soviet viewpoint, taking out some armaments, but leaving the manpower of Soviet units in place in eastern Europe might meet some of the worries of the Soviet and Pact leadership about the impact of large-scale Soviet withdrawals on political stability in eastern Europe. It might also minimize the involuntary retirement of large numbers of Soviet professional officers whose resentment of the Gorbachev leadership could become an important factor in Soviet domestic politics.

Notwithstanding these considerations, if a major objective of negotiated reductions is to build down the East/West military confrontation in a general sense, then a reduction in armaments should be paralleled by reduction in the personnel trained to operate them. It would not conform with the objective of the C.F.E. talks to permit an unlimited buildup of military personnel aimed at improving the effectiveness of remaining armaments, for example by building up the support infrastructure of fighter-bombers remaining after reductions, or strengthening the infantry component of tank units, or forming new units equipped with armaments not subject to reductions.

Moreover, the absence of manpower ceilings might make for a shifting scene of new personnel and changing military organization in which verification would become more difficult. Finally, manpower, which accounts for 50 to 60 percent of the defense costs of NATO states (far less for the Pact), must be cut if real savings are to be achieved. The savings from reductions in armaments alone would be limited.

These considerations argue for an overall ceiling on the full-time, active-duty ground and air-force manpower of all participants in both alliances, whether assigned to active-duty units or as cadre personnel of reserve units, above and beyond a cut in U.S. and Soviet manpower in central Europe. The NATO countries have justified their exemption of military manpower from negotiated cuts by citing the difficulty of reconciling data on military manpower and of verifying manpower ceilings. We shall discuss data exchange and verification in greater detail in later chapters. At this point, it can be said that, given the far-reaching positive shift of the Soviet positions on data exchange and verification, these problems do not seem to outweigh the good reasons for reducing military manpower; moreover, they have been overtaken by the decision to propose reduction of United States and Soviet manpower. If these cuts take place, they will have to be verified.

However, in the interest of reaching an early first agreement, it may prove feasible to reduce the active-duty ground and air force manpower of both alliances in an agreed central European sub-region to an equal ceiling for both alliances and under that equal ceiling also to reduce U.S. and Soviet stationed personnel to an equal level. If need be, all NATO stationed personnel as well as those of the U.S. could be brought under the stationed forces limit. But a stationed forces limit restricted to the United States or to the United States and Canada in the West would be preferable, because it would permit western European forces to form a single pool, an outcome more encouraging for western European defense cooperation. Under this approach, military manpower in the Atlantic-to-the-Urals area outside central Europe could be placed under a no-increase commitment and reduced in a second-phase agreement.

CEILINGS ON MILITARY UNITS

Vienna negotiators will have to resolve another question separate from those of manpower reductions or the disposal of armaments. This is the question of what will happen to the military units now holding armaments whose reduction is negotiated—in for example, tank divisions or air-force wings.

The question is both complicated and controversial. In the M.B.F.R. talks the Pact proposed reduction by units, as it has for the current talks. For its part, NATO argued in M.B.F.R. that the Soviet Union should reduce by divisions but that the United States and the Federal Republic should be free to take their manpower reductions by thinning out existing units. Both countries wished to retain maximum organizational structure to be filled out with reinforcements from the U.S. or with German reservists. And they wished to retain the freedom to vary the future mix and shape of units for maximum effectiveness. Federal Germany's desire to retain this freedom has, if anything, increased with the advent of manpower shortages from a declining birthrate, which could cut the number of young German males eligible for conscription in a given year by 200,000 as early as the 1990s—a shortfall equivalent to the personnel of ten of the Federal Republic's large ground-force divisions. However, thinout, where units continue to exist and the exact level of men and armaments has to be confirmed by on-site inspection, places a heavy burden on verification.

Reduction by complete units together with their armaments would make the greatest contribution to lowering the combat potential of both sides. But to assure that the effects of such reductions are enduring, residual ceilings should be placed on units of the type reduced. The unrestricted freedom to form new units could, for example, lead to reestablishment of reduced units and even a further increase of armored units in the Warsaw Pact, with smaller holdings of tanks but perhaps a larger number of infantry.

Reduction by units, disbanding reduced units and placing a residual ceiling on all units of the type reduced is also preferable to facilitate the verification mission. Men and arms can be dispersed and concealed. But for military effectiveness, they have to be combined and organized into military units and trained to work together. Moreover, verifying the elimination of the units to be cut and making sure that the number of units of the type remaining does not exceed residual limits are the most effective ways to assure compliance.

If there is to be a restriction on the maximum permitted number of units of the type reduced, then this is an additional argument for placing a general ceiling on manpower. In the absence of a general manpower ceiling, it would be necessary to place some limit on the number of personnel each type of unit could have, or Pact and even NATO units could double in size.

Should the overall level of active-duty military manpower permitted each alliance also be lowered by subtracting the manpower of disbanded units from the total permitted, thus establishing a new and lower overall manpower ceiling for each alliance? This would be logical. However, given the fact that current overall totals of ground and air-force manpower in the area to be covered by an agreement are approximately equal for NATO and the Pact but that the Pact would be expected to cut far more units than NATO, this tactic might result in giving NATO superiority in active-duty military manpower. A descending equal ceiling for both alliances, set at the total number of the numerically weaker side, may be the answer.

CEILINGS ON RESERVE UNITS

These arguments for reduction by units and for a residual ceiling on the number of units remaining are strong. But should negotiated reductions and residual ceilings affect not only active-duty units but also be applied to reserve units of the same type—tank, infantry, or artillery? This is one of the hardest questions NATO will be called on to answer.

For NATO, as we saw earlier, the very large number of reserve ground-force divisions that the Soviet Union can mobilize is a major source of worry. At the same time, using reductions to increase NATO's own reserve capacity would be one of the best ways of insuring against a negative shift in Soviet policy. It would be useful, for example, if Federal Germany could take its share of reductions by converting existing active-duty units to reserve units manned by a cadre of 25 percent or less of the manning level for wartime combat. In times of crisis, these reserve units could be activated and armed with weapons from storage in far less time than it would take opposing forces to move from the Soviet Union to central Europe. At a minimum, NATO would want to protect its present reserve capability if deep cuts are agreed.

However, NATO commanders are so worried by the capabilities of Soviet reserve forces and mobilization capacity that on balance they would probably prefer to forgo increasing their own reserves if Soviet reserves were also limited. Thus it seems better to restrict those reserves by completely disbanding reduced active-duty units and placing a ceiling on units of the type reduced and also at some stage in including the arms and manpower of reserve units in reductions, placing ceilings on the number, manpower, and armaments of reserve units in both alliances. Building down the military confrontation in Europe would be better served in this way, as well. This would mean, as a practical matter, that besides cutting some reserve units and setting limits on the number remaining it will be necessary to monitor the remaining units to make sure that they remain on reserve. This could be done by holding the number of active-duty military personnel in reserve units at 20 or 25 percent of wartime manning level, as well as by instituting other constraints on their equipment and activities. We will discuss these possibilities in Chapter 10.

An alternative treatment for reserves would be to permit each alliance to convert reduced active-duty units to reserve units together with their equipment. Under this approach, the total number of all units, active duty and reserve, would be limited, and the new Soviet reserve units would be confined to the area just west of the Urals, where they would be at a maximum distance from the line of confrontation but remain in the Atlantic-to-the-Urals area still subject to negotiated restrictions and inspection. This approach would be more favorable to NATO than placing no limits whatever on the number of Soviet active-duty or reserve units. But it might be difficult to negotiate with the Soviet Union given special restrictions on the treatment and location of Soviet units that are not applicable to western participants.

The discussion of many aspects of negotiated reductions, like ceilings on reduced units and the treatment of reserves, reflects serious concerns on both sides. Finding a pathway through these concerns, although by no means impossible, can be time-consuming.

What is needed at the C.F.E. talks is for the negotiators to carve out some manageable topics from the general subject matter of the talks and seek to reach early agreement on them, in order to give the C.F.E. talks that intangible but essential ingredient of success in negotiation: momentum.

In the next chapter, we shall discuss some steps that negotiators might be able to decide on parallel with their discussion of reductions to assure the success of the talks.

1.   Michael Gordon, "Soviets Shift on Limits on Conventional Forces", *New York Times*, June 30, 1989.
2.   Congressional Budget Office, *U.S. Ground Forces and the Conventional Balance in Europe*, June, 1988, p. 66.

9 Essential First Steps: Data Exchange, Early Warning, and Constraint Measures

The centerpiece of the talks in Vienna is force reductions. But there are several parallel steps other than reductions that participants in the talks would do well to take early on, in order to ease the way for maximum progress and to increase the effectiveness of reductions.

NATO negotiators should ask negotiators for the Warsaw Pact to join with them in establishing separate working groups, in addition to those working on reductions, to discuss the following matters:

- military doctrine, force posture, and the elements that each alliance fears most in the forces of the other;
- full data exchange; and
- measures for early warning and constraints on force deployments. (Early warning, which should encompass overflights at low altitude, can make the Atlantic-to-the-Urals area a "Zone of Military Openness" and help to confirm the unilateral Soviet reductions announced by General Secretary Gorbachev in December of 1988. Constraints, to include a "Restricted Military Area" along the Federal German border with East Germany and Czechoslovakia, can help to separate the main offensive forces of both alliances while reductions are worked out.)

We shall look in this chapter at each of these tasks in turn.

MILITARY DOCTRINE, FORCE POSTURE, AND PERCEIVED THREAT

This working group should seek to understand the military position in which each alliance perceives itself and identify the forces and weapons that each alliance finds most threatening. Its work can lead directly to more specific discussion of reductions by the negotiators and help them come to an agreement on what forces should be pared down or eliminated.

We described in Chapter 4 the Pact's frequent invitation to discuss doctrine. NATO fended off these offers with some embarrassment, because the Soviets were in fact responding to years of justified NATO criticism that the Pact's strategy of massive ground-force counterattack in the event of war placed it in a good position to launch an attack. NATO feared misuse of the doctrine theme for propaganda purposes, such as Pact critiques of NATO's flexible-response strategy or of the "follow-on forces attack" strategy of seeking to block the advance of Soviet reinforcements by deep interdiction. Finally, in late 1988, NATO agreed that the subject could be discussed on an East/West basis but in C.D.E.-2 rather than in the force-reduction talks.

This seems the less desirable venue, because a fruitful discussion of doctrine would facilitate agreement on reductions, while it is the doctrine and strategy of the two alliances rather than that of the neutrals and non-aligned which heightens the risks of the European confrontation.

According to the C.F.E. mandate, one of the main goals of the Vienna negotiations is the elimination of the capacity to initiate a large-scale offensive action. This topic is a central issue of military doctrine in very practical form. How should we go about measuring such a capacity? Both alliances state that they are defensive and that neither would initiate attack. But what about the capability of each to counterattack against an aggressive attacker? We saw in Chapter 4 that in the armies of the two alliances, the principal force components used for counterattack are the same as those used for attack: units equipped with surface-to-surface missiles, ground-attack aircraft, armed helicopters, tanks, artillery, and infantry-fighting vehicles. In sum, the forces used for counterattack are the same as those used for attack, for large-scale offensive action.

Here is a subject for the discussion of doctrine: How strong should counterattack capability be? Each alliance would surely wish to have sufficient military capability to halt an aggressor and to deny him success. But should each strive for the additional capacity to push the aggressor off its territory, even though that capacity could also be used for offensive purposes? To go further, should each alliance have the capacity to retaliate against the aggressor and to punish it by winning military victory over the aggressor's forces? This last point may be the key to successful discussion of doctrine. It would be wise in the nuclear age for each alliance deliberately to forgo the capacity to retaliate and punish with its conventional forces. It is forces of this organization and size that elicit fears of aggressive attack. The Soviet Union may have to revise the lesson it drew from the tragedy of World War II—not to fall back defensively and allow the destruction of home territory but to deploy well forward to give an immediate and decisive counterblow to any aggression.

Establishing acceptable objectives for defensive counterattack and defining the combination and number of armaments needed to achieve these objectives is one way each alliance can define a defensive posture. Individual weapons systems such as tanks can be used either offensively or defensively. However, as we argued in Chapter 4, it is possible to distinguish between forces configured for offense and for deep counterattack (forces composed of large numbers of armaments of considerable mobility, range, and reach) and forces configured for static defense and counterattack with limited objectives (emphasizing firepower with limited mobility and range). Certain weapons like tanks, surface-to-surface missiles, ground-attack aircraft, and armed helicopters, which can be classed as penetration weapons, are indispensable for attack and for deep counterattack. For defense, other armaments can substitute and the penetration armaments can be reduced or eliminated.

A mutually acceptable definition of counterattack objectives and the organization of forces for counterattack might therefore be a productive subject to discuss in a forum on doctrine. It is unlikely that in such a forum East and West could actually come to early agreement on the definition of a defensive posture, although in the long run they might. But even a preliminary discussion could help each alliance to articulate its objectives in the force-reduction talks, to identify the weapons they wish sooner or later to include in reductions, and to describe the type of forces each should have by the end of the reduction process.

Whether it takes place in the C.D.E. or C.F.E. forums, an exploratory look at military doctrine in practical rather than abstract terms can mitigate the tendency of each alliance to cling to its particular set of proposals without bending. After the alliances exchange and discuss data, a working group on doctrine could also be used to organize and present the views of NATO and the Pact on defining for the long term the force structure of both alliances following reductions in a situation of defense dominance.

DATA EXCHANGE

A revolutionary change seems to have taken place in the Soviets' attitude toward exchanging data on forces in Europe. For more than a decade during the M.B.F.R. talks the Soviet Union refused to release the more detailed figures on its forces in eastern Europe that could have ended its dispute with the West over the number of Warsaw Pact servicemen in central Europe and freed the talks from stalemate. Suddenly in 1987 Soviet officials began offering to exchange detailed data on military deployments, either on a bilateral or alliance-to-alliance basis, before the start of the current force-reduction talks. And at the Moscow summit in May of 1988, General Secretary Gorbachev backed up the offers by pledging the Soviet Union's willingness to resolve any disputes over the figures with on-site inspections.

The NATO countries, which were in some confusion about how to handle an exchange and which were making slow progress toward compiling data on their own forces, said they would not consider an exchange of data until the mandate for the force-reduction talks had been set and until the talks had started. Some NATO officials suspected that the Soviets were aware of NATO's internal difficulties and had designed their turnabout on the question of exchanging data to score propaganda points. That appraisal ignores how radical a shift the Soviets made; if NATO had accepted their offers and the Soviets had not been prepared to make good, their public-relations coup would have become a serious public-relations defeat.

To be sure, it was not clear at the outset that the Soviets were prepared to present more than aggregate totals for each type of weapon held by Pact forces. Such totals, like those presented by NATO for NATO and Pact forces late in 1988 in its publication *Conventional Forces in Europe: The Facts* and those presented by the Pact in January, 1989 (a comparison of the two publications is in Appendix I), amount only to assertions about the total level of weapons holdings of each alliance. As we have already seen, there are many differences between the two sets of figures.

Yet aggregate totals of this kind are of no value in resolving discrepancies. The figures each alliance has on the forces of its opponent consist of estimates of the strength of specific, identifiable units which are combined to form overall totals. If an alliance's holdings of information on the strength in men and weapons of individual units do not add up to the aggregate totals provided by its opponent, there is no way of finding out from a comparison of aggregate totals what the reason for the difference is. To find the reason for differences, each alliance must present information on each of its own major units and their strength in men and weapons.

In the fall of 1988 Soviet officials let it be known that detailed figures—not just aggregates—would be forthcoming. They were compelled, they said, by their own logic. They had offered on-site inspection to resolve disputes and such inspections would be impossible without specific information on the location and strength in men and major armaments of the units to be inspected. Consequently, this information would have to be made available. Some Soviet officials said that the exchange could reach down to the level of regiments.

In the spring of 1989, NATO decided to call for exchange of data in the less operational context of C.D.E.-2 and to offer to exchange more detailed data in the C.F.E. talks only after East/West agreement was reached as to types of armaments to be reduced. This approach seems mistaken. Whether or not data are exchanged in C.D.E.-2, NATO should make every effort to conduct a full exchange in the force-reduction talks early. Each alliance should present information, current as of some agreed date, on the location, official unit-name or designation, and numbers of troops and major weapons down to the level of brigade or regiment and comparable air-force units for all units in the Atlantic-to-the-Urals area, both active duty and reserve, to include armaments in storage, transit, and repair. The exchange should cover major ammunition stocks for ground and air forces.

There are many reasons for an early exchange of data in the force-reduction talks. A full exchange would test the commitment of the Soviets to openness as regards military forces. The on-site inspections that should follow an exchange of data would test the willingness of the Soviets to cooperate in carrying the inspections out. And they would give both alliances practice in handling one of the essential tools for verifying whatever reductions might be made later. Ultimately, an exchange of data together with on-site inspections will help the alliances to evaluate opposing forces realistically, mitigating the tendency on both sides to assume the worst.

There is another, highly practical reason for East/West data exchange early in the force-reduction talks: to prove to the satisfaction of western governments that the unilateral reductions announced by General Secretary Gorbachev in December of 1988 are actually taking place and that the forces withdrawn are not being replaced. Given the favorable impact on western opinion and the cost savings that the Soviet Union presumably is seeking, the Soviets will be motivated to carry the reductions out scrupulously and to avoid any hint of fraud. To that end the Soviets may invite western observers to follow some part of the reduction process.

But because their reductions are unilateral the Soviets will not be obliged by any formal commitment to freeze the number of their forces after the cutbacks are completed. The best way to deal with western doubts over the unilateral Pact reductions and their permanence is to exchange data early in the C.F.E. talks, valid as of January 1, 1989, before the unilateral reductions begin and to follow it with an update two years later, when the unilateral reductions are scheduled to be completed. A program of on-site inspections to validate the data exchanged will be necessary. Further assurance can be provided by early-warning inspections described later.

An exchange of data would clear the air of the many charges by the West during the M.B.F.R. talks that the Warsaw Pact falsified data. For a reduction agreement to be reached it will be necessary to get rid of this negative heritage. Sharing data is for both alliances a test of will to reduce forces. If the two alliances do not have enough confidence in each other to exchange specific information on the location and strength of their military units then it is doubtful that they are really ready to make deep cuts.

At present, specific figures on Soviet forces are not only withheld from the outside world but also from many civilian Soviet defense experts and economists. With a release of data to the West civilian Soviet officials and defense experts would have an opportunity to join the military in discussing how to scale down the overall size of Soviet armed forces and the resources allocated to them. In this way an exchange of detailed data could be even more important to long-term arms-control objectives than it would be to the force-reduction talks.

Both alliances have feared that differences over data exchanged could bring negotiators to an impasse as they did in the M.B.F.R. talks. It is always worthwhile to seek to avoid the mistakes of the past. But it is also possible to overreact to past mistakes and to draw the wrong lesson from them. As the current talks began, the NATO countries seemed to be doing just that. We pointed out in Chapter 5 that the M.B.F.R. talks broke down over the refusal of the Soviet Union and its allies to give the West the detailed data it needed to understand specifically why the Pact's total figures for its deployments in eastern Europe were smaller than NATO's. At the time there was no question of on-site inspection to help resolve the difference; the Pact was not even willing to agree in specific form to inspections for the purpose of verifying actual reductions, much less to verify preliminary data.

There are three important differences between the situation then and the situation now. The first is the readiness of the Pact to provide detailed information on its forces, including the strength and location of individual units. The second is the willingness of the Pact to permit on-site inspection to resolve any discrepancies. The third is the recognition by both the Pact and NATO that a perfect correspondence between the data of the two sides is not a necessary precondition of an agreement to establish a goal for reductions. Instead, as the West proposed during the M.B.F.R. talks in 1985, the alliances can agree on a numerical level to which both sides will reduce their holdings of a given armament and then verify the outcome. Since both sides have learned from the mistakes of the past, a new impasse over data can be avoided. In his concluding remarks at the Vienna C.S.C.E. review conference in January, 1989, Foreign Minister Shevardnadze distanced himself from the implication that full agreement on data would be needed to set reduction levels.

Data exchange will be needed early in the current force-reduction talks for all the reasons just described. It will also be needed for other practical reasons. Unless there is data exchange, it will not be possible to decide which types of aircraft should be reduced and in what combination or to decide the level of residual ceilings following reductions. Moreover, large-scale reductions in armaments will probably have to occur in phases over a period of years rather than at a single stroke, and these interim levels will have to be specified and verified. It will be insufficient for verification agencies merely to state that reductions are proceeding satisfactorily and that overall verification will take place only when all negotiated reductions have been completed. In addition, western parliaments and eastern governments are going to want to have some general idea of how much the opposing alliance will cut back. For this the data of both alliances will have to be in closer agreement.

The Warsaw Pact has urged that the alliances agree to eliminate asymmetries or imbalances in their arsenals which might be revealed by an exchange of data. We have pointed out that East/West agreement on data is not a requirement for setting new equal ceilings to which each alliance would have to cut its holdings. But what about a different issue: should NATO seek to use data exchange to document the existence of asymmetries and thus to buttress its argument that a given armament should be subject to reduction? NATO claims that the Pact has numerical superiority in many major weapons. The Pact's own figures (Appendix I) show it numerically superior to NATO in tanks, armored vehicles, artillery, combat aircraft of all types combined, as well as surface-to-surface missiles. But the Pact in its published data also maintains that NATO has more attack aircraft, combat helicopters, and anti-tank weapons than Pact forces. NATO's published data shows the opposite.

The answer to the question of whether data exchange should be used to identify the existence of numerical superiorities and thus as a guide to selection of armaments for reductions is probably no, for two reasons: each alliance already knows the armaments whose reduction it wishes to emphasize. NATO wants reductions in tanks, artillery, and armored troop carriers; the Pact wants reductions in attack aircraft, armed helicopters, and surface-to-surface missiles. Agreement on whether to include these armaments in reductions depends on factors other than numbers and in fact has already been reached, even though NATO has decided to postpone negotiation on reducing surface-to-surface missiles.

The second reason for not using data exchange to identify arms for reduction is the slowness of the data-comparison process. Even after definitional differences are resolved by discussion, the overall total figures presented by one alliance for its own holdings of a given type of armament—listing the holdings of that armament by individual units, including armaments in storage—may diverge widely from the assessments of the opposing alliance. In this case, the opposing alliance could request on-site inspections. These inspections would end in one of three ways: the alliance would find that its original assessments were incorrect; it would find that its original assessments were correct; or its doubts would persist unresolved. But the problem is that none of these findings could be conclusive. On-site inspection can only cover fragments of an alliance's total force. As a result, even if several on-site inspections indicated that the figures presented by the Pact were accurate for the individual units observed, more inspections and more research would be needed to convince western intelligence agencies that they should revise their estimates. Western intelligence agencies will be justifiably slow to change their minds and to revise estimates that they have spent years compiling. The slowness of this process is a major reason why data exchange validation inspections and the beginnings of agreed verification procedures should take place early in the C.F.E. talks.

A further question is whether an exchange of data should consist solely of each alliance presenting detailed figures for its own forces or whether each alliance should also be asked to present in the same degree of detail estimates of the forces of the opposing alliance? Western intelligence agencies will be reluctant to do the latter, because, as we have seen, the Pact's traditional secrecy on military forces has compelled NATO to base its assessments on information from various sources, some good and some bad. The Pact might be able to infer from the strengths and gaps in NATO's assessments the sources and methods on which the assessments were based. And some NATO intelligence agencies might also look inefficient. These considerations are sufficiently weighty for us to conclude that each alliance should present detailed figures on its own forces only.

Unavoidably, the resulting data comparison will be unsatisfactory from one viewpoint: each alliance will compare the detailed unit-by-unit presentations of the opposing alliance on its forces with the information it holds on the same units in its own classified dossiers. It will note for itself the degree to which the figures for individual units provided by the opposing alliance correspond or diverge from its own holdings for the same units. But neither side will be revealing the full extent of its knowledge of the other alliance's forces or the full reason for the questions it is asking about the data of the other. There will be no actual data comparison in the sense of both sides comparing two complete sets of figures on the same units.

Considerations like these are some of the reasons why NATO has not been enthusiastic about exchanging data with the Pact. But they overlook two cardinal points. First is the political importance of an exchange, just described. Second is its military importance. Over the long haul, the presentation of detailed figures combined with the right to question and discuss them and the right to make on-site inspections will ultimately contribute to a more accurate assessment of Warsaw Pact forces by NATO and, if rigorously pursued, to a closer correspondence between NATO and Pact figures. NATO must not take the defeatist position that it could learn nothing definitive about Pact forces, no matter how much data the Pact might present or how many inspections NATO might carry out or, alternatively, that no amount of on-site inspection, satellite photography, or human intelligence can compensate for the Pact's skill at cheating. For years NATO has asked the Pact to produce data. Now that the Pact is ready to do so NATO cannot say that *it* isn't ready or willing.

The alliances should also come to such an agreement on categories in which, for simplicity's sake, data probably will not be exchanged, such as small arms and light motor vehicles. Each alliance should have the right to specify the type of armament on which it wishes to exchange data. These nominations should be honored as long as they do not breach the mandate for the talks by specifying armaments not covered by it, such as naval forces.

DATA VALIDATION

In the C.F.E. talks, each alliance should have an annual quota of at least 100 divisional inspections at short notice over a period of two to three years to validate or evaluate each other's data. "Verification" would perhaps be a misnomer here; although each alliance would be obligated to present complete and accurate data on its forces, there would be no formal commitment or obligation to be verified. The figure of 100 inspections per year is based on the possibility of inspecting each Pact active-duty and reserve division and major air force units at least once in the three-year period. However, there would be no requirement to visit each unit and some might be visited repeatedly. The inspection quota should also allow an alliance to conduct as many as ten inspections at once of the units of its choice. No justification other than a generally-worded statement of a discrepancy in data should be required.

NATO personnel conducting the exchange of data and carrying out the inspections should be drawn from those who will later monitor reductions and compliance with residual ceilings. Data exchange and data validation are the foundation for the verification task. On-site inspection to resolve discrepancies in data will have to include direct access to barracks, messes, and equipment storage areas as well as to rosters of the men and equipment in a unit. The task will thus parallel the verification of reductions and will give each alliance valuable experience in verification before it is called on to make reductions.

We pointed out in Chapter 5 that the most important advantage to NATO of an exchange of detailed data is to give NATO verifiers an opportunity to see precisely how the Pact combines the strength in men and armaments of specific units into its overall totals. NATO verification officials need to have a clear understanding of how Pact data is articulated and of Pact information on the strength of individual units in order to establish their own verification data base on the same units. They will compare their own currently available information on the same units with Pact information and seek by discussion and inspections to reconcile differences between the two. They will need to have completed this laborious work well before they are called on to verify the manpower or armaments holdings of individual Pact units by on-site inspection following reductions. It will take a long time to achieve a data base acceptable to NATO intelligence agencies, which often have diverging assessments and analytical approaches among themselves that have to be resolved. If verifying officials do not have an acceptable data base before reductions begin, they will lack confidence in their ability to confirm compliance and will express this lack of confidence to parliaments. This problem may cause domestic political friction in some western countries. This scenario, too, is a compelling motive for NATO to begin exchanging full data early rather than later in the C.F.E. negotiations.

EARLY-WARNING MEASURES: ESTABLISHING A ZONE OF MILITARY OPENNESS

Because the force-reduction talks deal with a difficult, complex subject, negotiators should deliberately seek to identify and break off a manage-able segment and reach an agreement on that quickly, in order to build momentum. Early-warning and transparency measures are highly suited to this purpose, because agreeing on them would not require prior agreements on data or reductions. The operation of an effective set of early-warning measures would create mutual confidence, facili-tating difficult negotiation on force reductions. Usually such measures involve use of existing equipment or facilities and thus are relatively easy to organize and relatively low cost.

An agreement on early-warning measures could for a time also satisfy public opinion in the West and the East that the participants in the talks were actively seeking a positive outcome. For NATO govern-ments in particular, an agreement on early-warning measures could head off public pressure for unilateral troop cuts. Since the Pact, in general, appears more interested than NATO in achieving a specific outcome of the talks, it, too, would benefit from rapid agreement on early warning.

Early-warning and transparency measures should be considered autonomous actions to be carried out as soon as they are negotiated rather than put off until an agreement is reached on reductions. Even if negotiations for reductions are protracted or bog down, agreed early-warning measures will be extremely valuable contributions to the stability of the military confrontation in Europe.

Because of the greater openness of western societies and the traditional close hold of the Pact countries on military information, early-warning and transparency measures would bring the West a net gain in information. And they can help both West and East avoid miscalculation. Indeed, they are an essential complement of reductions to parity. As we discussed in the last chapter, bringing NATO and Pact forces to a state of parity will not by itself decisively enhance stability. Even at a lower level, rough equality in major armaments between the two alliances could increase incentives for preemptive attack in crisis situations and increase the intensity of the arms race. Therefore, in order to make an assured contribution to stability, reductions should be accompanied by early-warning measures (as well as by some degree of restructuring to make the forces of both alliances more defensive). As NATO forces become more equal to those of the Pact, the Pact's leaders will have as strong an interest as NATO's in such measures.

The 1986 Document of the Stockholm Conference on Confidence- and Security-Building Measures in Europe, which we reviewed in Chapter 6, provides for an extensive process of notifying the signers of military activities in the field. The follow-on C.D.E.-2 talks will provide an opportunity to improve and intensify these measures with the participation of the European neutral and nonaligned states as well as the members of both alliances. But a separate set of early-warning measures—measures designed to provide broad access to a whole range of military activities and to turn up evidence of preparations for conflict—needs to be discussed by NATO and the Pact in the force-reduction talks. Some of these measures would be better suited to this forum than to the C.D.E. conference for geographic reasons. Choosing between C.F.E. and C.D.E. should be based in part on which forum will allow more rapid progress. Here we leave aside that consideration and focus instead on the description of possible measures.

The most productive approach to early-warning measures in the NATO/Pact context would, in conformity with General Secretary Gorbachev's frequent application of the principle of *glasnost* or openness to the East/West military relationship, be a joint decision to make the entire Atlantic-to-the-Urals area a zone of military transparency or military openness. The establishment of such a zone would rest on the four measures described below. Together with data exchange and a continuing program of data validation inspections, this set of measures would have the additional function of providing confirmation that the announced Warsaw Pact unilateral reductions are taking place and that the reduced forces are not being replaced. The measures should therefore be viewed as having a dual function of early warning and verification, rather than painstakingly separating these two activities, as has been traditional western practice.

1 Overflights

The most important component of a Zone of Military Openness would be an annual quota of 150 short-notice, low-altitude flights by fixed-wing aircraft or helicopters over the eastern portion of the reduction area and the same number over the western portion. The eastern portion of that area would be divided into fifty quadrants for this purpose and the western portion into a lesser number of quadrants of similar size. The two alliances could use the same type of specialized aircraft, perhaps one provided and operated by the European neutrals. An alliance requesting an overflight would designate one or more quadrants for inspection. If it wished, its flight could cover a given quadrant repeatedly. As many as ten flights could be conducted simultaneously to check on widely spread activities. One third of these overflights could be supplemented by mobile ground observation in the same quadrant. This overflight program could be considered as a specific application of President Bush's proposal in the spring of 1989 to revive the Eisenhower open skies program.

In addition to the low-altitude overflights there might also be overflights at high altitude, using United States TR-1 aircraft. A few sweeps by this plane could provide timely coverage of military movements and activities in both the eastern and western portions of the large Atlantic-to-the-Urals area. For its high-altitude overflights the Warsaw Pact has no equivalent of the TR-1 but might be willing to use a two-seater version of the American plane if it could provide the co-pilot.

The Warsaw Pact might reject use of the TR-1 aircraft, the spyplane that succeeded the U-2, the model piloted by Gary Powers that was shot down over the Soviet Union in May of 1960. But the Pact would have considerable difficulty resisting the arguments NATO could make in favor of overflights at low altitude. These include the agreement of the two alliances in the C.F.E. mandate to give priority to preventing surprise attack; the apparent willingness of the Pact to allow overflights over the small zone of reduced armaments it has proposed within the

Atlantic-to-the-Urals area; the willingness of the Pact to allow observers at main traffic points; the Pact's willingness to allow on-site inspection to resolve disputes over data and for verification; the fact that, as early as 1958, in the conference on surprise attack, the Soviet Union itself proposed a zone for aerial photography to extend 800 kilometers on either side of the dividing line between the alliances; and finally, the repeated statements of the Soviet and eastern European leadership in support of *glasnost* in East/West military relations.

This system of overflights could be a very valuable supplement of satellite photography, which is often stymied by cloud cover in central and eastern Europe. And the capacity to carry out ten simultaneous flights over the western U.S.S.R. would provide close coverage of the activities of Soviet reserve units and help to meet NATO concerns about gradual covert training and preparation for full mobilization attack.

Some NATO countries, more sensitive politically than others to inspection by the Soviets, seem reluctant to support such a measure. But given the Pact's very thorough intelligence coverage of western Europe, these political objections do not outweigh the military benefits of overflights, which would also permit multilateral NATO participation and relieve some of the friction in the NATO alliance stemming from the U.S. monopoly over satellite photography.

2 Radar Surveillance

A component of a Zone of Military Openness would be a set of measures providing for undisturbed flights parallel to the line of contact between the alliances by radar-equipped aircraft like AWACs, which follow the movement of aircraft in the air; by aircraft equipped with synthetic-aperture radar, which follows activities at fixed sites; and, when they become available, by aircraft equipped with joint surveillance and target-attack systems (JSTARS), which will have the capacity to follow movement of large groups of military vehicles. The measure providing for such flights would preclude electronic jamming, which is sometimes done even in peacetime.

This group of measures could include forward aircraft-warning radar stations deployed deep in the territory of the opposing alliance, some manned with a small permanent contingent, and unmanned radars mounted on masts equipped with sensors against interference. Warning stations of this type would be put out of operation in a conflict situation, as would the communications of human observers, but interference with their operation would of itself provide warning.

3 Observation at Exit/Entry Points

The third component of a Zone of Military Openness would be arrangements to establish small, permanent groups of four to six observers at a restricted number of exit/entry points (ports, airfields, rail, and road) into the overall Atlantic-to-the-Urals area (or to a subregion like that suggested earlier for central Europe). All military personnel and armaments entering or leaving the area would be required to use these exit/entry points. The posts would do double duty, providing information on entry and departure of forces for warning purposes (for example, entry of Soviet forces from the area east of the Urals), and for purposes of verification, for example, by checking manpower and restricted armaments in and out of the reduction area. Such posts were proposed in the M.B.F.R. talks and agreed to in principle by Warsaw Pact negotiators. In the past NATO wanted a large number of exit/entry posts for its own logistic convenience, the Pact decidedly fewer. Given the cost, a smaller number is desirable.

4 Observation at Transportation Choke Points and at Military Headquarters

Permanent observer teams should also be posted at selected traffic choke points and at the headquarters of divisions and major combat airfields inside the reduction area. It may be difficult to gain agreement on posting observers at division headquarters and airfields but it does not seem impossible. Given at least limited permission to circulate and to observe such facilities as ammunition storage and aircraft loading, observers at these sites could provide valuable mutual assurance to both alliances. NATO observers at airfields where the Soviet Union conducts its semiannual troop rotation by flying in new conscripts would be in a better position than at present to ascertain whether the Soviet Union was flying new personnel but not taking back to the U.S.S.R. conscripts whose period of service was expiring. Concern over this possibility has been frequent in NATO. In Chapter 11 on verification, we describe these posts in more detail.

No one of these measures constituting a Zone of Military Openness would of itself fully guarantee warning of preparations for attack. But together—and in combination with activities of the intelligence apparatus of each alliance, including national technical means, and also in combination with the reporting system provided for by the Stockholm Document and eventually by whatever system is established to verify force reductions—they would provide a tight web of information on force activities of all kinds.

CONSTRAINTS

Constraints—negotiated restrictions on military activities or deployments—are not popular with military commanders in either alliance, because they restrict a commander's freedom to dispose over his military resources. Forced to choose between freedom from restrictions and restrictions imposed on the potential adversary, military commanders nearly always choose freedom from restrictions, even if the restriction would weigh more heavily on the adversary. This tendency may be stronger in NATO than in the Warsaw Pact, because NATO military commanders generally question the capacity of NATO political decision makers to rapidly counter potential Pact violations of constraints by suspending agreed restrictions on NATO forces. They assume, rightly or wrongly, that the Soviet Union would have far less difficulty in getting its Pact allies to agree to act.

The result is a decidedly negative attitude in NATO on constraints. This is unfortunate, because constraints once agreed upon can be rapidly applied, and at little or no economic cost. Only one such measure is now in effect: the prohibition negotiated in the first Stockholm C.D.E. conference against holding exercises involving more than 75,000 personnel without two years' notice. Constraints could be negotiated separately in advance of reductions and would be valuable in themselves if negotiation on reductions bogged down. If negotiated together with reductions, they would augment the contribution of reductions to security.

The objectives of negotiated constraints should be to:

1. Impede preparation for attack and to delay the attack in the event of violation. For example, a requirement to pull large ammunition depots exceeding a specified capacity of weight and volume back from the line of confrontation could make it more difficult

for an attacker to resupply its units to sustain forward movement. Such a requirement would not interfere with the dispersed storage of smaller amounts of ammunition for purposes of defense.

2. Provide unambiguous evidence of aggressive intent in the event of violation. Flagrant violation of a commitment not to undertake some specific action, like mounting more than 200 aircraft in training sorties at a given time or not to move tank-transporter trucks forward beyond a specified line, should be a warning of hostile intent, a clear enough warning to ease decisions even by the NATO alliance of sixteen sovereign states.

3. Restrict activities or deployments of higher value to an attacker than a defender, for example, forward deployment of mine-clearing equipment or heavy tank transporting trucks. However, to pass muster in negotiations, restrictions on activities like this should have some logical application to both alliances, not just one.

4. Extend the time available to a defender to prepare for attack. An example is secured, inspected storage of specialized major equipment, like assault bridging mounted on armored vehicles, often tanks, at sites pulled back from the line of confrontation. If one alliance broke such equipment out of storage, the other side could take that as a warning of hostile intent. The pulled-back position of the equipment would delay its deployment for combat. If in addition the equipment had been immobilized or partially dismantled before being put in storage there would be a further built-in delay in using it for combat purposes and more time for the defense to prepare for attack.

Constraints are not intrinsically different from reductions except in degree. Both are intended to delay an attacker. If the armament reductions negotiated in Vienna are confined to withdrawal, storage, or transfer to the custody of reserve units rather than destruction, they will not eliminate military capability. Instead, like many constraints, reductions of this kind would serve to delay an attack while equipment that had been cut from service was returned to duty. For that matter, if reduction agreements broke down, even destroyed armaments and disbanded units could be replaced eventually. Therefore, constraints and reductions should be seen not as different in kind but as located within a single spectrum of delay, with some measures causing more delay and others less.

Certainly the second round of C.D.E. confidence-building talks should deal with those constraints that are generally applicable to the territories of the thirty-five states participating. But some constraint measures are aimed specifically at coping with the NATO/Pact confrontation, in which large forces of opposing alliances are ranged on either side of a fixed line extending from Norway to Turkey. These would be best debated by C.F.E. negotiators. An example is the most general and perhaps most useful of the constraints proposed to date: a "Restricted Military Area," or R.M.A., for central Europe.

RESTRICTED MILITARY AREA

The main purpose of a Restricted Military Area is to stabilize the East/West military confrontation in Europe by disengaging the units of NATO and the Pact that are most valuable for offense, thus diminishing the possibility of misperception and preemptive action in crisis in the area of greatest force concentration. It is also a device for restructuring the confronting alliances at their line of contact toward a more defensive posture. Negotiation of a Restricted Military Area could also be linked to negotiation of reductions.

NATO's opposition to the nuclear- and chemical-free zones that the Warsaw Pact has proposed periodically has given the very concept of such zones a negative reputation. However, at least one of the Pact's suggestions has potential usefulness. In July of 1988 the Pact proposed establishing zones with a depth of between 100 and 150 kilometers on each side of the line of contact from which "the more dangerous, destabilizing types of weapons would be removed or reduced." The Pact did not then go into detail, so I shall proceed to describe my own version of such a Restricted Military Area, one that I have been recommending for some years before the Pact made its proposal. This version assumes that the Soviet withdrawal of six tank divisions and 5,000 tanks from eastern Europe announced at the end of 1988 will occur and builds on that.

To establish a Restricted Military Area, all NATO and Pact units equipped with surface-to-surface missiles, fixed-wing aircraft, helicopters, tanks, infantry-fighting vehicles (but not necessarily all armored personnel carriers), airborne units, and self-propelled, armored artillery, with the exception of rockets with ranges of fifty kilometers or less, would be pulled back from the line of confrontation in Federal Germany a distance of fifty kilometers on the NATO side and one hundred kilometers on the Warsaw Pact side. Withdrawals would normally be in the form of battalions, which are usually equipped with a single major armament. Major ammunition depots and bridging, tank-transporter, and pipeline units would be included in the withdrawals. If it is desired to make the restrictions even more stringent, all armored vehicles and all artillery or rocket launchers with a caliber of more than 110 millimeters could also be withdrawn from the area.

Two factors justify the difference between the hundred-kilometer width proposed for the Pact portion of the restricted military area and the fifty-kilometer width of the NATO portion. The first is the shallowness of the NATO area as compared with the depth of the Warsaw Pact territory to the Urals. The second is the relative closeness of the Pact's main reinforcing power, the Soviet Union, to the line of confrontation between the alliances and the distance of the United States, NATO's main source of reinforcements, from that line. NATO cannot accept for its own territory the broader 100 to 150 kilometer belt proposed by the Pact because of NATO's shallow area and the resulting dense deployments. There is some indication of Pact flexibility on the dimensions of a restricted area. When the Pact proposed a zone of this kind, it stated that the zone's breadth should be decided on the basis of unspecified "geostrategic" factors. Since then Soviet officials have informally spoken of their willingness to discuss asymmetrical dimensions, with greater depth on the Pact side.

All armaments of the types mentioned above would be prohibited from the restricted area. Should manpower also be restricted, given the difficulty of verifying manpower ceilings? One way to do so would be to allow the alliances to post as many active-duty personnel in the restricted area as NATO now has there—about 85,000—but no more. (This limitation would not include personnel of the Federal German Bundesgrezzschutz, the East German Volkspolizei, or the Czechoslovak border police. Instead their numbers could be frozen and prohibited armaments in their possession withdrawn.) This measure would not require any reduction in the number of NATO's personnel, but the reduction required of the Pact would be substantial. The Pact now has about 190,000 ground-force personnel deployed in the restricted area here proposed. Assuming that all six tank divisions with 50,000 personnel that the Soviets have scheduled for unilateral withdrawal will come from forces within the proposed hundred-kilometer belt in East Germany and Czechoslovakia, a restriction to 85,000 troops would require the Pact to withdraw an additional 55,000 men.

Unless the R.M.A. were part of a previously agreed reduction plan such as the proposal for U.S./Soviet reductions proposed by President Bush, also a possibility, finding barracks for these personnel might be a problem for East Germany and Czechoslovakia. These states might complain, too, that they were being compelled to defend an area twice the size of the NATO belt with no more troops than NATO. Yet to create a Restricted Military Area with no limits on manpower would leave open the possibility of a forward buildup of infantry units by the Pact. Consequently, a more easily negotiated solution might be to freeze manpower in the restricted area at 85,000 for NATO and at 140,000 for the Pact (its present strength of 190,000 less all 50,000 troops that the Soviets are withdrawing unilaterally, plus any additional active-duty East German and Czechoslovak personnel in this area which are to be reduced unilaterally).

In the R.M.A. each alliance would be free to deploy units equipped with armaments other than those restricted—for example, anti-aircraft and anti-tank units, infantry, and combat engineers—and to establish obstacles, barriers, and other counter-mobility devices. On its side NATO would maintain existing corps sectors, including all those manned by NATO allies of the Federal Republic. Both the Federal Republic and its allies would restructure the ground forces stationed forward in the restricted area, increasing the number of infantry, combat engineers, and other permitted forces to preserve a total strength of 85,000. Therefore, establishing an R.M.A. would not change the pattern or deterrent effect of forward deployments by NATO, nor would it call into question the commitment of the NATO allies, including the U.S. and the U.K., to involve themselves in any conflict in central Europe from the outset.

On both sides of the line of contact, the restricted area would be monitored by low-flying aircraft of the opposing alliance, by mobile inspectors inside the area, and by permanent posts on the western and eastern margins, through which all forces entering or leaving would be obliged to pass. Training areas of both alliances located in the R.M.A. could continue in use, provided both alliances gave sufficient advance notice, invited observers, and made sure that the troops using the areas passed through exit/entry posts.

Major violation of the restricted area through entry of additional units or prohibited equipment would be considered tantamount to opening hostilities. This point could be made explicit in the text of the agreement establishing the restrictions. This action would establish a line on the territory of each of the opposing alliances whose violation would justify the use of military force. (Such an approach could also be taken in connection with establishing sub-regions or the limit on stationed forces foreseen in NATO proposals.)

An R.M.A. would have many benefits for NATO, but also many for the Pact. It would result in NATO (and the Pact) deploying a screening force of infantry, obstacles, and barriers to take the first impact of possible attack, shifting NATO's scarce armored formations to a more effective role as rapid-response operational reserves, of which NATO now has too few. NATO members would be committed in advance, through their participation in the agreement, to recognize significant violation as a *casus belli*. Alternatively, the agreement could be worded to release all signatories from negotiated restrictions automatically and without notice following such a violation. Either way, decisionmaking in NATO would be improved.

What if the restricted area were in fact violated by the Pact? If both sides had a belt of obstacles and barriers manned mainly by infantry and combat engineers, the Pact's own infantry could theoretically be used in an attack with minimum preparation to soften up NATO's defenses for a tank attack as Pact tanks moved forward into the restricted area. But the concentrated firepower at the disposal of dug-in defensive forces and the attacking infantry's lack of armor would make the success of this initial attack unlikely.

NATO should have warning of the preparation for attack of Pact armored units outside the restricted area. It would have it immediately from its own observer personnel as soon as Pact forces entered the R.M.A. Pact tanks might be able to cross the 100-kilometer tank-free belt in about two days under NATO air attack. However, the gain in time to prepare for the armored attack could be vital for NATO. Moreover, the main thrusts of attack would be more clear than at present, where Pact armor can probe all along NATO's line. NATO could act to position its armored forces more effectively to counter the main direction of attack. Fewer of NATO's expensive armored forces would have to be tacked down along a defensive line awaiting an attack that might never come in that sector. In effect, the R.M.A. would move NATO's defensive frontier 100 kilometers to the east. NATO defense would in many respects gain the depth it now lacks.

The Pact for its part would obtain parallel benefits. As discussed in Chapter 7 the achievement of parity after reductions will not necessarily diminish the risk of war. For that reason the Pact might have as much interest as NATO in protecting itself against surprise attack.

Verification for the restricted area would be relatively easy, because withdrawals of the designated armaments would not be partial but total. A ceiling on manpower, if the alliances could agree to one, would present problems of verification but these would not be formidable, because the area would not be large.

The restricted area would be fairly easy to negotiate. There would be no need for participants to agree on data for armaments or to work out terms of reductions and no issues to resolve concerning the quality or age of equipment; all tanks would go.

When withdrawing armaments from the restricted area the two alliances could be given a choice. They could make the withdrawals either by pulling out entire battalions equipped with a given prohibited weapon and replacing them with other units, or by pulling out only armaments and retaining the units holding the armaments and restructuring them. If NATO chose to withdraw battalions from its fifty-kilometer strip, it would have to pull perhaps fourteen American tank and artillery battalions and perhaps fifty such Federal German battalions, equipped with about 1,700 tanks and 400 artillery pieces all told. If infantry-fighting vehicles were to be withdrawn in addition to these other armaments—and there is a good case for doing so—then the battalions holding them would not be withdrawn, but would remain in place. Withdrawal in this case would take out too many infantry and other units that should stay in the area.

From its hundred-kilometer belt, the Pact would have to withdraw units equipped with prohibited weapons—tanks, artillery, and, in its case, also surface-to-surface missiles, armed helicopters, aircraft, and bridging units—from (prior to unilateral reductions) three East German divisions, four Czechoslovak divisions, and eleven Soviet divisions, for a total of about 5,700 tanks, 4,200 artillery pieces, 108 missile launchers, and 300 attack helicopters.

For NATO, the establishment of an R.M.A. fifty kilometers deep would not require the relocation of many units or construction of new facilities. Tank and artillery battalions could be rotated out of the restricted area into installations in other parts of the Federal Republic, and infantry and combat engineer units could be rotated into the area from units already stationed elsewhere in the Federal Republic or nearby. Because the Pact's withdrawals would be much larger than NATO's, the Pact would be able to follow the same procedure only to some degree and would in any event have to restructure remaining forces into infantry units.

What should the alliances do with the armaments they withdraw? We have assumed here that the Soviet share of tanks to be withdrawn—

about 60 percent of the 5,700 total, or roughly 3,400 tanks, as well as the Soviet share of artillery pieces to be withdrawn—could be included in the already announced Soviet unilateral withdrawals and returned to Soviet territory. (At least two of the Soviet tank divisions announced for unilateral withdrawal are within the proposed 100-kilometer belt.) Soviet authorities have stated that the six Soviet tank divisions to be withdrawn will be disbanded and their tanks dismantled.

Withdrawn Czechoslovak and East German equipment could be transferred to active-duty or reserve units outside the restricted area or stored. If a force-reduction agreement is negotiated, its terms can dictate the fate of these armaments: either to destroy them or to place them in secured storage outside the restricted area. And, if the restricted area were negotiated as part of a broader reduction agreement or to fit into a subsequently negotiated agreement, the units withdrawn by both sides would be credited to overall reductions and disbanded.

One major benefit of an R.M.A., if it were negotiated early on before agreement on reductions can be reached, is that it would provide a basis for making Soviet and east European unilateral reductions an enduring treaty commitment.

WESTERN OBJECTIONS TO RESTRICTIVE ZONES

For years NATO has opposed the creation of zones 150 to 300 kilometers deep to be free of nuclear and chemical weapons because, given the shallowness of NATO territory, the zones would all but eliminate such weapons from NATO forces in central Europe, leaving Soviet and Pact forces outside the restricted zones still equipped with them. This would weaken NATO's deterrent capability without providing a comparable gain in stability. Unfortunately, NATO tends to lump all proposals for areas of disengagement with these Pact proposals for nuclear- and chemical-free zones and to dismiss them out of hand.

But even when the NATO allies have focussed on the question of more general zones of restricted armaments, as distinct from nuclear- and chemical-free zones, they have not been enthusiastic. Resistance has been strongest in the Federal Republic of Germany, where objections have fallen into four main categories:

- the worry that the creation of a special zone might deepen the division between the two Germanies;

- the potential for interference with NATO's strategy of forward defense;
- the economic and social impact of obstacles and barriers on Federal German territory within the zone; and
- the potentially negative political side effects of giving Federal Germany special status under an arms-control regime.

Federal Germany's concern about deepening its division from East Germany could probably be overcome by an East/West agreement in which both German states were contributing to stabilizing and controlling the military confrontation of which they are an important part.

The R.M.A. described here would not weaken NATO's strategy of forward defense. To the contrary, it would improve it. The Federal Republic's NATO allies would continue in their forward positions, and militarily, forward defense would become more viable with the withdrawal of the Pact's armored forces and the greater availability of NATO armor as operational reserves.

Federal Germany's concern that installing barriers in its portion of a restricted area could hinder tourism and would in any case be resisted by residents can be met by selecting less destructive and less visible emplacements than might otherwise be chosen. What would count most, in any case, would be having prepositioned materials and equipment like mines and pipe explosives immediately available in storage in the area and having troops trained and ready to build the barriers when necessary. Study after study has shown that placement of obstacles and barriers can make a critical difference for NATO at relatively low cost, especially in the early phases of Pact attack.[1]

Federal Germany's objection to being singled out for "special status" in arms control might be met if the R.M.A. were only one set of controls within a larger agreement that would also include (for example) controls on Soviet reserve forces in the U.S.S.R.

Besides the objections just outlined, NATO has argued that establishing a restricted area would hinder NATO forces from moving into the area during exercises to take up their readiness positions at the border. To this, it can be said that only some NATO forces would be affected. The personnel of armored units could themselves enter the area to familiarize themselves with readiness positions. In any case, the establishment of a restricted area would change the present pattern of readiness positions, shifting them back from the line of contact.

Some military experts on both sides believe that total withdrawal of the specified armaments from both eastern and western sectors of the

R.M.A. is too drastic. They concede that the pattern of deployments suggested here might be a reasonable posture for both alliances after deep cuts had been negotiated and carried out. But they believe that until then, military commanders on both sides would want to have some of the specified armaments, especially tanks and artillery, on hand for defensive purposes. They are sceptical of the capacity of minefields and infantry armed with anti-tank weapons to stop an attack by armored forces. They suggest for the interim period a zone in which the armaments would be thinned out but not eliminated.

This issue, which is part of the tank/anti-tank controversy described in Chapter 4, will not be resolved soon. But given NATO's interests, these objections to total withdrawal from an asymmetrical zone, deeper on the Pact side, do not seem to have decisive weight. In the event of a decision by NATO to prepare for attack—a decision which the establishment of a Restricted Military Area would facilitate—NATO's tanks and artillery would have only half as far to go to reach the line of contact as the Pact's forces and so could take up their positions much earlier. The Pact's interests would not be compromised by total withdrawal, either. The Pact's leaders have been less anxious about the possibility of an armored attack by NATO's unwieldy coalition army than about the possibility of a sudden attack by air. And in a restricted area of the sort described here, the Pact's ground-to-air defenses would not be weakened and indeed could be increased.

The less-radical alternative proposed by the skeptics would have some but not all of the benefits of the scheme described here and would impose some degree of delay on a surprise attack but not as much. What is more, a thin-out of armaments would be harder to verify than complete elimination.

SECURED STORAGE

Storing equipment in fenced compounds under surveillance by the opposing alliance could be one of the most versatile and flexible tools of arms control in Europe. C.F.E. working groups on early warning and constraints and on verification could begin to decide the terms of secured storage now, independent of negotiations on actual reductions. In that way an agreed system could be ready for presentation at the talks when appropriate.

Secured storage sites can be fenced with fiber-optic cables and equipped for continuous peripheral inspection by video and other cameras. Authorized exits can be equipped with a selection of sub-surface weight sensors, video cameras, and infrared sensors, some with continuous telemetry reporting. The compounds would have to be subject to on-site inspection by the opposing alliance from the ground or from low-flying aircraft. As we will see in discussing verification (Chapter 11), such compounds can also be established merely by ordinary wire fencing with a peripheral dirt road and a small resident observer group from the opposing alliance.

Secured storage can be used for equipment, like tanks, withdrawn from deployment with units in a force-reduction agreement, and for equipment already in storage, such as the prepositioned American armaments in Europe. It can be used to secure equipment of reserve units as a control on mobilization and to secure equipment, such as tank transporters, bridging equipment, and ammunition, whose forward deployment or location has been restricted.

Delay in the event of violation can be imposed by locating secured storage at maximum distance from the line of confrontation. Secured storage can also be used to delay an opponent by separating equipment from the units trained to use it. The delay factor can be increased by partially dismantling stored equipment in order to immobilize it: for example, by removing turrets or guns from tanks, rotors from helicopters, or engines from tank transporters.

Placing equipment in secured storage can be an important aid to verification. Violation of secured storage and breakout of secured equipment would provide early warning of intention to initiate hostilities. There is a trade-off between the intense control over secured storage sites provided by sensors and the considerable expense of installing and maintaining this equipment. On-site inspection is expensive, too. Nonetheless, however these sites might be monitored, the basic obligation of a country submitting its equipment to secured storage will be to hold the equipment at a designated site open to inspection by air or ground—or by satellite—and not to move it without notice.

PULLING BACK SPECIFIC TYPES OF EQUIPMENT

Secured storage could be the foundation of an alternative to the R.M.A. discussed earlier. Rather than pull all offensive armaments far from the line of contact, certain specialized types of armaments, like tank transporters, would be pulled back and placed in secured storage.

Pulling back major ammunition storage sites from the line of contact between the alliances would make a forward attack hard to sustain. Pulling back storage sites for aircraft munitions would have the same effect. Secured storage could be used even if the depots were left in their present location. Its effect would be intensified by requiring that advance notice be given of withdrawals. It might also be stipulated that only a certain amount of munitions could be withdrawn in any twenty-four-hour period.

A related measure would impose a fixed daily or weekly quota on the number of railroad cars carrying military equipment and personnel into a central European zone. This measure would be supervised by inspectors from the opposing alliance stationed permanently at designated exit/entry or internal traffic-control points. They would use direct observation and X-ray and radar sensors to monitor rail cargoes. This measure would check the ability of the Soviets to move materials into East Germany and Czechoslovakia by rail in a buildup prior to attack. Even if the transport of military equipment was not restricted, it would be the duty of inspectors at all exit/entry points to make sure that they were being given proper notice of all military traffic, including munitions transport, entering or leaving their area of responsibility.

In addition to major ammunition sites the alliances should consider agreement to pull back the following items: (1) military pipeline units; (2) tank-transporter units; and (3) nuclear-decontamination units, mine-clearing equipment, and combat bridging. All these items are needed to support forward moving forces and the Warsaw Pact is more dependent on them than NATO, which, for example, has its own static pipelines. Restrictions on the deployment of military bridging, proposed many years ago by a British officer, Colonel Jonathan Alford, constitute perhaps the most frequently considered constraint of modern times. Up to now, it has been blocked by NATO officers, who insist that bridging is needed equally for the defense. For a restricted area the answer is relatively easy. If tanks are to be pulled back, armored bridging can go with them. As an isolated measure, withdrawing bridging might be more acceptable to NATO if NATO bridging were pulled back fifty kilometers and Pact bridging one hundred kilometers and if only the stored combat bridging were pulled back, leaving in place bridging attached to armored vehicles.

Under a further constraint measure, armed helicopters could be pulled back beyond refuelling range. This would compel them to land to refuel before going into combat. Training would have to take place behind this line. Armed helicopters are a primary vehicle of surprise attack. Violation of the measure would be detected by surveillance aircraft, which could give early warning. The need to refuel would create a delay of several hours before all helicopters of a given unit could be combat-ready.

Main battle tanks, too, could be withdrawn fifty kilometers from the line of contact on the NATO side and 100 kilometers on the Pact side. The measure would check the speed with which an opponent could muster tanks for attack while giving the defender a day or two to prepare defenses. The delay would be increased by placing all or part of the tanks in secured storage. Zbigniew Brzezinski, who was national security adviser in the Carter administration, has proposed a tank-free zone in central Europe of larger dimensions than that suggested here.

My own view of proposals like these is that agreeing to pull back a single type of equipment means in practice establishing a restricted area for that type of equipment. It would be more effective and make more sense to establish an R.M.A. for the wider range of equipment suggested here earlier.

In this chapter we have discussed measures that participants in the C.F.E. force-reduction talks might discuss before they try to negotiate reductions. In the next chapter we shall present some specific suggestions on negotiated reductions. In that context we shall also discuss a further category of constraints: negotiated restrictions on reserve units. But before we turn to reductions, let us look at the possibilities for establishing a common NATO/Warsaw Pact risk-reduction center, as a further measure to stabilize the military confrontation in Europe and to reduce the risk of conflict through misperception and miscalculation.

A NATO/PACT RISK-REDUCTION CENTER

The flow of information and coordinating activity between East and West needed for repeated data exchanges, for the operation of early warning, constraint, and verification systems (including arranging for early warning and verification inspections), and for discussing complaints about compliance will be extensive. By itself this exchange will almost certainly be so large as to require some permanent alliance-to-alliance institution to handle it. In the M.B.F.R. talks there was East/West agreement in principle to establish a common organization to notify the signers of exercises and inspections and to deal with compliance issues. In the first C.D.E. talks at Stockholm the Pact suggested such an institution but NATO opposed it. In its proposals for both C.F.E. and C.D.E.-2 the Pact again proposed a center.

NATO's opposition at Stockholm was motivated in part by its longstanding apprehension toward any Soviet *droit de regard*—right of surveillance—over NATO's defense activities. European NATO members fear that if the Soviets were given the right to scrutinize and criticize certain defense activities, they might use their position to mount propaganda campaigns designed to arouse western public opinion against any aspect of NATO's defense programs.

These concerns are understandable. But what NATO has left out of account is its own *droit de regard* over the military activities of the Soviet Union and Warsaw Pact states, which it has been gaining in the C.D.E. confidence-building talks and would gain in greater measure with a force-reduction agreement and the establishment of a risk-reduction center.

Even without benefit of a risk-reduction center the Soviet Union has been exercising a *droit de regard* over the activities of NATO since the Cold War began. It has used its free access to information on defense issues vigorously to influence western public opinion—sometimes, as in the I.N.F. episode, with considerable effect. Given the Warsaw Pact's close control both of military information and the public media—a control that has extended to the jamming of western broadcasts—the NATO states have had no comparable advantage. Now NATO has a chance to negotiate access to information about the Pact's military activities. This, combined with the relaxation of the Pact's grip on its own media, can bring NATO a useful degree of oversight of the Pact's armed forces and a means to nurture and influence the increasingly active public debate inside Pact countries, including the Soviet Union, on those forces. These are openings that NATO should seize.

The NATO/Pact confrontation in Europe is sufficiently destructive and sufficiently prone to the consequences of human error and miscalculation to make the establishment of a risk-reduction center a requirement for any program designed to stabilize that confrontation. Nonetheless, the main function of such a center would not be to seek to manage a full-blown East/West crisis. Rather, it would be to prevent minor incidents and misunderstandings between the armed forces of the two alliances from developing into crises. Either the "crisis prevention" or "risk reduction" label would fit this function; here we use the term risk reduction.

In addition to coordinating compliance with a force-reduction agreement, participants in a joint risk-reduction center could query and discuss military activities not covered by existing reporting require-ments: extraordinary activities in border areas, unannounced force movements and concentrations, large-scale changes in deployments, border-crossing incidents of military significance by aircraft, missiles, or ground personnel, and other military activities that might constitute preparation for attack. They could also deal with acts of terrorism with international implications, like theft of nuclear weapons.

The objective of the center would be to clarify immediately the nature of such activities and correct misinterpretations that could lead to inflammatory reactions. It would deal with "low-level" incidents and would not substitute for more direct communications, including U.S./ Soviet communications, once a crisis developed. But it could develop tools that would help the superpowers to cope with crises after the terms of a treaty or agreement had been abrogated or suspended. Simply knowing each other's systems of response to crises could be of immense help to NATO and the Warsaw Pact if communications between them broke down.

BENEFITS OF A RISK-REDUCTION CENTER

A military confrontation on the immense scale of the NATO/Warsaw Pact confrontation in Europe, no matter how stable it might seem, can give rise to serious errors of interpretation. The possibility of human or mechanical error is high in a confrontation involving active-duty forces of more than six million men and hundreds of thousands of compli-cated weapons systems, all in a state of continual military activity.

In recent years there has been a steady stream of incidents capable of triggering a chain reaction leading to war. In early 1982 a NATO ship engaged in routine training off the Danish coast accidentally fired a missile that destroyed some buildings on the mainland. In early 1985 an errant Soviet cruise missile or drone crossed Norway and came down in Finland. In September 1986 an unarmed Soviet missile was reported to have landed in China. In 1987 a similar incident was reported in Poland. In early July, 1989, a Polish fighter aircraft crossed the whole NATO area and crashed in Belgium after its pilot ejected soon after takeoff in Poland.

To cite one incident descriptive of an entire class, in April of 1984 an American Army Cobra helicopter strayed from Federal Germany into Czechoslovakia. The pilot claimed he was fired on by Czechoslovak MIG-21 jets. Other witnesses in the Federal Republic reported that the

Czechoslovak aircraft did not fire on the helicopter but was firing around it to force it to the border. For their part the Czechoslovak authorities claimed that the border violation was a deliberate provocation by the U.S. Here is an incident of a type which is relatively frequent, which could have had serious consequences, and where the facts themselves are disputed—a classic case for clarification by a risk-reduction center.

In recent years the United States and the Soviet Union have been trying to improve their system for communication in a crisis, and they seem to be inching toward serious consideration of a risk-reduction center of their own. In July of 1984 the two countries concluded an agreement to improve the emergency hot line between Washington and Moscow, by establishing satellite transmission to speed communications and transmit maps and graphics. In May of 1987 they established separate risk-reduction centers in Moscow and Washington to give notice of missile tests. We can welcome any steps that could diminish the possibility of misperception and error between the nuclear superpowers. To do the same for NATO and the Warsaw Pact makes eminent sense.

A NATO/Warsaw Pact center should be staffed by senior officials with political and military experience from all participating countries, assisted by military officers and also by representatives of the international staffs of both NATO and the Warsaw Pact. It might have a permanent secretariat. The liaison officials from NATO and the Pact would have direct communication links with the operational headquarters of their own alliances, and each participating delegation would have direct communication links with political and military authorities in their national capitals.

POSSIBLE DRAWBACKS OF A CENTER

A risk-reduction center could have disadvantages and these must be evaluated.

One objection, often heard from American officials, is that such a center could sidetrack and blur discussion between the superpowers, allowing a bad situation to develop into a crisis. A risk-reduction center, these officials say, might be a "fifth wheel" that would actually interfere with resolution of the crisis. The officials feel this concern so strongly that they have prevented the establishment of a single U.S./Soviet center, insisting that each country have its own. Indeed, there is the possibility that a jointly operated center—even one that had been established for some time and whose staff was experienced—would be a source of confusing rather than clarifying information in time of crisis. But the work of a risk-reduction center in Europe would be on a mundane level—border infractions and the like—that would seldom if ever lead to crisis.

There remains the concern that a European risk-reduction center could interfere with and upset U.S./Soviet crisis discussions at a delicate stage. It would seem possible to deal with such an eventuality. The U.S. and the Soviet Union might stipulate as a condition of their participation in the center that, in the event of a bilateral crisis, either state could immediately change the venue of the discussion between them to any forum or channel it wished, including a strictly bilateral channel, provided only that both states kept the European center informed of their consultations.

Another objection often heard is that a country or an alliance could use a risk-reduction center to present deliberately misleading information. In the theoretical event that the Warsaw Pact were preparing a surprise attack on NATO, Pact officials could, it is feared, deliberately feed misinformation into a risk-reduction center, creating confusion and impeding perception of the real state of affairs. This possibility strikes an especially sensitive nerve with some NATO officials, whose abiding concern is that the governments of that democratic coalition would find it impossible to reach timely decisions in the event of threatening conflict. The Soviet Union and its allies might well have a similar worry about participating in a risk-reduction center.

There is no complete reply to this worry. Ideally, a risk-reduction center should produce clarity and make rational decision easier. The potential for abuse exists, but it is not unlimited. Each participating state would have at its disposal other sources of information than the center, means on which most would place primary reliance in making their decisions. Moreover, the center would not be without resources of its own. Chiefly, it could arrange to send out observers to confirm or deny information in question. If a state prevented access by observers, its refusal would in itself be significant. Use of the center to pass on misleading information would probably be revealed relatively soon. Thus the center's potential contribution to the store of knowledge between the two alliances probably outweighs its potential for disinformation.

A related concern is that a risk-reduction center might prove useless, because of the unwillingness of participants to present information they considered sensitive, with the result that the information actually exchanged would become less and less valuable, both on a routine basis and in a crisis. Participants could guard against this by stating clearly at the outset the information that would be required in specific situations and by monitoring compliance with particular care early in the center's existence. Persistent bilateral complaints to states that failed to present adequate information would also help. Once participants acquire the habit of giving adequate information and make that standard practice, the system contains built-in inhibitions to keep them from backsliding. In the final analysis, states can withdraw if the center is not performing adequately and the terms of agreement should deliberately make this easy.

Some say that citizens in the West might jump to the conclusion that a risk-reduction center constituted in itself such a significant gain in security that their support for necessary NATO efforts might weaken. In the era of the I.N.F. treaty and the Soviet Union's large unilateral troop withdrawals, an exaggerated evaluation of a rather prosaic measure like the establishment of a risk-reduction center seems unlikely. But while not overestimating the importance of a risk-reduction center, the people of both alliances are likely to welcome one. They will see it as giving their own governments a greater role in assuring the peace in Europe, reducing what many consider excessive dependence on superpower intelligence collection and bilateral communication. Establishing a center, whether under the auspices of the confidence-building talks or the force-reduction talks, will be considered by most as a desirable step toward "Europeanizing" the NATO/Pact confrontation and building a rudimentary European security system within the framework of the C.S.C.E. accords.

Cumulatively, the potential benefits of a risk-reduction center appear to outweigh the disadvantages.

CRISIS-MANAGEMENT MEASURES

The entire armory of arms-control measures—reductions, exchange of information, early-warning measures, residual ceilings, constraints, and verification by on-site inspection—is intended to stabilize the East/West confrontation, make it less dangerous, and build it down. Arms-control measures can bear witness to the relaxed state of East/West relations today, give it specific form, consolidate it, and encourage it.

But dispassionate analysis must acknowledge that these measures are essentially peacetime instruments for relatively tension-free situations. The system of protections advocated here could be swept away in an acute East/West crisis, stemming perhaps from a sharply negative turn in Soviet policies, even though it might well have kept many other crises from developing.

The alliances should take advantage of a risk-reduction center during a period of good relations to devise measures that might be used in genuine crises. Some of these measures would be forgotten and others discarded, but some might be remembered and tried.

To illustrate, one measure that could give the alliances time to cool off in a crisis and to open or resume political discussion would be an agreement that each alliance would have the right to call for a twenty-four- or forty-eight-hour freeze on forward movement toward the line of confrontation between the alliances by ground and air forces going beyond a line 100 kilometers from the line of confrontation. Forces inside the line could be moved to readiness positions, but aircraft and reinforcing and logistic ground force units could not be moved forward. Compliance with the measure could be verified by satellite, surveillance aircraft, and ground inspection. If an agreement to this effect, negotiated in a period of relatively good relations, were honored in crisis, it would give the alliances time to talk out their differences. If the agreement were violated, that would be a further, highly-visible proof of hostile intent.

If, as suggested in Chapter 7, we are thinking of the entire C.S.C.E. process as one in which many of various activities gradually develop into enduring institutions, then a joint risk-reduction center is a natural candidate. In the course of time, a joint center could perform a fact-finding or even a mediating function for disputes between participating countries—like the recurrent dispute between Hungary and Romania over treatment of the Hungarian minority in Romania—which might have serious destabilizing effects on the East/West relationship in Europe.

In this chapter we have considered a number of actions other than negotiated reductions that participants in the force-reduction talks might undertake in order to stabilize the East/West confrontation in Europe. Our main recommendations have been to have a full exchange of data early, to establish a Zone of Military Openness, and to establish a Restricted Military Area. In the next chapter we shall consider an approach to negotiated reductions designed to eliminate asymmetries, achieve deep cuts, reduce costs, and also to restructure forces in a more defensive mode, a stated objective of both alliances.

10 How to Cut NATO and Warsaw Pact Forces

We have urged in this book that the West make a deliberate decision in favor of building down the NATO/Pact military confrontation in Europe through deep cuts of its own as well as Pact forces, rather than limiting itself to an approach that could continue the confrontation at a high level.

If NATO countries wish to follow the course of deep cuts, mindful of uncertainties over the continuation of present, more constructive Soviet policy, they should think of an intermediate position midway between current levels and some ultimate minimum level. As discussed in Chapter 7, this position can be defined as an equal plateau of reduced forces, risks, and costs on which the West can rest more comfortably, with less strain and apprehension, while it observes the evolution of the Soviet system. This plateau should leave the West with substantial active-duty and reserve forces as protection against a negative turn in Soviet policy—a development for which, given the present state of openness and proliferation of Soviet contacts with the West, there would probably be many indications and clear political warning.

In May, 1988, General Secretary Gorbachev proposed that the first stage of reductions should consist of identifying the main asymmetries in weapons holdings of the two alliances that might emerge from an exchange of data and eliminating these imbalances by reduction to a level below that of the numerically weaker side. The Warsaw Pact confirmed this position in March, 1989, on entering the C.F.E. talks subsequently in more detail. Although the Pact proposal is not without complications, as we have seen in our earlier discussion, in general it is based on principles that the West had been urging since 1973 in the M.B.F.R. talks and which NATO itself proposed at the outset of C.F.E. Achieving parity in major armaments at lower numbers is a most important goal, resulting in enormous reductions in Soviet tanks, artillery, and armored personnel carriers as well as other armaments. We should vigorously support it.

Parity in selected armaments—even with very large Pact reductions—is not the full answer, however. As we saw in Chapter 7, parity in isolation, without the support of other measures, can be destabilizing, by encouraging competitive force improvements and increasing inducement for preemptive attack in a crisis. And parity based on the limited cuts of its own forces that NATO was offering when the C.F.E. talks began would not yield significant savings for the West. Something more is needed.

An important part of the answer lies in the transparency and early-warning measures discussed in the last chapter, as well as in constraint measures like the establishment of a Restricted Military Area along the dividing line between the opposing alliances in central Europe. But we must look still further if we are to achieve the greater stability—the reduced risk of war—that both alliances agreed should be the purpose of the C.F.E. talks. We must begin to reorient the forces of both alliances to defensive rather than offensive purposes.

How should this be done? Part of the answer lies in the selection of armaments for reductions. Given their statements, both alliances seem to wish to emphasize the reduction of armaments. We can support the logic of this approach. But then the question becomes, Which armaments? NATO's original selection of tanks, artillery, and armored troop carriers as candidates for reduction was good as far as it went, but too narrow. President Bush's NATO summit proposal to add aircraft, combat helicopters, and military personnel gave significant help.

Earlier we pointed out that, although individual weapons like tanks can be used either offensively or defensively, it is possible to distinguish between offensive force configurations emphasizing mobility, range, and reach and defensive forces emphasizing heavy firepower with limited mobility and range. The organization of forces and the "mix" of equipment—the amounts of specific types of armaments held by deployed forces—can favor either offense or defense. In addition, certain weapons like tanks and self-propelled armored artillery are more indispensable, because less substitutable, for attack than for defense. NATO refers to the Pact superiority in armor and artillery as "invasion capability." But armored forces are not the only ones that would be used for the offensive in modern warfare. In fact, as we have seen, hostilities would probably begin with air and missile attacks on the airfields and air defenses of the other side. If we wish to limit the Pact's offensive capability, these armaments, too, should be reduced.

The program of force reductions in Europe advanced by General Secretary Gorbachev in the May, 1988, Moscow summit urges the elimination of the "offensive core" of the forces of both sides. In December, 1988, when Gorbachev announced his large, unilateral

Soviet reductions, he said that "Soviet forces remaining in eastern Europe would be defensively structured." Since then, Soviet officials have indicated that the tanks of forward-deployed Soviet tank divisions will be reduced by 20 percent, from about 328 tanks to 260 per division, that the tanks of forward-deployed motorized rifle divisions will be reduced 40 percent, from about 270 to 160 per division, and that some active-duty motorized rifle divisions on Soviet soil will be converted to defensive infantry, machine gun/artillery divisions with only about forty tanks each. These changes might serve as models for later changes in organizing remaining Soviet and NATO forces, but they, too, are only part of the answer.

The NATO countries, too, have spoken of non-offensive defense. In a communiqué they issued in March, 1988, they declared that eliminating the capacity to initiate large-scale offensive action should be an objective of the force-reduction talks. As we have seen, the NATO position papers for C.F.E. issued in December, 1988, and March, 1989, urged that the long-term goal of the new talks should be to restructure forces to enhance defensive capabilities and reduce offensive capabilities.

The mandate agreed to by both alliances for the C.F.E. talks picks up the conceptual language suggested by NATO and speaks of eliminating "the capability for launching surprise attack and for initiating large-scale offensive action." Neither alliance upon entering the talks had specified what it had in mind with these formulations. Yet the willingness of both alliances to endorse the basic concepts of non-offensive defense in the mandate for the talks gives these concepts considerable status as a common East/West goal.

Yet the alliances should not wait until a final stage of the reduction process, as both the Soviets and NATO seem to be suggesting, to move decisively toward the goal of non-offensive defense. If specific action by the alliances to move toward a more defensive posture is in fact left until the end of the reduction process, the forces of the alliances will move through long periods of parity at a high level, with continuing high risks of clashing. Instead, the alliances should begin the task of restructuring their forces from the outset of negotiated reductions, both by focussing reductions on their more offensive weapons and by deliberately encouraging the development and deployment of defensive weapons.

To meet these various requirements, including the requirement for a reduction approach that can yield real cost savings for the West, I propose that NATO countries envisage a 50 percent cut in NATO's holdings of six armaments—surface-to-surface missiles, ground-attack aircraft, armed helicopters, as well as artillery, tanks, and armored troop carriers—and also in its active-duty ground- and air-force personnel, with Warsaw Pact forces coming down to NATO's new levels. Once agreed, the reductions would take place in stages over a ten-year period, or a shorter time if feasible. By the end of that period, they should yield substantial cuts, perhaps as high as 30 percent, in current western budgets for European defense.

The Pact's starting point for reductions would be its force levels following implementation of the unilateral Soviet reductions announced by General Secretary Gorbachev in December, 1988, and of accompanying eastern European unilateral reductions.

The overall reductions in the Atlantic-to-the-Urals area that would result from applying the opening positions of both sides at C.F.E. are shown in Appendix IX. Here, we illustrate the reduction process for the entire Atlantic-to-the-Urals area by using as a model a proposal for reductions in central Europe, the area of greatest NATO/Warsaw Pact force concentration, and the area of greatest United States and Soviet force presence. The process we describe for central Europe would be replicated at the same time in the other subregions into which the Atlantic-to-the-Urals area would be divided by East/West agreement. However, there might also be circumstances in which both sides agreed that it would be advantageous to begin the reduction in central Europe and follow it with reductions in other parts of the Atlantic-to-the-Urals area. For example, we suggested in Chapter 8 that it may prove more convenient to begin with manpower reductions in a central European sub-region for a first agreement and then to expand these cuts to the remaining Atlantic-to-the-Urals area in subsequent reductions stages.

The initial central European reduction would be a cut of 20 percent in NATO holdings of six key armaments with the greatest invasion or offensive capability, the capacity for attack by seizing and holding foreign territory or for preparing the way for such seizure. Combining the armament reduction proposals made by NATO with those made by the Pact, these armaments are surface-to-surface missiles; ground-attack aircraft; armed helicopters; artillery; tanks; and infantry-fighting vehicles. The Warsaw Pact would reduce its holdings of the same armaments and of the units equipped with them to the level of NATO after a 20 percent reduction. (Reduction amounts under this proposal are shown in Appendix X.)

In this approach, we are suggesting a 20 percent cut for the first phase. This reduction figure is illustrative; we want to make the point that NATO should be thinking throughout the reduction process of bigger cuts than it now projects. NATO is currently talking about new levels at 5 to 10 percent below its present holdings; the Pact has proposed cuts 10 to 15 percent below the numerically weaker side (in practice, nearly always NATO) and has moved toward the NATO position on some armaments. Some compromise figure between NATO and Pact percentages seems probable and should be acceptable as a first stage, provided there is a clear commitment from both sides to further reductions.

In later phases of the reduction approach suggested here, both alliances would reduce their holdings of the same armaments both in central Europe and in the remaining Atlantic-to-the-Urals area so that the ultimate outcome would be equal levels of these armaments for both alliances amounting to 50 percent of NATO's current holdings. Completion of a 50 percent manpower reduction would follow. (The numerical outcome of 50 percent cuts is also displayed in Appendix X.)

In the early phases of these reductions there would be no limit on the alliances' defensive deployments: anti-aircraft and anti-tank weapons, mines, obstacles, infantry, combat engineers, and transport helicopters with strictly defined characteristics. In fact, there would be incentives to strengthen them. Thus the restructuring of forces to emphasize defense over offense would be built into the reduction process from the outset. And any increases in the alliances' more defensive deployments would be underwritten by the step-by-step savings from reductions in more offensive deployments. To induce participants to give their more defensive forces priority they might be allowed in the early stages of reductions to reassign half the personnel from units cut in the course of armament reductions to units oriented to defense.

The lack of restrictions on defensive armaments and the opportunity early in the reduction process for defensive units to grow in troop strength may seem to invite an arms race in defensive weapons. But there is a safeguard against such a development in the completion of the 50 percent reduction in active-duty ground- and air-force personnel scheduled to follow the early stages of weapons reductions.

The approach I am suggesting provides for staged NATO reductions five to ten times larger than those now proposed by NATO. It would bring deep cuts in full-time, active-duty military manpower as well as armaments and cover three types of armaments whose reduction, at least at an early stage, has been opposed by NATO. Its rationale, moving toward a defensive posture from the outset, goes beyond the stated objective of both alliances to move toward a defensive posture at a later stage of negotiated reductions.

Let's look now at the first stage of the proposal from several angles: disposal of reduced armaments, reduction by units, and the treatment of manpower, reserve units, aircraft, and missiles. Then we can turn to the final stages, which would bring the forces of both alliances down to 50 percent of NATO's current strength.

IMPLEMENTATION

We have suggested that, for ease of understanding, we try to visualize the reduction process by using reductions in a central European zone as a model or surrogate for the first stage of reductions that would also be going on in other sub-regions of the Atlantic-to-the-Urals area.

As we have seen, there are many possibilities for defining a central European zone. Because this issue is under negotiation, with the outcome uncertain here, we will use for illustrative purposes a zone already described in Chapter 8. This zone, which we can call "Central Europe Extended," would cover forces deployed on the territory of France, the Federal Republic of Germany, the Benelux countries, and Denmark on NATO's side and, on the Pact side, the territory of East Germany, Czechoslovakia, Poland, Hungary, and the three Western Military Districts of the U.S.S.R. (the Baltic, Byelorussian, and Carpathian districts). In these territories NATO and the Warsaw Pact deploy most of the active duty and reserve forces that would be involved at an early stage in conflict on the Central Front.

Initial reductions in Central Europe Extended could take one of two forms. Under Alternative One, there would be a comprehensive 20 percent cut of specified armaments of both alliances in the suggested central European area, to include all holdings of these armaments in both combat-ready and reserve units and all armaments of these types stored by both alliances in the area. In tanks, for example, this would probably mean an equal level for both alliances of about 12,000. (See the charts in Appendix X; figures are rough illustrative calculations based mainly on data in the International Institute for Strategic Studies' *Military Balance, 1988–89.* Please note that IISS figures cover armaments stored by NATO but its figures for armaments stored by the Pact may not be complete.)

This new ceiling is calculated on the basis of about 10,000 tanks in NATO units in the area plus 5,800 NATO tanks in storage, including United States war reserves and United States POMCUS (Prepositioning of Material Configured to Unit Sets) stocks held in western Europe for reinforcement units stationed in the United States, whose personnel could be flown in a crisis to join up with their equipment. The starting tank figure for the Pact is about 25,000 after implementation of unilateral reductions announced in 1988. This figure includes the tank holdings of all organized Pact units whether classed as ready or not ready. The Pact figure might be increased to include further Pact tanks in storage when accurate figures are available from data exchange discussion and on-site inspection.

Like the present proposal, which we have called Alternative One, NATO's own starting approach for C.F.E. also provided for overall parity in armaments of both alliances whether deployed in units or stored. But NATO's proposals for geographic subregions, including those for central Europe, call for limits to be placed only on tanks held by "active units," excluding stored tanks. "Active" units as defined by NATO (*Conventional Forces in Europe: The Facts*) are units presently manned at above 5 percent of their full wartime strength. This definition includes both combat-ready and reserve units. The effect of this proposal is to omit NATO's own stored tanks from reductions, yet to count into the reduction base all known Soviet tank holdings, including those held in mobilization units with a cadre of caretaker personnel. In justifying this effort to gain exemption for its own stored armaments, NATO will correctly use the geographic argument that the Pact's main source of reinforcements, the Soviet Union, is close to the line of confrontation between the alliances while the United States, NATO's main source of reinforcements, is far from that line. Despite Soviet flexibility, this argument may not work since it could leave NATO with nearly 6,000 more tanks in central Europe than the Pact, about 50 percent more. That is why the Alternative One approach suggested here includes stored tanks as well as those in units even in subregions.

There is another problem with NATO's "active" unit definition. It may be suitable for a reduction approach where all reductions take place in a single stage and NATO reductions are held to a minimum. But for a multi-stage continuing process of negotiated reductions like that suggested here, with reduction by disbanding units, manpower reductions, and residual ceilings on units reduced, it could make it difficult for NATO to have an adequate number of low-manpower reserve units equipped with their own armaments.

A second approach, which we will call Alternative Two, may prove a more negotiable substitute for NATO's comprehensive approach of cutting all armaments in the Atlantic-to-the-Urals area, whether held by active-duty units, reserve units, or in storage, in one move. Alternative Two would also permit a distinction to be made between active-duty and reserve units in the event of deeper cuts, giving better protection to NATO's reserve capability.

Under Alternative Two, the first-stage reductions are on a narrower basis. They would consist of a 20 percent cut of the specified armaments held only by combat-ready NATO active-duty units, with Pact armaments held by the same type of active-duty units reduced to the new NATO level. The term combat-ready is used here as it was in Chapter 3: combat-ready active-duty units are equivalent to Pact Category I units, with over 75 percent of their wartime manpower, and Category II units, with over 50 percent of wartime manpower. Stored armaments and armaments of reserve units of both alliances deployed in the Atlantic-to-the-Urals reduction area, equivalent to Pact Category III units with no more than 20 percent of their manpower, as well as stored armaments not held by units, would not be reduced, but would be placed under a no-increase ceiling, subject to verification.

If applied to the Central Europe Extended area, under Alternative Two the proposed 20 percent reductions would leave the alliances with approximately 8,500 tanks each. This number is calculated on the basis of an estimated starting figure of roughly 10,000 NATO tanks in ready units in the reduction area and of 16,000 Pact tanks in Category I and II ready units in the area, following Soviet and Pact unilateral reductions. The big change is in the number to be cut by the Pact which, for example, drops from about 13,500 tanks under Alternative One's comprehensive approach to 7,500 under Alternative Two; Pact artillery and armored troop carrier reductions are also about 50 percent less under Alternative Two than under the comprehensive approach. Under Alternative Two, reductions of aircraft, armed helicopters, and surface-to-surface missiles do not change because in the Atlantic-to-the-Urals area these armaments are held by active-duty units rather than reserve units. Despite the forthcoming Soviet position at the outset of C.F.E., the negotiations may develop in such a way that a more easily negotiated first step is desirable for both sides.

Whatever approach might be used for initial reductions, at the end of the 50 percent reduction process total tank holdings of all NATO and Warsaw Pact states, not only of those in central Europe, would amount to about 11,000 of the present approximately 22,000 NATO total; in the Central Europe Extended region, each alliance would have about 5,000 tanks. (If a Restricted Military Area were in force, none of these

Pact tanks could be closer than 100 kilometers to the line of contact of the two alliances.)

In this suggested 50 percent reduction program, the reduction ratio of Pact to NATO reductions changes from about 17:1 in the current NATO proposal (2,000 NATO tanks to 37,000 Pact tanks before unilateral cuts) to 4:1 (47,000 Pact tanks to 12,000 NATO tanks) because under the 50 percent reduction approach, NATO is making sizable cuts as well as the Pact.

DISPOSAL OF REDUCED ARMAMENTS

As we saw in Chapter 8, one problem of negotiated reductions is what to do with the armaments retired from active duty. Here we present some solutions. Other solutions are, of course, possible and some may be easier for East and West to agree on. In that event, they should be accepted, assuming that negotiators have been aware in reaching these decisions of the range of other possibilities and their implications.

It is suggested that if aircraft are reduced, as is recommended here, they should be placed in secured storage—sealed hangars with a small observer contingent from the opposing alliance. Surface-to-surface missiles reduced by agreement should be destroyed. The armaments and armor of armed helicopters would be removed and the aircraft could be used for transport. The tanks, artillery, and infantry-fighting vehicles drawn from active service might also be destroyed. However, each alliance might be given the option of transferring these three types of equipment from active-duty units to reserve units and destroying instead an equivalent number of older weapons of the same type. This is not an ideal solution from the viewpoint of cutting combat capability, but it is likely to be what both alliances want to do. In Chapter 7, we reviewed the alternative method of reduction by withdrawal from the reduction area and found it impractical for most participating countries.

If Alternative Two, focussed on combat-ready units, is used for initial reductions, armaments of the type being reduced now held by reserve units (in the central European area, mainly Category III Pact divisions and Belgian and Dutch reserve divisions), as well as equipment in U.S. POMCUS storage and war reserve, would fall under a no-increase commitment and would be placed in secured storage in their present locations. On grounds of the distance of the United States from the reduction area, this would also be done with the armaments of United States units reduced by agreement.

Thus the phase-one reduction agreement would in one form or another restrict the level of reduced armaments deployed with units, in storage, repair, and transit. Reduced armaments found elsewhere in the reduction area would be a violation, with one exception—armaments at production plants. NATO's present proposals deal only with armaments deployed in units or in separate storage like POMCUS. They do not deal with continuing production in the reduction area of armaments reduced by agreement. Such production is a major possibility for circumvention and breakout from a reduction agreement.

Here, it is suggested that production plants in the Atlantic-to-the-Urals area producing armaments of the type reduced would not be restricted as to the amount of production, nor would the production process itself be subject to inspection—U.S. and Soviet production outside the reduction area would also not be restricted. But the armaments produced by these plants would have to be kept in designated, secured storage areas near the production plant. Removals from secured storage would be notified. When intended for transport outside the Atlantic-to-the-Urals area, these armaments would pass through exit/entry points manned by the opposing alliance. They could also be exchanged on a one-for-one basis to replace existing armaments deployed in the reduction area, whose destruction would have to be observed. United States, Canadian, and Soviet production outside the Atlantic-to-the-Urals area of armaments reduced by agreement inside the area would be subject to a reporting requirement.

Reporting production totals and making use of secured storage seems a reasonable course for production of reduced armaments inside the Atlantic-to-the-Urals area, given the two alternatives. One is to restrict the coverage of a reduction agreement only to armaments in deployed units. This would permit both alliances to manufacture and store as many reduction-category arms as they wished near active-duty and reserve units, a practice that would undermine the intent of the reductions. The other is to restrict production of reduction-category arms inside the Atlantic-to-the-Urals area, a scheme that would leave out of account the fact that many Soviet and all American and Canadian installations would not be so restricted. In later stages of negotiation, such restrictions should be considered. Despite their manifest complications, they would be an effective delaying obstacle to effort by a more aggressive Soviet leadership to rebuild Soviet forces.

REDUCTIONS BY UNITS, MANPOWER REDUCTIONS

To most effectively diminish combat potential and to aid verification, reductions should be by units (probably units of battalion size, the largest unit generally equipped with a single major armament) until the armament reduction quota is exhausted; that is, by battalions holding tanks and artillery, and by comparable air-force units. Residual ceilings would be placed on units of the type reduced. (As we have seen, NATO's opening proposal did not do this.) Reduction through cutting battalions holding reducible armaments will permit the alliances to retain in the area existing units of other types, like infantry, combat engineers, and antiaircraft. It will also require each alliance to restructure remaining forces, thus moving toward a more defensive orientation. To encourage this trend, as an exception, armored troop carriers would be withdrawn as armaments rather than in battalion form, and their infantry units left in the reduction area.

NATO forces would retain the forward-defense strategy. Present NATO corps sectors in Federal Germany, including those of the allies, would be maintained. Whether or not the Restricted Military Area proposed in Chapter 8 is established on both sides of the line of contact between the alliances, NATO's reduced force of armored divisions would be pulled back somewhat from frontline positions and a forward belt of infantry, combat engineers, rocket artillery, and rapidly emplaceable obstacles would be established.

Reduced units of both alliances should be disbanded, their manpower discharged from active duty, and the manpower ceiling for both alliances dropped accordingly. An initial agreement would also provide for an overall reduction to an equal ceiling for both alliances of 20 percent of active-duty ground and air force manpower of all member states of the two alliances. The present totals appear approximately equal if the same definitions are applied on both sides. (See IISS data in Appendix II.) The manpower of disbanded units would be credited to this overall manpower reduction quota. Deep cuts in manpower are necessary to cut defense budgets, and it is preferable that they should begin from the outset of reductions. The known difficulties of verifying manpower levels should be soluble, given greater Pact openness in providing data and permitting intrusive on-site inspection. Moreover, there is not much point in reducing units of one type and allowing limitless overall increase in units equipped with other armaments or in remaining artillery and tank units.

An alternative would be to permit the conversion of reduced battalions to reserve units by discharging their active-duty personnel down to a cadre staff of no more than 20 percent of their war-time manning level, placing their reduced armaments in secured storage. Soviet units of this type would have to be withdrawn to specified areas just west of the Urals. This approach would decrease active-duty forces on both sides, especially the Warsaw Pact's. But it would also increase the reserve holdings of both alliances. NATO is concerned already about existing Soviet reserve capability, and its concern will increase as unilateral Soviet reductions address NATO's other main worry—surprise attack. Moreover, it is improbable that the Soviets would agree to refrain from establishing new Soviet reserves while permitting NATO to increase its reserve units.

Therefore, it is preferable to reduce by disbanding units, mainly battalions, and by applying residual ceilings to units of the type reduced. Thus, Soviet ground-force reductions would take place through withdrawing active-duty units, disbanding these withdrawn units, and destroying their equipment or turning it over to existing reserve units and destroying the present holdings of these reserve units in reducible armaments.

TREATMENT OF RESERVE UNITS

NATO military officers are especially concerned about the Soviet Union's very large reserve capacity, mainly in Category III ground-force divisions. As we saw in Chapter 3, the speed with which these reserve units can be mobilized may well be lower than NATO analysts estimate. But it is safe to say that within about ninety days the Warsaw Pact could field a total of about 215 ground-force divisions in the area west of the Urals versus NATO's maximum of about 140, giving the Pact a considerable preponderance in numbers of organized ground-force combat units in a situation of full mobilization. Moreover, as we have seen, some western experts speculate that with a program of long-term, unobtrusive training to improve the readiness of Soviet reserve units, the Soviet Union could gain decisive advantage over the West and move to exploit it in an attack.

In theory the Soviet reserve problem would become less acute if conscription were eliminated in the U.S.S.R., thus cutting back the mobilization base of trained personnel. The Soviet government took the first step in this direction in March, 1989, by eliminating conscription of university students. But elimination still may be far off and both alliances will regard their reserves as insurance against a recurrence of East/West tensions.

The first phase of a C.F.E. agreement should therefore include measures that can provide NATO countries further reassurance on the issue of Soviet reserves. Under the Alternative One approach of reducing all types of units and storage of arms from the outset, Soviet and Pact reserve units would be reduced from the beginning with other types of units. Under the Alternative Two approach, where only ready units are reduced, we have already suggested two measures affecting Soviet (as well as NATO) reserve units that are subject to reduction: their overall number should be restricted and their holdings of armaments of the type reduced should be subject to a no-increase provision and placed in secured storage, periodically reported, and subject to verification.

As a further measure applicable to both alternatives, despite the difficulty of verifying manpower reductions, a ceiling should be placed on the active-duty manpower assigned to full-time duty in reserve units. This ceiling would hold the level of full-time, active-duty personnel in reserve units to no more than 20 percent of the wartime manning level of the unit. Reserve units in both alliances would also be obligated to give a year's notice before calling up reserve personnel for training and present calendars of reserve-unit training involving more than 8,000 men or two brigades. They would have to give six months' notice of small-unit training and invite observers to all training exercises involving 8,000 men or more. Verification of the 20 percent cadre would take place in intervals between reservist call-ups.

Finally, agreed limits might be placed on the number and size of out-of-garrison reserve-training activities. This numerical restriction would be the same type of limit as that which has been discussed for active-duty units, but with a lower ceiling, perhaps 20,000 men or the combat elements of two divisions. Only one such exercise could be held at a time, with no more than two larger exercises annually, prenotified a year in advance, as exceptions to permit training of reserve units together with active-duty units. NATO has in the past opposed restrictions on the size of out-of-garrison activities of active-duty units. It may be more willing to consider such restrictions for reserve units.

AIRCRAFT REDUCTIONS

In Chapter 8 we reviewed the many difficulties of reducing aircraft: NATO's reluctance after the I.N.F. treaty to eliminate any more nuclear delivery systems; the capability of aircraft to return rapidly to the reduction area if reduction is by withdrawal; opposition to destroying expensive aircraft as a reduction method; the problems of controls on aircraft production to avoid circumvention; the difficulties of working out trade-offs among aircraft of different types and quality; whether reductions should deal with aircraft in place or also consider reinforcement aircraft; the problem caused by the Pact's superior number of interceptor aircraft; and whether measures to restrict infrastructure should be sought.

Intrinsically, aircraft reduction is probably the knottiest problem of the current negotiations. Nonetheless, at the May, 1989, summit, NATO correctly decided to include aircraft in force reductions from the outset.

As reviewed in Chapter 8, the reasons for doing so appear conclusive: political leaders in the Soviet Union, and especially the Soviet military, will expect some quid pro quo for agreeing to make much larger tank and artillery reductions than NATO. Soviet and eastern European leaders have insisted on reduction of NATO aircraft as part of a C.F.E. agreement. If the West expects the Soviets to deal with its main concern—Pact armored attack—then it should be prepared to make at least a modest step toward meeting Soviet concerns. Moreover, if one major objective of reductions is to move toward greater stability in the East/West military confrontation and to provide greater security for the NATO alliance, then ground-attack aircraft, which were a primary weapon in Hitler's blitzkrieg attacks, and which would be the first wave of any future Pact attack on the West, should also be reduced.

Given the mobility of aircraft, it is logical to use the entire Atlantic-to-the-Urals area as a reduction area and this is the likely outcome in practice. Nonetheless, we will again use a central European area for illustrative purposes. Doing so will be consistent with our illustration of ground-force reductions. Moreover, as with the ground force example, if they are seeking an early first agreement, it may yet turn out to suit both alliances to start the reduction process in this area of greatest force concentration. (Appendix X shows the effect of the 15 percent aircraft reduction proposed by NATO using the reduction base proposed here, as well as the effects of a 50 percent reduction.) It is suggested that, in a phase-one agreement, ground-attack aircraft already deployed in the central European area, plus the aircraft deployed in the home territory of the U.K., a major base for NATO fighter-bombers, and those in the Kiev Military District of the Soviet Union, a major deployment area for Soviet fighter-bombers, be reduced by 20 percent of the numerically weaker force.

Using the reduction base suggested here, NATO is the numerically weaker force. Reductions would cover only aircraft already deployed in the reduction area. Reinforcement aircraft based outside the Atlantic-to-the-Urals area would be omitted because there is no objective way to determine in advance how many of their available aircraft U.S. and Soviet commanders would commit to conflict in Europe if war began.

The categories of aircraft to be covered by reductions might include tactical ground-attack aircraft, like the A-10 and Alphajet and the Pact's SU-25; fighter-bombers, such as the F-16, F-111, Tornado, and the Pact's SU-24; and the medium bombers—Badgers, Blinders, and Backfires—of the Smolensk Air Army deployed west of the Urals. To reduce ambiguity, the reduction base would also include multi-role aircraft on both sides, like the F-16 and MiG-21, which are built to function both as ground-attack aircraft and fighters.

Using this base, a 20 percent reduction would mean a NATO cut of about 400 aircraft to a common ceiling of approximately 1,600 for the Central Europe Extended reduction area, and a Pact reduction of about 1,000 aircraft to the same ceiling. In calculating these reductions, we have modified the figures in Appendix III to include multi-role aircraft of both sides in the reduction base. (See Appendix X for details of the suggested reduction base for aircraft.) These data indicate that before reductions, there may be about 1,800 aircraft for NATO and 2,600 for the Pact in the air reduction area defined above. This calculation also assumes that 400 aircraft, or half of the 800-aircraft unilateral Soviet reduction announced by General Secretary Gorbachev in December, 1988, plus 100 East European unilateral aircraft cuts—our rough estimate of the number of unilateral reductions which might be drawn from our reduction base—have already been withdrawn before reductions take place.

Using the same reduction base, under the 15 percent aircraft reduction proposed by President Bush for the whole Atlantic-to-the-Urals area, NATO's total becomes slightly larger than that of the Pact. NATO reduces 707 aircraft and the Pact, 548. Under a 50 percent reduction approach, NATO reduces 1,987 aircraft and the Pact, 1,827.

Despite the fact that Pact reductions under this approach would be larger than NATO's, whether the calculation is for central Europe only or for the entire Atlantic-to-the-Urals area, it is plausible that, given its interest in getting some hold over NATO air assets, the Pact would accept them. Refinement of data and definitions might alter these figures. In that case, following the general approach recommended here, reduction would be by 20 percent of the numerically weaker alliance, with the stronger alliance reducing to the new level. Reduction could be by secured storage in hangars or sheds in the reduction area; destruction might be politically unpalatable and withdrawal too easily reversed. However, here, too, destruction is the more definitive and therefore intrinsically more desirable form of reduction. NATO might find some older aircraft to fill out its reduction quota, but with a reduction as large as that shown by our figures, many of the aircraft destroyed by the Warsaw Pact would have to be recent models.

We have already suggested one measure to deal with the problem of the Warsaw Pact's large numerical superiority in interceptor aircraft, to include multi-role aircraft which can function as ground attack as well as air-to-air fighters in the reduction base. As a second step, the Pact could freeze the number of its interceptor aircraft and give NATO the right to increase to the Pact's level—"room at the top." NATO is not likely to exercise that option right now, but it might be useful to have some day as both sides configure their forces more defensively. The interceptor aircraft of both alliances should be subject to inspection to assure that they have not been equipped for ground combat. This approach would require an agreement on the distinctions between ground-attack and interceptor aircraft. For aircraft which may be deployed in the future, some Soviet experts suggest that the distinction between attack and interceptor aircraft might be made on the basis of restricting the takeoff gross weight measuring the lift or load-carrying capacity of interceptor aircraft.

Control of the production of aircraft would be as suggested here for ground-force armaments—reporting production, placing the aircraft in secured storage near the production plant, and reporting all movements inside the reduction area and departure from it. The U.S., Canada, and the U.S.S.R. could also be obligated to notify fellow participants in an agreement of their production of ground-attack aircraft outside the reduction area. Participants also might consider whether for the short-term some restriction could be imposed on the quantity of aircraft munitions stored in the area from the Atlantic to the Urals.

MISSILE REDUCTION

In earlier chapters we reviewed the pros and cons of negotiating missile reductions simultaneously with negotiation of conventional force reductions. It was suggested that the United States should in advance seek the agreement of the Soviet Union to reduce to a low equal ceiling. If that effort has been made and it is successful, simultaneous negotiations would, on balance, appear preferable. Reduction in the number of tactical-range surface-to-surface missiles in Europe could be negotiated separately by the U.S. and U.S.S.R. outside the alliance-to-alliance framework, with appropriate means of coordination with their respective allies and with the progress of the C.F.E. talks. An alternative, probably permissible under the terms of the agreed mandate, would be to negotiate in the C.F.E. talks themselves. However, the bilateral U.S./ Soviet framework might better meet the apprehensions of France and Britain, who fear a creeping process moving toward restrictions on their own nuclear forces. As in I.N.F., the U.S. should seek to exclude French tactical-range surface-to-surface missiles from reductions unless France ultimately proves willing to include its armaments in reductions.

The U.S./Soviet negotiations would cover all Warsaw Pact holdings and the holdings of all NATO countries deploying Lance (Belgium, the Netherlands, the U.K., the Federal Republic of Germany, and Italy), with the U.S. advised by a steering committee of these allies. As noted, a precondition for holding these talks, to be agreed among the NATO allies as well as between the U.S. and the Soviet Union, is an explicit understanding, to be reflected in the text of an agreement mandate, that their objective would be reduction of surface-to-surface missiles to an equal level somewhat lower than NATO's present holdings, rather than the complete elimination of these missiles.

As an alternative to beginning missile reduction talks immediately, in order to meet the concerns of some NATO states about the premature reduction of NATO's nuclear deterrent forces, the U.S./Soviet missile reduction talks could be timed to begin only after an agreement on reduction of conventional armaments had been signed and was entering the ratification process. But these talks cannot be omitted from the negotiating process and should be considered as part of it from the outset. There would be no lasting gain in Western security from a NATO/Pact force reduction in Europe that left the Warsaw Pact a superiority in surface-to-surface missiles under 500-kilometer range of over 5,000, with most northern European NATO countries within reach of these missiles. This large arsenal of missiles might well be used in a conventional mode at the outset of hostilities against NATO's air assets, command installations, and other critical facilities.

Conforming to the overall reduction approach suggested here, it is suggested that the present number of U.S. tactical-range missiles deployed in Europe—roughly 600—also be reduced by 20 percent to a level of about 480, and that the number of Pact missiles be reduced from about 6,000 to the new equal level of 480. It is proposed to cut missiles rather than launchers because launchers of this type usually have many easily usable reload missiles. The missiles eliminated would be destroyed as in I.N.F. A ceiling on missiles rather than launchers would also permit NATO more flexibility if it were decided to restrict both conventional and nuclear weapons; limiting reductions to launchers would require the development of a launcher other than the Multiple-Launcher Rocket System now planned for use with both the Lance follow-on and the A.T.A.C.M. missile. Restricting missiles rather than launchers would probably be more difficult to verify. Ultimately, it might require controls on production by the United States and the Soviet Union, an issue which in any case will have to be resolved for the negotiations on strategic missiles.

This outcome would permit some future deployment of the A.T.A.C.M. with conventional warheads and of a Lance follow-on using the same launcher as A.T.A.C.M., with freedom for NATO to decide how many should be nuclear and how many conventional, but only under this low ceiling.

NATO willingness to limit its deployment of conventional A.T.A.C.M.s, the cutting edge of Follow-on Forces Attack technology, to a low number could provide some negotiating leverage for the highly asymmetrical reductions of Pact missiles proposed here. The level of missiles equipped with conventional warheads should be limited, as in I.N.F., to promote verification. It should also be limited to avoid a large-scale proliferation of missiles equipped with conventional (or chemical) warheads, which would place the entire region on a hair trigger.

NATO would be trading a negotiated restriction on its right to deploy new American missiles in advance of their actual deployment against Pact reductions in missiles and armor, as it did in the I.N.F. talks, where, despite much criticism, this procedure ultimately proved successful. In later phases of reduction, the holdings of both alliances in nuclear bombs and standoff missiles for aircraft and in nuclear artillery shells would be reduced to a low equal level. Verifying such reduction, like verifying the reduction of tactical-range missiles, would be difficult; it might ultimately involve supervised destruction and controls over U.S. and Soviet production facilities.

FURTHER STAGES OF REDUCTION

So far, we have been discussing a first round of reductions in tanks, artillery, armored troop carriers, armed helicopters, ground-attack aircraft, and surface-to-surface missiles by both alliances to a new level 20 percent below NATO's present holdings. The first-phase agreement might provide for an implementation period of two to three years and contain a general commitment to move down to a final level representing 50 percent of NATO's current holdings. New negotiations on implementing this commitment would begin as soon as the first-phase agreement took effect. In these subsequent stages of negotiation, the designated armaments of both alliances in the Atlantic-to-the-Urals area would be cut by equal amounts through unit reductions with a sinking manpower ceiling at the level of the weaker alliance, until they included a further 30 percent of NATO's starting total in these armaments.

The objective would be to complete the reduction process within ten years of the first reduction. The implementation of each reduction phase would be dependent on the satisfactory implementation of the preceding phase. In the final phases of negotiation, which should begin in the eighth year from the beginning of the implementation of phase one, active-duty ground and air-force manpower of both alliances in the entire Atlantic-to-the-Urals area would be further reduced so that the total manpower reduction would amount to 50 percent of NATO's current level. Given their large size, these manpower reductions would require cutbacks in weapons and equipment not reduced by agreement, but the selection would be left to each alliance.

MILITARY EFFECTS OF A 50 PERCENT CUT

After the proposed reductions have taken place, both NATO and the Warsaw Pact would have forces in the Atlantic-to-the-Urals area of equal size in offensive weapons and active manpower, but forces of more limited mobility and range, with greater emphasis on defensive elements. Defensive restructuring would have taken place in the

Restricted Military Area and, as reductions proceeded, in forces throughout the reduction area. The defensive capacity of each alliance, untouched by negotiated reductions in armaments and by initial manpower cuts, would have increased in relationship both to each alliance's own offensive capacity and to the offensive capacity of the opposing alliance.

Each alliance would have a sizable number of penetration weapons for counterattack—for example, 10,000 tanks, about 1,400 ground-attack aircraft, and 300 surface-to-surface missiles. This would be enough to push back aggressive attack but not enough to prevail in an attack against the defensive capability of the opposing alliance. Constraints, transparency measures, including recurrent information exchange, a system of permanent observers, and a stringent verification system, would impede preparation for either surprise attack or full mobilization and give much increased warning if those preparations did take place.

NATO would have reached the stable plateau of reduced risks and costs proposed here as a goal for the C.F.E. talks. If the Soviets reversed their conciliatory policies at some future time, NATO would be considerably better off confronting Pact forces of the size and kind described here than as they are now. Because the proposals here provide for a more extensive system of early warning, constraints, and controls over Soviet mobilization capability, and deeper cuts of offensive armaments, NATO would also be better off than if the reduction process stopped with implementation of NATO's current proposals.

Skeptics may well comment that this account sounds plausible, but can NATO really afford militarily to reduce its forces by 50 percent? What would be the practical outcome if, after implementing the agreement, the Soviet Union actually decided ten years from now for whatever reason to attack NATO? After all, even after a 50 percent cut, the Soviet Union would still have about 700,000 active-duty ground-force personnel west of the Urals, over 6,000 tanks, and 1,500 combat aircraft, with perhaps ten divisions still in eastern Europe. As the attacker, it would decide on the point of attack. NATO might still have its decision-making problems; they could be even worse than today. History shows many cases where equal or smaller forces pushed through to victory.

The situation seems unrealistic, but it could happen. What could NATO do against it? Let's briefly compare a Soviet attack on central Europe in the new post-reduction situation with that we described in Chapter 3.

In a situation of deep cuts to an equal plateau, each alliance would have an equal number of active-duty personnel and major armaments in the Atlantic-to-the-Urals area and in its subregions. In Central Europe, the Soviet Union by itself would have smaller forces than the NATO allies in Federal Germany. The reduced forces of its Warsaw Pact allies would represent a small and diminishing asset. NATO would not be restricted in its defensive armaments and counter-mobility measures. With this balance of forces, and assuming a minimum NATO capacity for decisions, a Soviet attack using forces in place in central Europe would fail.

As for mobilized or reinforced attack, the entire Soviet mobilized ground forces west of the Urals would only roughly equal the mobilized forces of the NATO allies on the Central Front. There would be NATO overflights over the entire area to the Urals, constraints on the size and activity of Soviet reserve divisions, and perhaps a permanent observer presence in many Soviet headquarters. With measures of effective verification, violations of controls on Soviet reserves and mobilization activity would be immediately apparent. Even so, it could take months after this warning is given to the West for the Soviets to mobilize, expand, equip, and train reserves. There would be a considerable period for the West to take political action and to make its own military preparations.

If Soviet leaders decided to attack, NATO would know the main direction of attack through its own observers on the scene and through new air-mounted radar equipment for surveillance and target acquisition which should be in service soon.

Given violation of treaty restrictions, NATO's conventional missile and air forces, still effective after reductions, could begin interdiction while the attacking forces were still on Warsaw Pact territory.

The attacking Pact force would be further cut back by NATO's forward deployed defenses—obstacles, barriers, pipe and scatter mines, and rocket artillery. NATO's uncommitted mobile armored reserve, as large as the attacking Soviet force in its original state, would be focussed on the actual axis of attack, rather than spread out awaiting an attack in their sector which may not come. It would bring the attack to a halt and push it back. Taken together, the firepower of NATO air forces, forward defenses, and armored forces would considerably exceed that of the attacking Soviet force. The Pact, too, would have static forward defenses and minefields, but they would not help on the attack.

Because Soviet forces would have been so reduced, even in mobilized form, they would not have the momentum and weight of present forces. As a consequence, Soviet planners would have to calculate from the outset that the United States could maintain a secure reinforcement and logistics foothold in western Europe as long as war remained conventional.

A continuing nuclear deterrent would back this force. The odds favoring success of a Soviet attack on the West, now uncertain, would then be far worse—and NATO would be achieving this greater security at a much reduced cost.

CUTTING THE COSTS OF NATO DEFENSE

After completion of the proposed program for deep cuts, the reduction in 50 percent of NATO holdings of the specified armaments and by 50 percent of NATO active-duty ground and air-force personnel should enable European NATO countries to realize important savings in their current defense expenditures, perhaps up to 30 percent or more of their total expenditures. European savings would be considerably larger than those of the United States, because European NATO countries provide roughly 80 percent of NATO forces deployed in Europe. Given this larger saving, the European NATO countries might be willing to devote a certain proportion of these savings to additional payment for infrastructure and support costs for United States forces remaining in Europe.

Under the proposed reduction approach, United States ground and air force personnel in Europe would be reduced by 50 percent, to a level of about 150,000, with a reduction of two and one-half ground-force divisions and five air-force wings. To realize real savings for the United States, these units and a proportionate amount of supporting infrastructure in the U.S. should be disbanded and the personnel level of the U.S. Army and Air Force in the United States reduced accordingly.

Annual savings would begin in the first year of implementation of reductions. In a preliminary assessment (for details, see Appendix XI), the Defense Budget Project, a public interest group based in Washington, D.C., has estimated that annual savings on completion of reductions after ten years might be from $10 to $17 billion (fiscal 1989 dollars). These estimates include the following savings: withdrawing 100,000 Army troops ($4.8 billion); withdrawing five tactical air wings ($1.3 to $4.0 billion); converting two to three U.S.-deployed Army divisions to reserve status ($2.4 to $3.6 billion); converting five tactical

Air Force wings deployed in the United States to reserve ($1.3 to $4.0 billion); and reduced purchase of Army tactical missiles ($1.0 to $1.5 billion). Other analysts have calculated that additional savings from reductions in ground and air force units could total another $6 billion annually.

Increased contributions from European NATO countries (financed out of their own savings from reductions) to U.S. infrastructure in Europe might range up to $10 billion annually, yielding an upper estimate of about $30 billion in savings per year for the United States. If the United States were willing to forgo some modernization of U.S. units stationed in Europe or earmarked for European defense, still larger savings of about $10 billion annually could be made.

In the concluding chapter, we shall examine how these smaller forces might fit into the general framework of East/West relations. But first we should consider how the reductions can best be verified.

11 Verifying Deep Cuts[1]

Despite the difficulties that negotiators face in the C.F.E. talks, mounting political and economic pressures in both alliances and continued Soviet flexibility on details of negotiation could lead to success in a first agreement within three or four years and perhaps sooner. As we have seen in preceding chapters, such an agreement would probably comprise the following obligations:

- force reductions and residual ceilings on remaining forces of the type reduced;
- restrictions on military activities and deployments; and
- early-warning and transparency measures.

Compliance with these obligations will have to be verified by measures that apply to both sides equally. Fortunately, as the alliances strive to find effective and acceptable means of verification, they need not develop the whole process from the start. They can be guided by positive experience in verifying the I.N.F. treaty, in negotiating verification measures for U.S./Soviet reductions on strategic nuclear forces, in negotiations on chemical weapons and nuclear testing, and by the negotiation and successful verification of the Stockholm Document in its first years of implementation. The alliances also have in their favor the fact that they now seem equally willing to accept verification measures. In fact, the Pact may be somewhat ahead of European NATO members in its willingness to accept some of the more intrusive measures.

In order to develop and agree on a reasonable system of verification, participants in the force-reduction talks will have to cope with certain realities.

One reality is that complete knowledge of the other side's forces at a given time, whether for verification or for any other purpose, is impossible. An ideal verification system would be able to deliver a "snapshot" of all the deployments of each alliance at any given time—that is, it would be capable of gathering at a single stroke accurate data on all military forces significant for compliance. This might be possible for a small number of military installations or activities. But it is out of the question for all the numerous military forces in the large geographic area that will fall within the compass of a C.F.E. agreement. As a result, limited segments of the forces to be verified will have to be covered by verification activities at different times. The gap between the ideal and the possible will inevitably create discomforting uncertainty.

Beyond this built-in limitation, there are limits to what military leaders on both sides think the opposing alliance should see. Experience since the far-reaching changes in the Soviet position on verification under the Gorbachev leadership indicates that the political leaders on both sides often seek and agree to a more stringent level of verification than is acceptable to their own armed forces. At the December, 1987, Washington summit, President Reagan suggested and General Secretary Gorbachev agreed to "anywhere, anytime" suspect-site inspection for a strategic-reduction agreement. Yet in the fall of 1988, under the impact of objections from the United States armed forces and intelligence agencies, the Reagan administration pulled back from that position to a more circumscribed program of inspections relating to missile-production plants.

A second reality of verification is the intrinsic complexity of verification activities. Because verification strives for accuracy and precision, useful discussion must go into details. A frequent reaction from those who have not been able to follow the verification issue closely is that nothing so complicated can be negotiated between East and West. Yet negotiators overcame similarly complex issues in order to establish a system of verification for the I.N.F. treaty. And an even more complex system is being negotiated, although with real difficulty, in the U.S./ Soviet talks on reduction of strategic arms.

Nevertheless, as they plan a system for the verification of force reductions, to keep from being overwhelmed by the effort to cope with every possible evasive action of the opposing alliance, negotiators will have to keep constantly in mind the principles of simplicity and economy of effort and costs. Here too, the ideal cannot be achieved. Modern armed forces are complex organizations integrating a wide range of personnel, activities, and equipment, including weapons of overlapping capability. An effort to keep reductions and verification simple by identifying a single key armament or activity and restricting that could easily be frustrated if participants simply stepped up unrestricted activities and increased their holdings of unrestricted armaments. Fortunately, the principle of economy of effort and resources also applies to efforts to evade compliance—the means of cheating are nearly infinite, but most of them would represent dissipation of effort because they would not result in an effective concealed increment to permitted forces.

The costs of verification, too, in terms both of the personnel and equipment required, are considerable. Yet if negotiators practice a rigorous economy in designing verification measures there will be an unavoidable loss in coverage. In designing verification approaches, there is a continual trade-off between breadth of coverage and the constraints of cost. At the same time, even a stringent verification system would be cheap in comparison with the cost of maintaining forces at their present level.

The following discussion of verification emphasizes some frequent western concerns about verification and compliance, together with others that happen to be common to both alliances.

OBJECTIVES OF VERIFICATION

In the West it is generally agreed that the objectives of verification are to deter deliberate non-compliance (cheating), to detect militarily significant non-compliance in time to take counteraction, and to justify that counteraction. The deterrence function is important; as in public safety the fear of being caught is powerful. The ultimate objective of verification is, where feasible, to confirm compliance, leading to increased confidence by political leaders and publics on both sides that the agreement they have entered into has value. In this sense, successful verification of an agreement by mutually suspicious participants is an important confidence-building measure, perhaps the most important of all.

The agreed aim of the Atlantic-to-the-Urals talks will be to decrease the possibility of surprise attack or large-scale offensive action, including covert mobilization, by means of stabilizing measures and force reductions. Systems for the verification of an Atlantic-to-the-Urals agreement—indeed, of any arms-control agreement—should be deliberately arranged to contribute to the agreement's main objective. However, a system to verify residual ceilings after force reductions should not be expected on its own to do the entire job of detecting possible moves toward attack. Verification will be a valuable supplement of, but not a substitute for, a large, on-going collection of information in the national intelligence efforts of members of the NATO alliance. This effort, of course, will not stop simply because an East/West agreement to reduce forces in Europe has been concluded.

It is useful to keep in mind that the term "verification" covers a number of different activities. In American practice, the verification process is often divided into three components:

(1) Monitoring: collecting information on compliance with satellites, sensors, or inspectors, and analyzing the information to establish the facts;

(2) Verification as such: the political process of evaluating the information collected to assess whether there has been compliance or non-compliance; and

(3) Reaction of governments to indications of violation. Discussion in this chapter deals mainly with verification in the sense of monitoring compliance.

If the talks under way in Vienna do lead to an East/West agreement on force reductions, the central question about verification that NATO (and Pact) governments will be called on to answer will, in essence, be the same one asked in each of the bilateral U.S./Soviet nuclear arms-control agreements thus far concluded. Will the agreed verification measures be sufficient for NATO to detect a militarily significant degree of evasion or non-compliance in time to take counteraction, either to change the non-compliant behavior or to negate the military advantage it might have brought the offender?

In discussing how this question might be answered in the context of the Atlantic-to-the-Urals force-reduction talks, this chapter covers the following topics: (1) What is to be verified (a package of potential obligations is described); (2) How a participant might cheat; (3) Verification assets at the disposal of both alliances; (4) The shortcomings of these assets and political and technical factors that will complicate verification; (5) How a cutback in a specific armament—we use tanks for purposes of illustration—might be verified; (6) The cooperative measures from both sides needed to facilitate verification; (7) Organization, costs, and personnel requirements; and (8) An assessment of the potential effectiveness of the verification measures suggested here.

In this chapter, we will not deal with the verification of reductions in tactical-range surface-to-surface missiles or nuclear rounds for artillery. Many of the techniques described here for use in checking conventional-armament reductions, like the use of non-removable tags on permitted armaments and secured storage, could also be used to check reductions in nuclear warheads. But the production controls which might well be necessary for verifying reductions in warheads have not yet been tackled even in the U.S./Soviet strategic-reduction talks, although this will ultimately be necessary. For tactical-range missiles and artillery rounds, techniques will also have to be developed for checking nuclear storage sites despite reluctance in NATO—and presumably in the Pact—to reveal precise location of sites, techniques for securing them, and details of warhead design. In all, this is a topic that requires separate treatment.

1 WHAT IS TO BE VERIFIED?

To keep the scope of our discussion manageable, we shall focus on the verification of the first of successive stages of force reductions by the alliances, as described in the preceding chapter.

To do this we shall describe and number the separate obligations involved in a first-phase agreement to make it easier for readers to keep track of them.

In this first phase, all tanks, armored troop carriers, armed helicopters, artillery, and attack aircraft held in units or storage by NATO and the Pact would be subject to reduction, and, following reductions, residual no-increase commitments or ceilings would be placed on remaining armaments of this type which the alliances are permitted to have (Limit #1). There would be sub-ceilings on the number of these armaments that would be permitted in each of the sub-regions in which the Atlantic-to-the-Urals area is divided and on the amount of these armaments that can be held by a single participant. Let us say that as in the NATO program, there are six of these in all. Units holding these armaments would be disbanded, and the number of units of this kind remaining after reductions would also be restricted (Limit #2); sub-limits would apply here, too. (Under the Alternative Two approach suggested in Chapter 10, which focusses reductions on combat-ready units, both alliances would also promise not to increase the number of reduction-category armaments in reserve units or storage.)

Military manpower is the most mobile and concealable of all military resources and, consequently, the most difficult to verify; all soldiers have to do is to take off their uniforms and put on civilian clothing, blending with the civilian population, and they are virtually undetectable. Nonetheless, as we pointed out in the last chapter, some manpower restrictions appear both desirable and unavoidable in the first phase of a force-reduction agreement. They should include a ceiling on the active-duty manpower of each alliance (Limit #3). This ceiling would be lowered as units were disbanded and as the proposed 20-percent stage-one manpower reduction took place. There should also be a ceiling on the number of personnel assigned to all reduction-category units (Limit #4), to prevent the unchecked increase of this category of personnel and a buildup in the personnel strength of individual combat units. And there would be a separate ceiling restricting the number of active-duty personnel serving in each reserve unit holding reduction-category weapons to no more than 20 percent of wartime strength (Limit #5). Slow covert increase of the personnel of reserve units would be a major potential means of non-compliance.

We are suggesting a general sub-limit on all personnel assigned to combat-ready units like divisions (Limit #4), rather than a ceiling on the manpower of each individual unit, in order to create a pool of manpower and to leave some flexibility for changing the structure of individual units. Given a general ceiling on all personnel assigned to combat units and a ceiling on the number of units of this type, plus a requirement to periodically notify personnel strength of individual units, it might not be essential to limit the personnel assigned to individual tank, artillery, or other units following reductions. However, it would be highly desirable to do so for verification reasons. The absence of a limit of this type would mean that the Pact could assign more personnel to some active-duty tank or artillery battalions. Admittedly, imposing the tighter limit would restrict the flexibility of the NATO forces. This is yet another of the trade-offs so frequent in verification.

This reduction model could also include some obligatory constraints to be verified, like those we described in Chapter 9. These constraints might include a Restricted Military Area in which deployment of any armaments of the type reduced by agreement would be prohibited, or pulling back certain specialized equipment—ammunition, tank transporters, and mine-clearing and pipe-laying equipment—and placing it in secured storage supervised by the opposing alliance. In all there may be about ten overall ceilings for the 50-percent approach suggested here, with most of them applied with lower numerical thresholds in each of four or five subregions. The present NATO approach would have only slightly fewer obligations to monitor.

2 THE BREAKOUT PROBLEM

A necessary approach to designing a verification system is to dispassionately analyze the main possibilities for evasion by a determined adversary. Such analysis is value-free and says nothing about actual intentions. A pattern of repeated small-scale violations could indicate either a generally lax attitude toward compliance, a sloppy administrative system on the part of the inspected country, or a deliberate pattern of non-compliance. It is the task of verification analysts to imagine before a verification system is negotiated how residual ceilings might be violated in ways which could be successfully concealed, which would be militarily effective, and which would represent reasonable economy in using manpower and equipment resources—and to design verification measures to cope with these possibilities.

What degree of deliberate Pact non-compliance would be militarily significant? We might calculate as follows. Say that the first phase of reductions is set—as we have recommended—at a number equal to NATO's current holdings of tanks, armored troop carriers, artillery, armed helicopters, and attack aircraft less 20 percent. If the Warsaw Pact were then able to increase its holdings of these armaments—for example, its tanks—covertly in the reduction area so that it had a tank superiority of more than 20,000 tanks or so over NATO's new reduced level, NATO's post-reduction military position would be worse than it now is. That is a lot of tanks.

Measured on this scale, deliberate non-compliance on a small scale involving several hundred tanks dispersed in concealed hiding places would not bring a decisive military advantage. Logically, deliberate violation would have to involve a larger number of tanks to be militarily effective. It would theoretically be possible to deliberately disperse and conceal a still larger number of tanks in the Pact's portion of the area from the Atlantic to the Urals. Many might not be detected. Yet the longer such equipment is stored without regular opportunities for training and maintenance the less useful it would be. This would be an ineffective and uneconomic use of resources even for a policy of deliberate cheating. As we have pointed out, it is the combination of trained manpower and weapons in organized units that creates combat power; any one of these elements will by itself be inadequate.

Another possibility of systematic violation is the unreported existence and continued training in the Atlantic-to-the-Urals area of a large number of small, illicit units equipped with illicit armaments. The combination of overflights, mobile ground inspection, and the requirement to inform the opposing alliance of authorized training exercises in advance is a logical way to deal with this possibility. Yet this possibility makes clear the desirability of setting low the minimum size of exercises—especially reserve exercises—for which notice must be given.

A slow, covert buildup of restricted armaments might be accomplished by counterfeiting the "tags" of armaments scheduled for shipment to overseas buyers and diverting the weapons to hidden depots, where they would augment the permitted holdings of organized units. (We discuss tagging later in the chapter.) Forces might also be built up by ordering small platoon- or company-sized Soviet units to infiltrate the reduction area from east of the Urals and pick up equipment concealed in the reduction area at a time planned for attack.

The two most plausible and effective means of evading force-reduction limits in a C.F.E. agreement by the Soviet Union are also the most obvious ones. The first would be the sudden entry into the area from the Atlantic to the Urals of large Soviet units normally stationed east of the Urals, beyond the reach of negotiated restrictions. This threat can be diminished by the establishment of exit/entry points along the Urals, by satellite overflights of Soviet territory outside (and inside) the reduction area, by low-altitude observation overflights in the reduction area, and by suspect-site inspection. It is improbable that organized units of battalion size or larger could be introduced into the reduction area, without being identified in a relatively short period if they remained isolated from larger units already in the area.

The second plausible means of evasion would be to increase the armaments and personnel of organized units, whether combat-ready or reserve. Because the armament levels of organized units could be more easily checked, evasion would perhaps focus on concealing armaments elsewhere and on training additional personnel on permitted weapons. For a breakout attack, the trained personnel would be brought together with the concealed weapons to form new units. If the negotiators in Vienna do not set any limitations on manpower, the training of additional personnel beyond full unit strength would not be a violation of the agreement; this is an additional reason for manpower ceilings in a first reduction agreement. In fact, the existence of this violation possibility is also a rather strong argument for placing limits on the strength of individual units.

Assuring that reserve units remain reserve units can best be done by placing their equipment in secured storage and regulating the withdrawal of the equipment from storage for training purposes. Indeed, some Soviet experts have argued that verifying compliance with restrictions on manpower is so problematic that the best means of controlling the military potential of reserve units is not only to store their equipment in specified storage but to dismantle it as well.

However, a restriction on the number of active-duty personnel permitted to man reserve units also seems necessary. If Soviet reserve units were permitted to have on hand their full wartime strength of active-duty personnel whenever they wished, coordinated "breakout" would be possible. Thus, the overall number of Pact reserve units holding reducible armaments and the level of active-duty manpower of each of these reserve units, as well as of their armaments, should be subject to restriction and inspection on the basis of continually updated data on specific units provided by each alliance. As suggested in the last chapter, there should also be limitations on the size of out-of-garrison activities by reserve units; such restrictions may create fewer difficulties than similar restraints on active-duty units, and it could be made obligatory to invite observers.

Most of the other methods of possible non-compliance described here would probably either be visible or ineffective, expensive, and hard to organize. Consequently, efforts aimed at deterring the use of permitted centers of military activity for systematic non-compliance and detecting it if it occurs would appear to be the most effective use of verification resources.

NATO's reduction approach as presented in Vienna in March, 1989, did not foresee limitations on the number of units or on active-duty military personnel. Nor did it contain any restriction on continuing production in the Atlantic-to-the-Urals reduction area of armaments reduced by agreement. These omissions create real doubts as to the military effectiveness of the NATO approach in its original form. The absence of these ceilings also increases the possibility of non-compliance with a force-reduction agreement.

3 VERIFICATION ASSETS

To assess NATO's capability of dealing with deliberate non-compliance, we shall turn first to the verification assets or tools that both NATO and Pact governments would have available to monitor compliance. At this point, we shall limit ourselves to brief descriptions but it should be emphasized that all of these assets will be working together in a mutually reinforcing process. However, these assets have shortcomings and later in the chapter we shall describe some of them.

Professionals usually consider verification and early warning as two wholly separate activities. However, in Chapter 9, we described how early-warning and verification activities like overflights and data validation could be deliberately combined in measures agreed early in the talks for application before reductions take place. Doing so would have many benefits: among them, training and exercising verifiers on both sides at an early stage, enabling NATO to follow the significant Soviet unilateral reductions announced by General Secretary Gorbachev in December of 1988, and giving the West a means of assurance that unilaterally withdrawn Soviet units are not returned.

Among these dual-purpose verification and early-warning measures are exit/entry points. Exit from and entry to the Atlantic-to-the-Urals area could be through a limited number of checkpoints—airfields, ports, and road and rail junctions—permanently manned by personnel of the opposing alliance. The only authorized entry of organized Soviet units into the Atlantic-to-the-Urals area from Soviet territory east of the Urals would be through these posts. There could also be fixed observer posts at a number of major ports, airfields, and road and rail junctions *inside* the reduction area. Both types of observation posts would be designed with the double purpose of early warning and verification. To serve this same dual purpose, as discussed in Chapter 9, there should be provision in the initial agreement for several low-altitude overflight inspections per year to each of the geographic sectors into which the area from the Atlantic to the Urals would be divided, for a total of about 150 such flights for each alliance.

Among verification assets, national technical means—especially satellite photography and sensing as well as electronic intelligence—will remain the most important single resource for verifying a force-reduction agreement. For large ground-force armaments and aircraft, high-resolution satellite photography can give specific information on types and numbers of items stored in the open. It can also give precise dimensions of storage sheds and hangars, making it possible to estimate their capacity. And by showing the state of vegetation and grass cover, it can give useful information on the amount of activity going on in or near a given installation. However, because of the great number and mobility and the small size of conventional armaments, and also because of technical drawbacks and high cost, satellite imaging will probably not have the same salience for monitoring reductions in Europe that it has for monitoring reductions in nuclear arsenals.

In contrast, sensor- and camera-equipped fixed-wing aircraft and helicopters will have greater importance. The range of aircraft with potential value for verification on the NATO side—and the Warsaw Pact has or will have equivalents for most of these—includes the AWACS aircraft now in service, equipped with radar to monitor aircraft of the opposing alliance in flight; aircraft equipped with synthetic aperture radar, which can monitor stationary installations or objects on the ground; aircraft with the Joint Surveillance/Target Attack Radar System, or JStars, which the U.S. may be ready to deploy a decade from now and which will have the capacity to monitor moving columns of vehicles; and low-altitude fixed-wing aircraft and helicopters, from which objects on the ground may be photographed or observed directly.

Ground-based sensors (radar, infrared imaging devices, video monitors, and X-ray)—many equipped with cameras—can be used to provide information on the movement of objects across a given line or out of an enclosed area. Tamper-resistant fiber-optic seals and tags— non-reproducible identifying devices that can be affixed to armaments with epoxy resin with a unique holographic signature making imitation difficult—have been developed to identify nuclear missiles and could be used to identify permitted armaments carried by active-duty forces in the field. Some devices of this type could also contain microchips capable of broadcasting a signal on interrogation or of sending continual telemetry signals with a tamper-resistant authentication code. Naturally, all active tags and seals would be removed or destroyed in a situation of actual conflict.[2]

A major use of sensors could be for "secured storage," described in Chapter 9: armaments reduced by agreement but not destroyed can be kept inside a compound ringed by conventional or (in some cases) fiber-optic fencing and monitored by video and infrared cameras and by such devices as buried seismic weight sensors, dimension-measuring infrared imagers, and, at exits, by X-ray sensors. The compound would be subject either to permanent observation or to inspection on short notice by the opposing alliance either on the ground or from the air as well as satellite observation. Large-scale breakout of stored equipment from several sites would provide unambiguous indication of hostile intent.

Peripherally monitored secured sites similar to those described here have been established under the I.N.F. treaty at Votkinsk, in the U.S.S.R., and at Magna, Utah. The main problem is cost. Full-scale manned sensor monitoring systems would require tamper-resistant mechanisms that are quite expensive. The X-ray devices are not only costly but also difficult and expensive to maintain. The full range of possible equipment would probably not be needed for an ordinary equipment storage site. In any event, there will always be a trade-off between equipment cost and the assurance gained from using more sensors, one of the many trade-offs that have to be made in verification.

Some experts have raised the issue of whether secured storage sites would not create additional vulnerable and "lucrative" targets for air and missile attack if conflict occurs. This seems improbable. There are many more urgent targets on both sides. Moreover, as regards the Pact, both combat-ready and reserve divisions already use a form of secured storage for their major armaments.

Short-notice inspection by teams from the opposing alliance to "suspect sites" of their own choice will be an extremely important verification asset. Some interesting ways of calculating how much on-site observation is called for through relating the degree of concern over non-compliance to the intensity of the verification effort, including inspections, are being developed by the Lawrence Livermore Laboratories and others through decision analysis which, among other things, requires assigning probabilities to possible violations.

This work may in time produce greater precision, but decision analysis in its present state can give a misleading impression of dependability. I do not believe it is yet possible to quantify potential violations by their relative importance to the West, to quantify the information obtainable from each verification asset, and then to calculate quotients of certainty or uncertainty. My own estimate of how many on-site inspections will be needed is based, first, on an estimated number of major centers of military activity, which we have identified as the most plausible sites of deliberate non-compliance and, second, on an informed estimate of what each alliance may consider acceptable for on-site inspection. At the end of the chapter, I will attempt an assessment of the degree of assurance which can be expected from the verification system described here.

One major problem of monitoring reductions is the political acceptability to each alliance of intrusive aerial and ground inspection by the opposing alliance. Even if on-site inspection as such proves acceptable, if inspections are unlimited their number might create political and organizational difficulties for the host country, not to mention the cost. Therefore, as in previous arms-control negotiations, it is probable that neither NATO nor the Warsaw Pact will agree to an unlimited number of on-site inspections. Instead, participants may agree to limit the number of inspections to an annual quota for each alliance.

How big should this quota be? To verify the complex of obligations described here, an annual quota of about 350 short-notice inspections, ground or air, for each alliance may be necessary. This total is calculated on the basis of the obligations listed above, and assumes that the entire area from the Atlantic to the Urals will have to be covered. It allows for visits as follows:

- One inspection per year of each active-duty division. Depending on what is reduced and disbanded by agreement or unilateral action, there might be about a hundred of these on the Pact side and forty-odd on the NATO side;
- Inspection of up to 100 reserve units, including divisional secured-storage sites, and thirty to fifty separate storage sites, including those associated with production plants in the Atlantic-to-the-Urals area that produce reduction-category armaments. If secured storage sites are monitored by permanent inspection teams instead of sensors—this possibility is discussed below—it would not be necessary to subject them to additional on-site inspections. If aircraft reductions are included in an agreement, an additional number of storage sites might be added, although observation of major airfields through fixed observation posts would minimize the number of inspections called for, and possibly make them unnecessary; and
- Provision for 100 suspect-site inspections of the territory of each alliance at points other than designated sites in cases where there is suspicion that reduction-category armaments have been concealed.

Although the total annual quota of inspections is based primarily on the number of individual sites to be covered, there would be no requirement to visit each site. Some sites could be visited repeatedly. Moreover, there should be agreement to permit at least ten short-notice inspections simultaneously to sites of the inspecting side's own selection. The possibility of multiple simultaneous on-site inspections will intensify the deterrent effect of on-site inspection, although it also increases the number of inspecting teams each side must have available at one time.

As an alternative to a quota of suspect-site inspections carried out by outside inspectors flying or driving to a designated place, each alliance could authorize a specific number of resident inspectors. For NATO inspection of the Warsaw Pact, for example, there might be twenty to thirty inspectors for each country participating in an agreement and for each of the three Soviet military districts. Such teams would have the mission of carrying out suspect-site inspections on a continuing basis throughout the territory of the opposing alliance, using procedures somewhat similar to those used by the western military liaison missions in East Germany, which have since World War II been travelling ceaselessly to identify signs of preparation for attack by Soviet forces. This approach limits the number of inspectors rather than the number of inspections.

The considerable amount of information available to both alliances by combining unilateral collection with agreed inspection and data exchange will be further amplified through the force-activity notifications, invited observers, and on-site inspections provided for by the 1986 Stockholm Document. The NATO countries will seek in the current series of C.D.E. talks to obtain the information exchange they failed to obtain in the first series. Prospects are good that they will succeed in doing so and also in expanding the scope of obligatory notifications of force activities, of observer invitations, and of on-site inspections. Even the obligations in force now under the Stockholm Document are giving each side an authorized flow of information, especially on field activities, which adds considerably to the information obtained by unilateral means.

Rationale and Value of Data Exchange

The exchange of detailed data, with each alliance providing information on its own forces, including unit designation, location, and subordination, with strength in men and weapons accounted for down to the level of regiments or brigades or their equivalent, is essential for the force-reduction talks to succeed. For new reduction levels to be agreed, as we have seen, the numbers provided do not have to match precisely. Reduction obligations can instead be formulated through an obligation to reduce to the present NATO level minus some agreed number or, indeed, to some arbitrarily set numerical level for each reduced armament, without explicit reference to the data of either side. NATO proposed such a solution as early as December of 1985, when it suggested in the M.B.F.R. talks that a small number of American and Soviet personnel be withdrawn.

The real need for data exchange is verification. NATO's verification agencies need to have a clear understanding of the holdings of individual Pact units in men and reducible weapons before reductions actually take place. Only in this way can NATO establish a data base against which to monitor the holdings of units remaining after reductions take place, through on-site inspection and other means of information collection. For example, when a given Pact unit is inspected, the country deploying it will be expected to provide an up-to-date report of its strength in men and controlled armaments. This report and what the inspectors see directly will be compared with NATO's own current assessment of the unit's strength, refined and possibly changed through discussion of data on the same unit earlier provided by the Warsaw Pact in an overall exchange.

Owing to the Pact's secrecy on military issues, NATO has up to now had to piece together its estimates of Pact forces from fragments of information of varying quality. Consequently, its current figures may not be accurate for each Pact unit. In particular, NATO has to see from the data exchange early in the C.F.E. talks how the holdings in arms and men of specific Pact units combine into an overall total. It can then compare the Pact's information with its own estimates for specific units and, in the event of major discrepancies, conduct on-site data validation inspections, which will at the same time provide valuable experience and training for the personnel on both sides who will later verify compliance with an agreement.

These data-validation inspections, equivalent to the baseline inspections decreed in the I.N.F. agreement, should take place at a rate of about 100 per year to division-sized units over a two- to three-year period beginning early in the talks, while negotiation on reductions is proceeding. They should be sufficiently numerous to cover each active-duty and reserve division and comparable air-force units in both eastern and western portions of the reduction area.

The process of refining the data of both alliances is time-consuming and for that reason must begin early in the negotiation process. After comparing the figures provided by both alliances, discussing the figures, adjusting them, bringing them up to date, and confirming them by means of on-site inspections, the data holdings of each alliance on the forces of the other should move into closer correspondence.

General Secretary Gorbachev's December, 1988, announcement of unilateral Soviet reductions, many of them in the area west of the Urals, is an important additional reason for detailed data exchange at the outset of the new talks. Unless NATO can be given a detailed layout of Soviet forces prior to these reductions and a second updated Pact data presentation after the unilateral reductions have been completed, it is unlikely to be able to follow the course of the withdrawals with precision. For this purpose, neither the aggregate figures on Pact forces presented by NATO in November, 1988, nor the presence of western observers, official or unofficial, as units are withdrawn, is likely to suffice.

Among the most important of the West's assets for verification is the increasing openness of the Soviet Union and other Warsaw Pact countries. Although this factor cannot be quantified, it could deter deliberate cheating and will almost certainly provide extended warning of significant negative change in Soviet policy.

4 FACTORS COMPLICATING VERIFICATION

The information sources both unilateral and negotiated that we reviewed in the last section would produce a very large flow of information to verify compliance with a force-reduction agreement. Despite this impressive array, verification will be extremely difficult. Some of the obstacles are inherent in the task of verifying partial reductions in very large inventories of equipment spread over a wide area. Other obstacles are man-made: for example, the desire to exempt sensitive installations from inspection or resistance on political grounds to intrusive monitoring by the opposing alliance. The third category of obstacles are technical, arising from the limitations of sensors and national technical means. Let's look at each category in turn.

Inherent Difficulties from the Scope of the Task

The Atlantic-to-the-Urals area comprises all or part of the territory of twenty-one countries. It is very large: about 3.3 million square kilometers for NATO, 6.5 million square kilometers for the Pact. Agreed reductions of specified types of military and units would be partial. Many thousands of armaments of the same type and hundreds of similar units would remain in daily use throughout the reduction area. Even if reductions are limited to tanks, artillery, armored personnel carriers, armed helicopters, and ground-attack aircraft, as proposed here, verifiers will have to keep track of more than 100,000 pieces of equipment which continue to be deployed by each alliance in field units and at airfields. This is over sixty times the 1,600 delivery systems to which the United States and the Soviet Union would be limited in a strategic-reduction agreement. Moreover, production of these armaments in the C.F.E. reduction area will continue. To make the job still harder, these armaments are for the most part smaller than missiles, less dependent on visible ancillary equipment, and more mobile.

Moreover, compliance with residual ceilings will have to be verified in the built-up environment of industrial, urban countries containing hundreds of thousands of buildings and shelters, as well as wooded areas where tanks or other armaments can be readily concealed. Much of the equipment to be monitored is already stored in shelters, and both alliances have large stocks of camouflage material and regularly practice with it. Pact divisional formations, a natural verification unit, are often widely dispersed and sometimes quartered in as many as ten separate garrisons.

Negotiated definitions of armaments to be reduced will be as precise as possible, but there are bound to be "grey" areas open to dispute. For example, NATO wishes to focus on the Warsaw Pact's armor. But in modern armies, nearly all equipment intended for use in combat is armored: tanks, personnel carriers, artillery, anti-aircraft weapons, combat bridging, and reconnaissance vehicles. NATO itself has in service about twenty types of tanks and the Pact nine, and NATO has even more types of armored personnel carriers than it does of tanks. Although naval forces will be excluded from reductions by mutual agreement, they will be an additional source of confusion, because the navies of both alliances have aircraft, helicopters, and other equipment used by ground forces in the central European subregion; some is land-based.

Man-Made Complications of Verification

Among the complications of verification that are not inherent in the process itself, the issue of what is meant by a "reduction" may be one of the hardest to settle. If reduction means agreement to destroy equipment pulled from service, as is clearly preferable from the viewpoint of building down the military potential of both alliances, that is one thing. Then monitoring will focus on the equipment remaining. However, it was clear by the beginning of the talks that some NATO and Pact armies prefer to hand armaments over to reserve units as insurance against a downturn in East/West relations or to store them at designated locations rather than destroy them.

And if we are discussing reductions in tanks, armored troop carriers, artillery, helicopters, and ground-attack aircraft, what about continued production of these items in the reduction area? What will be done with new armaments produced—both those intended for forces in the area and for transfer or sale outside the area? As we have suggested in earlier chapters, one solution would be to place the output of these plants in secured storage adjacent to production facilities, subject to inspection by the opposing alliance. Withdrawals for sale or military aid outside the reduction area or to replace armaments in field units on a one-for-one basis would be allowed only if notice were given to all participants in the agreement.

Other requirements raised by one alliance or the other can cause serious difficulties for monitoring. For example, some NATO countries, including the U.S. and Federal Germany, have traditionally favored reductions by thin-out rather than by eliminating entire units outright. However, the task of verifying a reduction in tanks or other armaments by thin-out among all NATO or Pact units would be extremely hard. All tank units (for example) would continue to exist and to hold armaments whose number would fluctuate as repair and replacement were necessary. Consequently, for verification reasons, it would appear nearly essential to reduce by units. Reduction by units is also by far the more effective way to reduce the combat potential of the alliances.

Also for purposes of verification, ideally the barracks or garrisons of units pulled from service should remain unoccupied or put to civilian use. However, in crowded, garrison-short central Europe this is likely to be impractical.

Even if reduction by units prevails, NATO—and perhaps the Pact, as well—may insist on the flexibility to establish new units after reductions are finished and simply to equip them with a smaller number of armaments. If restructuring like this is permitted, it will complicate monitoring, no matter how much notice might be required in advance of any structural changes. (Moreover, unless there is a ceiling on military manpower, there could also be an increase in the personnel strength of individual units following reductions, although with a smaller number of tanks per unit.) Consequently, reduction by units in combination with enduring residual ceilings on remaining units of the type reduced will be necessary.

As we saw in Chapter 7, NATO wants to have collective, alliance-wide ceilings on reduced armaments in order to permit other members of the alliance to make up for unilateral reductions by one of its members that might take place subsequent to negotiated reductions and in order to avoid any implication of individual national ceilings. This practice would greatly complicate effective monitoring if it meant, as it did in the M.B.F.R. talks, that the alliances would supply collective alliance-wide data rather than totals for each country participating.

For example, NATO's March, 1979, proposal for C.F.E. foresaw decision within each alliance on the apportionment to each member state of agreed reductions in tanks and other armaments, with the exception of the "sufficiency" limit on Soviet forces. NATO took a similar approach in the M.B.F.R. talks. But there, it refused to agree to inform the Pact officially how large a share of total reductions each NATO country would undertake. If repeated in C.F.E., such a practice would make verification impracticable for both sides. One solution, if collective, alliance-wide residual ceilings are to be used, is to separate the obligation to maintain a ceiling from the obligation to supply data, so that national data can be provided by member states of all alliances without any implied obligation of national ceilings. This point could be confirmed by explicit East/West agreement.

Another man-made difficulty for verification is the increasing use by both alliances of covered storage for equipment, which can frustrate monitoring by satellite and aircraft. This would be a particular problem following reductions, when some storage facilities would no longer be full, because an alliance would not be able to estimate how many armaments were in a given installation by measuring its storage capacity.

One of the most vexing of the political difficulties for verification is the desire of both alliances to exempt certain areas and installations from inspection by aircraft or on the ground. (In practice, satellite observation cannot be prevented, although it can be made difficult by shelters and camouflage.) Areas designated off-limits to civilians and outsiders are far more plentiful in the Warsaw Pact than in NATO and their number will have to be cut drastically, either in the C.F.E. force-reduction talks or in the C.D.E.-2 confidence-building talks. But there will remain a large number of installations which both alliances will wish to exempt from low-flying aircraft or ground inspection, such as nuclear storage sites. The trouble is that many such exempt sites could be used to conceal equipment restricted by a force-reduction agreement.

As we have mentioned, in the I.N.F. negotiations the United States drew back from "anywhere, anytime" inspections of all facilities in the United States. In the force-reduction talks the same problem will arise—complicated, at least in the NATO countries, by differing national views as to the sensitivity of specific installations. To resolve the general issue of exempting sites from inspection, each alliance will have to settle for some trade-off between its desire to protect some of its own installations and its desire to have the right to inspect a maximum number of sites in the opposing alliance.

Shortcomings of Technical Assets

Technical monitoring devices have a number of shortcomings. Satellites are a limited resource. To place enough satellites in orbit to give continual close coverage of the area from the Atlantic to the Urals or even just the central European subregion may never be feasible for economic reasons. Given limitations on resources and on facilities and personnel for the interpretation of data transmitted by satellite, priorities will have to be set. Money is not the only impediment to satellite coverage. The weather also gets in the way. Central Europe is under cloud cover for an average of 60 percent of all daylight hours and most detectors on satellites cannot penetrate clouds or darkness. New generations of satellites will probably have infrared devices to overcome some of this difficulty, but even that will be inadequate if equipment is stored under cover or in forests. Ground-based sensors are fallible, too. Seismic, radar, infrared, and television sensors can be foiled and seals and identifying tags can be tampered with. Movement and camouflage can frustrate aerial inspection.

We have mentioned secured storage using peripheral fencing and sensors as a major verification asset for C.F.E. agreements. The main shortcoming of secured storage of this type is its high cost. Sensors are very costly to install and to maintain. There are nagging doubts as to whether they are as yet tamper-proof. And they have an additional complication: for sensor transmissions to be received and acted on, human inspectors must be on the site to receive them or the sensor information must be transmitted via a dedicated satellite. Either alternative—emplacing both sensors and human observers or installing sensors plus a satellite up-link—is very expensive. Consequently, until sensors and satellite connections can be employed more cheaply, the most practical means of securing equipment in storage may be ordinary wire fencing and patrols on roads surrounding the compounds. We will look at this option in more detail in the section on personnel and costs.

There is, of course, no single answer to all of these verification problems. To minimize them, some combination of national technical means, intelligence collection by people, and the growing pool of information for each side from authorized observation under the auspices of the Stockholm Document and from air and ground inspection and sensors must be devised. NATO experts will have to give the specific combination they select a great deal of thought.

To summarize, on the pattern of the I.N.F. treaty, the verification of a force-reduction agreement could consist of: baseline inspection or, as it is called here, data validation inspection of personnel and major equipment over a three-year period while reduction negotiations are continuing; supervision of destruction, dismantling, or immobilization of the equipment reduced by agreement; repeated on-site inspection of field units and storage sites; and suspect-site inspection. These measures would be augmented by agreed early-warning overflights, and by national technical means.

5 VERIFYING TANK REDUCTIONS

To understand the verification process better, let us consider how these procedures might be used to confirm reductions in tanks—the category of conventional weapons more threatening to NATO than any other.

The first step in verifying tank reductions would be for the alliances to exchange complete information on the number of tanks deployed by model number and type, their location, and their status—how many in specified active service and reserve units in repair, in storage, in transit, and in production (including tanks held at storage sites at production facilities), and to conduct baseline inspections to validate these figures.

Step two would be to establish the terms of reductions, setting the maximum number that each alliance will be allowed. As noted earlier, there is a discrepancy between NATO's estimate of the number of tanks held by the Pact before reductions and the total claimed by the Pact. However, as long as it is unambiguous that each alliance will reduce the number of its tanks to the same level—say 20,000 as proposed by NATO—some difference is tolerable, provided that the Pact reports the location of its tanks (and provided that the alliances can agree to the remaining steps in the scenario proposed here).

Step three would be to define the obligations attendant upon a residual ceiling on tanks. In one of the reduction models proposed in Chapter 10, for example, each alliance would pledge not to deploy in central Europe more than 10,000 tanks in active-duty units, reserve units, and in storage. These maximums would include tanks in transit across the subregion and tanks under repair. If the alliances choose not to destroy the weapons they withdraw, or if they choose some combination of destruction and storage, the storage sites will have to be designated. The alliances would also have to commit themselves to place the entire production of tank factories in the reduction area in secured storage and give notice of all withdrawals from these sites of tanks to be sent overseas or to replace a country's permitted holdings.

Finally, each alliance would pledge not to deploy tanks at locations other than those specified in the agreement.

Step four would be to construct facilities for secured storage early enough that they could be ready to receive armaments withdrawn. There are several ways to do this, but the best, as in the I.N.F. agreement, is for each alliance to build basic facilities in which to store its own armaments. The opposing alliance would install sensors if desired. Included in step four would be field inspection of sites for secured storage, including testing of sensors and imaging devices prior to their use. If exit/entry posts on the territory of the opposing alliance had not already been established as a measure of early warning, this would be done now.

Step five would be verification of agreed measures of reduction. Observers would watch over the destruction of tanks, their withdrawal from the reduction area, or their storage in secured compounds at specified sites. If so agreed between the alliances, observers would also make sure that tanks designated for storage were immobilized, by such means as removing gun turrets or guns from their mounts.

If withdrawal from the area is the agreed mode of reduction the weapons would have to be transported through the exit/entry checkpoints. The exit/entry posts would also be used to monitor the transfer of tanks produced in the subregion but sold or otherwise shipped to countries outside it. Replacement tanks entering the reduction area, whether by road, rail, sea, or air, would have to go through these checkpoints. Illicit entry into the reduction area would be possible, but use of agreed exit/entry posts would permit each alliance to focus its national technical means on other potential points of entry.

Step six would be to provide all tanks permitted under the residual ceiling with tamper-resistant identification tags. These could be attached by inspectors of the opposing alliance either at the exit/entry posts, at field units, or at production-plant storage sites. The tags might transmit a signal either continually or on interrogation by overflying aircraft. If tagging is employed, the discovery of tanks without tags inside the sub-region would be evidence of non-compliance.

Step seven would be on-site inspection for compliance with these obligations. Such inspection would be at short notice and at sites selected by the requesting alliance. The inspected country would be obliged to present current data on the tank strength of the inspected unit. In addition to about 250 inspections of divisions and storage sites per year, there would be a quota of about 100 suspect-site inspections per year. As we have seen, the negotiation of suspect-site inspections will raise the issue of whether some sites might be exempt. Suspect-site inspections will also raise problems of intrusiveness. For example, NATO may want to inspect storage areas normally used for armaments other than those reduced by agreement to assure that no tanks are hidden there.

6 COOPERATIVE MEASURES

Each alliance would commit itself to certain cooperative measures to facilitate inspection. On notice, tanks and other restricted armaments would be moved out of shelters and storage compounds and ranged in the open where they could be photographed by satellite or low-flying aircraft. At the same time, ground inspection of shelters, roofed storage, and repair facilities would take place; this would be easier and faster to accomplish if the equipment is removed from storage. Camouflage would be removed in units inspected and its use at the time of inspection forbidden. Where feasible, roofs would be removed from storage facilities. In cases of inspection of divisions and air units, as soon as a unit was designated for inspection there would be an immediate prohibition of movement in or out of the garrison within a radius of, say, 200 to 400 kilometers. Low-flying aircraft and satellite resources would check that this prohibition was being observed.

All participating countries would also be required to give notice of production of tanks in the reduction area, of the introduction of such equipment to the area from outside, and of the introduction of such equipment into units. Upon giving such notice a country would also have to give notice of the simultaneous withdrawal from the area of an equal number of tanks, in order to keep its holdings under the agreed limit. Withdrawal of tanks from secured storage for the purpose of training reserve units would also be reported in advance, together with specification of the number, period, and area of use. Each country would be allowed a maximum number of exercises per year and observers would have to be invited to all.

Inspections would, of course, cover holdings of all armaments reduced by agreement, not only tanks. Inspectors would do their work from low-flying aircraft or on the ground. They would have the right to enter shelters capable of harboring reduced armaments in all garrisons except any that might be specifically excluded and they could enter all storage, repair, and production sites. They would test seals and sensors at secured storage sites.

Verification of restrictions on military activities or deployments will also be required by a force-reduction agreement. The establishment of a Restricted Military Area from which all reduced armaments would be barred is such a measure. And it is one that would be far easier to verify than reductions in armaments, because the ban it imposed would not be partial but total. Other constraints, such as restricting the scale of out-of-garrison activities or reserve-unit training, would not be so easy to verify, though the task would be helped if the restrictions were expressed in terms of combat formations, as in the Stockholm Document.

7 ORGANIZATION, COSTS, AND PERSONNEL

A verification task of this complexity will require careful organization both within the alliances and between them. Inside NATO (and presumably inside the Warsaw Pact) it will be necessary to set up a specific institution to plan the use of NATO's inspection quota for Pact forces, to implement inspections, and to share and analyze information collected by national means, observers, and inspectors and provided by the opposing alliance. NATO inspection teams should be multilateral, although it will probably be sufficient to have only two to three allies represented on each team. The United States might well wish to be represented on many teams. It could also use the intra-NATO verification center as a place to share with its allies the information it obtains by national technical means and to receive information from them in turn.

NATO's intra-alliance center would also process information reported by the Pact and by its own observers and inspectors acting under the terms of the 1986 Stockholm Document and of whatever agreements might be made in the current C.D.E.-2 talks. The intra-alliance center would alert the NATO Council to any questions of compliance. It would also coordinate the 150 annual early-warning overflights and other early-warning and verification measures which each alliance might be authorized to make.

An East/West forum should be established for discussion of complaints of non-compliance. Serious complaints could also be handled bilaterally, but the NATO requirement for multilaterally shared information also argues for a multilateral organization here. NATO will have to overcome its apprehensions over a Soviet *droit de regard*, realizing that an East/West center will give it at least equal advantage with regard to the Pact's forces. As described in Chapter 9, this East/ West forum should be given the additional task of functioning as a risk-reduction center to investigate and clarify low-level incidents like border crossing by personnel and aircraft of the two alliances.

In this chapter we have proposed secured storage for aircraft, for reserve equipment, for ammunition stocks, for production sites, and for armaments and equipment such as tank transporters on which special restrictions might be imposed. But we have also discussed the high expense and impracticality of using fiber-optic fencing and sensors to enclose such sites under current conditions, where sensors would, in any event, have to be read by observer personnel or transmitted to a dedicated satellite. We have suggested instead a system of storage in which each compound would be fenced with wire fencing of some agreed type and its perimeter patrolled by a small resident team of soldiers, most of whom could be enlisted personnel instead of highly trained, officer-grade technicians. Such a system seems the cheapest and most effective option.

Equipment for sites like these would be limited to a couple of all-terrain vehicles, perhaps some portable photoelectric sensors, and field radios. Communication with a single base in each participating state (a selected embassy) could be by telephone. The host state would be responsible for installing ordinary wire-mesh fencing and cutting dirt roads; both would already exist in most cases. A complement of about twenty-five people might be needed for each site. There would be two teams of ten posted at the site in rotation and five substitutes who would fill in for people sick or on leave. Smaller teams might be possible.

The cost might be about $40,000 per man beyond normal pay and expenses for language training and special instruction, $10,000 per man for transport, $10,000 for rations, and $100,000 for two trucks and prefabricated housing, for a first-year total of about $1.5 million per site. For 100 sites, the total would be $150 million per year—the cost of four fighter aircraft.

At a cost of $1.5 million per site, monitoring up to 100 secured storage sites in the Pact's portion of area from the Atlantic to the Urals, plus personnel and equipment for perhaps 100 fixed observation posts at exit/entry points and other transport choke points inside the reduction area on the Pact side, would make for a initial annual expense of perhaps $300 million. Personnel for 100 secured storage sites at twenty-five men each and 100 permanent posts with a maximum of fifteen each (five men on duty, plus back-up personnel) would come to about 4,000, plus about 300 inspectors and 300 escort personnel, for a total of about 5,000 military personnel drawn from a total pool of nearly three million per side.

This calculation of the possible number of storage sites is generous. Divisional storage sites for reserve units could be combined to cut the total number by half or even less. The $300 million price tag is fairly large but it is only one-tenth of one percent of the $300 billion that NATO spends each year for the European confrontation. So it is surely affordable.

8 CONCLUSIONS

Still to be evaluated is the effectiveness of the verification system roughed out here against a deliberate, carefully planned attempt to evade it. At the beginning of this chapter we asked, will verification measures in combination with information from other sources be capable of detecting a militarily significant degree of Pact or Soviet evasion or non-compliance soon enough for NATO to react, either by seeing that the violations stop or by negating the military advantage they might have brought?

In the verification approach described here NATO would be able to rely on data supplied by the Pact in the course of periodic exchange, information supplied by inspection teams at as many as 300 exit/entry posts, transport choke points, and storage and production sites, information from approximately 350 annual inspections in the air or on the ground, and information from as many as 150 early-warning overflights annually. These sources would be buttressed by the considerable flow of information on military activities established by C.D.E.-1 and its successors, and by NATO's existing information-gathering assets, including national technical means, which have good prospects of improving, and also by "political warning," including statements of Pact leaders.

The additional information gained from negotiated measures in a force-reduction agreement would provide a great deal of assurance beyond the considerable amount of information already available through national intelligence collection that preparations for attack were not under way, thus serving the main objectives of a reduction agreement. A successful standing-start attack with minimal warning, now difficult, would be nearly impossible, and the warning time for a short-preparation attack would be extended by several days; for full mobilization by a much longer period.

However, even the exacting verification approach suggested here could not wholly eliminate the risk of a slow, covert buildup of forces over a long period. The verification system described might not register a slow "thickening" of the armaments and manpower of Pact forces by as much as 30 percent. Increases larger than that would be detected eventually. This acknowledged, we must also recognize that NATO would be better off militarily with an illicit Pact advantage in tanks of 20 to 30 percent over a common ceiling of 20,000 tanks per alliance than with the current Pact superiority of about 35,000 tanks.

Later in the reduction process, if the two alliances proceed to make deep cuts, as urged here, the potential gains from covert Pact buildup would become greater in relative terms. Yet to succeed, such an enterprise would take considerable skill and resources. It would also require a lot of luck, because the risk that such a complex, long-term scheme would be detected would be considerable. Given the growing openness of societies in the East, it would be very hard for the Pact's national leaders to maintain an impenetrable barrier between their outward amicability and inward determination to conquer western Europe by force of arms.

Even in a worst case, considerable political warning is likely to come out of the Soviet system. If the intent to attack was connected with an abrupt change of Soviet government, that change would in itself give political warning. And although some degree of slow, illicit buildup might escape the verification net, direct preparations for attack—mobilization of reserves, breakout of equipment from storage, forward movement of ammunition, loading of munitions and fuel by ground-attack aircraft and helicopters—certainly would not escape detection and would be all the more visible through the verification and early-warning measures contained in an agreement. So in all cases the system of reductions and verification outlined here would bring NATO a large net gain in security.

Several actions are needed to minimize the difficulty of reaching agreement on verification in the Atlantic-to-the-Urals talks:

(1) East/West negotiation on this subject should begin early in the new talks and be combined with discussion of data and early-warning measures;

(2) NATO needs to carry out some verification exercises in the field, complete with a "Red" Team doing its best to confuse and confound the inspectors;

(3) NATO needs to give more priority to developing and testing sensor and communications technology for secured storage. In the coming decades cheaper sensors and cheaper satellites should make it possible to monitor secured storage sites from a distance;

(4) As soon as is feasible, NATO and the Warsaw Pact should test their means of verification, by monitoring reductions in a single unit in each alliance;

(5) Finally, NATO should move now to establish an alliance-wide verification unit like that described earlier and charge it with the task of preparing a position for the alliance on verification.

In the final chapter of this book we'll try to look more deeply into the future that a build-down of the NATO/Pact military confrontation in Europe might bring.

12 The Way Ahead: The European Confrontation in a Global Framework

Given the complexity of negotiating force reductions, would unilateral action in each alliance on the lines of that decided on by the Soviet Union and its Warsaw Pact allies in the fall of 1988 be better? Can the United States and NATO do anything to make the challenges of negotiation, which include decisions about the future of nuclear deterrence in NATO, less formidable and less divisive? What would success in negotiating reductions mean for the long-term future of both alliances? Would build-down of the NATO/Pact military confrontation intensify instability in eastern Europe, the problem we identified in Chapter 3 as the most likely source of war in Europe if war comes? What effect would build-down have on the division of Europe and, more particularly, on the division of Germany? In this last chapter we will try to rough out some answers to these questions.

THE UNILATERAL ALTERNATIVE

To come within sight of the possibility of deep cuts in the NATO/Pact confrontation, we have had to work our way through a tangle of political and substantive problems: whether and how to cut back the number of nuclear delivery systems, including aircraft; how to dispose of armaments pulled from service; whether reductions should be by units; whether subceilings should be imposed on Soviet forces; and what constraints might buttress reductions most effectively. Owing to the large size of the armed forces that the Warsaw Pact will be deploying even after deep cuts, negotiators in Vienna would still have a briar patch of thorny issues with which to grapple even if verification were the only matter before them.

Having grasped the difficulty of questions like these, it is reasonable to conjecture whether there is not some simpler, less complicated way to build down the East/West military confrontation. What about unilateral action on both sides? Perhaps that could accomplish the job more easily and also more quickly, because it is evident that finding solutions to all these problems acceptable to both East and West will take a good deal of time. Unilateral action would also have a special advantage for NATO, at least theoretically: it would preserve NATO's freedom to reverse course rapidly if the Soviet Union should revert to an aggressive stance.

The question of whether unilateral action would be a better way to build down the confrontation is not easy to answer. Many of the advantages of unilateral action are also disadvantages. For example, just as NATO would be free to reverse a unilateral action, so would the Pact; neither side would have pledged not to do so. Under unilateral action, there would be no systems of verification, early warning, transparency measures, and constraints to insure against covert re-armament.

Moreover, a process of unilateral actions in both alliances to cut back the military confrontation in Europe is not as easy as it might appear. Uncoordinated unilateral decisions by individual NATO countries to cut NATO forces may come. But in the past, unilateral cuts by individual states acting on their own under domestic pressure have engendered great friction within the alliance. Some NATO states have argued against such actions by others as too risky, and, when individual states have proceeded to make unilateral cuts on their own, the response has been resentment on the part of other alliance members and their public and political opinion. In all, leaving the build-down in Europe to chance could seriously erode the alliance's main rationale, the capacity to enhance the strength of individual members by pooling it through voluntary cooperation.

What about parallel unilateral action internally coordinated by each of the alliances among its own members? Such a process is not easy. In fact, it comes close to formal negotiation in its difficulty, because each side, and especially NATO, would wish to assure that the other will carry out cuts of equal value. Negotiation among NATO members could be as tough as the preparation for the C.F.E. talks. But unilateral action need not be so formal. As we saw earlier, the Warsaw Pact has announced significant unilateral reductions for 1989 and 1990. What about a sequential process in which each side signals the other by taking some unilateral action and the opposing alliance decides on its own whether and what type of action to take in response? NATO could agree corporately to follow these Soviet examples by unilateral reductions of its own, also deciding within the alliance on the specific steps to be taken.

This process, too, would be complicated. Deciding on unilateral

reductions in a situation of longstanding East/West military confrontation requires one of two things. One is a leader like Mikhail Gorbachev
who wields enormous authority within a political system and who can
use it to put through an unpopular decision once reached. But the
NATO alliance is not organized on these lines of enlightened authori-
tarianism. For it, the second requirement would pertain: the capacity to
come to an official assessment that the Warsaw Pact and the Soviet
Union are not threatening attack and will not seek to draw military
advantage from NATO's unilateral reduction, and the capacity to
agree on the specific unilateral action to be taken. This means, first, an
official NATO finding that the Soviet Union has become more cooperative and, second, full agreement on what to do about it.

In the current situation of Warsaw Pact superiority, it will be hard
for NATO to come to such a consensus. Its reaction to Gorbachev's
December, 1988, announcement of unilateral Soviet cuts was, understandably, to point out that the Pact would still have large numerical
superiority if the cuts were carried out.

Later, if equality between the alliances is established by negotiated
asymmetrical cuts of Pact forces or if the Pact makes further unilateral
cuts having the same effect, then such NATO decisions may become
easier. In circumstances like these, NATO member states might be able
to decide that they could afford to cut their forces by a certain
percentage.

Yet the United States has an especially complicated budgetary
process in which Congress plays an exceptionally important role. There
is a tendency in American budgetary practice, when the objective is to
save money, to whittle the defense budget by stretching the period of
procurement for individual major weapons systems. Thus the United
States defense budget may decrease in response to economic pressures
and in competition with other budget programs in the absence of any
finding by the president that the threat from the Soviet Union has
decreased and in the absence of any direct link to specific defense or
arms-control policies of the Soviet Union. There is a link, of course, in
general information about Soviet actions shared by the president,
Congress, and the interested public, and often a loose consensus.

This rather autonomous process is likely to continue in coming
years. But some link with the defense budgets of other NATO states is
needed. Regardless of how the United States defense budget is decided
internally, United States government officials have to rationalize it for
the allies. Deciding within the alliance what budget cut for NATO
forces is feasible and thus which NATO forces to cut will be as difficult

as preparing for the C.F.E. talks—more so, because NATO would be trying to decide on real cuts, not possible ones.

And the Soviet Union would continue to have to take the lead in making unilateral cuts. That the Soviet Union will do so further, at least down to the level it has proposed for C.F.E. of 40 percent below current levels with further specific proposals designed to move the talks ahead, seems quite possible if the Gorbachev line continues to shape Soviet policy.

The entire thrust of Soviet policy on European force reductions that we have been describing in this book—the cooperative Soviet behavior in C.D.E.-1; the Soviet acceptance at the May, 1988, Moscow summit of the West's reduction concept for M.B.F.R. of reducing to equality below the level of the numerically weaker side; the Soviet announcement of unilateral reductions in December, 1988; and the March, 1989, Soviet C.F.E. proposals themselves, as well as the main trend of defense discussion in the Soviet Union itself—seem to argue that the Soviet leadership has decided to make a radical cut of 40 to 50 percent or more in Soviet forces in Europe (and possibly make unilateral cuts in its strategic nuclear forces as well) regardless of what NATO does in return.

If this assessment is correct, it means that the Soviet leadership may not wait much beyond the two-year period of implementation in 1989 and 1990 of the already announced unilateral reductions to see whether the C.F.E. talks may lead to a first agreement within one or two years thereafter. If the Soviet leadership decides that the C.F.E. talks are not productive, it seems likely to decide on a further large unilateral cut in Soviet forces.

If this is the likely outcome, why should NATO bother to undertake the difficult effort of negotiating reductions? There are five good reasons for doing so. Each of them addresses the uncertainties about the Soviet future that must be a central issue when the West considers reductions in its own forces.

First, a negotiated outcome will provide greater insurance—in the form of commitments not to exceed residual levels, early-warning and verification measures, and constraints on force activities—against the recurrence of a negative Soviet policy.

Second, in Chapter 3 we identified widespread unrest in eastern Europe followed by misperception and misunderstanding of military activities of the opposing alliances as the most likely trigger of war in Europe if war comes. A functioning force-reduction agreement would provide valuable, perhaps crucial safeguards against this contingency.

Third, negotiation seems likely to bring even deeper Soviet cuts than unilateral reductions would. NATO should be seeking to combine deep cuts, constraints, early-warning measures, and verification in such a way as to impose maximum delays in terms of years of highly visible military effort before Soviet forces could be restored to a level which would make a less conciliatory Soviet leadership confident that it could defeat remaining NATO forces.

Fourth, NATO will maintain its unity and cohesion better under the discipline of conducting negotiations—difficult as it is to do so—than in the more corrosive situation of competitive individual force cuts.

Fifth, a negotiated outcome would provide a stronger endorsement and confirmation within the Soviet system of the correctness of the Gorbachev line than a series of unilateral cuts. Like western publics, the Soviet public—and the Soviet military—like to see their country get something in return for its actions. Taken together, all these factors provide much more assurance than unilateral action would of continuation of a constructive Soviet approach and more protection against reversion to a negative one.

Although this is so, it is unnecessary for western leaders to make any final decision for or against negotiation, or for or against unilateral action. In the long term, once parity is reached the two methods should complement one another in the build-down process. After all, the NATO/Pact confrontation itself was built up in a series of unilateral actions and it is not necessary that every action to build it down be performed in lockstep. Yet a final point needs to be made: unilateral actions are a less dependable vehicle if the conscious intention of the leadership in both alliances is to cut back the NATO/Pact confrontation. This may be true even if the desire is stronger in one alliance than the other. If the Soviet Union wishes a positive effect on western political opinion, it probably would find that flexibility in negotiation would make a bigger impression than unilateral actions.

WHAT NATO NEEDS TO DO

After examining the pros and cons of unilateral action, we must conclude that there is no invisible regulating mechanism in the international system to replace the conscious decisions of NATO and Warsaw Pact governments. If the countries of the NATO coalition want to take advantage of the remarkable opportunity for building down the East/West military confrontation that has arisen from the convergence of the decline of the Cold War with the emergence of reform leadership in the Soviet Union—or, if we are more skeptically inclined, if the western governments want to make an effective test of whether that opportunity exists—then they will have to act vigorously.

The difficulties of the force-reduction talks that we have reviewed in this book are more numerous than those in nuclear arms control, but the two enterprises are similar in one important respect. Any agreement between potential adversaries on arms control is a remarkable achievement having two main characteristics: great intellectual ingenuity on the part of the negotiators and determination on the part of political leaders, who must drive negotiators to be creative, to overcome obstacles, and to achieve results.

Leadership is crucial to the process, and among the countries of the NATO coalition the United States must continue to play a leadership role. As we saw in our review of the impact of the I.N.F. treaty, over the past thirty years American prestige in Europe has declined from its high in the late 1950s and 1960s. The many reasons for this development include the emergence of economic strength in western Europe; the Soviet Union's achievement of nuclear parity with the United States; negative European reaction to American involvement in Vietnam, Watergate, and the Iranian hostage episode; the opposition of majority European opinion to specific American actions like the bombing of Libya and the invasion of Grenada; and the friction between the United States and Europe during the entire I.N.F. episode.

Yet, despite its decline, the United States continues to lead NATO. There is no substitute—no single European state and no coalition or grouping of European states, with equal authority. Acting together, the European NATO states can block and stalemate American initiatives, but they cannot—not yet, at any rate—supply positive leadership to the western coalition.

Even if the force-reduction talks are successful and a new basis of East/West equality is established after a cut of 50 percent of NATO's strength, as we have urged here, there will be a continuing need in the West for the NATO alliance. Even at that level, the Warsaw Pact will continue to have very powerful forces and the Soviet Union will continue to be a military superpower. If the administration of President George Bush wants the alliance to remain healthy even in a situation of contraction, it will have to come to an understanding with western European allies on two major, closely related issues: a larger role for Europe in NATO and the future of the western nuclear deterrent.

We will turn to these issues in a moment, but first there is a still more urgent step the new administration should take if it really wants to move the C.F.E. talks ahead. It needs to appoint a high level, Washington-based coordinator for these talks.

Until a U.S./Soviet agreement is achieved on reducing strategic nuclear armaments, the president will be giving his main attention to completing that agreement. Among all major issues in the field of foreign relations and arms control, it is likely that START will continue to be the most demanding on the president's time. It will require his daily supervision to succeed. Experience shows that it will be barely possible for the president to free enough time from other issues to watch over START. It is most improbable that he can give anything like the same degree of attention to NATO/Pact force-reduction negotiations.

Yet full-time attention from the top level of government is absolutely essential to break through the interagency and intra-alliance complexities of the C.F.E. talks.

The answer is to appoint a senior cabinet-level official with sole responsibility for the C.F.E. talks. This official should report directly to the president, should have assured access to him, and should have the political stature to work successfully with the secretaries of state and defense on this project. This Washington-based "expediter" should maintain close contact with top allied leaders and with the Soviet and Pact leadership to know when issues are ripe for decision and when compromise proposals may be needed.

To assure congressional support for the administration's management of the talks, it would be desirable to establish a bipartisan group in the Senate and also in the House of Representatives to review the administration's activities and give their advice.

During our examination in Chapter 7 of intra-alliance differences over preparation of positions for the C.F.E. talks, we concluded that these differences reflect underlying dissatisfactions in the alliance about the proper future shape of NATO. Consequently, to succeed in the C.F.E. talks and, more generally, in the process of building down the confrontation in Europe, the United States needs to reach a better understanding with its NATO allies over the future organization of U.S./European cooperation on defense. Unless it does, the talks may be stalled by disagreements over individual issues like the desirability of parity, unit reductions, and controls on production.

France's participation in the talks is a positive development. But it is evident that France, which has little experience in arms-control negotiations, wishes to avoid any appearance of American domination and aspires to take the lead in Europe. These attitudes are reflected in specific French positions in the C.F.E. talks, such as France's rejection of the alliance-to-alliance concept and of tight intra-alliance discipline in negotiations. Unless there is important change, France will continue to interfere with the achievement of consensus in NATO on the talks and to hold the alliance's policies to a conservative and unproductive minimum.

The United States should meet this problem head on, not only in the interest of the talks but also in the interest of keeping the alliance vigorous. American policy should be deliberately to encourage cooperation on defense among the European members of NATO, and to give clear support to the idea of a corporate European voice within NATO, with a major role for France. We are not talking here of "strengthening the European pillar" in some general sense, but of United States willingness to reorganize NATO procedures to permit use of NATO as a forum for coordinating defense and arms control policy between the United States and a western European grouping, rather than as a forum where the United States seeks to build a consensus among individual member states.

The United States has to find some way of dealing with western Europe corporately in the military sense as it will increasingly have to learn to deal with western Europe corporately on economic issues.

There is little prospect now or in the near future of the emergence of a formally organized "European Defense Union," which would take on independent responsibility for providing an effective defense of western Europe and for organizing that defense. This may well happen within a generation. But for such a concept to be workable, the diverse peoples of the European Community will have to have as much confidence in the capacity of their political executive, even if a group executive, to make decisions potentially involving the life and death of their system as the British and French populations now have in their own national governments.

Such a development seems possible, even probable, some decades from now. At the moment, what is needed is to assure that the long gestation of an autonomous European defense community does not result in the premature demise or incapacity of NATO. That could happen if the United States, by adhering to current NATO procedures, takes on the appearance of trying to block the development of an independent European defense. At present what is needed is a welcoming American attitude toward a European grouping.

More specifically, the administration should state its willingness to use NATO as a forum for coordinating the defense and arms-control policy of the United States with a European grouping as well as with those NATO states like Canada, Norway, and Turkey that may not be members of such a grouping. Such a position would dissatisfy the Turks, whose application to join the European Community has been kept by the Community at arm's length, but it might in fact accelerate Turkey's Community membership as well as Norway's. The Canadian voice has been, and will continue to be, valuable for NATO on its own. Whether this European group should be the Western European Union currently supported by France or something else would be for Europeans to decide.

In the past the United States has vigorously opposed the formation of a separate European caucus within NATO. It continues to do so, preferring the convenience of the moment to preparing the future. It argues that European members of NATO have a hard time agreeing among themselves and that, once members of the European Community have agreed with one another on some policy, their position becomes rigid and unchangeable, not a productive basis for U.S./ European discussion. European NATO members argue in turn that the process of interagency discussion in Washington is often so vigorously pursued that, when United States representatives in NATO finally address a topic, there is no give in *their* position. The answer, surely, is a basic understanding that positions advanced by either side will be preliminary and subject to change after discussion. In theory, these are the ground rules of the current process of consultation in NATO.

United States encouragement of a separate European defense grouping will also be the best way to encourage the western European countries to move toward military cooperation among themselves in areas outside Europe. This was done in a rudimentary way in 1987 and 1988, when western European states with naval units in the Persian Gulf worked together through the Western European Union to protect shipping through the Gulf. The United States has already benefited enormously from political and economic cooperation with NATO countries in areas outside of Europe. So have the European NATO states. But because European NATO members have feared American domination of coordinated military activities outside Europe, the United States has not been able to gain the agreement of European NATO members to cooperate militarily with the United States "out-of-area" under the formal coordination of NATO. The possibility of fruitful out-of-area cooperation between the United States and some corporate European entity like the Western European Union seems greater.

If the United States showed that it was serious about reorganizing NATO to give Europe a larger role within NATO, France would probably be willing in return to help in establishing a clear connection, rather than a rivalry, between a European defense grouping and NATO. The administration should first develop a model and then discuss it bilaterally with France and other NATO countries. In doing so, the United States should make clear its hope that a new structure for NATO will improve cooperation among NATO members on force reductions. It could move toward establishing a new structure by calling a NATO summit on the question.

THE NUCLEAR ISSUE IN NATO

NATO has been slow to agree on strengthening and modernizing its nuclear forces after the I.N.F. agreement or on the directly related issue of how to handle nuclear weapons in the force-reduction talks.

We have seen in this book that the belief that nuclear deterrence brings safety and the belief that deterrence through nuclear weapons is the ultimate risk are, for their respective adherents, tenets of faith approaching religion. Perhaps this is because nuclear weapons with their ultimate destructive capability have not been used in war in Europe and because it is highly improbable (although not impossible) that they would be used, two circumstances which give the debate over deterrence an abstract yet emotional quality. In any event, it is increasingly difficult to have dispassionate discussion of the future role of nuclear weapons in western defense. In practical terms, what is needed in the West is some way of balancing the views of the French, the British, and others, who see a vital role for nuclear deterrence, with the views of the Federal Germans and others, who want deep cuts in tactical-range nuclear weapons. Failure to come to some compromise on this issue can have destructive long-term effects on the alliance.

The United States should develop a policy that can bring a higher degree of agreement within NATO on the long-term role of nuclear weapons and that can also persuade France and the United Kingdom to relax their opposition to the tactical nuclear reductions desired by the Germans in connection with the C.F.E. talks. To achieve these goals, the French and the British need to be reassured about the future of their own nuclear deterrent in the face of the possibility of continuing U.S./Soviet negotiation on reductions both in strategic armaments and in tactical-range armaments deployed in Europe. One possible approach is for the United States to assure France and the U.K. that it will oppose reductions in French and British nuclear-delivery systems both in the C.F.E. talks and in any talks with the Soviets on nuclear reductions that might succeed the START talks. (This would not preclude some no-increase restrictions on French, U.K., and Chinese nuclear arsenals in the event the follow-on negotiations for strategic nuclear reductions succeeded.)

The United States should also seek a cooperative agreement with France and the U.K. to pool some part of American strategic resources with French and British nuclear armaments in a "Eurostrategic" nuclear triumvirate. Its goal would be to assure an effective western nuclear deterrent following whatever limited reductions might be negotiated in American nuclear-capable aircraft, nuclear-capable artillery, and surface-to-surface missiles deployed in Europe. One area of practical cooperation among the three countries would be in the development of an air-launched standoff missile of five- to six-hundred-mile range which could be used for interdiction with nuclear or conventional warheads. This project would be the focus of intense dispute in the West and with the Soviet Union, but it may be necessary to carry it out to demonstrate to the two European nuclear powers the seriousness of the United States' intention to protect and maintain their long-term nuclear capability.

Against the background of such an understanding with France and the U.K., the administration should attempt to gain NATO's acceptance of a compromise position on cutbacks in the deployment of shorter-range nuclear arms if the Soviets give clear evidence of their willingness to collaborate in practical ways to make sizable asymmetrical reductions in conventional forces.

The consideration underlying these suggestions is that, after the elimination of I.N.F. and probable further reductions in NATO nuclear armaments in the C.F.E. context or unilaterally, there will be a continued need for nuclear deterrence in Europe, but there will also be a need for NATO to modify, explicitly or implicitly, its strategy of flexible response.

The justification for a continued NATO nuclear deterrent is clear. As long as the Soviet Union remains a major nuclear power, there will be a need for a counterbalancing nuclear force in Europe, of which American nuclear weapons will be an essential element. The nuclear capabilities of Britain and France are not by themselves equal to the task. Nor is the confidence of non-nuclear western European states in British and French decisions over the possible use of nuclear weapons yet strong enough for non-nuclear states to forgo the added insurance of American participation in a NATO deterrent, even though the value of that participation may in the eyes of some Europeans have decreased.

The deployment of these weapons is needed to demonstrate the absolute determination of the West to resist to the ultimate consequence an attack or political intimidation by the Soviet Union. In actuality, either side would give serious consideration to the use of nuclear weapons if it were facing defeat in war in Europe.

This, rather than elaborate strategies for use of nuclear weapons, is the real substance of mutual nuclear deterrence. To implement it, NATO must continue to deploy nuclear weapons in Europe. And to convey this ultimate reality, the nature and deployment of these weapons must be such as to entail a realistic and practical possibility that NATO can use these weapons to strike militarily significant targets for rational operational purposes. But the strategy for possible use of these weapons must reflect their ultimate purpose and not be dictated by the technical availability of nuclear weapons for tactical war-fighting purposes.

So many changes have taken place in flexible response—NATO's current articulation of nuclear deterrence—that it no longer appears sustainable without modification.

As we saw in the opening chapters of this book, during the I.N.F. negotiations conservative Europeans lost a good deal of confidence in the reliability of the American nuclear deterrent. In reaction, there was a relative increase in their reliance on French and British nuclear forces. However, France continues to be opposed to flexible response and believes in "inflexible response": that the Soviet Union should be put on notice that *any* seriously intended military incursion will automatically bring a nuclear response. This important difference in view, and the related fact that France has regarded decisions on where and how to use its nuclear weapons as essential attributes of its national sovereignty, will create obstacles to efforts to substitute a European for a United States nuclear deterrent, or realistically to collaborate on a common United States, U.K., and French Eurostrategic nuclear deterrent. In either event, France would have to become less dedicated to autonomy.

As regards the material components of flexible response, the I.N.F. missiles have gone. NATO nuclear artillery is likely to be cut back through American withdrawals of nuclear artillery rounds whether or not the new talks are successful. If the C.F.E. talks fail, prospects for deployment in Europe of a modernized Lance missile are poor. If the new talks are successful, NATO's arsenal of tactical nuclear missiles and nuclear-delivery aircraft will also shrink. Thus, the material components of flexibility in NATO's flexible response strategy—the range of weapon types available—have been cut back and will probably be cut further. Restrictions on targeting are also likely to limit the flexibility of flexible response. Whereas in actual conflict any target may be selected, Federal Germany does not want missiles or air-delivered weapons to be targeted in peacetime on targets in East Germany with its population of fellow Germans.

Beyond these considerations is the still weightier one that if in fact the Soviet and Pact conventional superiority—which is the justification for NATO's reliance on nuclear deterrence—is eliminated through negotiated cuts or unilateral Soviet actions, this change will be as momentous in its way as the Soviet Union's achievement of strategic nuclear parity with the United States. This change must bring commensurate changes in NATO's strategy for nuclear deterrence.

For the reasons cited, much of the conceptual rationale of flexible response will have to be revised or dropped. The concept of coupling conventional conflict in Europe to strategic nuclear war through the "seamless web" of graduated nuclear response leading in an inevitable progression from the use of short-range nuclear artillery to strategic nuclear war is being leached away by these material changes, both existing and probable, and by the decline of confidence in the concept.

In practical terms, all these developments seem to rule out tactical use of NATO nuclear armaments at ranges below 200 kilometers. What is left is the possibility that western nuclear weapons launched by air, land-based missiles, or sea-launched cruise or ballistic missiles might be used in a more limited number of situations, like deep interdiction against supply lines and air bases and strikes on military targets in the western U.S.S.R.

Whether these factors will culminate in formal, explicit relinquishment of NATO's flexible-response strategy in favor of the position of no-first-use of nuclear weapons urged by the left in western Europe and by the Warsaw Pact is unclear. There will be good arguments for doing so, but their realization depends on the degree to which the thinking of conservative NATO defense officials evolves. The attitudes of the French and U.K. governments, which would form the core of a long-term nuclear capability for a future European Defense Union, will be critical, and some degree of agreement between their views and those of the European left will have to be maintained if the alliance is to continue to be effective.

Given this political requirement, perhaps the basic concept of maintaining uncertainty as to how, when, and whether western nuclear weapons will be used will be retained. If it is, NATO strategy will nonetheless probably be increasingly circumscribed by conditions and restrictions, like no early first use, the requirement for a high threshold of conventional resistance prior to possible use, or by statements that nuclear weapons will be used only as a last resort to preserve the territorial and political integrity of the NATO states.

THE WARSAW PACT SYSTEM AFTER A C.F.E. AGREEMENT

We have been discussing what the United States needs to do in NATO to clear the decks for effective negotiation with the Warsaw Pact in the force-reduction talks and what might happen to NATO's posture of nuclear deterrence in the event that agreement is reached there. What would be the effects of successful negotiation on the Warsaw Pact countries? Will reduced NATO/Warsaw Pact confrontation contribute to political instability in eastern Europe?

As we have seen, this was a concern of Warsaw Pact officials from the outset of the M.B.F.R. talks and it persists. As we mentioned at the beginning of this book, NATO officials, too, are increasingly worried that the relaxation of Soviet political control over the eastern European governments, which is a desirable by-product of Gorbachev's campaign to restructure the Soviet system, could lead to anarchic conditions in one or more eastern European states or even to conflict among them (for example, between Hungary and Romania over the treatment of the Hungarian minority in Romania). Pressures in eastern Europe are intensified by movements for autonomy inside the Soviet Union like those in the Soviet Baltic republics, the Ukraine, and Georgia.

Such developments could lead to Soviet military intervention in eastern Europe or, in the worst case, to war between NATO and the Soviet Union, in the classic pattern of the onset of World War I. Western policymakers have to address themselves seriously to this new range of problems in Europe.

In this context, some NATO officials worry that concluding and implementing NATO/Pact force-reduction agreements could intensify pressures making for blowup in eastern Europe. The impact on public opinion in eastern European countries of highly publicized Soviet withdrawals, of frequent visits by NATO military personnel on observation or verification missions, and of continued negotiations once the first phase of reductions has begun may be considerable. But that impact is more likely to be translated into direct pressures for more political and economic freedoms than into pressures for withdrawal of remaining Soviet forces or withdrawal of the eastern European states from the Warsaw Pact.

There are strong inhibitions on public pressures to eliminate the Soviet military presence in eastern Europe both in east European public opinion and governments. Even if Soviet forces in eastern Europe were cut in half, well over 250,000 troops would remain. And even if increases in these forces were prohibited in a C.F.E. agreement, thousands of Soviet troops would remain stationed in Soviet territory, at the borders of eastern European countries or within a few hundred miles of them. The memories of Budapest in 1956 and Prague in 1968 will long endure. With minor exceptions, even those dissidents in Poland and Hungary pressing most strongly for internal democratic reforms deliberately leave untouched the issue of membership in the Warsaw Pact. They may advance radical suggestions for negotiated mutual cuts in Pact and NATO forces and they may repeat with fervor the official Soviet and Warsaw Pact position that both NATO and the Warsaw Pact alliances should ultimately be dissolved. Some in Hungary and stronger groups in the Soviet-controlled Baltic states are pressing for a status of military neutrality. But most do not advocate unilateral withdrawal of their countries from the Warsaw Pact.

It seems probable that, as long as there is movement, or prospect of movement, on domestic reforms and some movement in arms control, there will be little serious pressure in eastern Europe for revision of the Warsaw Treaty link with the Soviet Union. Certainly, the eastern European governments will seek to control such pressures, because they are acutely aware that their own chances of survival would be radically cut if the Soviet military connection were eliminated or even if public pressures for withdrawal from the Warsaw Pact became so strong in their countries that the Soviet Union felt impelled to intervene militarily.

For its part, the Soviet Union under its present leadership seems likely to accept on a piecemeal basis nearly any change in the domestic political or economic systems initiated by the eastern European governments. It appears unlikely to intervene militarily in any but the most extreme conditions—those involving explicit withdrawal from membership in the Pact or outright anarchy and loss of political control.

The existence of these strong dynamics making for piecemeal change is why ideas of a high-level U.S./Soviet or East/West dialogue on the evolution of eastern Europe appear unwise. Such a dialogue would elevate to an issue of principle or to an issue of East/West relations the question of Soviet acceptance of a given innovation in eastern Europe and might well block the entire process.

The one way in which negotiated reductions do seem likely to generate pressure on Warsaw Pact governments is by opening the door to still larger cutbacks in the Pact's defense forces as a means of creating resources for domestic needs. Even in the early stages of the M.B.F.R. talks, officials of eastern European countries were unequivocal in their desire for cutbacks in Pact forces. They looked to an M.B.F.R. agreement to protect them from Soviet demands that they share more of the costs of defense, a kind of Warsaw Pact parallel to insistent United States demands on the NATO allies to share more of the burden of defending Europe. The pressures in Pact countries for more domestic spending have increased over time. All in all, despite very different mechanisms in eastern and western Europe for articulating public opinion and for bringing it to bear on political decisions, any reductions that might be negotiated in the Atlantic-to-the-Urals talks will lead to demands for more that will be as strong in eastern Europe as in western Europe.

THE FUTURE OF EAST GERMANY

Let us test our belief that the peoples and governments of eastern Europe will exercise restraint in pressing for changes which might trigger Soviet intervention by looking at the Warsaw Treaty country where the risks of developments which might trigger East/West conflict appear greatest—the German Democratic Republic. The risks are greatest in East Germany for two reasons: the fact that the border between the German Democratic Republic and the Federal Republic of Germany is the only line of direct contact between the forces of NATO and Warsaw Pact alliances, and the fact that the population on both sides of that border is German.

Other than Romania, under the wilful and increasingly ineffective leadership of Nicolae Ceausescu, East Germany under Erich Honecker has been the most vigorous opponent of economic reconstruction and *glasnost.* East German leaders have argued that they do not need these innovations because they have already undertaken their own restructuring of the East German economy—one they consider more promising than anything the Soviet Union has suggested. In 1987 and 1988 the East German leadership showed its distrust both of *glasnost* and economic restructuring by cracking down on dissenters and the Lutheran church and by refusing to publish many of Gorbachev's reform speeches or to permit the circulation in East Germany of Soviet publications in German containing the texts of statements by the Soviet leadership.

Yet East Germany's leaders may have an increasingly difficult time with the hitherto highly disciplined East German population. East Germans are being encouraged by what they see and experience on all sides—from Federal Germany, which five million East Germans visited in 1988 and whose television broadcasts are viewed daily by the majority of East Germans, and from the Soviet Union, and other states of eastern Europe—to urge more flexibility and openness on their government. Conceivably, they might take some new development in East/West relations, or in the Soviet Union, or cutbacks in the number of Soviet forces stationed in East Germany as a sign that they could afford some civil disobedience to achieve that end. Under the impact of improving East/West relations and under continuing pressure to modify its policies from its own population and, at some point, from the Federal German and Soviet governments to modify those policies before they failed, the East German government might begin to lose effective control over the country's policies and its population.

Widespread public unrest in East Germany and the inability of the government to control it are on the increasingly short list of developments that could ignite a NATO/Warsaw Pact conflict in Europe. But the chances that political discontent in East Germany would lead to widespread unrest and war are low. What seems more likely is that the East German government would be compelled to change its leaders and its domestic economic policies, perhaps with increasing frequency. The German Democratic Republic might join Poland and Hungary as a source of rapid domestic economic and political innovation.

Federal Germany, whose policy of trade credits and subsidies for communication and transport links with East Germany has long stabilized the internal situation in East Germany, will remain on the sidelines ready to help economically in especially difficult situations. Radical change in the international policies of the German Democratic Republic—for example, a push by groups in the East German public to withdraw from the Warsaw Pact—will be discouraged by all three governments most directly concerned, East Germany, Federal Germany, and the Soviet Union, as well as by the high degree of self-discipline and political realism of the East German population itself.

RELEVANCE OF ARMS CONTROL

However, no forecast can exclude the possibility of widespread unrest in an individual eastern European country. To be sure, the West has no interest in maintaining the internal status quo in eastern European countries in order to preclude a development of this kind; rather, it is interested in promoting change in that status quo. But East and West do share a common interest in insuring that the process of continuing change in Eastern Europe does not spill over into East-West conflict.

Arms-control agreements are not the problem here—the pressures that could lead to widespread unrest have already been released. But arms control is part of the solution. The entire approach proposed here—early-warning measures, agreed restrictions on force deployments, inspections, and the shift of each alliance to a more defensive posture through deep cuts—is designed to prevent a situation in which the huge military concentration in Europe is sparked into conflict by misperceptions of military activities during a crisis in eastern Europe.

An agreement such as we have proposed will provide additional treaty barriers to Soviet intervention in eastern Europe by limiting the size of Soviet forces deployed there. It will also provide for reciprocal restraints on western military activities, and many possibilities for checking actual force activities and departures from the norm. This should serve to diminish fears of a nervous Soviet leadership that the NATO alliance would seek a military advantage from eastern European unrest—fears that in a crisis might lead the Soviets to take preemptive military action, or that might in some cases lead the West to undertake alert or preparatory action based on a misperception. This important function of an agreement is all the more reason to press forward for early results in the C.F.E. talks.

There are two sets of circumstances in which self-imposed restraint by east Europeans or the Soviet leadership might weaken. The first is a situation of violent domestic insurrection (or civil war, if the term is preferred) in an eastern European country, perhaps Poland or Romania, where the government is unable even with heavy riot police and military forces to keep control and anarchy results. Here, the Soviet

Union would be pressed to intervene and might do so. Even then, however, it would be very reluctant to do so because of the political and economic costs and the possible military costs. There may be some possibility of cooperative East/West action as a substitute. We shall discuss this possibility shortly.

The other set of circumstances in which Soviet military intervention in eastern Europe is plausible is one in which the Soviet Union itself appears faced with a serious threat of secession by some of its components, and the Soviet government, perhaps after an abrupt change of leadership, intervenes militarily in eastern Europe in order to hold together the Soviet Union itself. This prospect is distant although perhaps not to be ruled out.

GERMAN REUNIFICATION?

But what about other long-term effects of successful arms-control negotiations in Europe? Might the successful negotiation of force reductions bring closer some negotiated change in the political map of Europe—that is, a reunification of Germany? Such an outcome is not likely for decades.

Hopes on the European left—and fears among western conservatives—of some Soviet proposal for the reunification of Germany under conditions of military neutrality and withdrawal from military alliances have increased as Europeans have observed the flexibility of the Gorbachev leadership in arms control and in domestic Soviet affairs. This possibility does not impress seasoned Federal German political leaders like Chancellor Kohl who, while repeatedly declaring that all Germans have a right to self-determination and unity, said in his October, 1987, "state of the nation" report that German reunification "is not now on the agenda of world history." This statement closely reflects the attitude of a large majority in the Federal German public who consider German reunification as something desirable but not attainable in practical terms. (In a public opinion poll taken in May, 1987, in the Federal Republic by the respected Emnid organization, 81 percent of the respondents said they wanted German reunification, but only 8 percent considered it possible in the next decade.)

But under conditions of expanding East/West arms control agreements, would a majority of Federal Germans find a military neutrality for Germany guaranteed by the United States and by a visibly more cooperative Soviet Union an acceptable price to pay for genuine self-determination for the East German population? This seems possible. From the very moment when Germany was divided in the late 1940s, at the peak of the Cold War, about one-third of adult Germans have been prepared to undertake the risk of military neutrality in order to achieve reunification of the country. That number is growing. A poll by the Allensbach Institute in July, 1988, showed that 44 percent of the respondents would accept military neutrality, as compared with 31 percent in 1980. Bundestag member Edvard Lintner, a Bavarian conservative who chairs the Bundestag committee on inner-German relations, in a talk in 1987 expressed the belief that 80 percent of Federal Germans would accept reunification with neutrality.

Yet public opinion polls cannot provide an accurate measure of Federal German opinion because they posit unstated but improbable preconditions for these changes in Germany's status. The polls do clearly show that Federal Germans are progressively less worried about issues of defense and security in connection with German reunification. But they rarely state the underlying assumption on which those Germans prepared to consider neutrality base their willingness—the assumption that the countries of Europe East and West, and the United States and the Soviet Union in particular, will welcome the reunification of Germany and will be ready to guarantee the security of this new arrangement.

This assumption appears unjustified. There is strong and continuing antipathy to any prospect of reunification of Germany in all European countries. Moreover, nearly all NATO governments, including that of the United States, would consider NATO defense of western Europe without the participation of the Federal Republic to be unworkable and German unity under conditions of neutrality a dangerous risk. Consequently, it is unlikely that they would be willing to back the arrangement or to guarantee its security. As for the Soviets, General Secretary Gorbachev told Federal German President Richard von Weizsäcker during the latter's July, 1987, visit to Moscow that the German question is not open. If "someone" nonetheless wants to go another way and seek to reunify Germany, there will be "serious consequences," Gorbachev said.

Neither NATO nor the Soviet Union is likely to trust the other sufficiently in the foreseeable future to undertake the risk of German reunification under conditions which, in each case, would render the respective alliances inoperable and then to guarantee the security of the resulting all-German state. The West will not in the foreseeable future trust the Soviet Union sufficiently to be willing to sacrifice the NATO alliance through the departure of Federal Germany. The Soviets, for their part, do not and will not trust the West sufficiently to be willing to sacrifice the Warsaw Pact and their defensive glacis in eastern Europe by letting East Germany depart from their alliance. Even if East/West relations improve much further, it remains most improbable that the Soviet Union would allow withdrawal of the G.D.R. from the Warsaw Pact or from bilateral security arrangements.

Without the most explicit guarantees from the United States and other major NATO governments for the security of a new Germany, Federal Germans would not have the slightest interest in a neutrality solution either. Moreover, Federal Germans show no readiness whatever to risk their present economic well-being and political freedoms in a reunification arrangement unless the Soviet Union were prepared to assure the population of East Germany political and economic freedoms equal to those enjoyed by the Federal Republic—in other words, to accept the elimination of Marxism/Leninism from the G.D.R., as well as to permit the G.D.R. to withdraw from the Warsaw Pact.

In short, there seems little prospect of German reunification on the basis of an explicit East–West deal. In the longer term, however, if there is a relatively smooth evolution toward pluralism in Poland, Hungary, and, ultimately, Czechoslovakia, the East German authorities will have to follow suit, however grudgingly. The institutions of the two German states may become more similar. At that distant point, with Federal Germany incorporated in a stronger European Community and many further changes in eastern Europe and the Soviet Union, the reunification of Germany by absorption of a demilitarized G.D.R. into the Federal Republic might no long appear so formidable a shift of the European balance.

THE COMING STRUCTURE OF EUROPE

But if it is unlikely that divided Germany will be reunited in the next decades, what effects would the build-down of the NATO/Pact military confrontation have on the alliances themselves? We have already mentioned the longstanding proposal of the Warsaw Pact for the dissolution of the alliances. If the C.F.E. talks are successful, will the need for the NATO alliance gradually fade away over the years?

Such a development is not at all likely for decades to come. In this book we have urged a 50-percent reduction in NATO forces, with Pact forces coming to the new NATO level, as a way of establishing an equal plateau from which western countries can safely and economically observe long-term developments in the U.S.S.R. We are talking of a situation in which each alliance will continue to have 1.5 million men under arms in the Atlantic-to-the-Urals area and arsenals of 10,000 tanks, 2,000 helicopters, and 1,500 fighter-bombers, as well as nuclear weapons—formidable forces in each case. More important, we are talking about a situation in which the Soviet Union will continue to be a major world military power, with about 10,000 strategic nuclear warheads at its disposal.

From the western point of view there will in these circumstances be a continuing need over an indefinite period for NATO or some successor organization to link the United States and Europe. A transatlantic alliance will be necessary to balance the military power of the U.S.S.R.

As we have seen in our earlier discussion of NATO nuclear strategy, it is unlikely that the western European states will be able to do this on their own, particularly in the nuclear sphere, for a long time to come. The question of nuclear protection for some European states by others will probably be the last to be resolved as a Western European Defense Union is gradually established. That question is a compound of all the insoluble issues of trust and reliability that have for years bedevilled American relations with the European non-nuclear states and which have been a main theme of this book. Consequently, although the NATO alliance will shrink in size and relative importance, it will continue. It will be largely up to the United States whether this continuing NATO alliance will be a healthy, trimmer NATO after forty years of successful existence or a hollow shell, eroded by U.S. frictions with western European member states.

Whatever we may think of the genesis of the Warsaw Treaty Organization as imposed by the Soviet Union, the continuation of that alliance for some time to come also appears a practical prerequisite for the political and economic evolution of each of the Pact countries. As long as the existence of the Pact is not questioned, the U.S.S.R. under its present leadership seems likely to tolerate and accept a great deal of domestic change in Pact countries. But if any member-states, particularly the more important ones—the G.D.R., Poland, and Czechoslovakia—seriously question continued membership in the Pact, Soviet flexibility will disappear and repression by force will be possible.

If the Soviet Union should ever evolve internally to a point at which it no longer elicits this fear of intervention, no longer insists that the existence of the Pact is necessary for Soviet security, and no longer forbids each member-state to make its own defense and foreign-policy decisions, then these benefits of the dual alliance system may have been outlived. But such an outcome is not now foreseeable.

In the meanwhile, the European order of the twenty-first century is likely to consist of a European Community growing in economic power and political cohesion, with a growing capacity for coordinating the military forces of those member-states who wish to participate (perhaps through the mechanism of the Western European Union). The NATO and Warsaw Pact alliances may lose power but will remain important. The United States and the Soviet Union will almost certainly continue to be major actors in Europe. The twenty-first-century European order is also likely to consist, as we suggested in Chapter 7, of a C.S.C.E. process taking on enduring structure and responsibilities by a process of slow accretion and which, like the NATO alliance, will give the United States a continuing, treaty-anchored role in contributing to the stability of Europe and thus to its own security.

As part of this C.S.C.E. process, it is possible that the two alliances may slowly develop some common institutions between them, notably a center for coordination of information or risk reduction. The United States, which up to now has sought to brake institution-building in the C.S.C.E. process, should instead encourage it. Eventually, if all goes well, such common C.S.C.E. institutions in all fields of C.S.C.E. activity—security, economic and cultural contacts—might play a larger role in assuring European stability, although such a development will be slow.

However, one possible role appears more timely. Earlier, we mentioned that the most dangerous development in eastern Europe over the next decades might be the emergence of persisting, violent conflict within an individual country whose government is not able to restore order. There might as a result be strong pressures on the Soviet government from inside the Soviet Union and from other Pact governments to intervene.

Theoretically, the Soviet Union, if it felt obliged to intervene, might seek to cut the very high political costs of doing so by bringing in the United States or western European countries into some form of co-responsibility, like bringing in western observers to help establish a new type of government in the eastern European country. It is more likely that Soviet intervention would be of classic repressive nature. Such an intervention could be a disaster for the reform line within the Soviet Union and for East/West relations and could in some circumstances lead to East/West conflict.

Here, there is a possibility that East/West dialogue or top-level U.S./

Soviet dialogue might be helpful in leading to some expanded use of the C.S.C.E. apparatus. The East/West risk-reduction center that we discussed in Chapter 9 might be useful for fact-finding and the mediation of a conflict between two eastern European states. In an extreme situation, the C.S.C.E. system might be used to organize and coordinate the use of armed forces of European neutral states to intervene temporarily and symbolically to restore public order in an eastern European country. All those involved in such a problem, including the United States, the Soviet Union, the east European states, and the European neutrals, are already participants in the C.S.C.E. machinery. In such a situation, using the forces of European neutrals like Sweden, Switzerland, or Austria would be far preferable to intervention by either Warsaw Pact or NATO forces.

WORLDWIDE EFFECTS OF BUILD-DOWN IN EUROPE

Ambitious as it may seem, a program of 50-percent reductions in the forces of NATO and the Pact must be only the beginning of a far more exacting program. As we have seen, the reduction in Europe of ground-attack aircraft, if seriously pursued, will bring pressure to limit aircraft production not only in the Atlantic-to-the-Urals area but also in the territory of the U.S.S.R. east of the Urals and in the United States. Similarly, a serious reduction in forces in Europe will cause participants on both sides to argue also for reductions in naval forces and in the air-, sea-, and ground-transport capability of East and West—reductions that would have a bearing on the ability of the United States and the Soviet Union to intervene in Third World countries. In fact, any successfully pursued disarmament effort on any portion of the spectrum of East/West military confrontation will sooner or later engender parallel activity to regulate the other sectors of confrontation, and this tendency should be encouraged.

Therefore, in the long run we will have to plan for the consequences of building down the NATO/Pact confrontation not only for Europe but worldwide. This pressure to deal with other aspects of the confrontation may lead the U.S. and the U.S.S.R. to reach some understanding providing for mutual restraint on direct intervention in Third World countries and to make greater use instead of the United Nations peacekeeping forces. It will also entail agreed restrictions on arms sales and on providing military advisers and trainers by NATO and Warsaw Pact countries to Third World countries and some agreed scheme for making reductions in American and Soviet forces—including naval forces—not covered in the Atlantic-to-the-Urals framework. It should entail a second round of U.S./Soviet negotiations on strategic nuclear reductions, one that might reach out to freeze the holdings of the other declared nuclear powers—China, the United Kingdom, and France.

In sum, building down the confrontation in Europe should point the alliances toward a transition from a world dominated by intense military competition in every type of armed forces to an international system characterized by mutual military restraint between East and West and at least partial cooperation in dealing with regional conflicts.

But these issues are clouded in the future. What is important now is to build on the achievements of the past decades—the Helsinki accords, the Stockholm Document, the I.N.F. treaty, and even the M.B.F.R. talks to the degree that the latter moved the alliances closer to force reductions. The time has come for deep cuts in the NATO/Warsaw Pact military confrontation in Europe. I hope this book has given readers some useful ideas on how to go about the job.

Appendix I: NATO and Warsaw Pact Forces in Europe—Data Published by the Two Alliances

Type	NATO Estimates[a]		WTO Estimates[b]	
	NATO	WTO	NATO	WTO
Personnel	2,213,593[c]	3,090,000	3,660,200	3,573,100[d]
Combat aircraft	3,977[e]	8,250	7,130	7,876[f]
Total strike aircraft	NA	NA	4,075	2,783[g]
Helicopters	2,419[h]	3,700	5,270	2,785[i]
Tactical missile launchers	NA	NA	136	1,608
Tanks	16,424[j]	51,500	30,690	59,470[k]
Anti-tank weapons	18,240[l]	44,200	18,070	11,465[m]
Armored infantry fighting vehicles	4,153[n]	22,400	46,900	70,330[p]
Artillery	14,458[q]	43,400	57,060	71,560[r]
Other armored vehicles	35,351[s]	71,000		
Armored vehicle launch bridges	454[t]	2,550		
Air defense systems	10,309[u]	24,400		
Submarines			200	228[v]
Submarines—nuclear powered			76	80
Large surface ships			499	102[w]
Aircraft-carrying ships			15	2
Aircraft-carrying ships armed with cruise missiles			274	23
Amphibious warfare ships			84	24[x]

Sources: [a] *Conventional Forces in Europe: The Facts*, November, 1988.
[b] "Warsaw Pact Releases Figures on Force Strengths," *Foreign Broadcast Information Service: Soviet Union*, January 30, 1989, pp. 1–8.

Notes for Data Published by the Alliances
The following explanatory notes may be helpful to explain differences in the data presented by the two alliances caused by differences of definition:

[c] "Covers full-time military personnel of land forces, including Army personnel who perform ground-based air defence duties. Also included are

command and general support troops and other ministry of defence troops. Paramilitary forces are excluded."

ᵈ WTO definition: "Total of armed forces in Europe and adjoining waters."

ᵉ Includes: F–16, F–4, F–5, NF–5, F–104, F–100, F–18, CF–18, F–111, F–35/RF–35, T–2E, A–7/TA–7, A–10, Alphajet, G–91, Buccaneer, Harrier, Jaguar, Mirage F1/3/5, Tornado, F–15, Mirage 2000, Lightning, RF–4, TR–1, C–212, PD808, EF–111, EC–130H, DC–8, Sarigue, C–160 Gabriel, RF–5, RF–16, RF–84, Hunter and Canberra for NATO. NATO has 530 combat aircraft in storage.

MIG–15, MIG–17, MIG–21, MIG–23, MIG–25, MIG–27, MIG–29, MIG–31, SU–7, SU–15, SU–17, SU–22, SU–24, SU–25, SU–27, YAK–28, YAK–28P, L–29, L–39, IL–28, AN–12, TU–16, TU–22, TU–128 and TU–22M for WTO. Also included is the TU–22M (Backfire) land-based naval aircraft.

Excluded in the figures given are combat-capable training aircraft: 530 for NATO and 5,700 for WTO.

ᶠ WTO classification: "Combat aircraft of front-line (tactical) Air Force aviation and Air Defense forces and naval aviation." Types include: fighter-bombers (Buccaneer, Tornado, F–111, Mirage 5, F–4, F–15, F–16, F–18, Jaguar, Mirage III, F–104, Mirage 2000, F–100, F–35 Draken, F–5, F–84, and G–91), ground attack aircraft (A–7, A–10, Harrier, and Alphajet), fighters (F–16, Tornado, Mirage 2000, F–4, F–104, Mirage F–1, F–5), Air Defense Forces fighter-interceptors (Lightning), reconnaissance and electronic warfare aircraft (EF–111, RF–4, Tornado, Jaguar, Mirage F–IR, RF–5, Mirage IIIR, RF–16, Nimrod, Orion P–3, G–91, RF–104, RF–84, EC–130, DC–8, Canberra, and Shackleton), naval aviation (A–4, A–6, A–7, F/A–18, Sea Harrier, AV–8, Etendard, Super Etendard, F–4, Tornado, F–104, F–14, Crusader, ASW aircraft, reconnaissance, and electronic warfare planes), and combat support aircraft for NATO.

Front-line bombers (Su–24), fighter-bombers (Su–22, Su–76, Su–17, MiG–27), ground-attack aircraft (Su–25), fighters (MiG–29, MiG–23, MiG–21, Su–27), Air Defense forces fighter interceptors (MiG–31, MiG–25, Su–27, Su–15, Tu–128, Yak–28), reconnaissance and electronic warfare planes (MiG–25, MiG–21, Su–17, Su–24, Yak–28), naval aviation (Tu–16, Tu–22, Tu–142, Il–38, Be–12, Yak–38, Su–17, MiG–21, MiG–23, MiG–29, Su–27) for WTO.

ᵍ Includes: bombers, fighter-bombers, ground-attack aircraft within front-line (tactical) Air Force aviation aircraft and naval aviation aircraft.

ʰ Includes: attack helicopters equipped with anti-tank guided missiles and machine guns and assault/transport helicopters. Not included in the given NATO figure are 180 helicopters held in storage.

ⁱ WTO definition: "Combat helicopters, including naval." Types include: gunships (Apache, Huey Cobra, Cobra-TOW, Bo–105P, Lynx, Mangusta, and Gazelle), multi-role (Iroquois, Black Hawk, Bo–105M, Alouette, Lynx, AB–204, AB–205, AB–206 and AB–212), reconnaissance (Kaiowa, Gazelle, Alouette), assault transport and specialized (Puma, EH–IH, and EH–60), Navy helicopters (Sea King, Wessex, Lynx, Super Frelon, Alouette, AB–212, Sea Cobra, Sea Stallion, Sea Hawk, and Iroquois) for NATO and gunship

(Mi–24), assault transport (Mi–8), reconnaissance and force adjustment [razvedka i korrektirovka] (Mi–24 and Mi–8), electronic warfare (Mi–8), and Navy helicopters (Ka–25, Ka–27, Ka–29, and Mi–14) for WTO.

j Includes: Challenger, M–1, Leopard I and II, AMX–30, M–60, Chieftain, Centurion, M–47 and M–48 for NATO and T–80, T–72, T–62, T–64, T–55/54 and T–10/10M for WTO. Not included in the given NATO figure are 5,800 tanks held in storage.

k WTO definition: "All types of tanks with which the Warsaw Pact and NATO are equipped."

l Includes vehicle mounted and non-vehicle mounted anti-tank guided missile launchers, anti-tank guns and recoilless rifles. Armored fighting vehicles and helicopters whose primary purpose is not anti-tank but which are equipped with anti-tank guided missiles are also covered. Not included in the figure are NATO's 2,700 anti-tank weapons held in storage.

m WTO defines this category as: "Antitank missile complexes." Includes: "ATGM combat vehicles of frontline, army, divisional, and regimental echelon and portable systems of the battalion echelon" for WTO and "systems similar in terms of designation and characteristics" for NATO.

n Includes: Marder, AMX–10P, M–2 (Bradley) and YPR–765 (25 mm) for NATO and BMP–1/2 and BMD1 for WTO. Not included in the given NATO figure are 575 AIFV held in storage.

p WTO definition: "Infantry combat vehicles and armored transports"; includes "infantry combat vehicles, armored personnel carriers, combat assault vehicles, combat reconnaissance patrol vehicles, and combat reconnaissance vehicles," yet excludes light tanks from this category.

q Includes: artillery, mortars, and multiple rocket launchers with tubes of 100 mm and above. Not included in the given figure are 2,870 artillery pieces held in storage.

r WTO includes much smaller armaments in the definition of this category: "Rocket propelled salvo-fired systems, field pieces (75 mm and above), and mortars (50 mm and above)."

s Includes: light tanks, armored personnel carriers, armored command vehicles and military support carriers that are not covered in the preceding category. Not included in the given figure are 7,560 Armored Vehicles held in storage.

t Includes assault bridges mounted as an integrated system on armored carriers. Not included in the given figure are 160 Armored Vehicle Launch Bridges held in storage.

u Includes anti-aircraft artillery and fixed and mobile surface-to-air missiles. Not included in the given figure are 770 Air Defense Systems held in storage.

v Excludes submarines armed with strategic ballistic missiles.

w Includes aircraft carriers, battleships, cruisers, destroyers, frigates, amphibious warfare ships with a displacement of 1,200 tons and over.

x Includes those with a displacement of 1,200 tons and over.

Appendix II: NATO and Warsaw Pact Forces in Europe—Data Published by the International Institute of Strategic Studies

	NATO guidelines Area (NGA)[a]		Jaruzelski Area[b]		Atlantic to Urals		Global	
	NATO[c]	WP	NATO[c]	WP	NATO[c]	WP	NATO[c]	WP
1. Land/Air								
Manpower (000)								
Total active ground forces[d]	786	995	803	1,137	2,340	2,143	3,197	2,744
Total ground force reserves[e]	1,167	1,030	1,222	1,157	4,543	4,239	5,710	5,340
Divisions[f]								
Manned in peacetime[g]	29⅔	49⅔	31⅓	58	105⅔	101½	125	127⅔
Manned on mobilization of reserves[h]	10⅔	12	12⅔	14	36	113	54⅓	158
Total war mobilized	40⅓	61⅔	44⅓	72	141⅔	214⅔	179⅓	285⅔
Ground Force Equipment[i]								
Main battle tanks	12,800	18,800	13,000	21,300	22,200	53,000	33,600	68,900
MICV[j]	4,400	8,700	4,400	9,800	6,200	23,600	9,900	31,400
Artillery (incl MRL)[k]	3,100	11,100	3,500	12,200	10,600	36,000	17,000	48,700
Mor (120 mm and over)	1,100	2,100	1,200	2,400	2,900	8,300	2,900	11,700

[illegible]	6,200	[illegible]	6,300	3,100	11,000	13,700	28,300	22,400
AA guns[m]	3,100	2,200	3,200	2,400	9,000	11,000	9,900	14,100
SAM[m]	1,100	2,600	1,200	3,000	2,400	12,400	3,400	15,500
Armed hel[n]	516	545	516	635	864	1,220	3,208	2,105
Land Combat Aircraft[o]								
Bombers[p]	84	225	84	225	350	888	489	1,020
FGA/CAS	978	915	1,017	1,005	2,865	2,330	4,895	3,180
Air defence/fighters[q]	309	1,422	347	1,737	1,178	4,432	2,861	5,755

	European/Atlantic waters		*Global*	
	NATO	*WP*	*NATO*	*WP*
2. Maritime				
Naval Forces				
Submarines[r]	206	190	241	272
Carriers[s]	15	2	22	4
Battleships/cruisers[s]	23	24	46	36
Destroyers/frigates[s]	327	193	435	257
Amphibious[t]	69	84	107	117
Naval Air[o]				
Bombers	–	286	–	400
Attack	433	} 188	899	} 290
Air defence/fighter	161		347	
ASW fixed-wing ac	232	137	700	219
ASW hel	349	274	704	387

Source: The International Institute of Strategic Studies, *The Military Balance, 1988–1989* (London: IISS, 1988) pp. 236–7.

Notes by IISS:

a The territories of FRG, the Benelux countries, GDR, Poland and Czechoslovakia.

b NGA plus territory of Denmark and Hungary.

c French and Spanish Forces are not part of NATO's integrated military command, but are included in relevant totals.

d Ground Forces exclude paramilitary forces, such as border guards and security troops, though these include formations of up to divisional size, hold heavy equipment and would probably fulfil some rear area security functions in war. Warsaw Pact figures could also be increased considerably by the inclusion of a proportion of the men forming railroad, construction, Kommandatura etc. troops. Marines and Naval Infantry have been included, but troops manning air-defence units, when these are part of an Air Force or a separate service, are not.

e Normally only men within 5 years of their active service period are included, unless a country entry specifies a different parameter. Home Guard manpower has not been included.

f Divisions are not a standard formation between armies; manpower and equipment totals vary considerably. For the purposes of this table we have counted divisional equivalents as being either 3 manoeuvre brigades (normally of 3 battalions plus some supporting units) or 4 regiments (normally groups of battalions of infantry or armour only).

g Includes all Soviet and WP Category A and B divisions and NATO formations manned at over 50% of war establishment.

h Comprises only forces mobilized within the relevant geographical area. North American-based US and Canadian forces earmarked for reinforcement of Europe are shown under the 'Global' heading.

i Totals include all known stocks of material whether manned by active or reserve forces, held as maintenance reserves, or in prepositioned sets (POMCUS). It should be noted that information on WP reserve holdings is much more limited than for NATO and the relevant figures much lower. This may be at least in part accounted for by the WP operational practice of replacing spent divisions by follow-on echelons rather than topping them up from reserve stocks.

j MICV comprise all armoured wheeled or tracked infantry fighting vehicles armed with a cannon of not less than 20mm calibre.

k ATK guns have not been included with artillery this year.

l ATGW proliferation presents particular difficulties for realistic counting rules. The figures shown are estimated aggregates of all dismounted ATGW and those vehicle-mounted weapons with a primary ATK role. Soviet Category 3 divisions have been assumed to hold full scales.

Totals exclude ATGW on MICV (e.g., M-2/-3 Bradley BMP BMD) or fired by main battle tank main armament (e.g., T-80) and do not, therefore, represent total available ATGW for either side. The substantial reduction in WP numbers from those presented in *The Military Balance 1987–1988* reflects a revised estimate of the TO & E for BMP-equipped regiments together with an increase in m SAM launchers exclude shoulder-launched weapons (e.g., *Javelin*, *Blowpipe*, *Stinger*, SA-7/-14/-16). Air Force and separate Air Defence force SAM and AA guns are included.

n Comprises all helicopters whose primary function is close air support or anti-tank. IISS date no longer allows us confidently to discriminate between categories for aggregation purposes. Moreover, some can readily reconfigure between roles.

o Totals include OCU and training aircraft of the same type as those in front-line squadrons.

p Long-range strategic bombers have been excluded (e.g., B-1, B-52, Tu-95, Mya-4 and *Mirage* IVP).

q Comprises aircraft with the capability (weapons, avionics, performance) to engage in aerial combat. Dual-role aircraft with a ground-attack capability are included in the FGA category unless specified in the national entry as belonging to an AD unit.

r Excludes only SSB and SSBN.

s The difference in the totals from the figures given in *The Military Balance 1987–88* can be accounted for by the changed rules for designating warships. See pp. 7–8.

t Only amphibious ships (i.e., over both 1,000 tonnes full-load displacement and 60 metres overall length) are included.

Appendix III: NATO and Warsaw Pact Air Forces in Central Europe

A. Overall Aircraft in Europe

Reduction Area		Warsaw Pact (*current*)	NATO
Atlantic to the Urals	Ground attack	2570 (+400)[a]	2881 (+1034)[b] (+18)[e]
	Fighter-interceptor	2620 (+970)[c]	1245 (+216)[b]
		5190 (+1370)	4126 (+1268)
Central Europe Extended	Ground attack	1445 (+180)[d] (+400)[a]	1655 (+1034)[b] (+18)[e]
	Fighter-interceptor	1975 (+970)[c]	787 (+216)[b]
		3420 (+1550)	2442 (+1268)

Source: Edward Warner, "Approaches to Conventional Arms Reductions," *Conventional Arms Control and East-West Security*, F. Stephen Larrabee and Robert Blackwill, eds. (Durham, North Carolina: Duke University Press, 1989).

Notes
  [a] Soviet medium bombers of the Smolensk Air Army based in the European USSR.
  [b] U.S.-based aircraft earmarked for reinforcement deployment to Europe according to the 1988 CBO study: *U.S. Ground Forces and the Conventional Balance in Europe*, Congressional Budget Office, June, 1988, pp. 97–8.
  [c] Soviet fighter-interceptors of the Air Defense Forces for homeland defense based in the European USSR.
  [d] Fencer fighter-bombers of the Vinnitsa Air Army based in the Kiev military district.
  [e] French Mirage IV P strategic bombers based in France.

B. NATO Air Forces in Central Europe Extended

	Fighter-bombers		Fighter-interceptors	
	Aircraft (location)	#	Aircraft (location)	#
United States	F-111E/F	140	F-5E (UK)	19
	A-10A (UK)	108	F-15C/D	
			(FRG/Na)	96
	F-16C/D (FRG)	96[a]	F-16C/D (FRG)	60[a]
	F-4G (FRG)	36		
	Total	380		175
Belgium	F-16A/B	36[a]	F-16A/B	36[a]
	Mirage 5 BA/BD	50		
	Total	86		
Canada	CF-18 (FRG)	18[a]	CF-18 (FRG)	18[a]
Denmark	F-16A/B	26[a]	F-16 A/B	26[a]
	Draken/F-35	15[a]	Draken/F-35	10
	Draken/RF-35	18		
	Total	59		36
France	Mirage IIIE	80[b]	Mirage F-1C	135
	Mirage 5F	30	Mirage IIIE	26
	Jaguar A	127[b]	Mirage 2000B/C	45
	Mirage 2000N	13[b]		
	Total	250		206
Federal Republic of Germany	Tornado (FRG/UK)	190	F-4F	71[a]
	T-4F	71[a]		
	Alpha Jet	153		
	Total	414		
Netherlands	F-16A/B	86[a]	F-16A/B	61[a]
	NF-5	47		
	Total	133		
United Kingdom	Tornado (FRG/UK)	149	Tornado	36
	Harrier (FRG/UK)	51	F-4 (FRG/UK)	114
	Jaguar	63	Hawk	72
	Buccaneer	34		
	Total	297		222
	TOTAL	1637[c]		825[c]

Meeting Gorbachev's Challenge

Source: Edward Warner, "Approaches to Conventional Arms Reductions," *Conventional Arms Control and East-West Security*, F. Stephen Larrabee and Robert Blackwill, eds. (Durham, North Carolina: Duke University Press, 1989).

Notes

[a] Multirole Belgian, Danish, and Dutch F-16s and Danish Draken F-35s are split between the ground attack and air defense categories in accordance with mission specialization data from the International Institute of Strategic Studies, *The Military Balance, 1988–1989* (London: IISS, 1988). The multirole US F-16s, Canadian CF-18s, and German F-4Fs, whose pilots are trained for both air-to-air and air-to-ground combat, have been split evenly between the two mission areas.

[b] Includes French 15 Mirage IIIE, 45 Jaguar, and 13 Mirage 2000N fighter-bombers that are identified by IISS as "prestrategic" nuclear delivery systems. Does not include the 18 French Mirage IV P "strategic" bombers that are configured solely for nuclear delivery.

[c] Includes combat-capable aircraft used in training and conversion units.

C. Warsaw Pact Air Forces in Central Europe Extended

	Fighter-bombers		Fighter-interceptors	
	Aircraft	#	*Aircraft*	#
Soviet Union				
In GDR, Poland	MiG-27	135	MiG-21	90
Czechoslovakia	Su-17	225	MiG-23	315
& Hungary	Su-24	90	MiG-25	45
	Su-25	45	MiG-29	90
	Total	495		540
In Legnica Air Army	Su-24	225	n.a.	
In Baltic,	MiG-27	180	MiG-21	90
Belorussian &	Su-17	45	MiG-23	135
Carpathian MDs	Su-25	45	MiG-29	135
	Total	270		360
Poland	Su-17	125	MiG-21	360
	Su-7	30	MiG-23	40
	LIM-6	70		
	Total	225		400

	Fighter-bombers		Fighter-interceptors	
	Aircraft	#	*Aircraft*	#
GDR	MiG-27	25	MiG-21	225
	Su-17	35	MiG-23	45
	Total	60		270
Czechoslovakia	MiG-27	40	MiG-21	225
	MiG-21	45	MiG-23	45
	Su-25	40		
	Su-7	45		
	Total	170		270
Hungary	n.a.		MiG-21	45
			MiG-23	90
			Total	135
TOTAL		1,445[a]		1,975[b]

Source: Edward Warner, "Approaches to Conventional Arms Reductions," *Conventional Arms Control and East-West Security*, F. Stephen Larrabee and Robert Blackwill, eds. (Durham, North Carolina: Duke University Press, 1989).

Notes

[a] Does not include the 120 Backfire, 120 Blinder, and 160 Badger bombers of the Strategic Air Army headquartered at Smolensk in Belorussia, although many of these bombers are based in the "central Europe Extended" area and would very likely be employed to deliver conventionally armed bombs and missiles against NATO targets in Central Europe during a conventional war. A portion or all of the 180 Fencer fighter-bombers of the air army headquartered at Vinnitsa in the Ukraine might also be deployed forward to carry out conventional bombing missions in central Europe.

[b] Does not include the 135 fighter-interceptors of the Air Defense forces based in the Baltic, Belorussian, and Carpathian Military Districts that protect the Soviet homeland.

Appendix IV: Warsaw Pact and NATO Ground Forces in the Atlantic-to-Urals Area

A. WP Readiness by Division June 1988[a]

	Category I T	MR	AB	Category II T	MR	AB	Category III T	MR	Total
Non-Soviet Forces in Eastern Europe:									
Bulgaria	0	2	0	0	3	0	0	3	8
Czech	1	3	0	2	1	0	2	1	10
GDR	2	4	0	0	0	0	0	0	6
Hungary[b]	0	0	0	1.7	3.3	0	0	0	5
Poland	5	3	0	0	0	0	0	5	13
Romania	1	1	0	1	3	0	0	4	10
EE total	9	13	0	4.7	10.3	0	2	13	52
Soviet Forces in:									
WESTERN STRATEGIC THEATRE:									
Western TVD									
Czechoslovakia	2	3	0	0	0	0	0	0	5
GDR	11	8	0	0	0	0	0	0	19
Poland	1	1	0	0	0	0	0	0	2
Baltic MD	0	0	2	1	3	0	2	4	12
Belorussian MD	0	1	0	3	1	0	7	0	12
Carpathian MD	1	0	0	1	6	0	2	3	13
−subtotal	15	13	2	5	10	0	11	7	63
South-Western TVD									
Hungary	2	2	0	0	0	0	0	0	4
Kiev	0	0	0	0	0	0	8	8	16
Odessa	0	0	0	0	0	1	0	8	9
−subtotal	2	2	0	0	0	1	8	16	29
North-Western TVD									
Leningrad	0	0	1	0	0	0	0	11	12

	Category I			Category II			Category III		
	T	MR	AB	T	MR	AB	T	MR	Total
CENTRAL RESERVE									
Moscow	0	0	1	0	0	0	2	7	10
Urals	0	0	0	0	0	0	1	5	6
Volga	0	0	0	0	0	0	0	4	4
− subtotal	0	0	1	0	0	0	3	16	20
SOUTHERN STRATEGIC THEATRE:									
North Caucasus	0	0	0	1	0	0	0	7	8
Transcaucasus	0	0	1	0	3	0	0	8	12
− subtotal	0	0	1	1	3	0	0	15	20
USSR total	17	15	5	6	13	1	22	65	144
WTO TOTAL	26	28	5	10.7	23.3	1	24	78	196

Sources: This chart was derived using the Institute of Strategic Studies, *The Military Balance, 1988–1989* (London: IISS, 1988), pp. 39–52, and was adapted for the study by the Congressional Budget Office, *U.S. Ground Forces and the Conventional Balance in Europe*, June, 1988, p. 92.

Notes by the Congressional Budget Office
  [a] The Soviet Army can be categorized into three types of combat readiness. Category I units are at 75–100% strength in manpower and can reach full strength after 24 hours' notice. Category II units are manned at 50–70% strength with some equipment in storage. Divisions can be ready in 30 days after mobilization. Category III units are manned at 10–33% personnel strength with about 30–50% of their equipment. Most of their equipment is held in storage. Divisions can be ready 60 or more days after mobilization. Divisions are being reduced with the implementation of the WTO unilateral reduction announcements of December, 1988.
  [b] Hungary's ground forces have been reorganized to simplify the command structure. Instead of a standard army/divisional/regimental organization of most Warsaw Pact armies, a corps/brigade structure has been introduced. Hungary has 5 tank brigades and 10 motorized rifle brigades. Assuming 3 brigades equals 1 division, Hungary has 1.7 tank divisions and 3.3 motorized rifle divisions. In 1987–88 Hungary's divisions were established to be in Category II level of readiness, by IISS, and it is assumed readiness level has not changed.

B. NATO Readiness by Division

| | | Divisions[a] Reinforcements | | |
	In Place[b]	Active[c]	Reserve[d]	Total
BEL	2/3	2/3	2/3	2
CAN	1/3	0	0	1/3
DEN	0	2	0	2
FRA[e]	3	12	0	15
FRG	12	0	3 1/3	15 1/3
NETH	1/3	1 2/3	1 1/3	3 1/3
UK	3	2/3	0	3 2/3
US	5 1/3	10	15	30 1/3
Total	24 2/3	27	20 1/3	72

Source: Adapted from Congressional Budget Office, *U.S. Ground Forces and the Conventional Balance in Europe*, U.S. Government Printing Office, June, 1988.

Notes
  [a] Includes separate brigades and armored cavalry regiments (ACRs). Three brigades or three ACRs are considered equivalent to one division.
  [b] All of these forces could be available within one to three days after NATO starts to mobilize. A small fraction (about one-eighth) are on constant alert, however, and would be available immediately.
  [c] All of these forces, except those of the United States, could be available within a week after NATO starts to mobilize. Six of the U.S. divisions would be available within 10 days of NATO's mobilization.
  [d] The European reserves could be available within one week after NATO starts to mobilize. The last U.S. reserve unit included here would arrive 79 days after mobilization.
  [e] France, although not a military member of NATO, does have bilateral agreements with West Germany stating that France will come to West Germany's aid if the latter is attacked.

Appendix V: Soviet and Eastern European Unilateral Withdrawals from Eastern Europe

Soviet, April 1989

	CSSR	GDR	HU	POL	TOTAL
Armed Forces (Personnel)	5,300	34,700[a]	10,000[d]		50,000
Artillery Systems		330	200		530
Chemical Defense Battalions	1		1		2
Fighter Aircraft Regiments			1		1
Combat Aircraft	20				20
Interceptor Squadrons			1		1
Vehicles		5,000	3,000		8,000
Motor Transport Battalions	1				1
Parachute Battalions	1		1		2
Tanks	708	3,842[b]	450		5,000
Tank Divisions	1	4[c]	1		6
Tank Training Regiments		3	1	1	5
Instructor Regiments		2			2
Airborne Assault Battalions	1	1	1	1	4
Engineers Battalions	1				1
Landing/Assault Brigades				1	1
Independent Battalions		11			11
Helicopter Regiment				1	1
Anti-Aircraft Missile Regiments			1	1	

Notes

[a] Total Soviet personnel reductions from CSSR, GDR, and HU are 50,000. CSSR and HU account for 15,300, thus, the remainder of 34,700 men is assumed to be withdrawn from the GDR.

[b] Total Soviet tank reductions from CSSR, GDR, and HU are 5,000. CSSR and HU account for 1,158, thus, the remainder of 3,842 is assumed to be withdrawn from the GDR.

[c] The Soviet 7th, 12th, 25th, and 32nd tank divisions are being withdrawn. Each tank division has four short-range nuclear missiles, thus, 24 missiles would be reduced. *The New York Times*, January 24, 1989.

[d] Among the 10,000 soldiers are 2,400 officers and ensigns, and over 8,000 non-commissioned officers and soldiers.

Eastern Europe February, 1989

	BU	CSSR	GDR	HU	POL	TOTAL
Defense Spending % Cut	12	15	10[e]	17	4	
Armed Forces (Personnel)	10,000	12,000[a]	10,000	9,300[f]	40,000	81,300
Combat Aircraft	20	51[b]	50	9	80	210
Artillery Systems	200			430	900	1,530
Aircraft Squadron			1	1[g]		2
Armored Personnel Carriers		165		30	700	895
Jet Fighter Divisions				1		1
Tanks	200	850[c]	600	251	850	2,751
Tank Divisions		2 1/2				2 1/2
Tank Regiments			6		2	8
Tank Brigades				1		1
Motorized Rifle Divisions		3[d]			4[h]	7
Missile Launch Pads				6		6
Naval Units	5					5

Notes

[a] Men will be transferred from combat units to Army construction organizations. Their equipment will be stored and mothballed in depots.

[b] Reduction concerns type MiG 21s and Su-7Bs.

[c] Tank reductions include T–54 and T–55 series.

[d] The Motorized Rifle divisions are to be reorganized into military depots. Their arms and equipment are to be mothballed.

[e] The GDR's defense budget is scheduled to be $8.8 billion in 1989, up by 3.4% from 1988. *The Washington Post*, January 24, 1989.

[f] The 9,300 figure included between 2,000–2,100 professional soldiers. Half of this number are officers, and half are non-commissioned officers.

[g] In the case of Hungary, one aircraft squadron amounts to 9 interceptor fighter jets.

[h] The 2nd and the 15th mechanized divisions will be dismantled, while the manning level of the 10th and 16th armored divisions will be reduced.

Further plans
CSSR:
1. Army construction organizations will be strengthened by 20,000.
2. The number of divisional and regimental tactical exercises is to be reduced by 50 percent, the number of live rounds fired by 25–30 percent, and the number of reservists called up for exercises by 15,000 people.

GDR:
1. The GDR National People's Army will be reconstructed in such a way that it will have a "still more strictly defensive character."

POL:
1. Dismantling will affect a dozen regiments of various kind of forces, including armored, artillery, and air force regiments. Furthermore, 30 territorial defense, engineering, construction, road and rail units will be transformed into civil defense formations.
2. Two armored regiments, a brigade of operational and tactical missiles, a mechanized training regiment, and several other units will be dismantled.

Sources
Bulgaria
"Zhivkov Announces Military Budget, Forces Cut," *Foreign Broadcast Information Service: East Europe*, January 30, 1989, p. 8.
Czechoslovakia
"Defense Council Announces Arms Reductions," and "Minister Vaclavik Details Cuts," *Foreign Broadcast Information Service: East Europe*, January 30, 1989, p. 16.
"Chief of General Staff Details Arms, Troop Cuts," *Foreign Broadcast Information Service: East Europe*, February 6, 1989, p. 7.
"Chief of Staff Notes CSLA Troop, Arms Cuts," and "Vacek on Timetable for Soviet Troop Withdrawal," *Foreign Broadcast Information Service: East Europe*, February 7, 1989, pp. 7–8.
German Democratic Republic
"Honecker on Troop Withdrawal," *Foreign Broadcast Information Service: East Europe*, January 24, 1989, p. 33.
"General Outlines Troop Withdrawal from GDR," *Foreign Broadcast Information Service: Soviet Union*, April 19, 1989, p. 9.
Hungary
"Karpati on Soviet Cuts, Defense Budget Cuts," *Foreign Broadcast Information Service: East Europe*, December 9, 1988, p. 23.
"Defense Ministry Details Cuts," and "Karpati Comments on Measure," *Foreign Broadcast Information Service: East Europe*, January 31, 1989, p. 33.
"News Briefing on Partial USSR Troop Pullout," *Foreign Broadcast Information Service: East Europe*, January 31, 1989, p. 34.
"Hungarian Officials, Soviet Envoy on Troop Cut," *Foreign Broadcast Information Service: Soviet Union*, February 2, 1989, p. 42.
"Soviet Commander, Envoy on Hungarian Withdrawal," *Foreign Broadcast Information Service: Soviet Union*, February 3, 1989, p. 5.
"Defense Minister Details Soviet Troop Pullout," *Foreign Broadcast Information Service: East Europe*, February 3, 1989, p. 15.
Poland
"PAP Reports Defense Reductions," *Foreign Broadcast Information Service: East Europe*, January 25, 1989, pp. 40–41.
"3 Soviet Army Regiments to Leave 'This Year'," *Foreign Broadcast Information Service: East Europe*, February 1, 1989, p. 39.
"Siwicki Queried on Military Structural Changes," *Foreign Broadcast Information Service: East Europe*, February 28, 1989, pp. 26–32.

Appendix VI: C.S.C.E. Documents: The Stockholm Document; The Agreed Mandate for the C.F.E. Force-Reduction Talks and for the C.D.E.-2 Talks on Confidence- and Security-Building Measures

DOCUMENT OF THE STOCKHOLM CONFERENCE
(September 19, 1986)

On Confidence- and Security-Building Measures and Disarmament in Europe Convened in Accordance with the Relevant Provisions of the Concluding Document of the Madrid Meeting of the Conference on Security and Cooperation in Europe

1.. The representatives of the Participating States of the Conference on Security and Cooperation in Europe, Austria, Belgium, Bulgaria, Canada, Cyprus, Czechoslovakia, Denmark, Finland, France, the German Democratic Republic, the Federal Republic of Germany, Greece, The Holy See, Hungary, Iceland, Ireland, Italy, Liechtenstein, Luxembourg, Malta, Monaco, the Netherlands, Norway, Poland, Portugal, Romania, San Marino, Spain, Sweden, Switzerland, Turkey, the Union of Soviet Socialist Republics, the United Kingdom, the United States of America and Yugoslavia, met in Stockholm from 17 January 1984 to 19 September 1986 in accordance with the provisions of the Concluding Document of the Madrid meeting relating to the Conference on Confidence- and Security-Building Measures and Disarmament in Europe.

2. The participants were addressed by the Swedish Prime Minister, the late Olof Palme, on 17 January 1984.

3. Opening statements were made by the Ministers of Foreign Affairs and other Heads of Delegations. The Prime Minister of Spain as well as ministers and senior officials of other Participating States addressed the Conference later.

4. The Secretary-General of the United Nations addressed the Conference on 6 July 1984.

5. Contributions were made by the following non-participating Mediterranean states: Algeria, Egypt, Israel, Lebanon, Morocco, Syria and Tunisia.

6. The Participating States recalled that the aim of the Conference on Confidence- and Security-Building Measures and Disarmament in Europe is, as a substantial and integral part of the multilateral process initiated by the Conference on Security and Cooperation in Europe, to undertake, in stages, new, effective and concrete actions designed to make progress in strengthening confidence and security and in achieving disarmament, so as to give effect and expression to the duty of States to refrain from the threat or use of force in their mutual relations as well as in their international relations in general.

7. The Participating States recognize that the set of mutually complementary confidence- and security-building measures, which are adopted in the present Document and which, in accordance with the relevant provisions of the Madrid Concluding Document, will by their scope and nature and by their implementation serve to strengthen confidence and security in Europe and thus to give effect and expression to the duty of States to refrain from the threat or use of force.

8. Consequently, the Participating States have declared the following:

Refrain from the Threat or Use of Force

9. The Participating States, recalling their obligation to refrain, in their mutual relations as well as in their international relations in general, from the threat or use of force against the territorial integrity or political independence of any State, or in any other manner inconsistent with the purposes of the United Nations, accordingly reaffirm their commitment to respect and put into practice the principle of refraining from the threat or use of force, as laid down in the Final Act.

10. No consideration may be invoked to serve to warrant resort to the threat or use of force in contravention of this principle.

11. They recall the inherent right of individual or collective self-defense if an armed attack occurs, as set forth in the Charter of the United Nations.

12. They will refrain from any manifestation of force for the purpose of inducing any other State to renounce the full exercise of its sovereign rights.

13. As set forth in the Final Act, no occupation or acquisition of territory resulting from the threat or use of force in contravention of international law will be recognized as legal.

14. They recognize their commitment to peace and security. Accordingly, they reaffirm that they will refrain from any use of armed forces inconsistent with the purposes and principles of the Charter of the United Nations and the provisions of the Declaration of Principles Guiding Relations Between Participating States, against another Participating State, in particular from invasion of or attack on its territory.

15. They will abide by their commitment to refrain from the threat or use of force in their relations with any State, regardless of that State's political, social, economic or cultural system and irrespective of whether or not they maintain with that State relations of Alliance.

16. They stress that non-compliance with the obligation of refraining from the threat or use of force, as recalled above, constitutes a violation of international law.

17.   They stress their commitment to the principle of peaceful settlement of disputes as contained in the Final Act, convinced that it is an essential complement to the duty of States to refrain from the threat or use of force, both being essential factors for the maintenance and consolidation of peace and security. They recall their determination and the necessity to reinforce and to improve the methods at their disposal for the peaceful settlement of disputes. They reaffirm their resolve to make every effort to settle exclusively by peaceful means any dispute between them.

18.   The Participating States stress their commitment to the Final Act of the C.S.C.E. and the need for full implementation of all its provisions which will further the process of increasing security and developing cooperation in Europe, thereby contributing to international peace and security in the world as a whole.

19.   They emphasize their commitment to all the principles of the Declaration on Principles Guiding Relations Between Participating States and declare their determination to respect and put them into practice irrespective of their political, economic or social systems as well as of their size, geographical location or level of economic development.

20.   All these ten principles are of primary significance and, accordingly, they will be equally and unreservedly applied, each of them being interpreted taking into account the others.

21.   Respect for and the application of these principles will enhance the development of friendly relations and cooperation among the Participating States in all fields covered by the provisions of the Final Act.

22.   They reconfirm their commitment to the basic principle of the sovereign equality of States and stress that all States have equal rights and duties within the framework of international law.

23.   They reaffirm the universal significance of human rights and fundamental freedoms. Respect for and the effective exercise of these rights and freedoms are essential factors for international peace, justice and security, as well as for the development of friendly relations and cooperation among themselves as among all States, as set forth in the Declaration of Principles Guiding Relations Between Participating States.

24.   They reaffirm that, in the broader context of world security, security in Europe is closely linked with security in the Mediterranean area as a whole; in this context, they confirm their intention to develop good neighborly relations with all States in the region, with due regard to reciprocity, and in the spirit of the principles set forth in the Declaration of Principles Guiding Relations Between Participating States, so as to promote confidence and security and make peace prevail in the region in accordance with the provisions contained in the Mediterranean chapter of the Final Act.

25.   They emphasize the necessity to take resolute measures to prevent and to combat terrorism, including terrorism in international relations. They express their determination to take effective measures, both at the national level and through international cooperation, for the prevention and suppression of all acts of terrorism. They will take all appropriate measures in preventing their respective territories from being used for the preparation, organization or commission of terrorist activities. This also includes measures to prohibit on their territories illegal activities, including subversive activities, of persons,

groups and organizations that instigate, organize or engage in the perpetration of acts of terrorism, including those directed against other States and their citizens.

26. They will fulfill in good faith their obligations under international law; they also stress that strict compliance with their commitments within the framework of the C.S.C.E. is essential for building confidence and security.

27. The Participating States confirm that in the event of a conflict between the obligations of the members of the United Nations under the Charter of the United Nations and their obligations under any treaty or other international agreement, their obligations under the Charter will prevail, in accordance with Article 103 of the Charter of the United Nations.

28. The Participating States have adopted the following measures:

Prior Notification of Certain Military Activities

29. The Participating States will give notification in writing through diplomatic channels in an agreed form of content, to all other Participating States 42 days or more in advance of the start of notifiable* military activities in the zone of application** for confidence- and security-building measures.

30. Notification will be given by the Participating State on whose territory the activity in question is planned to take place even if the forces of that State are not engaged in the activity or their strength is below the notifiable level. This will not relieve other Participating States of their obligation to give notification, if their involvement in the planned military activity reaches the notifiable level.

31. Each of the following military activities in the field conducted as a single activity in the zone of application for CSBMs at or above the levels defined below, will be notified:

31.1. The engagement of formations of land forces*** of the Participating States in the same exercise activity conducted under a single operational command independently or in combination with any possible air or naval components.

31.1.1. This military activity will be subject to notification whenever it involves at any time during the activity:

—at least 13,000 troops, including support troops, or
—at least 300 battle tanks

if organized into a divisional structure or at least two brigades/regiments, not necessarily subordinate to the same division.

31.1.2. The participation of air forces of the Participating States will be included in the notification if it is foreseen that in the course of the activity 200 or more sorties by aircraft, excluding helicopters, will be flown.

31.2. The engagement of military forces either in an amphibious landing or in a parachute assault by airborne forces in the zone of application for CSBMs.

31.2.1. These military activities will be subject to notification whenever the amphibious landing involves at least 3000 troops or whenever the parachute drop involves at least 3000 troops.

---

* In this Document, the term "notifiable" means subject to notification.
** See Annex I.
*** In this context, the term "land forces" includes amphibious, airmobile and airborne forces.

31.3. The engagement of formations of land forces of the Participating States in a transfer from outside the zone of application for CSBMs to arrival points in the zone, or from inside the zone of application for CSBMs to points of concentration in the zone, to participate in a notifiable exercise activity or to be concentrated.

31.3.1. The arrival or concentration of these forces will be subject to notification whenever it involves at any time during the activity:

—at least 13,000 troops, including support troops, or

—at least 300 battle tanks

if organized into a divisional structure or at least two brigades/regiments, not necessarily subordinate to the same division.

31.3.2. Forces which have been transferred into the zone will be subject to all provisions of agreed CSBMs when they depart their arrival points to participate in a notifiable exercise activity or to be concentrated within the zone of application for CSBMs.

32. Notifiable military activities carried out without advance notice to the troops involved, are exceptions to the requirement for prior notification to be made 42 days in advance.

32.1. Notification of such activities, above the agreed thresholds, will be given at the time the troops involved commence such activities.

33. Notification will be given in writing of each notifiable military activity in the following agreed form:

34. General Information

34.1. The designation of the military activity

34.2. The general purpose of the military activity

34.3. The names of the States involved in the military activity

34.4. The level of command, organizing and commanding the military activity

34.5. The start and end dates of the military activity

35. Information on Different Types of Notifiable Military Activities

35.1. The engagement of land forces of the Participating States in the same exercise activity conducted under a single operational command independently or in combination with any possible air or naval components:

35.1.1. The total number of troops taking part in the military activity (i.e., ground troops, amphibious troops, airmobile and airborne troops) and the number of troops participating for each State involved, if applicable.

35.1.2. Number and type of divisions participating for each States

35.1.3. The total number of battle tanks for each State and the total number of anti-tank guided missile launchers mounted on armored vehicles

35.1.4. The total number of artillery pieces and multiple rocket launchers (100 mm calibre or above)

35.1.5. The total number of helicopters, by category

35.1.6. Envisaged number of sorties by aircraft, excluding helicopters

35.1.7. Purpose of air missions

35.1.8. Categories of aircraft involved

35.1.9. The level of command, organizing and commanding the air force participation

35.1.10. Naval ship-to-shore gunfire

35.1.11. Indication of other naval ship-to-shore support

35.1.12.   The level of command, organizing and commanding the naval force participation

35.2 .   The engagement of military forces either in an amphibious landing or in parachute assault by airborne forces in the zone of application for CSBMs:

35.2.1.   The total number of amphibious troops involved in notifiable amphibious landings, and/or the total number of airborne troops involved in notifiable parachute assaults

35.2.2.   In the case of a notifiable amphibious landing, the point or points of embarkation, if in the zone of application for CSBMs

35.3.   The engagement of formations of land forces of the Participating States in a transfer from outside the zone of application for CSBMs to arrival points in the zone, or from inside the zone of application for CSBMs to points of concentration in the zone, to participate in a notifiable exercise activity or to be concentrated:

35.3.1.   The total number of troops transferred

35.3.2.   Number and type of divisions participating in the transfer

35.3.3 .   The total number of battle tanks participating in a notifiable arrival or concentration

35.3.4.   Geographical coordinates for the points of arrival and for the points of concentration

36.   The envisaged Area and timeframe of the Activity

36.1.   The area of the military activity delimited by geographic features together with geographic coordinates, as appropriate

36.2.   The start and end dates of each phase (transfers, deployment, concentration of forces, active exercise phase, recovery phase) of activities in the zone of application for CSBMs of participating formations, the tactical purpose and corresponding geographical areas (delimited by geographical coordinates) for each phase

36.3.   Brief description of each phase

37.   Other Information

37.1.   Changes, if any, in relation to information provided in the annual calendar regarding the activity

37.2.   Relationship of the activity to other notifiable activities

Observation of Certain Military Activities

38.   The Participating States will invite observers from all other Participating States to the following notifiable military activities:

38.1.   The engagement of formations of land forces* of the Participating States in the same exercise activity conducted under a single operational command independently or in combination with any possible air or naval components.

38.2.   The engagement of military forces either in an amphibious landing or in a parachute assault by airborne forces in the zone of application for CSBMs.

38.3.   In the case of the engagement of formations of land forces* of the Participating States in a transfer from outside the zone of application for CSBMs to arrival points in the zone, or from inside zone of application for

---

* In this context, the term "land forces" includes amphibious, airmobile and airborne forces.

CSBMs to point of concentration in the zone, to participate in a notifiable exercise activity or to be concentrated, the concentration of these forces. Forces which have been transferred into the zone will be subject to all provisions of agreed confidence- and security-building measures when they depart their arrival points to participate in a notifiable exercise activity or to be concentrated within the zone of application for CSBMs.

38.4.   The above-mentioned activities will be subject to observation whenever the number of troops engaged meets or exceeds 17,000 troops, except in the case of either an amphibious landing or a parachute assault by airborne forces, which will be subject to observation whenever the number of forces engaged meets or exceeds 5,000 troops.

39.   The host State will extend the invitations in writing through diplomatic channels to all other Participating States at the time of notification. The host State will be the Participating State on whose territory the notified activity will take place.

40.   The host State may delegate some of its responsibilities as host to another Participating State engaged in the military activity on the territory of the host State. In such cases, the host State will specify the allocation of responsibilities in its invitation to observe the activity.

41.   Each Participating State may send up to two observers to the military activity to be observed.

42.   The invited State may decide whether to send military and/or civilian observers, including members of its personnel accredited to the host state. Military observers will, normally, wear their uniforms and insignia while performing their tasks.

43.   Replies to the invitation will be given in writing not later than 21 days after the issue of the invitation.

44.   The Participating States accepting an invitation will provide the names and ranks of their observers in their reply to the invitation. If the invitation is not accepted in time, it will be assumed that no observers will be sent.

45.   Together with the invitation the host State will provide a general observation programme, including the following information.

45.1.   The date, time and place of assembly of observers;

45.2.   Planned duration of the observation programme;

45.3.   Languages to be used in interpretation and/or translation;

45.4.   Arrangements for board, lodging and transportation of the observers;

45.5.   Arrangements for observation equipment which will be issued to the observers by the host State;

45.6.   Possible authorization by the host State of the use of special equipment that the observers may bring with them;

45.7.   Arrangements for special clothing to be issued to the observers because of weather or environmental factors.

46.   The observers may make requests with regard to the observation programme. The host State will, if possible, accede to them.

47.   The host State will determine a duration of observation which permits the observers to observe a notifiable military activity from the time that agreed thresholds for observation are met or exceeded until, for the last time during the activity, the thresholds for observation are no longer met.

48.   The host State will provide observers with transportation to the area of the notified activity and back. This transportation will be provided from either the capital or another suitable location to be announced in the invitation, so that the observers are in position before the start of the observation programme.

49.   The invited State will cover the travel expenses for its observers to the capital, or another suitable location specified in the invitation, of the host State, and back.

50.   The observers will be provided equal treatment and offered equal opportunities to carry out their functions.

51.   The observers will be granted, during their mission, the privileges and immunities accorded to diplomatic agents in the Vienna Convention on Diplomatic Relations.

52.   The host State will not be required to permit observation of restricted locations, installations or defence sites.

53.   In order to allow the observers to confirm that the notified activity is non-threatening in character and that it is carried out in conformity with the appropriate provisions of the notification, the host State will:

53.1.   At the commencement of the observation programme, give a briefing of the purpose, the basic situation, the phases of the activity and possible changes as compared with the notification and provide the observers with a map of the area of the military activity with a scale of 1 to not more than 500,000 and an observation programme with a daily schedule as well as a sketch indicating the basic situation;

53.2.   Provide the observers with appropriate observation equipment; however, the observers will be allowed to use their personal binoculars, which will be subject to examination and approval by the host State;

53.3.   In the course of the observation programme, give the observers daily briefings with the help of maps on the various phases of the military activity and their development and inform the observers about their positions geographically; in the case of a land force activity conducted in combination with air or naval components, briefings will be given by representatives of these forces;

53.4.   Provide opportunities to observe directly forces of the State/States engaged in the military activity so that the observers get an impression of the flow of the activity; to this end, the observers will be given the opportunity to observe major combat units of the participating formations of a divisional or equivalent level and, whenever possible, to visit some units and communicate with commanders and troops; commanders or other senior personnel of participating formations as well as of the visited units will inform the observers of the mission of their respective units;

53.5.   Guide the observers in the area of the military activity; the observers will follow the instructions issued by the host State in accordance with the provisions set out in this Document;

53.6.   Provide the observers with appropriate means of transportation in the area of the military activity.

53.7.   Provide the observers with opportunities for timely communication with their Embassies or other official missions and consular posts; the host State is not obligated to cover the communication expenses of the observers;

53.8. Provide the observers with appropriate board and lodging in a location suitable for carrying out the observation programme and, when necessary, medical care.

54. The Participating States need not invite observers to notifiable military activities which are carried out without advance warning to the troops involved unless these notifiable activities have a duration of more than 72 hours. The continuation of these activities beyond this time will be subject to observation while the agreed thresholds are met or exceeded. The observation programme will follow as closely as practically possible all the provisions for observation set out in this Document.

Annual Calendars

55. Each Participating State will exchange, with all other Participating States, an annual calendar of its military activities subject to prior notification,* within the zone of application for CSBMs, forecast for the subsequent calendar year. It will be transmitted every year, in writing, through diplomatic channels, not later than 15 November for the following year.

56. Each Participating State will list the above-mentioned activities chronologically and will provide information on each activity in accordance with the following model:

56.1. Type of military activity and its designation;

56.2. General characteristics and purpose of the military activity;

56.3. States involved in the military activity;

56.4. Area of the military activity, indicated by appropriate geographic features and/or defined by geographic coordinates;

56.5. Planned duration of the military activity and the 14-day period, indicated by dates, within which it is envisaged to start;

56.6. The envisaged total number of troops engaged in the military activity;

56.7. The types of armed forces involved in the military activity;

56.8. The envisaged level of command, under which the military activity will take place;

56.9. The number and type of divisions whose participation in the military activity is envisaged;

56.10. Any additional information concerning, inter alia, components of armed forces, which the Participating State planning the military activity considers relevant.

57. Should changes regarding the military activities in the annual calendar prove necessary, they will be communicated to all other Participating States no later than in the appropriate notification.

58. Information on military activities subject to prior notification not included in an annual calendar will be communicated to all Participating States as soon as possible, in accordance with the model provided in the annual calendar.

Constraining Provisions

59. Each Participating State will communicate, in writing to all other Participating States, by 15 November each year, information concerning

---

* As defined in the provisions on Prior Notification of Certain Military Activities

military activities subject to prior notification* involving more than 40,000 troops, which it plans to carry out in the second subsequent calendar year. Such communication will include preliminary information on each activity, as to its general purpose, timeframe and duration, area, size and States involved.
60.   Participating States will not carry out military activities subject to prior notification* involving more than 75,000 troops, unless they have been the object of communication as defined above.
61.   Participating States will not carry out military activities subject to prior notification* involving more than 40,000 troops unless they have been included in the annual calendar, not later than 15 November each year.
62.   If military activities subject to prior notification* are carried out in addition to those contained in the annual calendar, they should be as few as possible.

Compliance and Verification

63.   According to the Madrid mandate, the confidence- and security-building measures to be agreed upon "will be provided with adequate forms of verification which correspond to their content."
64.   The Participating States recognize that national technical means can play a role in monitoring compliance with agreed confidence- and security-building measures.
65.   In accordance with the provisions contained in this Document, each Participating State has the right to conduct inspections on the territory of any other Participating State within the zone of application for CSBMs.
66.   Any Participating State will be allowed to address a request for inspection to another Participating State on whose territory, within the zone of application for CSBMs, compliance with the agreed confidence- and security-building measures is in doubt.
67.   No Participating State will be obliged to accept on its territory within the zone of application for CSBMs, more than three inspections per calendar year.
68.   No Participating State will be obliged to accept more than one inspection per calendar year from the same Participating State.
69.   An inspection will not be counted if, due to *force majeure*, it cannot be carried out.
70.   The Participating State which requests an inspection will state the reasons for the request.
71.   The Participating State which has received such a request will reply in the affirmative to the request within the agreed period of time, subject to the provisions contained in paragraphs 67 and 68.
72.   Any possible dispute as to the validity of the reasons for a request will not prevent or delay the conduct of an inspection.
73.   The Participating State which requests an inspection will be permitted to designate for inspection on the territory of another State within the zone of application for CSBMs, a specific area. Such an area will be referred to as the "specified area." The specified area will comprise terrain where notifiable military activities are conducted or where another Participating State believes a notifiable military activity is taking place. The specified area will be defined and

---

* As defined in the provisions on Prior Notification of Certain Military Activities

limited by the scope and scale of notifiable military activities but will not exceed that required for an Army-level military activity.

74.   In the specified area, the representatives of the inspecting State accompanied by the representatives of the receiving State will be permitted access, entry and unobstructed survey, except for areas or sensitive points to which access is normally denied or restricted, military and other defense installations, as well as naval vessels, military vehicles and aircraft. The number and extent of the restricted areas should be as limited as possible. Areas where notifiable military activities can take place will not be declared restricted areas, except for certain permanent or temporary military installations which, in territorial terms, should be as small as possible, and consequently, those areas will not be used to prevent inspection of notifiable military activities. Restricted areas will not be employed in a way inconsistent with the agreed provisions on inspection.

75.   Within the specified area, the forces of Participating States other than the receiving State will also be subject to the inspection conducted by the inspecting State.

76.   Inspection will be permitted on the ground, from the air, or both.

77.   The representatives of the receiving State will accompany the inspection team, including when it is in land vehicles and in aircraft from the time of their first employment until the time they are no longer in use for the purposes of inspection.

78.   In its request, the inspecting State will notify the receiving State of:

78.1.   The reasons for the request;

78.2.   The location of the specified area defined by geographical coordinates;

78.3.   The preferred point(s) of entry for the inspection team;

78.4.   Mode of transport to and from the point(s) of entry and, if applicable, to and from the specified area;

78.5.   Where in the specified area the inspection will begin;

78.6.   Whether the inspection will be conducted from the ground, from the air, or both simultaneously;

78.7.   Whether aerial inspection will be conducted using an airplane, a helicopter, or both;

78.8.   Whether the inspection team will use land vehicles provided by the receiving State or, if mutually agreed, its own vehicles;

78.9.   Information for the issuance of diplomatic visas to inspectors entering the receiving State.

79.   The reply to the request will be given in the shortest possible period of time, but within not more than twenty-four hours. Within thirty-six hours after the issuance of the request, the inspection team will be permitted to enter the territory of the receiving State.

80.   Any request for inspection as well as the reply thereto will be communicated to all Participating States without delay.

81.   The receiving State should designate the point(s) of entry as close as possible to the specified area. The receiving State will ensure that the inspection team will be able to reach the specified area without delay from the point(s) of entry.

82.   All Participating States will facilitate the passage of the inspection teams through their territory.

83. Within forty-eight hours after the arrival of the inspection team at the specified area, the inspection will be terminated.

84. There will be no more than four inspectors in an inspection team. While conducting the inspection, the inspection team may divide into parts.

85. The inspectors and, if applicable, auxiliary personnel, will be granted, during their mission, privileges and immunities in accordance with the Vienna Convention on Diplomatic Relations.

86. The receiving State will provide the inspection team with appropriate board and lodging in a location suitable for carrying out the inspection, and, when necessary, medical care; however, this does not exclude the use by the inspection team of its own tents and rations.

87. The inspection team will have the use of its own maps, own photo cameras, own binoculars, and own dictaphones, as well as own aeronautical charts.

88. The inspection team will have access to appropriate telecommunications equipment of the receiving State, including the opportunity for continuous communication between the members of an inspection team in an aircraft and those in a land vehicle employed in the inspection.

89. The inspecting State will specify whether aerial inspection will be conducted using an airplane, a helicopter or both. Aircraft for inspection will be chosen by mutual agreement between the inspecting and receiving States. Aircraft will be chosen which provide the inspection team a continuous view of the ground during the inspection.

90. After the flight plan, specifying, inter alia, the inspection team's choice of flight path, speed and altitude in the specified area, has been filed with the competent air traffic control authority, the inspection aircraft will be permitted to enter the specified area without delay. Within the specified area, the inspection team will, at its request, be permitted to deviate from the approved flight plan to make specific observations provided such deviation is consistent with paragraph 74 as well as flight safety and air traffic requirements. Directions to the crew will be given through a representative of the receiving State on board the aircraft involved in the inspection.

91. One member of the inspection team will be permitted, if such a request is made, at any time to observe data on navigational equipment of the aircraft and to have access to maps and charts used by the flight crew for the purpose of determining the exact location of the aircraft during the inspection flight.

92. Aerial and ground inspectors may return to the specified area as often as desired within the forty-eight hour inspection period.

93. The receiving State will provide for inspection purposes land vehicles with cross country capability. Whenever mutually agreed, taking into account the specific geography relating to the area to be inspected, the inspecting State will be permitted to use its own vehicles.

94. If land vehicles or aircraft are provided by the inspecting State, there will be one accompanying driver for each land vehicle, or accompanying aircraft crew.

95. The inspecting State will prepare a report of its inspection and will provide a copy of that report to all Participating States without delay.

96. The inspection expenses will be incurred by the receiving State, except

when the inspecting State uses its own aircraft and/or land vehicles. The travel expenses to and from point(s) of entry will be borne by the inspecting State.

97.   Diplomatic channels will be used for communications concerning compliance and verification.

98.   Each Participating State will be entitled to obtain timely clarification from any other Participating State concerning the application of agreed confidence- and security-building measures. Communications in this context will, if appropriate, be transmitted to all other Participating States.

99.   The Participating States stress that these CSBMs are designed to reduce the dangers of armed conflict and of misunderstanding or miscalculation of military activities and emphasize that their implementation will contribute to these objectives.

100.   Reaffirming the relevant objectives of the Final Act, the Participating States are determined to continue building confidence, to lessen military confrontation and to enhance security for all. They are also determined to achieve progress in disarmament.

101.   The measures adopted in this Document are politically binding and will come into force on 1 January 1987.

102.   The Government of Sweden is requested to transmit the present Document to the follow-up meeting of the C.S.C.E. in Vienna and to the Secretary-General of the United Nations. The Government of Sweden is also requested to transmit the present Document to the Governments of the non-participating Mediterranean States.

103.   The text of this Document will be published in each Participating State, which will disseminate it and make it known as widely as possible.

104.   The representatives of the Participating States express their profound gratitude to the people and Government of Sweden for the excellent organization of the Stockholm Conference and warm hospitality extended to the delegation which participated in the Conference.

Stockholm, 19 September 1986

Annex I

Under the terms of the Madrid mandate, the zone of application for CSBMs is defined as follows:

On the basis of equality of rights, balance and reciprocity, equal respect for the security interests of all C.S.C.E. participating States, and of their respective obligations concerning confidence- and security-building measures and disarmament in Europe, these confidence- and security-building measures will cover the whole of Europe as well as the adjoining sea area* and air space. They will be of military significance and politically binding and will be provided with adequate forms of verification which correspond to their content.

* In this context, the notion of adjoining sea area is understood to refer also to ocean area adjoining Europe.

As far as the adjoining sea area* and air space is concerned, the measures will be applicable to the military activities of all the Participating States taking place there whenever these activities affect security in Europe as well as constitute a part of activities taking place within the whole of Europe as referred to above, which they will agree to notify. Necessary specifications will me (*sic*) made through the negotiations on the confidence- and security-building measures at the Conference.

Nothing in the definition of the zone given above will diminish obligations already undertaken under the Final Act. The confidence- and security-building measures to be agreed upon at the Conference will also be applicable to all areas covered by any of the provisions in the Final Act relating to confidence- and security-building measures and certain aspects of security and disarmament.

Whenever the term "the zone of application of CSBMs" is used in this Document, the above definition will apply.

Annex II

Chairman's Statement

It is understood that, taking into account the agreed date of entry into force of the agreed confidence- and security-building measures and the provisions contained in them concerning the timeframes of certain advance notifications, and expressing their interest in an early transition to the full implementation of the provisions of this Document, the Participating States agree to the following:

The annual calendars concerning military activities subject to prior notification and forecast for 1987 will be exchanged not later than 15 December 1986.

Communications, in accordance with agreed provisions, concerning military activities involving more than 40,000 troops planned for the calendar year 1988 will be exchanged by 15 December 1986. Participating States may undertake activities involving more than 75,000 troops during the calendar year 1987 provided that they are included in the annual calendar exchanged by 15 December 1986.

Activities to begin during the first 42 days after 1 January 1987 will be subject to the relevant provisions of the Final Act of the C.S.C.E. However, the Participating States will make every effort to apply to them the provisions of this Document to the maximum extent possible.

This statement will be an annex to the Document of the Stockholm Conference and will be published with it.

Stockholm, 19 September 1986

* In this context, the notion of adjoining sea area is understood to refer also to ocean area adjoining Europe.

Annex III

Chairman's Statement

It is understood that each Participating State can raise any question consistent with the mandate of the Conference on Confidence- and Security-Building Measures and Disarmament in Europe at any stage subsequent to the Vienna C.S.C.E. follow-up meeting.

This statement will be an annex to the Document of the Stockholm Conference and will be published with it.

Stockholm, 19 September 1986

Annex IV

Chairman's Statement

It is understood that the Participating States recall that they have the right to belong or not to belong to international organizations, to be or not to be a party to bilateral or multilateral treaties of alliance; they also have the right of neutrality. In this context, they will not take advantage of these rights to circumvent the purposes of the system of inspection, and in particular the provision that no Participating State will be obliged to accept on its territory within the zone of application for CSBMs, more than three inspections per calendar year.

Appropriate understandings between Participating States on this subject will be expressed in interpretive statements to be included in the Journal of the Day.

This statement will be an annex to the Document of the Stockholm Conference and will be published with it.

Stockholm, 19 September 1986

* * *

THE AGREED MANDATE FOR THE C.F.E. FORCE REDUCTION
TALKS AND FOR THE C.D.E.-2 TALKS ON CONFIDENCE- AND
SECURITY-BUILDING MEASURES
(Adopted January 10, 1989)

CONFIDENCE- AND SECURITY-BUILDING MEASURES AND
CERTAIN ASPECTS OF SECURITY AND DISARMAMENT IN
EUROPE

STOCKHOLM CONFERENCE: ASSESSMENT OF PROGRESS ACHIEVED

The participating States,
    In accordance with the relevant provisions of the Madrid Concluding Document, assessed progress achieved during the Conference on Confidence-

and Security-building Measures and Disarmament in Europe, which met in Stockholm from 17 January 1984 to 19 September 1986.

They welcomed the adoption at Stockholm of a set of mutually complementary confidence- and security-building measures (CSBMs).

They noted that these measures are in accordance with the criteria of the Madrid mandate and constitute a substantial improvement and extension of the confidence-building measures adopted in the Final Act.

They noted that the adoption of the Stockholm Document was a politically significant achievement and that its measures are an important step in efforts aimed at reducing the risk of military confrontation in Europe. They agreed that the extent to which the measures will in practice contribute to greater confidence and security will depend on the record of implementation. They were encouraged by initial implementation and noted that further experience and detailed review will be required. They reaffirmed their determination to comply strictly with and apply in good faith all the provisions of the Document of the Stockholm Conference.

They reaffirmed their commitment to the provisions of the Madrid Concluding Document relating to the Conference on Confidence- and Security-building Measures and Disarmament in Europe and agreed to resume the work of the Conference with a view to achieving further progress towards its aim.

NEW EFFORTS FOR SECURITY AND DISARMAMENT IN EUROPE

The participating States,

Recalling the relevant provisions of the Final Act and of the Madrid Concluding Document according to which they recognize the interest of all of them in efforts aimed at lessening military confrontation and promoting disarmament,

Reaffirming their determination expressed in the Final Act to strengthen confidence among them and thus to contribute to increasing stability and security in Europe,

Stressing the complementary nature of the efforts within the framework of the C.S.C.E. process aimed at building confidence and security and establishing stability and achieving progress in disarmament, in order to lessen military confrontation and to enhance security for all,

Stressing that in undertaking such efforts they will respect the security interests of all C.S.C.E. participating States inherent in their sovereign equality,

Having also considered ways and appropriate means to continue their efforts for security and disarmament in Europe,

Have reached the understanding that these efforts should be structured as set forth below:

NEGOTIATIONS ON CONFIDENCE- AND SECURITY-BUILDING MEASURES

The participating States have agreed that Negotiations on Confidence- and Security-building Measures will take place in order to build upon and expand the results already achieved at the Stockholm Conference with the aim of elaborating and adopting a new set of mutually complementary confidence- and security-building measures designed to reduce the risk of military confrontation in Europe. These negotiations will take place in accordance with the Madrid mandate. The decisions of the Preparatory Meeting held in Helsinki from 25 October to 11 November 1983 will be applied *mutatis mutandis* (see Annex II).

These negotiations will take place in Vienna, commencing in the week beginning on 6 March 1989.

The next Follow-up Meeting of the participating States of the C.S.C.E., to be held in Helsinki, commencing on 24 March 1992, will assess the progress achieved in these negotiations.

NEGOTIATION ON CONVENTIONAL ARMED FORCES IN EUROPE

The Negotiation on Conventional Armed Forces in Europe will take place as agreed by those States named in the mandate contained in the Chairman's statement in Annex III of this document, who among themselves have determined the agenda, the rules of procedure and the organizational modalities of these negotiations, and will determine their timetable and results. These negotiations will be conducted within the framework of the C.S.C.E. process.

These negotiations will take place in Vienna, commencing in the week beginning on 6 March 1989.

The next Follow-Up Meeting of the participating States of the C.S.C.E., to be held in Helsinki, commencing on 24 March 1992, will exchange views on the progress achieved in these negotiations.

MEETINGS IN ORDER TO EXCHANGE VIEWS AND INFORMATION CONCERNING THE
COURSE OF THE NEGOTIATION ON CONVENTIONAL ARMED FORCES IN EUROPE

It has been agreed that the participating States will hold meetings in order to exchange views and information concerning the course of the Negotiation on Conventional Armed Forces in Europe.

These meetings will be held at least twice during each session of the Negotiation on Conventional Armed Forces in Europe.

Provisions on practical modalities relating to these meetings are contained in Annex IV of this document.

At these meetings, substantive information will be provided by the participants in the Negotiation on Conventional Armed Forces in Europe on developments, progress and results in the negotiations with the aim of enabling each participating State to appraise their course.

The participants in these negotiations have undertaken to take into consideration, in the course of their negotiations, the views expressed at such meetings by other participating States concerning their own security.

Information will also be provided on a bilateral basis.

The next Follow-up Meeting of the participating States of the C.S.C.E., to be held in Helsinki, commencing on 24 March 1992, will consider the functioning of these arrangements.

Taking into account the relevant provisions of the Final Act and of the Madrid Concluding Document, and having considered the results achieved in the two negotiations, and also in the light of other relevant negotiations on security and disarmament affecting Europe, a future C.S.C.E. follow-up meeting will consider ways and appropriate means for the participating States to continue their efforts for security and disarmament in Europe, including the question of supplementing the Madrid mandate for the next stage of the Conference on Confidence- and Security-building Measures and Disarmament in Europe. ....

Annex II

CHAIRMAN'S STATEMENT

NEGOTIATION ON CONFIDENCE- AND SECURITY-BUILDING MEASURES

With reference to the provision that the decisions of the Preparatory Meeting held in Helsinki from 25 October to 11 November 1983 will be applied *mutatis mutandis* to the Negotiations on Confidence- and Security-building Measures, which will take place according to the relevant provisions of the subchapter "Confidence- and Security-building Measures and Aspects of Security and Disarmament in Europe", it is understood that

*the meetings of the Plenary during the first two weeks will be held according to the work programme attached to this statement. The first Plenary will be held on 9 March 1989 at 10:30 a.m. The first session will end on 23 March 1989,

*subsequent work programmes will be adopted by the Plenary,

*in conformity with the rules of procedure, the Government of Austria will designate an Executive Secretary, the designation being subject to approval by the participating States,

*the Chair at the first Plenary meeting will be taken by the representative of the host country and thereafter in daily rotation, in French alphabetical order, starting with the representative of ... (drawn by lot at the Vienna Meeting).

This statement will be an Annex to the Concluding Document of the Vienna Meeting and will be published with it. ...

Annex III

CHAIRMAN'S STATEMENT

NEGOTIATION ON CONVENTIONAL ARMED FORCES IN EUROPE

It is understood that the following mandate has been agreed by the States participating in the future Negotiation on Conventional Armed Forces in Europe:

MANDATE FOR NEGOTIATION ON CONVENTIONAL ARMED FORCES IN EUROPE

The representatives of Belgium, Bulgaria, Canada, Czechoslovakia, Denmark, France, the German Democratic Republic, the Federal Republic of Germany, Greece, Hungary, Iceland, Italy, Luxembourg, the Netherlands, Norway, Poland, Portugal, Romania, Spain, Turkey, the Union of Soviet Socialist Republics, the United Kingdom and the United States of America, held consultations in Vienna from 17 February 1987 to 10 January 1989.

These States,

Conscious of the common responsibility which they all have for seeking to achieve greater stability and security in Europe,

Acknowledging that it is their armed forces which bear most immediately on the essential security relationship in Europe, in particular, as they are signatories of the Treaties of Brussels (1948), Washington (1949) or Warsaw (1955), and accordingly are members of the North Atlantic Alliance or parties of the Warsaw Treaty;

Recalling that they are all participants in the C.S.C.E. process; Recalling that, as reaffirmed in the Helsinki Final Act, they have the right to belong or not to belong to international organizations, to be or not to be a party to bilateral or multilateral treaties including the right to be or not to be a party to treaties of alliance;

Determined that a Negotiation on Conventional Armed Forces in Europe should take place in the framework of the C.S.C.E. process;

Reaffirming also that they participate in negotiations as sovereign and independent States and on the basis of full equality;

Have agreed on the following provisions:

PARTICIPANTS

The participants in this negotiation shall be the 23 above-listed States hereinafter referred to as "the participants."

OBJECTIVES AND METHODS

The objectives of the negotiation shall be to strengthen stability and security in Europe through the establishment of a stable and secure balance of conventional armed forces, which include conventional armaments and equipment, at lower levels; the elimination, as a matter of priority, of the capability for launching surprise attack and for initiating large-scale offensive action. Each and every participant undertakes to contribute to the attainment of these objectives.

These objectives shall be achieved by the application of militarily significant measures such as reductions, limitation, redeployment provisions, equal ceilings, and related measures, among others.

In order to achieve the above objectives, measures should be pursued for the whole area of application with provisions, if and where appropriate, for regional differentiation to redress disparities within the area of application and in a way which precludes circumvention.

The process of strengthening stability and security should proceed step-by-step, in a manner which will ensure that the security of each participant is not affected adversely at any stage.

SCOPE AND AREA OF APPLICATION

The subject of the negotiation shall be the conventional armed forces which include conventional armaments and equipment, of the participants based on land within the territory of the participants in Europe from the Atlantic to the Urals.

The existence of multiple capabilities will not be a criterion for modifying the scope of the negotiation:

*No conventional armaments or equipment will be excluded from the subject of the negotiation because they may have other capabilities in addition to conventional ones. Such armaments or equipment will not be singled out in a separate category:

*Nuclear weapons will not be a subject of this negotiation.

Particular emphasis will initially be placed on those forces directly related to the achievement of the objectives of the negotiation set out above.

Naval forces and chemical weapons will not be addressed. The area of application* shall be the entire land territory of the participants in Europe from the Atlantic to the Urals, which includes all the European island territories of the participants. In the case of the Soviet Union the area of application includes all the territory lying west of the Ural River and the Caspian Sea. In the case of Turkey, the area of application includes the territory of Turkey north and west of the following line: the point of intersection of the border with the 39th parallel, Muradiye, Patnos, Karayazi, Tekman, Kemaliye, Feke, Ceyhan, Dogankent, Gozne, and thence to the sea.

EXCHANGE OF INFORMATION AND VERIFICATION

Compliance with the provisions of any agreement shall be verified through an effective and strict verification regime which, among other things, will include on-site inspections as a matter of right and exchanges of information.

Information shall be exchanged in sufficient detail so as to allow a meaningful comparison of the capabilities of the forces involved.

Information shall also be exchanged in sufficient detail so as to provide a basis for the verification of compliance.

The specific modalities for verification and the exchange of information, including the degree of detail of the information and the order of its exchange, shall be agreed at the negotiation proper.

PROCEDURES AND OTHER ARRANGEMENTS

The procedures for the negotiation, including the agenda, work programme and timetable, working methods, financial issues and other organization modalities, as agreed by the participants themselves, are set out in Annex 1 of this mandate. They can be changed only by consensus of the participants.

The participants decided to take part in meetings of the States signatories of the Helsinki Final Act to be held at least twice during each round of the Negotiation on Conventional Armed Forces in Europe in order to exchange views and substantive information concerning the course of the Negotiation on Conventional Armed Forces in Europe. Detailed modalities for these meetings are contained in Annex 2 to this mandate.

The participants will take into consideration the views expressed in such meetings by other C.S.C.E. participating States concerning their own security.

Participants will also provide information bilaterally.

The participants undertake to inform the next C.S.C.E. Follow-up Meeting of their work and possible results and to exchange views, at that meeting, with the other C.S.C.E. participating States on progress achieved in the negotiation.

The participants foresee that, in the light of circumstances at the time, they will provide in their timetable for a temporary suspension to permit this exchange of views. The appropriate time and duration of this suspension is their sole responsibility.

Any modification of this mandate is the sole responsibility of the participants, whether they modify it themselves or concur in its modification at a future C.S.C.E. Follow-up Meeting.

The results of the negotiation will be determined only by the participants.

---

* The participants will be guided by the language on non-circumvention as set out in the section on Objectives and Methods.

CHARACTER OF AGREEMENTS

Agreements reached shall be internationally binding. Modalities for their entry into force will be decided at the negotiation.

VENUE

The negotiation shall commence in Vienna no later than in the seventh week following the closure of the Vienna C.S.C.E. Follow-up Meeting.

The representatives of the 23 participants, whose initials appear below, have concluded the foregoing mandate, which is equally authentic in the English, French, German, Italian, Russian and Spanish languages.

The representatives, recalling the commitment of their States to the achievement of a balanced outcome at the Vienna C.S.C.E. Meeting, have decided to transmit it to that Meeting with the recommendation that it be attached to its Concluding Document.

(Initialed by the representatives of the 23 States at the Palais Liechtenstein, Vienna, Austria, the 10th day of January 1989).

Annex I (Mandate)

PROCEDURES FOR THE NEGOTIATION ON CONVENTIONAL ARMED FORCES IN EUROPE

The representatives of the 23 states listed in the mandate, hereinafter referred to as "the participants", held consultations in Vienna from 17 February 1987 to 10 January 1989, and agreed on the following procedural arrangements for the conduct of the Negotiation on Conventional Armed Forces in Europe.

These procedural arrangements have been adopted by the consensus of the participants. They can be changed only by consensus of the participants.

I. AGENDA

1. Formal opening.
2. Negotiations, including presentation of proposals by the participants, elaboration of measures and procedures for their implementation, in accordance with the provisions of the mandate of the Negotiation on Conventional Armed Forces in Europe.

II. WORK PROGRAMME

The first plenary of the Negotiation on Conventional Armed Forces in Europe will open in Vienna at 3 pm on the Thursday of the week referred to in the section of the mandate on Venue. A work programme for the meetings of the plenary during the first fourteen days of the round is attached. Thereafter, the plenary will agree further work programmes for the remainder of the first round, and for subsequent rounds. A decision on the date for conclusion of the round will be taken at the first plenary.

In 1989, there will in principle be four rounds.

The participants will, in setting their timetable, take due account of the practical needs of all delegations, including those participating in other negotiations within the framework of the C.S.C.E. process.

III. WORKING METHODS

With the exception of the formal opening, all business under the agenda will—unless otherwise agreed—be dealt with in closed plenary and in such subsidiary working bodies as are established by the plenary. The work of such subsidiary bodies will be guided by the plenary.

Decisions shall be taken by consensus of the participants. Consensus shall be understood to mean the absence of any objection by any participant to the taking of the decision in question.

The proceedings of the negotiation shall be confidential unless otherwise agreed at the negotiation.

Unless otherwise agreed, only accredited representatives of the participants shall have access to meetings.

During the plenary meetings all participants shall be seated in the French alphabetical order.

IV. LANGUAGES

The official languages of the negotiation shall be: English, French, German, Italian, Russian and Spanish. Statements made in any of these languages shall be interpreted into the other official languages.

V. ROLE OF THE CHAIRMAN

The Chairman of the first plenary will be the representative of Poland.

The Chair thereafter will rotate weekly according to the French alphabetical order.

The chairman of each meeting shall keep a list of speakers and may declare it closed with the consent of the meeting. The chairman shall, however, accord the right of reply to any representative if a speech made following closure of the list makes this desirable.

If any representative raises a point of order during a discussion, the chairman shall give that representative the floor immediately. A representative raising a point of order may not speak on the substance of the matter under discussion.

The chairman shall keep a journal which shall record the date of the plenary, and the names of the chairman of the plenary and of speakers in the plenary. The journal shall be handed from chairman to chairman. It shall be made available only to participants.

VI. FINANCIAL ISSUES

The following scale of distribution has been agreed for the common expenses of the negotiation subject to the reservation that the distribution in question concerns only this negotiation and shall not be considered a precedent which could be relied on in other circumstances:

9.95% for France, Federal Republic of Germany, Italy, Union of Soviet Socialist Republics, United Kingdom, United States of America.

6.25% for Canada

5.0 % for Spain

3.85% for Belgium, German Democratic Republic, Netherlands, Poland

2.25% for Czechoslovakia, Denmark, Hungary, Norway

0.85% for Greece, Romania, Turkey

0.65% for Bulgaria, Luxembourg, Portugal

0.15% for Iceland

Payment of contributions by the participants shall be made into a special account of the negotiation. Accounts shall be rendered by the host country in respect of each round or at intervals of 3 months, as appropriate. Accounts shall be expressed in the currency of the host country and shall be rendered as soon as technically possible after the termination of a billing period. Accounts shall be payable within 60 days of presentation in the currency of the host country.

VII. HOST COUNTRY SUPPORT

The government of Austria shall provide security and other necessary support services for the negotiation.

The host country shall be asked to appoint an administrator, agreed by the participants, to make and manage arrangements for the negotiation. The administrator shall be a national of the host country. The task of the administrator shall include, in liaison with the appropriate host country authorities:

a. to arrange accreditation for the participants,
b. to manage the facilities of the negotiation,
c. to ensure the security of, and control access to, the facilities and meetings,
d. to employ and manage interpretation staff,
e. to make available appropriate technical equipment,
f. to ensure the availability of translation services in all official languages; the practical arrangements for their use being agreed at the negotiation,
g. to deal with financial matters,
h. to make available to participants as necessary facilities for press briefings and to arrange appropriate media accreditation.

The administrator shall act at all times in conformity with these rules of procedure. Liaison between the administrator and the plenary will be effected by the chairman.

Annex II (Mandate)

MODALITIES FOR MEETINGS TO EXCHANGE VIEWS AND INFORMATION CONCERNING THE COURSE OF THE NEGOTIATION ON CONVENTIONAL ARMED FORCES IN EUROPE

The participants have, for their part, agreed the following modalities for the meetings which are to be held between participants in the Negotiation on Conventional Armed Forces in Europe and other C.S.C.E. participating States.

Unless otherwise agreed, meetings will take place at least twice in the course of each round of the negotiation.

Meetings will not be extended beyond the day on which they convene, unless otherwise agreed.

The chair at the first meeting will be taken by the delegation chosen for this purpose by lot. The chair will then rotate among the 35 States represented in alphabetical order according to the French alphabet.

Further practical arrangements may, if necessary, be agreed by consensus, taking due regard of relevant precedents.

STATEMENT OF THE REPRESENTATIVE OF DENMARK

On behalf of the government of Denmark, I wish to confirm that the Faroe Islands are included in the area of application for the Negotiation on Conventional Armed Forces in Europe.

STATEMENT OF THE REPRESENTATIVE OF NORWAY

On behalf of the government of Norway, I confirm that Svalbard including Bear Island, is included in the area of application for the Negotiation on Conventional Armed Forces in Europe.

STATEMENT OF THE REPRESENTATIVE OF PORTUGAL

The islands of Azores and Madeira have by right the status of European Islands. It has been agreed in the mandate that all the European island territories of the participants are included in the area of application. I can therefore state on behalf of my government that the Azores and Madeira are within the area of application for the Negotiation on Conventional Armed Forces in Europe.

STATEMENT OF THE REPRESENTATIVE OF SPAIN

On behalf of the government of Spain, I confirm that the Canary Islands are included in the area of application for the Negotiation on Conventional Armed Forces in Europe.

STATEMENT OF THE REPRESENTATIVE OF THE UNION OF SOVIET SOCIALIST REPUBLICS

On behalf of the government of the Union of Soviet Socialist Republics, I confirm that Franz Josef Land and Novaya Zemlya are included in the area of application for the Negotiation on Conventional Armed Forces in Europe.

This statement will be an Annex to the Concluding Document of the Vienna Meeting and will be published with it.

Source: Concluding Document of the Vienna Meeting 1986 of Representatives of the Participating States of the Conference on Security and Co-operation in Europe, Held on the Basis of the Provisions of the Final Act Relating to the Follow-up to the Conference, pp. 14–16, 42–57.

Appendix VII: The Warsaw Pact's July, 1988, and March, 1989, Position Papers on C.F.E., and its October, 1988, and March, 1989, Position Papers on C.D.E.-2

STATEMENT BY THE MEMBERS OF THE WARSAW TREATY
ORGANIZATION
on Talks on the Reduction of Armed Forces and Conventional Armaments
in Europe
July 1988

The Warsaw Treaty member states believe that the interests of European and universal security urgently call for sizable cuts in armed forces and conventional armaments in Europe—from the Atlantic to the Urals. They are for talks on this issue to open without delay, in 1988.

The allied states are convinced that the priority objective of these talks is to ensure a radical reduction in the military potentials of both alliances and secure such a situation in the continent in which the NATO and Warsaw Treaty countries would have the forces and armaments needed for defence but insufficient for a surprise attack and offensive operations. This would enhance military–political stability and security in Europe in conditions where the U.S.S.R.–U.S. Treaty on the Elimination of their Intermediate-Range and shorter-Range Missiles is in effect, and facilitate further movement along the path of promoting disarmament, strengthening trust and lowering the threat of war.

The Warsaw Treaty member states proceed from the premise that cuts in armed forces and conventional armaments will be accompanied by a corresponding curtailment of military spending.

Acting on the basis of their joint programme for reducing armed forces and conventional armaments in Europe, which they put forward in Budapest in June 1986 and supplemented in Berlin in May 1987, the Warsaw Treaty member states are for the following issues to be resolved during the first phase of the relevant talks.

1. Achieving Equal Lowered Levels

The ultimate goal of the first phase of the talks should be achieving roughly equal (balanced) collective levels as regards troop strength and the amount of conventional armaments for the states members of the two military–political alliances. These levels would be lower than those currently existing on either side.

The process of attaining such levels would be taking place by phases on the European and the regional scale. First of all, it would be expedient to concentrate on the issues of mutually eliminating the imbalances and asymmetries in individual types of conventional arms and in the armed forces of the two military–political alliances in Europe.

The imbalances and asymmetries would be removed by withdrawing forces from the reduction area and subsequently disbanding them or by disbanding them on the spot, as well as by using other possible measures. The arms and military equipment to be reduced would be eliminated on specially assigned sites or be turned over by agreement to be used for peaceful purposes. Provision could be made for storing part of the arms and equipment on a temporary basis. Such storage sites would be kept under constant international control.

The attainment of the final goal of the first phase would lay the groundwork for further significant mutual cuts in troops and armaments. At the second phase the armed forces of each side would be reduced by approximately 25 per cent (by some 500,000 men) with their organic armaments; at the third phase the reduction of the armed forces and conventional armaments would be continued and the armed forces of both sides would acquire a strictly defensive nature.

The Warsaw Treaty member states consider it expedient that all the participants in the talks should not, from the moment they begin and until the agreements achieved at them become effective, take steps running counter to the objectives of the talks, in particular should not build up their armed forces and conventional armaments from the Atlantic to the Urals.

With the agreement's entry into force, all the participants in the negotiations would pledge not to build up their armed forces and conventional armaments in the territory that might be left outside that covered by the initial cuts.

2. Preventing a Surprise Attack

Measures to reduce and eliminate the danger of surprise attack would be an integral part of the process of reducing armed forces and conventional armaments in Europe.

For this purpose, starting from the first phase, corridors (zones) with a lower arms level would be created along the line of contact between the two military–political alliances, from which the more dangerous destabilising types of conventional arms would be removed or reduced. As a result, military potentials in these corridors (zones) would be kept at a level ensuring only a defensive capability but ruling out the possibility of a surprise attack.

The depth of the corridors (zones) with a lowered arms level could be agreed on the basis of geostrategic factors, the combat and technical characteristics of the principal types of arms and other criteria.

These steps would be accompanied by agreed confidence-building measures which would limit military activity in the corridors (zones), providing correspondingly a stiffer regime closer to the line of contact. They would cover, in particular, the scale and number of simultaneous exercises, the duration and frequency of exercises, as well as a ban on major exercises, and restrictions on troops movements.

3. Data Exchange and Verification

With a view to determining the correlation of forces between the two military–political alliances and detecting imbalances and asymmetries in the armed forces and conventional armaments on the European and the regional scale early in the talks or, if possible, even before their commencement, relevant initial data essential for conducting the negotiations would be mutually exchanged. Provision would also be made for the possibility of verifying these data with the start of the talks by means of on-site inspections.

An effective system would be created for verifying compliance with the accords to be reached at the talks, by using national technical means and international procedures, including on-site inspections without the right to refuse them. Checkpoints would be set up both along and inside the corridors (zones) with a lowered arms level and in the reduction area (at railway stations and junctions, airfields and ports). Verification would be effected of the process of reducing, eliminating (dismantling) and storing arms and of disbanding military units, as well as of troop activities and the limit on the number of troops and armaments remaining after the cuts.

An international verification commission would be formed and vested with extensive powers (in terms of monitoring, inspections, dealing with contentious issues, etc.).

The Warsaw Treaty member states believe that a considerable reduction and subsequent elimination of tactical nuclear weapons, including munitions for dual-capable systems, would be an important measure towards reducing the war danger and creating a more stable situation in Europe. They reaffirm their proposal for an early opening of relevant talks and conducting them with a view to concluding a mutually acceptable agreement.

The Warsaw Treaty member states proceed from the premise that there is a close relationship between the process of reducing armed forces and conventional armaments from the Atlantic to the Urals and the continued development and broadening of confidence- and security-building measures in Europe within the C.S.C.E. framework. They maintain that the second phase of the Conference on Confidence- and Security-Building Measures and Disarmament in Europe should continue to examine the issues left unresolved at the Conference's first phase, particularly those concerning the extension of confidence-building measures to cover the activity of air forces and navies, and to agree on new-generation confidence-building measures, including those of a restrictive nature. All these measures would contribute to lowering the risk of a surprise attack and promoting openness and predictability in the military field.

The Warsaw Treaty member states are prepared to discuss other possible measures and proposals for strengthening stability in Europe at ever lower levels of armed forces and armaments, with the principles of equality and equal security being observed and the agreements reached being made effectively verifiable.

Source: Documents of the Meeting of the Political Consultative Committee of the Warsaw Treaty Member States (Moscow: Novosti Press Agency Publishing House, 1988).

*   *   *

Eduard Shevardnadze's Address in Vienna

March 6, 1989

Mr. Chairman, Ladies and Gentlemen:

We are opening unique negotiations—unique not only as regards their formula, format, and set of participants. Memory prompts us that never before has an undertaking with so momentous an objective been conceived.

Reason convinces us that the road leading to that objective is the right one.

Instinct tells us that the willingness to reach the end of the road is common to all of us.

The very opportunity that has been offered to us is unique.

Political intuition and objective analysis make us conclude that if we make use of this opportunity, we will obtain a Europe of a new quality and value.

We are in effect opening negotiations not just on reducing troops and conventional arms and on confidence-building measures—we are undertaking the task of overcoming the split of Europe.

As we get under way, it is appropriate to present our vision of the current state of affairs and of the goals shared by all.

The better we know each other's views, the easier it will be to identify reasonable defense requirements of the European countries. Furthermore, reasonable requirements can only be identified on the basis of reasonable perceptions.

Well, today more than ever before, reason is a solid pillar of politics, and this, I believe, is also a unique feature of the moment and the greatest achievement of the new times. Being very different in terms of outlook, convictions, and value systems, and having no intention of giving them up, we have finally been able to perceive ourselves as a single nucleus of the European entity.

The negotiations of 35 and of 23—the two new branches of Helsinki—are starting at a time when things in Europe that only a few years ago seemed impossible have become routine.

The routine nature of these things reveals new standards of international existence.

Soviet and American nuclear missiles are being destroyed as a matter of routine.

Inspections of military facilities are being conducted on a workaday basis.

Notifications of planned military exercises, troop movements and strategic missile launches are being sent in an equally ordinary way.

These routine things have become the norm, the rule, the canon. It is our duty to extend that also to the reduction of conventional armed forces.

In fact, they are already being reduced—reduced unilaterally by the Soviet Union, Bulgaria, Hungary, the German Democratic Republic, Poland, Rumania and Czechoslovakia—reduced on a large scale. Thus deeds come ahead of words; obligations precede agreements.

Already during this year the Soviet armed forces deployed in the allied countries of Eastern Europe will be cut by over 20,000 men, 2,700 tanks and 300 combat airplanes. Twenty-four tactical missile launchers will be withdrawn from the German Democratic Republic.

By 1991 the armed forces of the Warsaw Treaty countries will have been reduced by 300,000 men, 12,000 tanks, and 930 combat airplanes.

The composition of the remaining Soviet units and formations in those countries will also change substantially. There will be 40 per cent fewer tanks in motorized rifle divisions and 20 percent fewer tanks in tank divisions.

This diplomacy of example, diplomacy of deeds, calls for something more than just a chorus of praise and approval. Let those in the West who are applauding our unilateral steps respond with a step of their own in those categories of arms where they have an advantage.

However substantial the numerical reductions may be, their main significance probably lies in the political signal that they send.

The actions taken by the Soviet Union and other socialist countries reflect, above all, a new approach to assessing the probability and degree of military threat posed by the West. They reflect growing confidence that security can to an increasing extent be assured by nonmilitary means. The outdated criterion that the more weapons, the better the guarantee of security has been replaced by a single and ever-present resource—an emerging factor of trust.

For our part we would like to hope that our way of thinking and acting is no longer identified in the west with ill will or evil intentions.

The mutual "image of the enemy" that used to pervade both Western and our propaganda is giving way to a more objective and serious look at each other.

Let us together pledge that, that image, which not only affects people's feelings but also leaves a grave imprint on policy making, dialogue and communication, shall not burden these negotiations.

Now, let me present to you our specific positions.

They call for a three-stage reduction of armed forces in Europe down to a level sufficient exclusively for defense.

Recently NATO, too, has put forward a proposal of stability at lower levels of armaments.

These two approaches can be bridged. Notwithstanding serious differences, they can be brought together. For both NATO and the Warsaw Treaty Organization call for eliminating the potential for carrying out a surprise attack and for launching large-scale offensive operations. Furthermore, both sides believe that a lower level of over-all military confrontation is Europe has to be attained.

That is already a kind of starting point for the negotiations, which isn't bad.

This is what we propose. In the first phase, with a duration of two or three years, imbalances and asymmetries would be eliminated, as regards both troop numbers and the main categories of arms.

To achieve this, it is proposed that reduction focus on the most destabilizing kinds and categories of arms, such as attack combat airplanes of tactical aviation, tanks, combat helicopters, combat armored vehicles, armored personnel carriers, and artillery, including multiple rocket launcher systems and mortars.

NATO and the Warsaw Treaty would reduce their armed forces and conventional arms down to equal collective ceilings, which would be 10–15 percent lower than the lowest levels possessed by either of the political–military alliances.

A small remark here. We do not know what proposals our negotiating partners from NATO will bring to this rostrum, but it is clear from our discussions that they would prefer not to affect troop numbers and would artificially restrict the list of destabilizing armaments subject to priority reductions.

Let me ask: What kind of reductions are these if they do not affect the main component of armed forces—their personnel? And surely airplanes and helicopters can be used for a surprise attack.

The next element: Along the line of contact of the two political–military alliances, strips (zones) with lower levels of arms would be set up, in which the most dangerous destabilizing kinds of arms would be subject to withdrawal, reduction, or limitation, and limitations would be imposed on military activities.

Tactical nuclear arms would also be withdrawn from these zones. Nuclear weapon delivery vehicles would be pulled back from the line of contact to a distance that would make it impossible for them to reach the other side's territory.

All of these elements are treated in detail in the proposals of our allies.

In the second phase, also lasting two or three years, further cuts would be carried out to reduce the equal levels attained during the first phase on an equal-percentage basis.

During this stage the armed forces of each side would be reduced by another 25 per cent, that is, by approximately 500,000 men, with their organic armaments. At the same time, other categories of arms would be reduced, and further steps would be taken to restructure the armed forces based on the principles of sufficiency for defense.

Finally, during the third phase, the armed forces would be given a strictly defensive character, and agreements would be reached on ceilings limiting all other categories of arms and based on the principles of armed forces development by which the participating countries would have to abide.

One of the most difficult problems, it would seem, is how to avoid the sterile data debate which Vienna has already heard as the requiem for talks on disarmament in Central Europe.

Even now it is clear that the published figures are causing a great deal of mutual arguments and objections. That is understandable. Differing approaches were applied, and, hence, the conclusions turned out to be different. We would think that it is not productive now to argue who is right and who is wrong.

Wouldn't it be better just to avoid sterile arguments about data while giving priority to strategy and big politics?

We are not citing any absolute figures for future ceilings. This is what experts should work on. It is up to them to develop a common approach, a single method of account, which must be scientific, fair, and objective.

Any ingenious stratagem or undisguised attempt to retain an advantage in a particular kind of arms could torpedo the negotiations.

This is not a matter of arithmetic but more properly of morality. Honesty and fair play are indispensable components of the process of negotiations.

If we—both in the West and in the East—are convinced that growing trust creates an opportunity to lower military confrontation, that conviction should be translated in practice into greater openness and *glasnost*, and lower levels of troops and armaments. The only correct and acceptable way to achieve security is to create a situation that rules out mutual threats.

That is why we are saying that at each stage of the process of disarmament the interests of mutual security must be observed. Without that we shall not be able to stop the arms race. It cannot be stopped selectively. True, we can move faster in one area while postponing a decision in another, but it would be naive to think that one has no relation to the other. And since that is so, we have to take, so to say, a broad-spectrum approach, to move ahead, across the broadest front of disarmament, ridding ourselves of nuclear, chemical, conventional, and any other weapons.

We continue to be fully confident of an early conclusion of the Soviet–American treaty to reduce strategic offensive arms by 50 percent. We hope that the day of the signing of the convention banning and eliminating chemical weapons is not far off.

I also want to emphasize that the Vienna mandate is based on the Madrid mandate, which provides that confidence- and security-building measures must apply not only to Europe but also to the adjacent sea area and the air space above it.

In going back to this question it is not at all our aim formally to reaffirm our position about the need to include naval armaments, too, within the context of confidence-building measures.

Technological advances are changing the role of those armaments. As ships are equipped with long-range cruise missiles, which even conventionally armed can perform strategic tasks, attack capabilities of naval fleets will be even more powerful than they are now. Surface ships and submarines are becoming ideal offensive weapons, best fit for surprise attack.

Measures that give ground forces a strictly defensive structure, withdrawals of tanks and artillery, and all other steps to rule out surprise attack logically bring about the need for serious efforts to limit destabilizing functions and capabilities of naval forces.

The issue of naval forces has been raised on the eve of these negotiations, not as a condition but with only one aim in mind: We have to understand clearly even now that the scope of eventual agreements will, to some extent, be affected by, among others things, the factor of naval arms.

This is equally true of the question of modernizing tactical nuclear arms, if such plans are translated into practical actions.

The reason is not only that modernization is a way to maintain and build up nuclear arsenals.

What is more, it can destroy the fragile trust that has just begun to emerge in

Europe as a result of decisions that are genuinely significant militarily, and important politically and psychologically.

If that happens, Europe will be pushed back to what it was before the conclusion of the Soviet–American treaty eliminating I.N.F. missiles.

The Soviet Union proposes that separate negotiations be started as soon as possible on reducing and completely eliminating tactical nuclear weapons in Europe.

What Europe needs is not modernization of missiles but a modernized system of security based on drastic reductions of troops and armaments.

But even then, we would, of course, have to be confident that the new formula for security would work in all situations.

To have such confidence, the most rigorous and reliable verification must be assured. As we see it, that should not be a big problem. In principle we know how it could be done. What is more, we have systems in operation and well-tested methods of control and verification. The implementation of the Stockholm Agreements and the practice of monitoring compliance with Soviet–American agreements make us confident that the problem of verification can be solved in this area as well.

We shall insist on the most stringent and rigorous verification, including inspections without right of refusal, aerial monitoring of the situation and checking the routes of communication used to reinforce troops and equipment.

In other words, there is no verification measure that we would not be ready to consider and to accept on the basis of reciprocity.

Such is our long-term program for reducing conventional armed forces.

Its implementation begins, naturally, with first steps. Let us try to take them and to conclude the initial agreement within a short time.

We have all that is needed for that.

At the negotiations of 35 we would like not only to improve what was done in Stockholm but also to reach agreement on a new generation of large-scale confidence-building measures under which openness and *glasnost* would go hand in hand with limitations of all kinds of military activities and with confidence-building measures extended to naval and air forces.

Neutral and nonaligned countries could play an important role here. We for our part will do our best to make sure that their security interests are fully taken into account.

Let me add another remark.

The evolution of the situation in some regions adjoining Europe makes one think of new dimensions of European security.

In the Middle East and Southwest Asia, that is, in close proximity to Europe, powerful weapons arsenals are being created. It is not enough just to mention that 25,000 tanks and 4,500 aircraft are deployed and ready for combat in the Middle East, and there is a real danger of nuclear and chemical weapons appearing there: Missiles have already appeared with an operational range of 2,500 kilometers, that is to say, of precisely the same class that is being eliminated from Europe. This new situation is emerging against the background of the mounting trend toward European disarmament. The conclusion is obvious: The processes of disarmament in Europe and settlement in the Middle East have to be synchronized.

While the Mediterranean is, in some way, joining in the C.S.C.E. process, the

Middle East and Southwest Asia remain outside our collective concern. I say collective concern because certain attempts are being made on an individual basis.

Today they are clearly insufficient.

While welcoming the Europeans' Middle East initiative, the Soviet Union is calling for joining the efforts of all permanent members of the United Nations Security Council, the U.N. Secretary-General, and the European community and helping the peoples of the region to establish peace, put an end to the arms race and initiate wide-range economic and environmental cooperation. To do so, it is imperative to get rid of the rudimentary mentality that requires acting against each other rather than together with others. There should be no playing on any contradictions—whether it is Israel's conflict with the Arabs or the difficulties in the West's relations with Iran.

There should be respect for the values of those with whom we coexist on our planet—even if they do not fit our own standards.

Going back now to the topic of the coming negotiations of 23 and 35, let me express confidence that they have good chances for success.

I want to assure you that the Soviet Union will do its best to help them succeed. It will do so guided by our view of today's world and of ways to assure its security and solve global and regional problems, as set forth by Mikhail Gorbachev at the session of the United Nations General Assembly.

We have a difficult road ahead of us. Our experience—the experience of five Soviet–American summits and more than 30 ministerial meetings—tells us that without such intensive work on problems of real disarmament, there would be no treaty eliminating I.N.F. missiles today.

These negotiations will require something similar, but on a larger scale. At certain stages the matter could be considered at the highest level. It is possible that more than one C.S.C.E. summit meeting would be required. We have to anticipate that at decisive moments, possibly twice a year, foreign ministers might have to meet in order to keep the fire burning at these negotiations and to prepare for the summit.

In this area, which is of major importance for the future of Europe, there is a need for maximum concentration of efforts and active cooperation among all states participating in the Helsinki process.

We are firmly counting on that.

Let me wish the participants in these negotiations an early and productive implementation of the mandate.

Our wholehearted gratitude goes to Austria, which has assumed the difficult function of hosting these talks. We thank the government of the republic and the Austrian people.

* * *

WARSAW PACT POSITION PAPER ON C.F.E.

Conceptual Approach to the Reduction of Conventional Armed Forces in
Europe
March 9, 1989

The parties to the agreement will be: Belgium, Bulgaria, Canada, Czechoslo-
vakia, Denmark, France, the German Democratic Republic, the Federal
Republic of Germany, Greece, Hungary, Iceland, Italy, Luxembourg, the
Netherlands, Norway, Poland, Portugal, Romania, Spain, Turkey, the Union
of Soviet Socialist Republics, the United Kingdom, and the United States of
America.

The Warsaw Treaty member States believe that the agreement should have
the following objectives: to strengthen stability and security in Europe through
deep cuts in conventional armed forces, including conventional armaments and
equipment, of the Warsaw Treaty member States and of the NATO member
countries so as to establish in this way a balance at lower levels at which both
military alliances will keep forces and systems necessary solely for defense and
insufficient to launch surprise attack or conduct offensive operations; to
restructure and redeploy their armed forces on strictly defensive principles.

The process of strengthening stability and security on the European continent should proceed stage by stage and in a manner that will not upset the
overall balance or prejudice anyone's security at all stages of the negotiations.

These objectives could be achieved through reductions, limitations, appropriate redeployment measures, equal collective ceilings on armed forces and
conventional armaments both throughout the European zone and in its
individual regions. The scope and procedure of reduction of national and
foreign troops down to agreed levels would be decided upon with each alliance
on the basis of the principles and criteria to be agreed at the negotiation.

The reductions in conventional armed forces and armaments will be effected
on the basis of reciprocity, with all the Participating States without exception
making their appropriate contributions with account taken of their military
potentials.

The reductions will be accompanied by corresponding cuts in military
expenditures and by measures to convert their conventional armed forces and
armaments.

These objectives can be achieved both through agreed steps and unilateral
measures to reduce their armed forces and armaments.

The zone of application of agreement would cover the entire land territory of
the Participating States in Europe from the Atlantic to the Urals, including a
part of the Asian territory of Turkey and the Soviet Transcaucasus as well as all
the European Island territories of the Participating States including the Faroe
Islands, Svalbard, the Islands of Azores and Madeira, the Canary Islands,
Franz Josef Land and Novaya Zemlya.

At the first stage of reductions which would begin not later than 1991 and
end in 1994 all the Participating States would eliminate imbalances and
asymmetries between NATO and the Warsaw Treaty as regards both troop
numbers and main armaments and would make steps to eliminate the capability to launch surprise attack or initiate large-scale offensive action.

To this end attention would be focused on reducing the most destabilizing types and categories of armaments such as attack combat aircraft of short-range tactical aviation, tanks, combat helicopters, combat armoured vehicles and armoured personnel carriers, artillery including multiple launch rocket systems and mortars.

The Participating States would reduce their conventional armed forces and armaments down to equal collective ceilings that would be 10–15% lower than the lowest levels possessed by the military political alliances. These ceilings would be agreed between the Participating States in absolute terms. They believe that after the first-stage reductions, by 1994 such collective ceilings for member States of either of the military political alliances could be approximately established for strength of the armed forces, number of attack aircraft, tanks, combat helicopters, combat armoured vehicles and armoured personnel carriers, artillery including multiple launch rocket systems and mortars.

Definitions would be worked out for each category of armaments including a list of concrete systems pertaining to them as well as rules of accounting for the purposes of unified data exchange. Such data can be presented with regard to each individual Participating State including data on the troops stationed in the territory of any other Participating State in the zone of agreements. Both general and random verification of data can be undertaken following their presentation.

The reduction of armed forces could be implemented through disbandment of the troops being reduced or their withdrawal from the territory of another State and subsequent disbandment.

The armaments and equipment being reduced are eliminated under agreed procedures at specially assigned locations or are converted for civilian use. A part of the armaments and equipment are put in temporary storage under international control.

As regards surprise attack prevention measures, starting with the first stage onwards, zones of reduced levels of armaments would be established along the line of contact between the two military political alliances, from where the most dangerous destabilizing types of conventional armaments and equipment would be pulled out, reduced, or limited and where limitations would be

The establishment of such zones in Central Europe and in other regions of the European continent could be effected on the basis of the existing and possible new proposals.

The depth of such zones could be agreed with account taken of geographical factors and performance characteristics of the main types of armaments.

Confidence- and security-building measures would limit military activities within the strips (zones) and would, appropriately, provide for an increasingly rigorous regime as the line of contact is approached. In particular, they would affect the scope and number of concurrent exercises, the duration and frequence of exercises and envisage a ban on large-scale exercises and limitations on troop transfers.

The Second Stage (1994–1997). Subject to the attainment, as a result of the first stage, of lower equal ceilings, the Participating States will implement subsequent reductions on an equal-percentage basis.

At the second stage the armed forces of each side would be cut approximately by 25% (by about 500,000 men) with their organic armaments.

Along with further substantial lowering of the levels of the most destabilizing types and categories of armaments the Participating States shall take steps to reduce other categories of armaments not affected by the first-stage cuts.

The Participating States will make further steps to restructure their armed forces on the basis of the principle of sufficiency for defense.

They will elaborate and make agreed steps to develop predictability and openness in day-to-day military activities and to lower their levels.

The Third Stage (1997–2000). During the third stage further reductions of armed forces and conventional armaments shall be implemented and the armed forces of the Participating States will be given a strictly defensive character.

The Participating States will reach agreement on ceilings on all other categories of armaments.

The Participating States will reach agreements on the principles of armed forces development by which they will abide in the future for the purposes of maintaining a secure and stable peace in Europe.

Verification. The Participating States will agree to exchange data regarding manpower strength, number of conventional armaments, and deployment of military formations and to verify them, including through on-site inspections.

There would be envisaged the establishment of a comprehensive and effective system of verification of compliance with agreements including land and air on-site inspections without the right to refuse. There would be created checkpoints to monitor entry/exit both along and inside the strips (zones) of reduced levels of armaments and in the reduction area (at railway stations, junctions, airfields, ports). Such technical means of verification as artificial Earth satellites, aircraft, helicopters, ground automatic recording systems, including the ones developed through international cooperation, could also be used for the purposes of verification.

There would be verification of the process of reduction, elimination (Dismantlement, conversion) and storage of armaments, disbandment of formations and units, non-excess of the strength of armed forces and the number of armaments as well as of the activities of the troops remaining after reductions.

An international verification (consultative) commission would be set up and given wide powers (observation, inspection, consideration of disputes, etc.), which would be made up of representatives of the Participating States.

A prominent part in the implementation of verification and control measures should be played by the highest representative bodies—Parliaments, National Assemblies and the Supreme Soviet—which could act as guarantors of the reductions and redeployment of the armed forces and conventional armaments of the appropriate countries. Related matters could be discussed within the framework of foreign and military affairs committees and be reflected in appropriate statements to be made on behalf of the parliaments.

The Warsaw Treaty member States also envisage that the provisions of the Agreement will not be aimed against any other countries or their security interests and will not be construed as prejudicial to other international treaties concluded by the Participating States.

For the purposes of ensuring the viability and effectiveness of agreements each Participating State will not circumvent their provisions or assume international obligations which would conflict with the Agreement.

* * *

STATEMENT OF THE COMMITTEE OF MINISTERS FOR FOREIGN AFFAIRS OF THE WARSAW TREATY ON CONFIDENCE- AND SECURITY-BUILDING MEASURES AND DISARMAMENT IN EUROPE

October 28–29, 1988

The States party to the Warsaw Treaty believe that confidence- and security-building measures as significant means and stimulating factors can facilitate the reduction of military threat and the achievement of real disarmament, as well as the strengthening of peace and stability in relations between States.

From the point of view of improving the political atmosphere, the importance of measures adopted at the Stockholm Conference on Confidence- and Security-Building Measures and Disarmament in Europe in September 1986 is becoming apparent to the extent of their implementation. The Stockholm Document demonstrates that important security issues can be solved by political will and mutual efforts by all interested States in the Spirit of new thinking. The resumption of the work of the Conference on Confidence- and Security-Building Measures and Disarmament in Europe and the further implementation of the Stockholm Document and its provisions broaden the perspectives for negotiations concerning both more significant confidence- and security-building measures and the reduction of armed forces and conventional armaments in Europe.

Further improvement of confidence- and security-building measures on the European continent is of particular significance today when the 23 States parties to the Warsaw Treaty and NATO are preparing to enter into negotiations of a unique scope and importance on armed forces and conventional armaments in Europe from the Atlantic to the Urals. In the view of the allied socialist countries military confidence- and security-building measures and efforts towards the reduction of armed forces and conventional armaments are interrelated. Further steps in the field of confidence- and security-building measures facilitate progress towards the reduction of armed forces and conventional armaments in Europe and the solution of other disarmament issues, which in turn would create favorable conditions to increased confidence.

The Ministers for Foreign Affairs of the States party to the Warsaw Treaty believe that the negotiations on confidence- and security-building measures in Europe should be continued as early as 1988. In order to reduce military confrontation and the risk of an armed conflict in Europe, to reduce and avert the danger of a surprise attack and to enhance mutual security, to lend a strictly defensive character to military activities and to increase their openness and predictability as well as to promote the implementation of disarmament measures, the negotiations should make it possible that the measures elaborated ultimately cover the activity of all elements of armed forces (ground, air and naval forces) of the States participating in the process of security and co-operation in Europe (C.S.C.E.). The creation, on an equal basis, of mechanisms and procedures for contacts and consultations would also serve these objectives.

Confidence- and security-building measures should be applied to all the military activities of the participating States that affect European security or constitute part of military actions taking place within the boundaries of

Europe. These measures should be substantial, militarily effective and politically binding.

The military confidence- and security-building measures should be worked out and introduced gradually, taking into account the military and geographical realities in Europe and the level of mutual understanding among States.

Being an important element of the all-European process the negotiations should be conducted on the basis of the Madrid mandate, including the objectives, the principles, the subject of negotiations, the zone of application of confidence- and security-building measures, the rules of procedure contained in the mandate, and should be in accordance with the Concluding Document of the Vienna follow-up meeting.

It would be expedient to continue efforts at the negotiations to develop and expand the existing confidence- and security-building measures, and a new set of measures could also be worked out on the basis of proposals by the participating States.

Agreements to be reached in the course of the negotiations by the 23 and the 35 States respectively should be in harmony with each other and should complement and reinforce each other.

In the view of the States party to the Warsaw Treaty a new generation of confidence- and security-building measures could be worked out in the following main directions:

1. *Constraining measures*

These measures would apply to the size and number of simultaneous military exercises, the duration and frequency of military exercises, ban large-scale military exercises and restrict the redeployment of troops and technical equipment. Moreover, they would envisage the limitation of the number of combat-readiness (alertness) military exercises and the number of troops engaged; they would affect the series of large-scale military exercises constituting a unified military exercise by concept, and would also envisage restraint on military activities in the vicinity of the borders of the participating States.

2. *New confidence- and security-building measures*

These would include prior notification of independent activities by air and naval forces, invitation of observers according to appropriate parameters, inspection of such activities and agreement on restricting measures, modalities of the exchange of annual calendars of such activities; extension of confidence- and security-building measures to the territories of all the countries participating in the C.S.C.E. process; creation of zones of confidence and security in Europe and the adjoining seas and oceans; and also the possibility of working out such confidence- and security-building measures that envisage more stringent regimes on the basis of the closeness to line of contact between the military–political alliances or other States. Measures to avoid incidents on seas and oceans adjoining Europe and in the airspace thereof would also be co-ordinated.

Different aspects of military doctrines could be discussed and compared in the course of or in connection with the negotiations. Issues related to freeze on and reduction of military budgets could also be explored.

The States party to the Warsaw Treaty believe that the establishment of a European center for reducing military threat and preventing surprise attack would signify a qualitatively new step in reinforcing mutual confidence. The task of such a center would be to exchange information and to maintain contacts as well as to hold consultations primarily for the operative settlement of events giving rise to concern or suspicion.

3. *Measures to increase the openness and predictability of military activities: inspection, exchange of information and consultations*
These measures would cover regular exchange of data on armed forces and their activities, including forces deployed at military bases around Europe; exchange of information on the structure and substance of military budgets; refraining from building up armed forces and renouncing the establishment of new military bases on the territories of foreign States; setting up observation posts at agreed sites (points) within the zone of application of confidence- and security-building measures; creation of special operative communication links between the interested countries; improving conditions for inspection and working opportunities for observers; the use of the latest technical equipment; developing relations between political and military representatives of the participating States; and broadening the present practice of exchange of military–diplomatic representations and military delegations.

Other measures promoting mutual understanding and enhancing confidence and security could also be adopted.

The idea and proposals by the States party to the Warsaw Treaty concerning confidence- and security-building measures are based on the defensive nature of their military doctrine. Their implementation is meant to make the military potentials of the participating States become strictly defensive in nature.
In connection with this, the States represented at the meeting stand for the elimination of military bases on foreign territories and reaffirm their position concerning the simultaneous dissolution of the military–political alliances.
In the opinion of the States party to the Warsaw Treaty, the convening of an all-European summit meeting to explore issues concerning the reduction of armed forces and conventional armaments in Europe, with the participation of the United States and Canada, would also contribute to the elaboration and implementation of new confidence- and security-building measures.
The States party to the Warsaw Treaty are ready to study other possible proposals aiming to enhance mutual confidence and security and to accelerate the process of disarmament in Europe.

Budapest, October 29, 1988

*   *   *

WARSAW PACT PROPOSALS FOR C.D.E.-2 OF MARCH 9, 1989
(As Summarized by Western Participants)

Bulgaria introduced the Eastern proposal on behalf of the Warsaw Pact. The proposal was cosponsored by Bulgaria, Hungary, the German Democratic Republic and Czechoslovakia, but supported by all Pact members. The main elements (taken from an unofficial translation) are:

SECTION 1: Constraining Measures
  1. Limitation of notifiable military activities including practice alerts, involving over 40,000 troops.
  2. No more than 3 notifiable activities to be carried out simultaneously on the territory of a participating state. The total number of troops involved concurrently to be limited to 40,000.
  3. No more than 2 notifiable activities involving 25,000 troops to be carried out on the territory of each participating state annually.
  4. No more than 40,000 troops at any one time to be engaged in a series of exercises carried out in close proximity to one another, even if the exercises have no formal link.

SECTION 2: Naval and Air CSBMs
  1. Notification of air exercises involving over 150 combat aircraft, or 130 combat aircraft in the air simultaneously, or more than 500 sorties.
  2. Notification of transfers of more than 70 combat aircraft into the zone or within it.
  3. Observation of air exercises involving over 300 combat aircraft or over 600 sorties.
  4. Limits on air exercises involving more than 600 combat aircraft or 1800 sorties.
  5. Inclusion of air activities in annual calendars.

B. Naval Forces
  1. Notification of naval exercises involving over 20 combat ships of more than 1500 tons each, or over 5 ships with at least one over 5000 tons and equipped with cruise missiles or aircraft, or over 80 combat aircraft.
  2. Notification of transfers into or within the zone of naval groups of over 10 ships of more than 1500 tons each, or over 5 ships of which at least one is over 5000 tons and equipped with cruise missiles or aircraft.
  3. Notification of "Marine Force Transfers" involving over 3000 men to the territory of another state.
  4. Notification of transfers to the territory of another state of over 30 naval combat aircraft.
  5. Observation of exercises involving over 25 combat ships of more than 1500 tons each or over 100 combat aircraft.
  6. Limitation of exercises of over 50 combat ships.
  7. Naval exercises to be limited to 10 to 14 days.
  8. No more than 6 to 8 naval exercises by each state annually.
  9. Prohibition of notifiable naval exercises in areas of intense civil activity or areas of "international significance."
  10. Inclusion of naval activities in annual calendars.

11. Conclusion of an agreement on prevention of incidents in Sea areas and air space adjoining Europe.

SECTION 3: Development and amplification of Stockholm Document
  1. Lower thresholds for notification and observation of land force activities.
  2. Additional information in annual calendars.
  3. Improved observation modalities, including aerial observation and aerial survey of the exercise area.

SECTION 4: Zones
  1. Establishment of zones involving special limits on force levels and activities.
  2. Possible measures to include restructuring of formation, stricter notification and observation thresholds and stricter constraint measures. Verification to include e.g., observation posts in agreed locations. A central European zone to include e.g., FRG, Belgium, the Netherlands, Luxembourg, Denmark, GDR, Czechoslovakia, Poland and Hungary.

SECTION 5: Improved openness and predictability of military activities, exchange of information and consultations and verification
  1. Regular exchanges of information on the number, structure and deployment of land, naval and air forces disaggregated to brigade/regiment or equivalent formations.
  2. Voluntary provision of additional information not covered by the agreement.
  3. Periodic discussion of military doctrine and other aspects of policy.
  4. Enhanced arrangements for exchange of official visits.
  5. Regular bilateral or multilateral consultations on CSBM issues.
  6. Use of automatic/remote-control verification equipment.
  7. Establishment of a risk-reduction center.
  8. Development of a special communication system e.g., for resolving disputes.

Appendix VIII: NATO's December, 1988, and March, 1989, Position Papers on C.F.E. and C.D.E.-2

STATEMENT ISSUED BY THE NORTH ATLANTIC COUNCIL
MEETING IN MINISTERIAL SESSION AT NATO HEADQUARTERS,
BRUSSELS

DECEMBER 8–9, 1988

In their statement, "Conventional Arms Control: The Way Ahead," the Heads of State and Government participating in the meeting of the North Atlantic Council in March 1988 emphasized that the imbalance in conventional forces remains at the core of Europe's security concerns. We shall be presenting specific proposals at the negotiating table to redress this imbalance.

We look forward to the early commencement of the two negotiations we have proposed: one on conventional stability between the 23 members of the two military alliances in Europe and one on confidence- and security-building measures among all 35 signatories of the Helsinki Final Act.

In these negotiations we will be guided by:
— the conviction that the existing military confrontation is the result, not the cause, of the painful division of Europe;
— the principle of the indivisible security of all our nations. We shall reject calls for partial security arrangements or proposals aimed at separate agreements;
— the hope that the new thinking in the Soviet Union will open the way for mutual agreement on realistic, militarily significant and verifiable arrangements which enhance security at lower levels.

TOWARDS STABILITY

The major threat to stability in Europe comes from those weapons systems which are capable of mounting large-scale offensive operations and of seizing and holding territory. These are above all main battle tanks, artillery and armoured troop carriers. It is in these very systems that the East has such a massive preponderance. Indeed, the Soviet Union itself possesses more tanks and artillery than all the other members of the Warsaw Pact and the Alliance combined. And they are concentrated in a manner which raises grave concerns about the strategy which they are intended to support as well as their role in maintaining the division in Europe.

The reductions announced by the Soviet Union are a positive contribution to correcting this situation. They indicate the seriousness with which the conventional imbalances which we have long highlighted as a key problem of European security are now also addressed by the Soviet government. We also welcome the declared readiness of the Soviet Union to adjust their force posture. The important thing is now to build on these hopeful developments at the negotiating table in order to correct the large asymmetries that will still remain and to secure a balance at lower levels of forces. For this, it will be necessary to deal with the location, nationality and the state of readiness of forces, as well as their numbers. Our proposals will address these issues in the following specific ways:

—We shall propose an overall limit on the total holdings of armaments in Europe. This limit should be substantially lower than existing levels, in the case of tanks close to a half. This would mean an overall limit of about 40,000 tanks.

—In our concept of stability, no country should be able to dominate the continent by force of arms. We shall therefore also propose that no country should be entitled to possess more than a fixed proportion, such as 30 percent, of the total holdings in Europe of the 23 participants in each equipment category. In the case of tanks, this would result in an entitlement of no more than about 12,000 tanks for any one country.

—Our proposal will apply to the whole of Europe. In order to avoid undue concentration of these weapon categories in certain areas of Europe, we shall propose appropriate sub-limits.

To buttress the resulting reductions in force levels in the whole of Europe, we shall propose stabilizing measures. These could include measures of transparency, notifications and constraint applied to the deployment, movement, and levels of readiness of conventional armed forces, which include conventional armaments and equipment.

Finally, we shall require a rigorous and reliable regime for monitoring and verification. This would include the periodic exchange of detailed data about forces and deployments, and the right to conduct on-site inspections.

TOWARDS TRANSPARENCY

Greater transparency is an essential requirement for real stability. Therefore, within the framework of the C.S.C.E. process, the negotiations on confidence- and security-building measures form an essential complement to those on conventional stability. We are encouraged thus far by the successful implementation of the Stockholm Document and we consider that the momentum must be maintained.

In order to create transparency of military organization, we plan to introduce a proposal for a wide-ranging, comprehensive annual exchange of information concerning military organization, manpower and equipment as well as major weapon deployment programmes. To evaluate this information we will propose modalities for the establishment of a random evaluation system.

In addition, in order to build on the success of the Stockholm Document and to create greater transparency of military activities, we will propose measures in areas such as:

—more detailed information with regard to the notification of military exercises,
—improvements in the arrangements for observing military activities,
—greater openness and predictability about military activities,
—a strengthening of the regime for ensuring compliance and verification.

Finally, we shall propose additional measures designed to improve contacts and communications between participating states in the military field; to enhance access for military staffs and media representatives; and to increase mutual understanding of military capabilities, behavior and force postures. We will also propose modalities for an organized exchange of views on military doctrine tied to actual force structures, capabilities and dispositions in Europe.

A VISION FOR EUROPE

We will pursue these distinct negotiations within the framework of the C.S.C.E. process, because we believe that a secure peace cannot be achieved without steady progress on all aspects of the confrontation which has divided Europe for more than four decades. Moreover, redressing the disparity in conventional forces in Europe would remove an obstacle to the achievement of the better political relationship between all states of Europe to which we aspire. Conventional arms control must therefore be seen as part of a dynamic process which addresses the military, political, and human aspects of this division.

The implementation of our present proposals and of those we are making for further CSBMs will involve a quantum improvement in European security. We will wish to agree and implement them as soon as possible. In the light of their implementation we would then be willing to contemplate further steps to enhance stability and security in Europe, for example:
—further reductions or limitations of conventional armaments and equipment,
—the restructuring of armed forces to enhance defensive capabilities and further reduce offensive capabilities.
Our vision remains that of a continent where military forces only exist to prevent war and to ensure self-defense, not for the purpose of initiating aggression or for political or military intimidation.

Source: "Statement issued by the North Atlantic Council Meeting in Ministerial session at NATO Headquarters, Brussels, December 8–9, 1988," Press Communiqué-Conventional Arms Control, Federal Information Systems Corporation.

*   *   *

C.F.E.: WESTERN POSITION PAPER
MARCH 1989

NEGOTIATION ON CONVENTIONAL ARMED FORCES IN EUROPE

Position paper provided by the delegations of Belgium, Canada, Denmark, Federal Republic of Germany, France, Greece, Iceland, Italy, Luxembourg, Netherlands, Norway, Portugal, Spain, Turkey, United Kingdom and United States.

OBJECTIVES

The objectives of these negotiations, as agreed in the mandate, are:
—The establishment of a secure and stable balance of conventional forces at lower levels;
—The elimination of disparities prejudicial to stability and security;
—The elimination, as a matter of high priority, of the capability for launching surprise attack and for initiating large-scale offensive action.

Through the approach outlined below the Western delegations will seek to establish a situation in which surprise attack and large-scale, offensive action are no longer credible options. We pursue this aim on the basis of equal respect for the security interests of all. Our approach offers a coherent whole and is intended to be applied simultaneously and in its totality in the area of application.

RATIONALE

The rationale for our approach is as follows:
—The present concentration of forces in the area from the Atlantic-to-Urals (ATTU) is the highest ever known in peacetime and represents the greatest destructive potential ever assembled. Overall levels of forces, particularly those relevant to surprise attack and offensive action such as tanks, artillery and armored troop carriers, must therefore be radically reduced. It is the substantial disparity in the numbers of these systems, all capable of rapid mobility and high firepower, which most threatens stability in Europe. These systems are also central to the seizing and holding of territory, the prime aim of any aggressor.
—No one country should be permitted to dominate Europe by force of arms: No participants should therefore possess more than a fixed proportion of the total holdings of all participants in each category of armaments, commensurate with its needs for self-defense.
—Addressing the overall number and nationality of forces will not by itself affect the stationing of armaments outside national borders: additional limits will also be needed on forces stationed in other countries' territory.
—We need to focus on both the levels of armaments and state of readiness of forces in those areas where the concentration of such forces is greatest, as well as to prevent redeployment of forces withdrawn from one part of the area of application to another. It will therefore be necessary to apply a series of interlocking sub-limits covering forces throughout the area, together with further limits on armaments in active units.

SPECIFIC MEASURES

The following specific weapons in each of the three categories identified below will at no time exceed:

Rule 1: Overall limit

> The overall total of weapons in each of the three categories identified below will at no time exceed:
> —Main Battle Tanks   40,000

—Artillery Pieces	33,000
—Armored Troop Carriers	56,000

Rule 2: Sufficiency

No one country may retain more than 30 percent of the overall limits in these three categories, i.e.

—Main Battle Tanks	12,000
—Artillery Pieces	10,000
—Armored Troop Carriers	16,800

Rule 3: Stationed Forces

Among countries belonging to a treaty of alliance neither side will station armaments outside national territory in active units exceeding the following levels:

—Main Battle Tanks	3,200
—Artillery Pieces	1,700
—Armored Troop Carriers	6,000

Rule 4: Sub-limits

In the area indicated below, each group of countries belonging to the same treaty of alliance shall not exceed the following levels:

1. In the area consisting of Belgium, Denmark, The Federal Republic of Germany, France, Greece, Iceland, Italy, Luxembourg, The Netherlands, Norway, Portugal, Spain, Turkey, The United Kingdom, Bulgaria, Czechoslovakia, The German Democratic Republic, Hungary, Poland, Romania and the territory of the Soviet Union west of the Urals comprising the Baltic, Byelorussian, Carpathian, Moscow, Volga, Urals, Leningrad, Odessa, Kiev, Trans-Caucasus, North Caucasus military districts:

—Main Battle Tanks	20,000
—Artillery Pieces	16,500
—Armored Troop Carriers	28,000 (of which no more than 12,000 AIFVs)

2. In the area consisting of Belgium, Denmark, the Federal Republic of Germany, France, Italy, Luxembourg, The Netherlands, Portugal, Spain, The United Kingdom, Czechoslovakia, The German Democratic Republic, Hungary, Poland and the territory of the Soviet Union west of the Urals comprising the Baltic, Byelorussian, Carpathian, Moscow, Volga, Urals military districts in active units:

—Main Battle Tanks	11,300
—Artillery	9,000
—Armored Troop Carriers	20,000

3. In the area consisting of Belgium, Denmark, The Federal Republic of Germany, France, Italy, Luxembourg, The Netherlands, The United Kingdom, Czechoslovakia, The German Democratic Republic, Hungary, Poland and the territory of the Soviet Union comprising the Baltic, Byelorussian, Carpathian military districts in active units:

-Main Battle Tanks 10,300
-Artillery 7,600
-Armored Troop Carriers 18,000

4. In the area consisting of Belgium, The Federal Republic of Germany, Luxembourg, The Netherlands, Czechoslovakia, The German Democratic Republic, and Poland in active units:
-Main Battle Tanks 8,000
-Artillery 4,500
-Armored Troop Carriers 11,000

5. Rule 4 is to be seen as an integrated whole which will only be applied simultaneously and across the entire area from the Atlantic-to-the-Urals. It will be for the members of each alliance to decide how they exercise their entitlement under all of these measures.

Rule 5: Information Exchange

Each year holdings of main battle tanks, armored troop carriers and artillery pieces will be notified, disaggregated down to battalion level. This measure will also apply to personnel in both combat and combat support units. Any change or notified unit structures above battalion level, or any measure resulting in an increase of personnel strength in such units, will be subject to notification, on a basis to be determined in the course of the negotiations.

MEASURES FOR STABILITY, VERIFICATION AND NON-CIRCUMVENTION

As an integral part of the agreement, there will be a need for:
-Stabilizing measures:
To buttress the resulting reductions in force levels in the ATTU area. These should include measures of transparency, notification and constraint applied to the deployment, movement, storage and levels of readiness of conventional armed forces which include conventional armaments and equipment.
-Verification arrangements:
To include the exchange of detailed data about forces and deployments, with the right to conduct on-site inspection, as well as other measures designed to provide assurance of compliance with the agreed provisions.
-Non-Circumvention provisions:
Inter alia, to ensure that the manpower and equipment withdrawn from any one area do not have adverse security implications for any participant.
-Provisions for temporarily exceeding the limits set down in rule 4 for prenotified exercises.

The Longer Term

In the longer term, and in the light of the implementation of the above measure, we would be willing to contemplate further steps to enhance stability and security in Europe, such as:
-Further reductions or limitations of conventional armaments and equipment.
-The restructuring of armed forces to enhance defensive capabilities and further to reduce offensive capabilities.

* * *

TEXT OF THE NATO PROPOSAL FOR C.D.E.-2 AS TABLED AT THE
VIENNA NEGOTIATIONS ON CONFIDENCE- AND
SECURITY-BUILDING MEASURES ON MARCH 9, 1989

The Delegations of Belgium, Canada, Denmark, France, the Federal Republic
of Germany, Greece, Iceland, Italy, Luxembourg, the Netherlands, Norway,
Portugal, Spain, Turkey, the United Kingdom, and the United States of
America:
—Recalling that the adoption of the Stockholm Document in September 1986
 was a politically significant achievement and that its measures are an
 important step in efforts aimed at reducing the risk of military confrontation
 in Europe,
—Encouraged by the satisfactory implementation of these measures thus far,
—Determined to build upon and expand the results achieved at the Stockholm
 Conference and to carry forward the dynamic process of confidence building,
—Stressing the complementary nature within the framework of the C.S.C.E.
 process of negotiations on further confidence- and security-building
 measures and negotiations on conventional armed forces in Europe,
—Determined
  —to create greater transparency about military organization;
  —to create greater transparency and predictability about military activities;
  —to improve contacts and communications between the participating states;
  —and determined, in the forthcoming negotiations, to promote an exchange
   of views on military policy,
—In conformity with the Madrid Mandate of 1983 as confirmed by the
 C.S.C.E. Review Meeting in Vienna 1989, propose confidence- and security-
 building measures including the following:

I. Transparency about Military Organization

These measures are designed to create more openness and confidence about the
military force disposition of each participating state. This will be achieved by
regular exchanges of information on forces on land in the zone and on major
weapon deployment programmes. The information exchanged will be subject
to evaluation.

Measure 1: Exchange of Military Information
Participating states will exchange information concerning military organization, manpower and equipment in the zone. This will include annual information on:
—land forces command organization in the zone;
—the designation of major ground units, down to below divisional level;
—the normal peacetime locations of these units;
—the personnel strength of these units;
—the major weapons systems and equipment belonging to these units;
—land-based air units and their aircraft strength.
  It will also include immediate notification of:
—the relocation in the zone of major ground units as specified above from one
 normal peacetime location to another;
—the calling up of a significant number of reservists.

Measure 2: Information Exchange on Major Conventional Weapon Deployment Programmes
Each participating state will inform the others of those major conventional weapons systems and equipment specified in Measure 1 which it intends to introduce into service with its armed forces in the C.D.E. zone in a specified period.

Measure 3: Establishment of a Random Evaluation System
In order to evaluate the information provided under Measures 1 and 2, participating states will establish a random evaluation system in which:
—they will have the right to conduct a number of pre-announced visits to normal peacetime locations specified under Measure 1;
—these visits, of a limited duration, will be carried out by personnel already accredited to the host state or designated by the visiting state;
—evaluators will be allowed to observe major weapons systems and equipment;
—appropriate arrangements for the evaluation visit will be made by the host state, whose representatives will accompany the evaluation teams at all times.

II. Transparency and Predictability of Military Activities

These measures will build upon those agreed in Stockholm by refining them in order to enhance openness and produce greater predictability of military activities.

Measure 4: Enhance Information in the Annual Calendar
Participating states will provide in their annual calendars more information, and in greater detail, about future military activities. This will include the designation, number and type of ground units down to divisional level scheduled to take part in notifiable military activities in the zone.

Measure 5: Enhance Information in Notification
To improve the notification concerning military activities, participating states will communicate more information, and in greater detail, about the engagement of their armed forces as well as their weapons systems and equipment in such ground force activities.

Measure 6: Improvements to Observation Modalities
Participating states will facilitate observation by organizing more detailed briefings, providing better maps and allowing more observation equipment to be used. Furthermore, in order to improve the observers' opportunities to assess the scope and scale of the activity, the participating states are encouraged to provide an aerial survey of the area of the activity. Moreover, the duration of the observation programme will be improved.

Measure 7: Lowering of the Observation Threshold
Participating states will invite observers to notified activities whenever the number of troops engaged meets or exceeds 13,000 or if more than 300 tanks participate in it.

Measure 8: Improvements to Inspection Modalities
Participating states will adopt measures for a substantial improvement of the inspection which include:

—increasing the number of passive inspections;
—shortening the period between the inspection request and access of the
    inspectors to the specified area;
—permitting, on request by inspectors, an aerial survey before the commence-
    ment of the inspection;
—improving the equipment and communications facilities that the inspection
    team will be permitted to use;
—improving the briefings to inspectors.

Measure 9: Lowering the Thresholds for Longer Notice of Larger Scale
Activities
Participating states will not carry out military activities subject to prior
notification involving more than 50,000 troops unless they have been the object
of communication stipulated in the Stockholm Document.

III.   Contacts and Communication

These measures are designed to increase the knowledge about the military
capabilities of the participating states by developing communications and
military contacts.

Measure 10:   Improved Access for Accredited Personnel Dealing With Military Matters
In order to implement the principle of greater openness in military matters and
to enhance mutual confidence, the participating states will facilitate the travel
arrangements of accredited personnel dealing with military matters and assist
them in obtaining access to government officials. Restrictions on the activities
of accredited personnel in the C.D.E. zone should be reduced.

Measure 11: Development of Means of Communication
Participating states, while using diplomatic channels for transmitting communications related to agreed measures (calendars, notifications, etc.) are encouraged to consider additional arrangements to ensure the speediest possible
exchange of information.

Measure 12: Equal Treatment of Media Representatives
Participating states will be encouraged to permit media representatives to
attend observed military activities; if media representatives are invited, the host
state will admit such representatives from all participating states and treat them
without discrimination.

IV.   Exchanges of Views on Military Policy

Confidence-building is a dynamic process which is enhanced by the free and
frank interchange of ideas designed to reduce misunderstandings and misrep-
resentation of military capabilities. To this end, participating states will, in the
forthcoming negotiations, avail themselves of the following opportunities:
—to discuss issues concerning the implementation of the provisions of the
    Stockholm Document;
—to discuss, in a seminar setting, military doctrine in relation to the posture
    and structure of conventional forces in the zone, including inter alia:

—exchanging information on their annual military spending;
—exchanging information on the training of their armed forces, including references to military manuals;
—seeking clarification of developments giving rise to uncertainty, such as changes in the number and pattern of notified military activities.

Appendix IX: Reductions Under the NATO and Warsaw Pact Proposals of 1989

A. NATO's Reduction Proposal Using NATO's Data[a]

	Main Battle Tanks	Armored Personnel Carriers	Artillery/ Multiple Rocket Launchers
NATO Holdings	22,224	47,639	17,328
Reductions	2,224	19,639	828
Proposed NATO/WTO Level[b]	20,000	28,000	16,500
WTO Holdings	39,249[c]	93,400	33,370[c]
Reductions	19,249	65,400	16,870

[a] Data from NATO's *Conventional Forces in Europe: The Facts*, November 1988.

[b] NATO's proposal outlines an overall holdings level for these armaments, and NATO and the Warsaw Pact must reduce to meet these levels.

[c] Announced WTO unilateral reductions totaling 12,251 main battle tanks, and 10,030 artillery pieces have been subtracted from these totals.

B. Warsaw Pact's 10% Reduction Proposal Using WTO Data[a]

	Main Battle Tanks	Armored Personnel Carriers	Artillery/Multiple Rocket Launchers	Armed Helicopters	Combat Aircraft	Armed Forces Personnel
NATO Holdings	30,690	46,900	57,060	5,270	7,130	3,660,200
Reductions	3,069[b]	4,690[b]	5,706[b]	2,764	951	733,580
Proposed NATO/WTO Level	27,621	42,210	51,354	2,506	6,179	2,926,620
WTO Holdings	47,219[c]	70,330	61,530[c]	2,785	6,866[c]	3,251,800[c]
Reductions	19,598	28,120	10,176	279[b]	687[b]	325,180[b]

[a] Data from "Warsaw Pact Releases Figures on Force Strengths," *Foreign Broadcast Information Service: Soviet Union,* January 10, 1989, pp. 1–8.

[b] Indicates a 10% reduction for the side possessing the smaller number of holdings in each of the categories as outlined by the WTO reduction proposal.

[c] Announced WTO unilateral reductions totaling 12,251 main battle tanks, 10,030 artilery pieces, 1,010 combat aircraft, and 321,300 personnel have been subtracted from these totals.

C. NATO and Warsaw Pact First-Stage Reduction Proposals Using the International Institute of Strategic Studies Data[a]
1. NATO's Proposal

	Main Battle Tanks	Armored Personnel Carriers[b]	Artillery/ Multiple Rocket Launchers
NATO Holdings	22,200	47,639	13,500
Reductions	2,200	19,639	—
Proposed NATO/WTO Level[c]	20,000	28,000	16,500
WTO Holdings	40,749[d]	93,400	34,270[d]
Reductions	20,749	65,400	17,770

[a] Data from the International Institute of Strategic Studies, *The Military Balance, 1988–1989*, London: IISS, 1988. (See Appendix II.)

[b] The working definition for Armored Personnel Carriers is different in interpretation by NATO and IISS. Therefore, the figure given is in compliance to NATO's definition and is used from NATO's *Conventional Forces in Europe: The Facts*, November, 1988.

[c] NATO's proposal outlines an overall holdings level for these armaments, and NATO and the Warsaw Pact must reduce to meet these levels.

[d] Announced WTO unilateral reductions of a total of 12,251 main battle tanks and 10,030 artillery pieces have been subtracted from these totals.

2. Warsaw Pact 10% Reduction Proposal[a]

	Main Battle Tanks	Armored Personnel Carriers[b]	Artillery/ Multiple Rocket Launchers	Armed Helicopters	Combat Aircraft	Armed Forces Personnel
NATO Holdings	22,200	46,900	13,500	864	3,215	2,340,000
Reductions	2,220[c]	4,690[c]	1,350[c]	86[c]	1,228	700,470
Proposed NATO/WTO Level	19,980	42,210	12,150	778	1,987	1,639,530
WTO Holdings	40,749[d]	93,400[b]	34,270[d]	1,220	2,208[d]	1,821,700[d]
Reductions	20,769	51,190	22,120	442	221[c]	182,170[d]

[a] Data from International Institute of Strategic Studies, *The Military Balance, 1988–1989*, London: IISS, 1988. (See Appendix II.)

[b] The working definition for Armored Personnel Carriers is different in interpretation by WTO and IISS. Therefore, the figure given is from NATO's *Conventional Forces in Europe: The Facts*, November, 1988.

[c] Indicates a 10% reduction for the side possessing the smaller number of holdings in each of the categories as outlined by the WTO reduction proposal.

[d] Announced WTO unilateral reduction of a total of 12,251 main battle tanks, 10,030 artillery pieces, 1,010 combat aircraft, and 321,300 personnel have been subtracted from these figures.

396

D. WTO May 1989 Reduction Proposal Compared to NATO's March and May 1989 Proposals

1. NATO and WTO Proposals for Overall Alliance Holdings of Reducible Armaments

a. Overall Units Proposed by NATO[a]

	Main Battle Tanks	Armored Personnel Carriers	Artillery/Multiple Rocket Launchers	Armed Helicopters[d]	Strike Aircraft[d]	Armed Forces Personnel[c]
NATO Holdings[b]	22,224	47,639	17,328	2,185	6,600	305,000
Reductions	2,224	19,639	828	285 (15%)	900 (15%)	30,000
Proposed NATO/WTO Level	20,000	28,000	16,500	1,900	5,700	275,000
WTO Holdings[b]	51,500	93,400	43,400	3,100	13,950	625,000
Reductions	31,500	65,400	26,900	1,200	8,250	350,000

[a] Appendix VIII provides the Western Position paper for the C.F.E. talks where NATO outlines overall alliance limits in three armament categories. (See Appendix VIII: Rule 4, 2.) In May, 1989, President Bush proposed including armed helicopters, strike aircraft and armed forces personnel in the C.F.E. talks, and they are added here.

[b] Data from NATO's *Conventional Forces in Europe: The Facts*, November, 1988.

[c] The Armed Forces Figures are those of the United States and Soviet Forces in Europe.

[d] Estimates; official figures not released.

b. *Overall Limits Proposed by the WTO*[a]

	Main Battle Tanks	Armored Personnel Carriers	Artillery/Multiple Rocket Launchers	Armed Helicopters	Strike Aircraft	Armed Forces Personnel
NATO Holdings[b] Reductions	30,690 10,690	46,900 18,900	57,060 33,060	5,270 3,570	4,075 2,575	3,660,200 2,310,200
Proposed NATO/WTO Level	20,000	28,000	24,000	1,700	1,500	1,350,000
WTO Holdings[b] Reductions	59,470 39,470	70,330 42,330	71,560 47,560	2,785 1,085	2,783 1,283	3,573,100 2,223,100

[a] Appendix VIII provides the Western Position paper for the C.F.E. talks where NATO outlines limits in three armament categories. In May, 1989, the Soviet Union proposed figures for these levels that parallel the NATO levels.

[b] Data from "Warsaw Pact Releases Figures on Force Strengths," *Foreign Broadcast Information Service: Soviet Union,* January 10, 1989, pp. 1–8.

2. Sufficiency Level Proposed by the WTO[a]

	Main Battle Tanks	Armored Personnel Carriers[b]	Artillery/ Multiple Rocket Launchers[b]	Armed Helicopters	Combat Aircraft	Armed Forces Personnel
Soviet Holdings[b]	41,580	45,000	50,275	2,200	5,955	2,458,000
Announced Unilateral Soviet Cuts	10,000	—	8,500	—	800	240,000
Remaining Holdings	31,580	45,000	41,775	2,200	5,155	2,218,000
Proposed Further Soviet Reductions[c]	17,580	27,000	24,775	850	3,955	1,298,000
New Soviet Holdings Level	14,000	18,000	17,000	1,350	1,200	920,000
Proposed NATO Sufficiency Level[a]	12,000	16,800	10,000	—	—	—

[a] NATO's March, 1989, Position Paper (see Appendix VIII) proposes in Rule 2 a "sufficiency" level according to which no one country would possess more than 30 percent of the overall limit totaling the holdings of both alliances in the three categories. The overall limit was established at 40,000 for Main Battle Tanks, 33,000 for Artillery Pieces, and 56,000 for Armored Troop Carriers. In May, 1989, the Soviet Union accepted this idea in principle, but advanced somewhat different numbers for it, including numbers for helicopters, combat aircraft, and military personnel.

[b] Figures from "Warsaw Pact Releases Figures on Force Strengths," *Foreign Broadcast Information Service: Soviet Union,* January 10, 1989, pp. 1–8.

[c] Gorbachev in May, 1989, proposed further reductions at these levels. *Washington Post,* May 24, 1989.

3. Limits on NATO and the WTO Armaments Stationed Outside National Territory

	Main Battle Tanks	Artillery Pieces	Armored Troop Carriers
NATO Limits[a]	3,200	1,700	6,000
WTO Limits[b]	4,500	4,000	7,500

[a] Appendix VIII Rule 3 outlines the NATO stationed forces limits of armaments in active units.

[b] The WTO has in principle accepted these limits on stationed forces. *Washington Post*, May 25 and 28, 1989.

Sub-limits by Geographic Zone

NATO Position
Maximum number of armaments in active units for each alliance in each of three zones in limited to:

Zone 1
West: Belgium, FRG, Luxembourg, Netherlands
East: Czechoslovakia, GDR, Poland

  8,000 main battle tanks
  4,500 artillery pieces
11,000 armored troop carriers

Zone 2
West: Belgium, Denmark, FRG, France, Italy, Luxembourg, Netherlands, and Great Britain
East: Czechoslovakia, GDR, Hungary, Poland, Baltic-, Belorussian-, Carpathian Military Districts

10,000 main battle tanks
  7,600 artillary pieces
18,000 armored troop carriers

Warsaw Pact Position
Maximum number of armaments (including stored arms) for each alliance in each of three zones is limited to:

Central Zone
West: Belgium, FRG, Luxembourg, Denmark
East: Czechoslovakia, GDR, Hungary, Poland
  8,700 tanks
  7,600 artillery pieces
14,500 armored troop carriers
     420 strike aircraft
570,000 troops

Forward Zone
West: Belgium, Denmark, FRG, Italy, Luxembourg, Greece, Turkey and Norway
East: Czechoslovakia, GDR, Hungary, Poland, Romania, Bulgaria, Odessa-, North and Trans Caucasus-, Lenin-, Baltic Military Districts

Zone 3
West: Belgium, Denmark, FRG,
   France, Italy, Luxembourg,
   Netherlands, Portugal, Spain,
   Great Britain
East: Czechoslovakia, GDR,
   Hungary, Poland Baltic-,
   Belorussian-, Carpathian-,
   Moscow, Volga-, Ural Military
   Districts

11,300 main battle tanks
 9,000 artillery pieces
20,000 armored troop carriers

16,000 tanks
16,500 artillery pieces
20,500 armored troop carriers
 1,100 strike aircraft
 1,300 combat helicopters
 1 million troops

Rear Zone
West: Belgium, Denmark, FRG,
   France, Italy, Luxembourg,
   Netherland, Portugal, Spain,
   Great Britain, Greece, Turkey,
   and Iceland
East: Czechoslovakia, GDR,
   Hungary, Poland, Romania,
   Bulgaria, Odessa-, North & Trans
   Caucasus-, Lenin-, Baltic-,
   Belorussian-, Carpathian-, Kiev-,
   Moscow-, Volga-, Urals Military
   Districts
 4,000 tanks
 7,500 artillery pieces
 7,500 armored troop carriers
   400 strike aircraft
   400 combat helicopters
350,000 troops

Warsaw Pack Position on Alternative Zones
Tabled in June, 1989

Central Zone
West: Belgium, Denmark, FRG, France, Luxembourg, Netherlands, and great
   Britain
East: Czechoslovakia, GDR, Hungary, Poland, Baltic-, Belorussian-, Carpath-
   ian Military Districts

13,300 tanks; 11,500 artillery pieces; 20,750 armored troop carriers; 1,120 strike
aircraft; 1,250 combat helicopters; 910,000 troops

North Zone
West: Norway
East: North half of Leningrad Military District

200 tanks; 1,000 artillery pieces; 150 armored troop carriers; 30 strike aircraft;
30 combat helicopters; 20,000 troops

South Zone
West: Italy, Greece, and Turkey
East: Romania, Bulgaria plus Odessa, Trans- and North Caucasus Military
  Districts

5,200 tanks; 8,500 artillery pieces; 5,750 armored troop carriers; 290 strike
  aircraft; 360 combat helicopters; 270,000 troops

Rear Zone
West: Spain, Portugal, and Iceland
East: South half of Leningrad Military District plus Moscow, Volga, and Ural
  Military Districts

1,300 tanks; 3,000 artillery pieces; 1,350 armored troop carriers; 60 strike
  aircraft; 60 combat helicopters; 150,000 troops

Source: Arms Control Association.

Appendix X: NATO and Warsaw Pact Reductions Proposed in This Book

I. NATO and Warsaw Pact Ground Force Reduction Proposal
   A. Comprehensive 20% Build Down Reduction Proposal for Central Europe Extended (including armaments held by reserve units and in storage).
      1. NATO Forces in Central Europe Extended
      2. WTO Forces in Central Europe Extended
   B. Alternate 20% Build Down Reduction Proposal for Central Europe Extended (excluding armaments held by reserve units and in storage).
      1. NATO Forces in Central Europe Extended
      2. WTO Forces in Central Europe Extended
   C. NATO and Warsaw Pact 50% Build Down Reduction Proposal for the Atlantic to Urals Area (including armaments held by reserve units and in storage).
      1. NATO Forces in the ATTU area
      2. WTO Forces in the ATTU area

II. NATO and Warsaw Pact Air Force Reduction Proposal
   A. NATO and WTO 20% Build Down Reduction Proposal for Central Europe Extended.
      1. NATO Air Forces in Central Europe Extended
      2. WTO Air Forces in Central Europe Extended
   B. NATO and WTO 50% Reduction Proposal for the Atlantic to Urals Area.
      1. NATO Air Forces in the ATTU Area
      2. WTO Air Forces in the ATTU Area

I. NATO and Warsaw Pact Ground Force Reduction Proposal

A. Comprehensive 20% Build-Down Reduction Proposal for Central Europe Extended (including armaments held by reserve units and in storage)

1. NATO Forces in Central Europe Extended[a]

	Main Battle Tanks	Armored Personnel Carriers[b]	Artillery/Multiple Rocket Launchers	Armed Helicopters[c]	Surface-to-Surface Missiles[d]	Personnel Ground	Air
Belgium	334	1,267	256	0		65,100	18,700
Canada	77	191	26	32		4,400	2,700
Denmark	210	641	450	14		17,000	6,900
France	1,340	3,010	1,406	215	100[d]	280,900	95,000
FRG	4,937	3,636	2,344	210		332,100	108,700
Luxembourg	0	5	0	0		800	0
Netherlands	913	1,995	789	0		66,000	18,100
UK	700	1,792	228	48		69,700	0
US	6,151	4,268	1,100	234	600	206,790	44,500
Total	14,662	16,805	6,599	753	700	1,042,790	294,600
Minus 20%	2,932	3,361	1,320	200[e]	140	208,558	58,920
New Joint NATO/WTO Level	11,730	13,444	5,279	553	560	834,232	235,680

2. WTO Forces in Central Europe Extended

		Main Battle Tanks	Armored Personnel Carriers	Artillery/ Multiple Rocket Launchers	Armed Helicopters[c]	Surface- to- Surface Missiles	Personnel Ground	Air
Czechoslovakia		3,400[h]	2,500	2,391	45		145,000	52,000
Cat.	I	1,141	893	558			53,760	
	II	927	336	396			37,520	
	III	927	336	396			37,520	
GDR		2,850[h]	3,750	1,657	100		120,000	37,000
Cat.	I	1,740	1,206	728			79,520	
	II	0	0	0			0	
	III	0	0	0			0	
Hungary		1,300[h]	1,000	635	40		77,000	22,000
Cat.	I	0	0	0			0	
	II	1,452	996	689			66,192	
	III	0	0	0			0	
Poland		3,950[h]	2,700	2,385	30		230,000	92,000
Cat.	I	2,453	985	1,062			100,800	
	II	0	0	0			0	
	III	1,355	1,450	720			70,000	
USSR		20,398[h]	9,034	15,440	476	6,000	1,029,920	172,500[f]
Cat	I	10,030	4,741	4,302			422,920	
	II	3,840	2,242	2,070			198,800	
	III	5,148	2,051	2,394			227,360	
Total		31,898	18,984	22,508	691	6,000	1,601,920	375,500
WTO Unilateral Reductions[g]		7,551	895	5,530	—	—	80,533	40,767
Remaining Total		24,347	18,089	16,978	691	6,000	1,521,387	334,733
WTO Reductions		12,617	4,645	11,699	138	5,440	687,155	99,053
New Joint NATO/WTO Level		11,730	13,444	5,279	553[e]	560	834,232	235,680

406

Notes for Table A:

ᵃ NATO figures are for holdings of active duty units and include stored NATO tanks, which NATO's *Conventional Forces in Europe: The Facts* of November, 1988, estimates at 5,800. This storage figure includes 2,887 U.S. war reserve and 1,464 U.S. prepositioned POMCUS tanks. Also, NATO figures include 409 APCs and 165 artillery pieces in storage.

ᵇ This figure is illustrative. NATO is using a new category for reductions which appears to combine armored infantry fighting vehicles and armored personnel carriers. NATO has not yet made available specific figures for this new category.

ᶜ For NATO the following types of helicopters were counted: SA-330 Puma, SA-341/-342 Gazelle, UH-1 Iroquois, AH-1 Cobra/Sea Cobra, AB Bell 205, Hughes 500 m, PAH-1 Bo-159P, CH-124 SH-3, H-53 Stallion, HA-15 Bo105, and CH-47 Chinook. For the WTO the following were counted: Mi-24 Hind, Mi-14 Haze, Mi-8 Hip, Mi-6 Hook, Mi-2 Hoplite, Mi-1Hare, Ka-25 Hormone, and Ka-27 Helix.

ᵈ Surface-to-surface missiles are listed here in terms of missiles instead of launchers. It is estimated that NATO has about 700 missiles for its 127 launchers including French missiles. We include French missiles in the NATO total, but also recommend that they should be excluded from actual reductions. The total of Pact missiles is estimated at 6,000.

ᵉ Throughout this book, we follow a standard approach reducing from the level of the numerically smaller side. In this case, 20% is reduced from the totals of the smaller side (WTO), and NATO must reduce 200 helicopters to meet the new WTO level.

ᶠ The International Institute for Strategic Studies specifies the given Soviet Air Force personnel figure of 315,000 for the four Groups of Soviet Forces (in the GDR, Czechoslovakia, Hungary, and Poland), and the sixteen military districts of the USSR. Here we assume half of the total or 157,500 is deployed in Central Europe Extended.

ᵍ In his speech to the U.N. on 12/7/88, Gorbachev announced a unilateral reduction of 10,000 tanks, 8,400 artillery pieces from Soviet forces west of the Urals including those in Eastern Europe. For the purposes of this estimate of unilateral cuts in Soviet forces in Eastern Europe we have deducted half of the armament totals. Gorbachev also announced a cut of 50,000 in Soviet personnel in Eastern Europe. He did not specify the breakdown totals of ground, air, and naval personnel within the 50,000 figure. Therefore, we assume that at least two-thirds or 33,000 of the 50,000 to be reduced are ground force personnel. We subtract the other one-third from the Air Force total with a caveat that some naval personnel may have been included in the 50,000 total. We have deducted the unilateral reductions listed in Appendix V from national totals.

ʰ The total of main battle tanks, armored personnel carriers, artillery, and ground personnel for Category I, II & III Warsaw Pact units is somewhat less than the total aggregate figures shown for each of these armaments in the chart. This mismatch, which we are pursuing, probably has several causes. There may be some allowance in IISS figures for training units, repair and storage.

B. Alternate 20% Build-Down Reduction Proposal for Central Europe Extended (excluding armaments held by reserve units and in storage)

1. NATO Forces in Central Europe Extended[a]

	Main Battle Tanks	Armored Personnel Carriers[b]	Artillery/Multiple Rocket Launchers	Armed Helicopters[c]	Surface-to-Surface Missiles[d]	Personnel Ground	Personnel Air
Belgium	320	1,058	248	0		65,100	18,700
Canada	77	191	26	0		4,400	2,700
Denmark	210	641	450	14		17,000	6,900
France	1,340	3,010	1,266	215		280,900	95,000
FRG	4,937	3,636	2,344	210	100[d]	332,100	108,700
Luxembourg	0	5	0	0		800	0
Netherlands	750	1,795	772	0		66,000	18,100
UK	700	1,792	228	48		69,700	0
US	1,800	4,268	1,100	234	600	206,790	44,500
Total	10,134	16,396	6,434	721	700	1,042,790	294,600
Minus 20%	2,027	7,277[e]	1,950[e]	168[e]	140	301,580[e]	58,920
New Joint NATO/WTO Level	8,107	9,119	4,484	553	560	741,210	235,680

2. WTO Forces in Central Europe Extended

	Main Battle Tanks	Armored Personnel Carriers	Artillery/Multiple Rocket Launchers[c]	Armed Helicopters[c]	Surface-to-Surface Missiles	Personnel Ground	Personnel Air
Czechoslovakia Cat.	3,400[h]	2,500	2,391	45		145,000	52,000
I	1,141	893	558			53,760	
II	927	336	396			37,520	
III	927	336	396			37,520	
GDR Cat.	2,850[h]	3,750	1,657	100		120,000	37,000
I	1,740	1,206	728			79,520	
II	0	0	0			0	
III	0	0	0			0	
Hungary Cat.	1,300[h]	1,000	635	40		77,000	22,000
I	0	0	0			0	
II	1,452	996	689			66,192	
III	0	0	0			0	
Poland Cat.	3,950[h]	2,700	2,385	30		230,000	92,000
I	2,453	985	1,062			100,800	
II	0	0	0			0	
III	1,355	1,450	720			70,000	
USSR Cat.	20,398[h]	9,034	15,440	476	6,000	1,029,920	172,500[f]
I	10,030	4,741	4,302			422,920	
II	3,840	2,242	2,070			198,800	
III	5,148	2,051	2,394			227,360	
Total Cat. I and II	31,898	18,984	22,508	691	6,000	1,601,920	375,500
	21,583	11,399	9,805	—	—	959,512	—
WTO unilateral reductions[g]	5,000	—	4,200	—	—	33,000	17,000
Remaining total	16,583	11,399	5,605	691	6,000	926,512	358,500
WTO reduction	8,476	2,280	1,121	138	5,440	185,302	122,820
New Joint NATO/WTO Level	8,107	9,119[e]	4,484[e]	553[e]	560	741,210[e]	235,680

Notes for Table B

[a] NATO figures are for holdings of active duty units and exclude stored NATO tanks, which NATO's *Conventional Forces in Europe: The Facts* of November, 1988, estimates at 5,800. This storage figure includes 2,887 U.S. war reserve and 1,464 U.S. prepositioned POMCUS tanks. Also, NATO figures do not include 409 APCs, 165 artillery pieces in storage.

[b] This figure is illustrative. NATO is using a new category for reductions which appears to combine armored infantry fighting vehicles and armored personnel carriers. NATO has not yet made available specific figures for this new category.

[c] For NATO the following types of helicopters were counted: SA-330 Puma, SA-341/-342 Gazelle, UH-1 Iroquois, AH-1 Cobra/Sea Cobra, AB Bell 205, Hughes 500m, PAH-1 Bo-159P, CH-124 SH-3, H-53 Stallion, HA-15 Bo105, and CH-47 Chinook. For the WTO the following were counted: Mi-24 Hind, Mi-14 Haze, Mi-8 Hip, Mi-6 Hook, Mi-2 Hoplite, Mi-1 Hare, Ka-25 Hormone, and Ka-27 Helix.

[d] Surface-to-surface missiles are listed here in terms of missiles instead of launchers. It is estimated that NATO has about 700 missiles for its 127 launchers including French missiles. We include French missiles in the NATO total, but also recommend that they should be excluded from actual reductions. The total of Pact missiles is estimated at 6,000.

[e] Throughout this book, we follow a standard approach reducing from the level of the numerically smaller side. In this case, 20% is reduced from the totals of the smaller side (WTO), and NATO must reduce 7,277 APC, 1,950 artillery pieces, 168 armed[?] helicopters, and 301,580 ground personnel to meet the new WTO level.

[f] The International Institute for Strategic Studies specifies a Soviet Air Force personnel figure of 315,000 for the four Groups of Soviet Forces (in the GDR, Czechoslovakia, Hungary, and Poland), and for the sixteen military districts of the USSR. Here we assume half of the total or 157,500 is concentrated in Central Europe Extended.

[g] In his speech to the U.N. on 12/7/88, Gorbachev announced a unilateral reduction of 10,000 tanks, 8,400 artillery pieces from Soviet forces West of the Urals including those in Eastern Europe. For the purposes of this estimate of unilateral cuts in Soviet forces in Eastern Europe we have deducted half of the armament totals. Gorbachev also announced a cut of 50,000 in Soviet personnel in Eastern Europe. He did not specify the breakdown totals of ground, air, and naval personnel within the 50,000 figure. Therefore, we assume that at least two-thirds or 33,000 of the 50,000 to be reduced are ground force personnel. We subtract the other one-third from the Air Force total with a caveat that some naval personnel may have been included in the 50,000 total. East European unilateral reductions are not subtracted from Category I, II & III units but only from National totals, since it is unclear from which type of units they will be reduced.

[h] The total of main battle tanks, armored personnel carriers, artillery, and ground personnel for Category I, II & III Warsaw Pact units is somewhat less than the total aggregate figures shown for each of these armaments in the chart. This mismatch, which we are pursuing, probably has several causes. There may be some allowance in IISS figures for training units, repair and storage.

C. NATO and Warsaw Pact 50% Build-Down Reduction Proposal for the Atlantic to Urals Area (including armaments held by reserve units and in storage)

1. NATO Forces in the ATTU area[a]

	Main Battle Tanks	Armored Personnel Carriers[b]	Artillery/ Multiple Rocket Launchers	Armed Helicopters[c]	Surface-to-Surface Missiles[d]	Personnel Ground	Personnel Air
Belgium	334	1,267	256	0		65,100	18,700
Canada	77	191	26	32		4,400	2,700
Denmark	210	641	450	14		17,000	6,900
France	1,340	3,010	1,406	215	100[d]	280,900	95,000
FRG	4,937	3,636	2,344	210		332,100	108,700
Greece	1,893	2,245	1,336	10		170,500	24,000
Italy	1,720	4,416	1,618	15		265,000	73,000
Luxembourg	0	5	0	0		800	0
Netherlands	913	1,995	789	0		66,000	18,100
Norway	122	150	405	0		19,000	9,100
Portugal	66	232	167	0		44,000	13,600
Spain	838	1,196	1,845	46		232,000	32,500
Turkey	3,607	3,300	2,115	0		522,900	57,400
UK	700	1,792	228	48		69,700	0
US	6,151	4,268	1,100	234	600	216,810	92,800
Total	22,908	28,344	14,085	824	700	2,306,210	552,500
Minus 50%	11,454	14,172	7,043	412	350	1,153,105	276,250[e]
New Joint NATO/ WTO Level	11,454	14,172	7,042	412	350	1,153,105	276,250

	Main Battle Tanks	Armored Personnel Carriers	Artillery/ Multiple Rocket Launchers	Armed Helicopters[c]	Surface-to-Surface Missiles	Personnel Ground	Air
Bulgaria	2,550[h]	1,035	1,890	40		115,000	34,000
Cat. I	542	580	288			28,000	
II	813	870	432			42,000	
III	813	870	432			42,000	
Czechoslovakia	3,400[h]	2,500	2,391	45		145,000	52,000
Cat. I	1,141	893	558			53,760	
II	927	336	396			37,520	
III	927	336	396			37,520	
GDR	2,850[h]	3,750	1,657	100		120,000	37,000
Cat. I	1,740	1,206	728			79,520	
II	0	0	0			0	
III	0	0	0			0	
Hungary	1,300[h]	1,000	635	40		77,000	22,000
Cat. I	0	0	0			0	
II	1,452	996	689			66,192	
III	0	0	0			0	
Poland	3,950[h]	2,700	2,385	30		230,000	92,000
Cat. I	2,453	985	1,062			100,800	
II	0	0	0			0	
III	1,355	1,450	720			70,000	
Romania	1,860[h]	3,000	675	0		140,000	32,000
Cat. I	599	313	270			25,760	
II	1,139	893	558			53,760	
III	1,084	1,160	576			56,000	

[continued overleaf]

2. WTO Forces in the ATTU area — continued

	Main Battle Tanks	Armored Personnel Carriers	Artillery/ Multiple Rocket Launchers	Armed Helicopters[c]	Surface-to-Surface Missiles	Personnel Ground	Personnel Air
USSR	36,200[h]	28,005	31,950	835	6000	1,912,440	345,000[f]
Cat. I	10,690	4,741	4,302			442,420	
II	5,048	3,908	2,628			259,060	
III	21,516	19,356	12,132			1,030,120	
Total	52,110	41,990	41,583	1,090	6,000	2,739,440	614,000
WTO Unilateral Reductions[g]	12,751	895	10,030	—	—	214,200	107,100
Remaining Total	39,359	41,095	31,553	1,090	6,000	2,366,840	506,900
WTO Reductions	27,905	26,923	24,511	678	5,650	1,213,735	230,650
New Joint NATO/WTO Level	11,454	14,172	7,042	412	350	1,153,105	276,250[e]

Notes for Table C

a NATO figures are for holdings of active duty units and includes, stored NATO tanks, which NATO's *Conventional Forces in Europe: The Facts* of November, 1988, estimates at 5,800. This storage figure includes 2,887 US war reserve and 1,464 US prepositioned POMCUS tanks. Also, NATO figures include 559 APCs and 457 artillery pieces in storage.

b This figure is illustrative. NATO is using a new category for reductions which appears to combine armored infantry fighting vehicles and armoured personnel carriers. NATO has not yet made available specific figures for this new category.

[c] For NATO the following types of helicopters were counted: SA-330 Puma, SA-341/-342 Gazelle, UH-1 Iroquois, AH-1 Cobra/Sea Cobra, AB Bell 205, Hughes 500m, PAH-1 Bo-159P, CH-124 SH-3, H-53 Stallion, HA-15 Bo105, and CH-47 Chinook. For the WTO the following were counted: Mi-24 Hind, Mi-14 Haze, Mi-8 Hip, Mi-6 Hook, Mi-2 Hoplite, Mi-1 Hare, Ka-25 Hormone, and Ka-27 Helix.

[d] Surface-to-surface missiles are listed here in terms of missiles instead of launchers. It is estimated that NATO has about 700 missiles for its 127 launchers including French missiles. We include French missiles in the NATO total but also recommend that they should be excluded from actual reductions. The total of Pact missiles is estimated at 6,000.

[e] Throughout this book, we follow a standard approach reducing from the level of the numerically smaller side. In this case, 50% is reduced from the totals of the smaller side (NATO), and WTO must reduce to meet the new NATO levels.

[f] The International Institute for Strategic Studies specifies the given Soviet Air Force personnel figure of 315,000 for the four Groups of Soviet Forces (in the GDR, Czechoslovakia, Hungary, and Poland), and the sixteen military districts of the USSR. We estimate 100,000 are located in the other military districts outside the Atlantic-to-Urals area leaving 215,000 concentrated in the area.

[g] WTO unilateral reductions in the Atlantic-to-Urals area of 12,751 tanks, 895 armored personnel carriers, 10,030 artillery pieces and 321,300 ground and air personnel (see Appendix V) have been deducted from the National totals. The breakdown totals of ground, air and naval personnel within the 321,300 figure have not been provided. For this estimate, we assume that at least two-thirds or 214,200 are ground force personnel and the remaining one-third constitute an Air Force total with a caveat that some personnel may have been included in the 321,300 total.

[h] The total of main battle tanks, armored personnel carriers, artillery, and ground personnel for Category I, II & III Warsaw Pact units is somewhat less than the total aggregate figures shown for each of these armaments in the chart. This mismatch, which we are pursuing, probably has several causes. There may be some allowance in IISS figures for training units, repair and storage.

II. NATO and Warsaw Pact Air Force Reduction Proposal
A. NATO and WTO 20% Build-Down Reduction Proposal for Central Europe Extended[a]
1. NATO Forces in Central Europe Extended

Location	Aircraft[b]		
Belgium	F-16		97* (36)
	Mirage-5F		50
		total	147
Canada (in the FRG)	F-18		36* (18)
Denmark	F-16		52* (26)
	Draken		43* (8)
		total	95
France	Jaguar		127
	Mirage F-1		135
	Mirage III		106* (26)
	Mirage 5-F		30
	Mirage 2000B/C		58* (45)
		total	456
FRG	AlphaJet		153
	F-4		142* (71)
	Tornado		190
		total	485
Netherlands	F-5		47
	F-16		147* (61)
		total	194
United Kingdom	Harrier		51
(in FRG)	Tornado		293
	F-4		96
	Buccaneer		52
	Jaguar		108
		total	600
United States	F-4		36
(in FRG)	F-16		156* (60)
		total	192
	NATO Total		2,205
	Minus 20%		441
	New Joint NATO/WTO Level		1,764

2. WTO Air Forces in Central Europe Extended

Soviet Union Location		Aircraft[b]		Eastern European States Location		Aircraft[b]	
CSSR, GDR,	Fencer	Su-24	315	Czecho-			
Poland	Fishbed	MiG-21	(90)*	slovakia	Fishbed	MiG-21	270* (225)
(including	Fitter	Su-17,			Flogger	MiG-27	40
HQ Legnica)		20 22	225		Frogfoot	Su-25	40
and Hungary	Flogger	MiG-27	135		Fitter A	Su-7	45
	Frogfoot	Su-25	45				
						total	395
		total	810				
				GDR:	Fishbed	MiG-21	(225)*
Baltics	Fishbed	MiG-21	(90)*		Fitter	Su-17,	
Belorussia	Fitter	Su-17,				20, 22	35
(including HQ		20,22	45		Flogger	MiG-27	25
Smolensk),	Flogger	MiG-27	180				
and	Frogfoot	SU-25	45			total	285
Carpathians	Backfire	Tu-26	120				
	Badger	Tu-16	160	Hungary:	Fishbed	MiG-21	(90)*
	Blinder	Tu-22	120				
				Poland:	Fishbed	MiG-21	(360)*
		total	760		Fitter	Su-17,	
						20, 22	125
Kiev MD	Fencer	Su-24	180		Fitter A	Su-7	30
including	Flogger	MiG-27	45			LIM 6	70
HQ Vinnitsa		total	225			total	585

Total Soviet Union	1,795	Total Eastern Europe	1,355

Warsaw Pact Total 3,105[c]

Warsaw Pact Total after Deleting Unilateral Soviet Reduction[d] 2,650

WTO Reduction   886

New Joint NATO/WTO Level   1,764

B. NATO and WTO 50% Air Force Reduction Proposal for the Atlantic to Urals Area.[a]
1. NATO Air Forces in the ATTU Area

Location	Aircraft[b]		
Belgium	F-16		97* (36)
	Mirage-5F		50
		total	147
Canada (in the F.R.G.)	F-18		36* (18)
Denmark	F-16		52* (26)
	Draken		43* (8)
		total	95
France	Jaguar		127
	Mirage F-1		135*
	Mirage III		106*
	Mirage 5-F		30
	Mirage 2000B/C		58* (45)
		total	456
FRG	AlphaJet		153
	F-4		142* (71)
	Tornado		190
		total	485
Greece	A-7		59
	F-4		50* (15)
	F-5		76* (20)
	F-104		76
	Mirage F-1		(38)*
		total	299
Italy	F-104		126* (96)
	G-91		141
	Tornado		98
		total	365
Netherlands	F-5		47
	F-16		147* (61)
		total	194
Norway	F-5		30
	F-16		65* (32)
		total	95
Portugal	A-7		42
	G-91		47
		total	89
Spain	F-4		(32)*
	F-5		39
	F-18		46
	Mirage F-1		(62)*
	Mirage III		(48)*(24)
		total	227

B. NATO and WTO 50% Air Force Reduction Proposal for the Atlantic to Urals Area.[a]—*continued*

Location	Aircraft[b]		
Turkey	F-4		124
	F-5		80
	F-100		95
	F-104		234* (42)
		total	533
United Kingdom	F-4		(96)*
(in U.K. and F.R.G.)	Buccaneer		52
	Harrier		51
	Jaguar		108
	Tornado		293* (36)
		total	600
United States	A-10		108
(in Europe)	F-4		36
	F-5		19*
	F-16		228* (96)
	F-111		140
		total	531

NATO Total 4,152

NATO 15% Reduction	1,002[e]	NATO 50% Reduction	2,300[e]
New Joint NATO/WTO Level	3,150	New Joint NATO/WTO Level	1,852

2. WTO Forces in the ATTU Area

Soviet Union				Eastern European States			
Location		Aircraft[b]		Location		Aircraft[b]	
CSSR, GDR, Poland (including HQ Legnica) and Hungary	Fencer	Su-24	315	Bulgaria:	Fishbed	MiG-21	(110)*
	Fishbed	MiG-21	(90)*		Flogger	MiG-27	45
	Fitter	Su-17, 20, 22	225		Fresco	MiG-17	15
	Flogger	MiG-27	135		Frogfoot	Su-25	45
	Frogfoot	Su-25	45				
						total	215
		total	810	Czecho-slovakia:	Fishbed	MiG-21	270* (225)
Baltics, Belorussia (including HQ Smolensk), and Carpathians	Fishbed	Mig-21	(90)*		Flogger	MiG-27	40
	Fitter	Su-17, 20, 22	45		Frogfoot	Su-25	40
	Flogger	MiG-27	180		Fitter A	Su-7	45
	Frogfoot	Su-25	45				
	Backfire	Tu-26	120			total	395
	Badger	Tu-16	160	GDR:	Fishbed	MiG-21	(225)*
	Blinder	Tu-22	120		Fitter	Su-17, 20, 22	35
					Flogger	MiG-27	25
		total	760				
						total	285
Leningrad MD	Fishbed	MiG-21	45				
	Fitter	Su-17, 20, 22	45	Hungary:	Fishbed	MiG-21	(90)*
	Flogger	MiG-27	45				
		total	135				
Odessa and Kiev MDs including HQ Vinnitsa	Fencer	Su-24	180	Poland:	Fishbed	MiG-21	(360)*
	Flogger	MiG-27	135(45)*		Fitter	Su-17, 20, 22	125
	Fishbed	MiG-21	45		Fitter A	Su-7	30
						LIM 6	70
		total	360			total	585
Trans-Caucasus MD	Fencer	Su-24	45				
	Fitter	Su-17, 20, 22	225	Romania:	Fresco	MiG-17	85
	Flogger	MiG-27	135		Orao	IAR-93	35
	Frogfoot	Su-25	45				
						total	120
		total	450				

Total Soviet Union	2,515	Total Eastern Europe 1,690

Warsaw Pact Total 4,205
Warsaw Pact Total after Deleting Unilateral Soviet Reduction[d] 3,705

WTO 15% Reduction	555	WTO 50% Reduction	1,853
New Joint NATO/WTO Level	3,150	New Joint NATO/WTO Level	1,852

Notes for Section II

ᵃ Charts II–A and B are derived using Appendix III as the base, and *The Military Balance, 1988–1989*. We have included in the reduction base all ground-attack aircraft, fighter-bombers, and medium bombers, as well as multi-role aircraft which can be used for ground attack. We have excluded air-to-air fighters, training, air-defense, and strategic-bomber-aircraft. For NATO the total aircraft not counted are: 69 F-4, 20 F-5, 120 F-15, 40 Mirage IV, and 72 Hawk. For the WTO the following were not counted: 1025 MiG-23, 360 MiG-29, 90 MiG-25, and 45 Su-15.

ᵇ For the purposes of the reduction proposal set forth in this book, multi-role aircraft normally classed as fighter aircraft and listed as Fighter–Interceptors in Appendix III have been added to the category of attack aircraft in this chart, and are indicated by asterisks. The number of aircraft of each type shifted is shown in parenthesis. Stored aircraft are included in the totals.

ᶜ To arrive at the 3,705 Warsaw Pact total, we have added to the WTO Fighter–Bombers total in Appendix III of 1,445 the 1,080 multi-role MiG–21s from the fighter–interceptors column, the 400 Soviet medium-range bombers from the Smolensk Air Army based in European USSR, and the 225 aircraft located in the Kiev military district.

ᵈ According to Gorbachev's reduction proposal, 800 Soviet combat aircraft of unspecified type would be unilaterally withdrawn. Eastern European members of the Warsaw Pact have announced unilateral reductions of 200 aircraft. We have arbitrarily subtracted one-half of the total 1,000 aircraft, or 500 aircraft from the Warsaw Pact reduction base set forth here.

ᶜ For Central Europe Extended, NATO is the numerically smaller side, and the WTO must reduce more aircraft to meet the new NATO level. For the ATTU area, the roles are reversed and it is NATO which must reduce more to meet the new joint WTO level.

Main sources for Appendix X:

The International Institute for Strategic Studies, *The Military Balance, 1988–1989* (London: IISS, 1988).

Conventional Forces in Europe: The Facts, (NATO: November, 1988).

U.S. Ground Forces and the Conventional Balance in Europe, Congressional Budget Office, June, 1988.

Appendix XI: Possible Savings from United States Force Reductions

Based on the reduction proposal described in Chapter 10, the Defense Budget Project has prepared the following estimate:

Savings in the year 2000, Fiscal year 1989 in billions.

Operations and Support (O&S) Savings from
Withdrawing 100,000 Army troops: $4.8 billion

From Congressional Budget Office (CBO) data, adjusted to FY 1989 dollars

O&S Savings from Withdrawing 5 tactical air wings: $1–3 billion

CBO, *Reducing the Deficit* (February 1989) shows annual O&S savings of $700 million from cutting 3 air wings, or $233 million for each wing. The range was provided because CBO's methodology yields a conservative result. The upper range is derived using the following method: Take the total FY 1989 O&S budget for the active duty Air Force (roughly $42 billion), assume that half of this amount is for strategic forces, and that 30% of the $21 billion in remaining costs for tactical forces are fixed. Thus, divide $14.7 billion by 25 active duty air wings, for O&S costs of $588 million per wing.

O&S savings from converting 2–3 U.S.-deployed Army
divisions to reserve: $2.4–$3.6 billion

Assume that the entire FY 1989 active duty Army O&S budget (roughly $46 billion) supports 18 divisions, and that 30% of these costs are fixed. Savings from eliminating two active duty divisions would therefore be $3.6 billion, and eliminating three would save $5.4 billion. Assume that the O&S budget for Army reserves (roughly $8.2 billion) supports 10 divisions, with 30% fixed costs. Adding two reserve divisions would therefore cost $1.2 billion, and adding three would cost $1.8 billion. Net savings would be between $2.4 billion and $3.6 billion.

O&S Savings from converting 30 U.S. tactical Air
Force squadrons (10 wings) to reserve $1.3–4 billion

Using the assumptions above, cutting 10 active duty air wings would save between $2 billion and $6 billion annually. Assume that reserve forces cost one-third as much as active duty forces to operate and support (the ratio derived above for Army divisions).

ATACMs $1–1.5 billion

CBO, *Alternatives for Improving NATO's Ground Forces* (June 1988), shows

420

purchases of 11,254 ATACMs between 1994 and 2008 at a cost of $17.55 billion in FY 1989 dollars. This averages out to $1.25 billion per year.

Total: $10.5–16.9 billion

POTENTIAL SAVINGS FROM ADDITIONAL FORGONE MODERNIZATION

Initial calculations and assumptions:

Army procurement budget is $15 billion in FY 1989.

Air Force procurement budget is $31 billion in FY 89. Assume that roughly $11 billion is in the black (classified) budget, and that 25% of the remaining $20 billion is in strategic programs, satellite programs, and airlift and therefore not affected by the reductions. Thus, the portion of Air Force procurement used for these calculations is also $15 billion.

Assume that future procurement savings for equipment going from active forces to POMCUS sets are 85% of what would otherwise be expected, to allow for spare parts and for lower efficiency (hence greater per unit costs) resulting from reduced production rates.

Assume that future procurement savings for equipment going from active forces to reserves are 70% of what would otherwise be expected, on the same basis as above, but also allowing for some equipment to be purchased expressly for the reserves. Assume that POMCUS and reserves will get the most modern equipment not needed by active duty forces.

1. Savings from withdrawing 100,000 Army troops. Two ways to calculate: 100,000 troops out of 772,000 = 13%. 0.13 (proportion of force) × $15 billion (procurement budget) × 0.85 (to account for the fixed costs) = $1.6 billion. Alternatively, 3 divisions of 18 = one-sixth, or 17%. 0.17 × $15 billion × 0.85 = $2.2 billion.
2. Savings from withdrawing 5 of 25 active tactical air wings. Assuming all procurement goes to active wings, and the reserves get the leftovers: 0.2 (proportion of the force) × $15 billion (adjusted procurement budget) × 0.85 (to account for fixed costs) = $2.6 billion.
3. Savings from converting 2–3 U.S. deployed Army divisions to reserve. Assume 30% fixed costs. 2–3 divisions out of 18 = one-ninth (11%) to one-sixth (17%). If two divisions: 0.11 (proportion of force) × $15 billion (procurement budget) × 0.17 (to account for fixed costs) = $1.2 billion. If three divisions: 0.17 × $15 billion × 0.7 = $1.8 billion. Range of estimates = $1.2–$1.8 billion.
4. Savings from converting 30 U.S. tactical Air Force squadrons to reserve. Assume 30% fixed costs. 30 squadrons = 10 wings. 10 of 25 active wings = 40%. 0.4 (proportion of forces) × $15% billion (procurement budget) × 0.7 (to account for fixed costs) = $4.2 billion.

Summary of estimated modernization savings:

1. From withdrawing 100,000 Army troops: $1.6–$2.2 billion
2. From withdrawing 5 tactical air wings: $2.6 billion

3. From converting 2–3 U.S. deployed Army
   divisions to reserve: $1.2–$1.8 billion
4. From converting 30 U.S. tactical Air Force
   squadrons to reserve: $4.2 billion

Total: $9.6–$10.8 billion

This estimate was prepared in March, 1989, by Gordon Adams, Alexis Cain, and Natalie Goldring of the Defense Budget Project, Washington, D.C.

Notes and References

1 Beginning the Build-Down in Europe: Negotiating the I.N.F. Treaty

1. The text of the I.N.F. treaty, together with a fuller description of the I.N.F. negotiations, is published in my article on the subject for the *SIPRI Yearbook 1988: World Armaments and Disarmament*, on which this chapter is based. The best general sources on I.N.F. are: (1) Lawrence Freedman, *The Evolution of Nuclear Strategy* (New York: St. Martin's Press, 1983); (2) Raymond Garthoff, *Detente and Confrontation* (Washington, D.C.: The Brookings Institution, 1985); (3) David N. Schwartz, *NATO's Nuclear Dilemmas* (Washington, D.C.: The Brookings Institution, 1983; (4) Gerard Smith, *Double Talk* (Lanham, MD: University Press of America, 1985, paperback ed.); (5) Strobe Talbott, *Deadly Gambits* (New York: Knopf, 1984); and (6) Thomas Risse-Kappen, *The Zero Option* (Boulder, CO: Westview Press, 1988). My own book, *Watershed in Europe* (Lexington, MA: Lexington Books, 1987), contains a detailed description of the development of the I.N.F. talks up to the spring of 1986.

3 Starting Point: The Current NATO/Warsaw Pact Force Relationship

1. James A. Thomson, "An Unfavorable Situation: NATO and the Conventional Balance", (Santa Monica, CA: The Rand Corporation, November, 1988).
2. William Kaufmann, "Who Is Conning the Alliance?," paper for the Aspen Strategy Group.
3. "NATO Center Region Military Balance Study 1978–1984" Washington, D.C.: Office of the Assistant Secretary of Defense, Program Analysis and Evaluation, July 13, 1979, declassified) pages II-2, 5, 6.
4. See William Mako, "United States Ground Forces and the Defense of Central Europe" (Washington, D.C.: The Brookings Institution, 1985).
5. The categories, developed in 1973 by U.S. analysts from Soviet models, are described in many places. See, for example, William Kaufmann, "Non-Nuclear Deterrence," in John Steinbrunner and Leon Sigal, eds., *Alliance Security: NATO and the No First Use Question* (Washington, D.C., The Brookings Institution, 1983).
6. David M. Shilling, "Europe's Conventional Defenses," *Survival*, March/April, 1988.
7. Malcolm Chambers and Lutz Unterseher, *Is There a Tank Gap?*, Peace Research Report, no. 19, University of Bradford. A version of this study was also published in *International Security*, 1988, 13:1.

4 The New Thinking About Armed Forces in West and East: Can It Help in East/West Negotiations?

1. For a general review of the main proposals and criticisms of them, see Jonathan Dean, "Alternative Defence: Answer to NATO's Central Front Problems?," London, *International Affairs*, vol. 64 (Winter 1987/88) 1.

2. Early proposals for reform of NATO's military posture are described on page 271 of Adam Roberts's *Nations in Arms* (New York: St. Martin's Press, 1986 2nd ed.).

3. The "Bonin Plan" is briefly described in David Gates's "Area Defense Concepts: The West German Debate," in *Survival*, July–August, 1987. The article provides an excellent short survey of the alternate defense issue.

4. Horst Afheldt, *Defensive Verteidigung*, Reinbek, Rowohlt Taschenbuch Verlag, 1983; Norbert Hannig, *Verteidigen Ohne Zu Bedrohen*, November, 1986, AFES, Institut für Politik und Wissenschaft, Universität Stuttgart.

5. Studiengruppe Alternative Sicherheitspolitik, *Strukturwandel der Verteidigung*, Opladen, Westdeutcher Verlag, 1984; Lutz Unterseher, *Defending Europe: Toward a Stable Deterrent*, Studiengruppe Alternative Sicherheitspolitik, Bonn, 1986; John Grin and Lutz Unterseher, "The Spiderweb Defense," *Bulletin of the Atomic Scientists*, September 1988.

6. Albrecht A. C. von Mueller, *The Integrated Forward Defense*, Starnberg, 1985; "Confidence Building by Hardware Measures," paper for the 34th Pugwash Conference on Science and World Affairs, July 1984; "Structural Stability at the Central Front," Paper no. 13, Niels Bohr Centennial, University of Copenhagen, September, 1985.

7. Karsten Voigt, Konventionelle Stabilisierung und strukturelle Nightangriffsfähigkeit, Bonn, *Beilage Zum Parliament*, Aus Politik und Zeitgeschehen, 1988.

8. The text of both letters is published in the Federation of American Scientists, *Public Interest Report* 41:2, February 1988.

9. The text, entitled "An East–West Negotiating Proposal," has been published in the *Bulletin of the Atomic Scientists*, September, 1988.

10. See Vitaly Zhurkin, Sergei Karaganov, Andrei Kortunov, "Reasonable Sufficiency—or How to Break the Vicious Circle," Moscow, *New Times*, Oct. 12, 1987.

11. Cited by Paul Dibb, "Is Soviet Military Strategy Changing?," Adelphi Papers 235, Spring, 1989, London, International Institute for Strategic Studies.

12. See A. Kokoshin and V. Larionov, "The Battle of Kursk from the Standpoint of Defensive Doctrine," in *World Economy and International Relations*, Moscow, no. 8, 1987; and A. Kokoshin and V. Larionov, "The General Setting of Opposing Forces in the Context of Guaranteeing Strategic Stabilization," *World Economy and International Relations*, Moscow, June, 1988.

13. See David Holloway, "Gorbachev's New Thinking," in *Foreign Affairs*, America and the World, 1988/89.

5 Lessons from Failure: Vienna One and What We Can Learn From It

1. The Soviets presented figures in 1975 and, in slightly more detailed form, again in 1980. In 1980, NATO counted its own ground-force manpower at 744,000 (the figures are rounded and they exclude 50,000 French troops whom France prohibited from consideration in the talks) and its air-force manpower at 198,000. NATO counted Warsaw Pact ground-force manpower at 956,000 and air-force manpower at 224,000. The Pact claimed it had only 815,000 ground-force personnel and 182,000 air-force personnel. Thus the Pact's estimate of its superiority over NATO in manpower was lower than NATO's estimate by about 183,000. As for the reductions that the Pact would have had to make to come down to the ground-force ceiling of 700,000 proposed by NATO, if the Pact ground-force total was 815,000, as the Pact claimed, the Pact would have had to withdraw 115,000 men. Since about half of the Pact's military personnel in the M.B.F.R. reduction area were Soviet, this would have worked out to a cutback of about 57,000 Soviet forces. But using NATO's estimates that Pact ground forces numbered about 956,000, a total Pact reduction of 256,000 men would have been required to reach the 700,000-man common ceiling proposed by NATO, more than double the number calculated on the basis of Pact figures. About half of these troops, or 128,000, would have been Soviet, and thus the Soviet reduction, too, would have to have been doubled.

6 The C.D.E. Parallel Track: Success of the Stockholm Conference

1. C.S.C.E. participants are: Austria, Belgium, Bulgaria, Canada, Cyprus, Czechoslovakia, Denmark, Finland, France, the German Democratic Republic, the Federal Republic of Germany, Greece, The Holy See, Hungary, Iceland, Ireland, Italy, Liechtenstein, Luxembourg, Malta, Monaco, the Netherlands, Norway, Poland, Portugal, Romania, San Marino, Spain, Sweden, Switzerland, Turkey, the Union of Soviet Socialist Republics, the United Kingdom, the United States of America, and Yugoslavia.
2. For more background on the Helsinki talks and the C.D.E. negotiations, see the author's *Watershed in Europe* (Lexington, MA: Lexington Books, 1987, Chapters 5 and 8; and John Borawski, *From the Atlantic to the Urals: Negotiating Arms Control at the Stockholm Conference*, (Washington, D.C.: Pergamon-Brassey's International Defense Publishers, 1988).

7 The Two Alliances Ready Themselves

1. The text of the Gorbachev speech of April 18, 1986, is contained in FBIS of April 18, 1986, USSR International Affairs, Eastern Europe,

426 *Meeting Gorbachev's Challenge*

pp. F1–F9; the text of relevant sections of the Budapest Declaration is in FBIS of June 13, 1986, USSR International Affairs, Communist Relations, pp. B8–12, and in *Warsaw Treaty New Initiatives*, Novosti Press Agency Publishing House, Moscow, 1986.
2. The text of this portion of Shevardnadze's U.N. speech is in *Tass Bulletin A-20*, June 8, 1988.

8 Negotiators' Headaches: Substantive Problems of Force Reductions

1. Michael Gordon, "Soviets Shift on Limits on Conventional Forces," *New York Times*, June 30, 1989.
2. Congressional Budget Office, *U.S. Ground Forces and the Conventional Balance in Europe*, June, 1988, p. 66.

9 Essential First Steps: Data Exchange, Early Warning, and Constraint Measures

1. See Congressional Budget Office, *U.S. Ground Forces and the Conventional Balance in Europe*, June, 1988.

11 Verifying Deep Cuts

1. Earlier versions of this chapter have appeared in *The Handbook of Verification Procedures*, edited by Frank Barnaby (London: Macmillan, 1989), and in *Conventional Arms Control and East/West Security*, edited by F. Stephen Larrabee and Robert Blackwill (Durham, North Carolina: Duke University Press, 1989).
2. See Richard L. Garwin, "Tags and Seals for Verification," *Bulletin of the Council for Arms Control*, London, October, 1988.

Index

427